Andrea Daniel

Perception Gaps between Headquarters and Subsidiary Managers

GABLER RESEARCH

mir-Edition

Herausgeber / Editors:

Prof. Dr. Andreas Al-Laham
Universität Mannheim,
Prof. Dr. Johann Engelhard
Universität Bamberg,
Prof. Dr. Michael Kutschker
Universität Eichstätt, Ingolstadt,
Prof. Dr. Profs. h.c. Dr. h.c. Klaus Macharzina
Universität Hohenheim, Stuttgart,
Prof. Dr. Michael-Jörg Oesterle
Universität Mainz,
Prof. Dr. Stefan Schmid
ESCP Europe Wirtschaftshochschule Berlin,
Prof. Dr. Martin K. Welge
Universität Dortmund,
Prof. Dr. Joachim Wolf
Universität Kiel

In der mir-Edition werden wichtige Ergebnisse der wissenschaftlichen Forschung sowie Werke erfahrener Praktiker auf dem Gebiet des internationalen Managements veröffentlicht.

The series mir-Edition includes excellent academic contributions and experiential works of distinguished international managers.

Andrea Daniel

Perception Gaps between Headquarters and Subsidiary Managers

Differing Perspectives on Subsidiary Roles and their Implications

GABLER

RESEARCH

Bibliografische Information der Deutschen Nationalbibliothek
Die Deutsche Nationalbibliothek verzeichnet diese Publikation in der
Deutschen Nationalbibliografie; detaillierte bibliografische Daten sind im Internet über
<http://dnb.d-nb.de> abrufbar.

Bibliographic information published by the Deutsche Nationalbibliothek
The Deutsche Nationalbibliothek lists this publication in the Deutsche Nationalbibliografie;
detailed bibliographic data are available in the Internet at http://dnb.d-nb.de.

Dissertation ESCP Europe Wirtschaftshochschule Berlin, 2009

Abonnenten von mir – Management International Review erhalten auf die in der mir-Edition veröffentlichten Bücher 10% Rabatt.

Subscribers to mir – Management International Review are entitled to a 10 % price reduction on books published in mir-Edition.

1. Auflage 2010

Alle Rechte vorbehalten
© Gabler | GWV Fachverlage GmbH, Wiesbaden 2010

Lektorat: Ute Wrasmann | Jutta Hinrichsen

Gabler ist Teil der Fachverlagsgruppe Springer Science+Business Media.
www.gabler.de

Das Werk einschließlich aller seiner Teile ist urheberrechtlich geschützt. Jede Verwertung außerhalb der engen Grenzen des Urheberrechtsgesetzes ist ohne Zustimmung des Verlags unzulässig und strafbar. Das gilt insbesondere für Vervielfältigungen, Übersetzungen, Mikroverfilmungen und die Einspeicherung und Verarbeitung in elektronischen Systemen.

Die Wiedergabe von Gebrauchsnamen, Handelsnamen, Warenbezeichnungen usw. in diesem Werk berechtigt auch ohne besondere Kennzeichnung nicht zu der Annahme, dass solche Namen im Sinne der Warenzeichen- und Markenschutz-Gesetzgebung als frei zu betrachten wären und daher von jedermann benutzt werden dürften.

Umschlaggestaltung: KünkelLopka Medienentwicklung, Heidelberg
Gedruckt auf säurefreiem und chlorfrei gebleichtem Papier
Printed in Germany

ISBN 978-3-8349-2071-3

Vorwort der Herausgeber

Für viele Unternehmen ist es heutzutage unerlässlich, sich auf ausländischen Märkten zu betätigen. Ein erfolgreiches Management der Internationalisierung stellt Unternehmen allerdings immer wieder vor neue Herausforderungen. Die Herausgeber beabsichtigen mit der Schriftenreihe **mir-Edition**, die vielfältigen und komplexen Managementanforderungen der internationalen Unternehmenstätigkeit wissenschaftlich zu begleiten. Die **mir-Edition** soll zum einen der empirischen Feststellung und der theoretischen Verarbeitung der in der Praxis des Internationalen Managements beobachtbaren Phänomene dienen. Zum anderen sollen die hierdurch gewonnenen Erkenntnisse in Form von systematisiertem Wissen, von Erklärungen und Denkanstößen sowie von Handlungsempfehlungen verfügbar gemacht werden.

Diesem angewandten Wissenschaftsverständnis fühlt sich seit nunmehr 50 Jahren auch die in über 40 Ländern gelesene internationale Fachzeitschrift **mir** – Management International Review – verpflichtet. Während in der Zeitschrift allerdings nur kurzgefasste englischsprachige Aufsätze publiziert werden, soll der breitere Raum der vorliegendenden Schriftenreihe den Autoren und Lesern die Möglichkeit zur umfänglichen und vertieften Auseinandersetzung mit dem jeweils behandelten Problem des Internationalen Managements eröffnen. Der Herausgeberkreis der **mir-Edition** wurde 2008 um weitere renommierte Fachvertreter des Internationalen Managements erweitert. Geblieben ist jedoch die Herausgeberpolitik für die **mir-Edition**, in der Schriftenreihe innovative und dem Erkenntnisfortschritt dienende Beiträge einer kritischen Öffentlichkeit vorzustellen. Neben Forschungsergebnissen, insbesondere des wissenschaftlichen Nachwuchses, können auch einschlägige Werke von Praktikern mit profundem Erfahrungswissen im Internationalen Management einbezogen werden. Wissenschaftliche Sammelbände, etwa zu Tagungen aus dem Bereich des Internationalen Managements, sind ebenso sehr gerne in der Reihe willkommen. Die Herausgeber laden zu Veröffentlichungen sowohl in deutscher als auch in englischer Sprache ausdrücklich ein.

Das Auswahlverfahren sieht vor, dass die Herausgeber gemeinsam über die Veröffentlichung eines für die Reihe eingereichten Werkes entscheiden. Wir freuen uns auf Ihre Manuskripte und hoffen, mit dieser seit langer Zeit renommierten Schriftenreihe die wissenschaftliche Diskussion und die praktische Lösung von Problemen des Internationalen Managements weiter zu stimulieren.

Andreas Al-Laham, Johann Engelhard,
Michael Kutschker, Klaus Macharzina,
Michael-Jörg Oesterle, Stefan Schmid,
Martin K. Welge, Joachim Wolf

Preface

Nowadays, it is essential for a multitude of companies to engage in foreign markets. However, the successful management of internationalization processes constantly poses new challenges. By publishing the book series "mir-Edition", the editors attempt to provide academic guidance on the manifold and complex requirements of international business activities. The book series' purpose hence is twofold. Firstly, the "mir-Edition" is to provide empirical assessment and theoretical elaboration on the phenomena which can be observed in international management practice. Secondly, the findings obtained are to be made available in the form of systematised knowledge, explanations, thought-provoking impulses as well as recommendations for further courses of action.

For the past 50 years, the international journal "mir – Management International Review", which is read in more than 40 countries, has seen itself committed to promoting an understanding of international management as an applied academic discipline. As of now, the journal only publishes articles in English. The wider range of the existing book series ought to give authors and readers the opportunity to deal with the various problems of international management in a comprehensive and thorough manner. The editorial board of the "mir-Edition" was extended in 2008 through the addition of renowned experts from the domain of international management. Yet, the established editors' policy for the "mir-Edition" of presenting innovative work to a critical audience, which support the scientific advancement, has remained unchanged.

Besides the academic contributions of young scholars, the editors also welcome the relevant works of practitioners, who possess a profound knowledge in the area of international management. Furthermore, edited volumes, collecting for instance presentations held at conferences in the field of international management, are invited for publication. The editors explicitly welcome books both in the English and the German language.

The selection process stipulates that the editors jointly decide on the publication of any book manuscript submitted for the series. As editors of this well established and renowned book series, we are looking forward to receiving your manuscripts and we hope to further stimulate the academic discussion and to provide applied solutions for the challenges in the area of international management.

Andreas Al-Laham, Johann Engelhard,
Michael Kutschker, Klaus Macharzina,
Michael-Jörg Oesterle, Stefan Schmid,
Martin K. Welge, Joachim Wolf

Foreword

Within the literature on international management, headquarters-subsidiary relationships have been a central research area for some decades now. Furthermore we can rely on various contributions in the international management field which have shown that there is a great variety of subsidiary roles. Surprisingly, it is often assumed that headquarters and subsidiaries have the same understanding of the role a specific subsidiary plays. However, this assumption may be questioned. While subsidiaries can take on different roles, we should not take for granted that headquarters and subsidiaries share the same perceptions of these roles.

Andrea Daniel focuses on differences in perception between headquarters' and subsidiaries' managers. She reviews the relevant literature and finds out that, so far, not many contributions in international management research have concentrated on perception gaps. While some studies have covered some antecedents and/or some consequences of perceptions gaps, they are usually not particularly strong in their theoretical development. To fill this research gap is one of Andrea Daniel's objectives. Another major objective is to contribute to the research area on perception gaps in MNCs in an empirical way. The conceptual as well as the empirical focus of the dissertation is on perception gaps regarding a subsidiary's role and on conflict as one major potential consequence of perception gaps.

To me, the present book offers highly valuable insights in headquarters-subsidiary relationships, by departing from the assumption that headquarters and subsidiaries have the same understanding of subsidiary roles. Andreas Daniel gives new theoretical insights by transferring Katz and Kahn's "open system approach" to network MNCs. Using a case study approach, she not only adds rich empirical material on how perception gaps can cause conflicts; she also demonstrates how important it is to differentiate between different types of conflicts. Interestingly, headquarters and subsidiaries do not only have differing perceptions when it comes to subjective dimensions. Even for dimensions that we may interpret as rather objective – such as the type of value-adding activities carried out by a subsidiary – differences in perception between headquarters and subsidiaries appear.

I highly appreciate the work done by Andrea Daniel and I am sure that the work will have an impact on the international management field. The contribution gives us a more realistic picture of the complex nature of MNCs, it focuses on the two main groups of actors within MNCs (i.e. headquarters and subsidiaries) and also stresses the roles of individuals within headquarters and subsidiaries for negotiating reality (as exemplified in the current case by the subsidiary's role). I am convinced that the ideas and the results presented in this book will influence future research and management practice alike.

Berlin, November 2009   Stefan Schmid

Preface

This thesis was written while I was working as a research assistant at the Chair of International Management and Strategic Management at ESCP Europe Wirtschaftshochschule Berlin. I would like to use this preface to thank all persons who accompanied me during that time and who supported my project.

First of all, I would like to thank my supervisor Prof. Dr. Stefan Schmid. He guided me in exploring the field of headquarters-subsidiary relationships and immediately supported the idea to study the perception of subsidiary roles. Through valuable ideas and critical questions, he inspired many new thoughts that influenced the final shape of my thesis. He encouraged me to look for original solutions and was open for less conventional directions. Thank you very much!

I am also indebted to Prof. Dr. Wolfgang Dorow who accepted the task to function as second reviewer and who provided insightful comments from a different perspective on the manuscript.

The empirical study which is a central part of this thesis would not have been possible without the generous support of the top managers of two multinational companies. I am grateful for the opportunity to take a look behind the scenes of these companies and I wish to thank each one of my interview partners who invested a significant amount of time in answering my questions and discussing their point of view on the headquarters-subsidiary relationships in their company.

Words of thanks also go to my colleagues and fellow Ph.D. students at ESCP Europe. They contributed to my thesis through discussions, ideas, questions and by critically revising selected parts of the manuscript. Moreover, they played an important role by creating a very pleasant working environment in which mutual support could be taken for granted. I would like to mention Monika Dammer-Henselmann, Dr. Matthias Daub, Tobias Dauth, Ruben Dost, Philipp Grosche, Swantje Hartmann, Dr. Katharina Hefter, Thomas Kotulla, Dr. Mario Machulik, Julia Maurer, Renate Ramlau, and Stephan Schulze. Thanks to all of you!

The most critical reviewer of the manuscript was Michael. Thank you for your honest opinion, your endless encouragement and your patience! Finally, I would like to thank my family and my friends for their support and backing throughout the time of my dissertation.

Munich, November 2009   Andrea Daniel

Brief Contents

1. **Introduction** 1
   - 1.1 Context 1
   - 1.2 Goals of the Study 2
   - 1.3 Outline of the Study 3

2. **Central Concepts** 5
   - 2.1 Multinational Network Corporations 5
   - 2.2 Subsidiary Roles in Multinational Network Corporations 13
   - 2.3 Perception Gaps Concerning Subsidiary Roles 27
   - 2.4 Headquarters-Subsidiary Conflict 39
   - 2.5 Summary and Conclusions 52

3. **Conceptual Framework** 54
   - 3.1 Open System Approach According to Katz and Kahn 54
   - 3.2 Multinational Network Corporations as Open Systems 77
   - 3.3 Research Framework 93

4. **Empirical Study** 111
   - 4.1 Research Design 111
   - 4.2 Data Collection 118
   - 4.3 Data Analysis 135
   - 4.4 Scientific Quality Criteria 142

5. **Empirical Findings** 147
   - 5.1 Introduction 147
   - 5.2 The Cases 155
   - 5.3 Perception Gaps Concerning the Subsidiary's Role 203
   - 5.4 Implications of Perception Gaps for the Headquarters-Subsidiary Relationship 219

6. **Discussion** 240
   - 6.1 Limitations of the Present Study 240
   - 6.2 Implications for the International Business Literature 245
   - 6.3 Avenues for Future Research 250
   - 6.4 Managerial Implications 253
   - 6.5 Summary 256

Appendix 257

References 267

Contents

1. **Introduction** 1
   1.1 Context 1
   1.2 Goals of the Study 2
   1.3 Outline of the Study 3

2. **Central Concepts** 5
   2.1 Multinational Network Corporations 5
      2.1.1 General Characteristics of Multinational Corporations 5
      2.1.2 Towards a Network Model of Multinational Corporations 6
      2.1.3 Characteristics of Multinational Network Corporations 10
   2.2 Subsidiary Roles in Multinational Network Corporations 13
      2.2.1 The Subsidiary Role Concept in the International Business Literature 13
      2.2.2 Subsidiary Role Typologies 16
      2.2.3 Approach to Subsidiary Roles in the Present Study 20
         2.2.3.1 Selection of Subsidiary Role Typologies 20
         2.2.3.2 Differentiation of Subsidiary Roles According to Bartlett and Ghoshal 22
         2.2.3.3 Differentiation of Subsidiary Roles According to Gupta and Govindarajan 25
   2.3 Perception Gaps Concerning Subsidiary Roles 27
      2.3.1 Attributes of Perception Gaps 27
         2.3.1.1 The Subjective Nature of Perception 27
         2.3.1.2 Perception Gaps vs. Perception Errors 28
      2.3.2 Perception Gaps in the International Business Literature 30
         2.3.2.1 Approaches to Perception Gaps 30
         2.3.2.2 Contributions on Perception Gaps Concerning Subsidiary Roles 32
         2.3.2.3 Overview of the Research Field 37
      2.3.3 Approach to Perception Gaps in the Present Study 38
   2.4 Headquarters-Subsidiary Conflict 39
      2.4.1 General Conflict Literature 39
      2.4.2 Headquarters-Subsidiary Conflict in the International Business Literature 43
      2.4.3 Approach to Headquarters-Subsidiary Conflict in the Present Study 46
         2.4.3.1 Overview 46
         2.4.3.2 Conflict Issues 47
   2.5 Summary and Conclusions 52

3. **Conceptual Framework** 54
   3.1 Open System Approach According to Katz and Kahn 54

- 3.1.1 Selecting a Conceptual Approach for the Present Study 54
  - 3.1.1.1 Categories of Organizational Theories 54
  - 3.1.1.2 System Theoretical Approaches to Organizations 58
- 3.1.2 Overview of the Open System Approach 60
  - 3.1.2.1 Point of Departure 60
  - 3.1.2.2 Characteristics of Open Systems 61
  - 3.1.2.3 Social Organizations as Open Systems 64
- 3.1.3 Role Theoretical Framework 67
  - 3.1.3.1 Overview of Role Theory 67
  - 3.1.3.2 Role Theoretical Framework Within the Open System Approach 70
- 3.1.4 Conflict Model 74
- 3.2 Multinational Network Corporations as Open Systems 77
  - 3.2.1 Applicability of the Open System Approach 77
    - 3.2.1.1 Parallels Between Network Perspectives and the Open System Approach 77
    - 3.2.1.2 Specific Demands of Multinational Network Corporations 79
    - 3.2.1.3 Dealing with the Duality of Individuals and Organizational Units 83
  - 3.2.2 Subsidiary Roles from a Role Theoretical Perspective 85
  - 3.2.3 Headquarters-Subsidiary Conflict from an Open System Perspective 89
- 3.3 Research Framework 93
  - 3.3.1 Overview 93
  - 3.3.2 Likelihood of Perception Gaps 94
    - 3.3.2.1 Perception Gaps Concerning the Subsidiary's Overall Role 94
    - 3.3.2.2 Perception Gaps Concerning the Importance of the Subsidiary's Market 96
    - 3.3.2.3 Perception Gaps Concerning the Subsidiary's Capabilities 97
    - 3.3.2.4 Perception Gaps Concerning Knowledge Flows 97
    - 3.3.2.5 Summary 99
  - 3.3.3 Consequences of Perception Gaps 99
    - 3.3.3.1 Conflict as General Consequence Proposed by the Conceptual Framework 99
    - 3.3.3.2 Perception Gaps Concerning the Importance of the Subsidiary's Market 101
    - 3.3.3.3 Perception Gaps Concerning the Subsidiary's Capabilities 104
    - 3.3.3.4 Perception Gaps Concerning Knowledge Inflow 106
    - 3.3.3.5 Perception Gaps Concerning Knowledge Outflow 108
  - 3.3.4 Summary 110

4. Empirical Study 111

- 4.1 Research Design 111
  - 4.1.1 Rationale for a Case Study Approach 111
  - 4.1.2 Overview of the Case Study Design 113
    - 4.1.2.1 Unit of Analysis 113

	4.1.2.2	Case Selection	114
	4.1.2.3	Types of Data	116
4.1.3		Operationalization of the Conceptual Framework	117
4.2	Data Collection		118
4.2.1		Questionnaire	118
	4.2.1.1	Goals	118
	4.2.1.2	Procedure	119
	4.2.1.3	Operationalization of the Subsidiary Role Dimensions	120
	4.2.1.4	Operationalization of Headquarters-Subsidiary Conflict	124
4.2.2		Interviews	129
	4.2.2.1	Goals	129
	4.2.2.2	Procedure	130
	4.2.2.3	Interview Guideline	131
4.2.3		Respondents	133
4.3	Data Analysis		135
4.3.1		Questionnaire	135
	4.3.1.1	Overview	135
	4.3.1.2	Subsidiary Role Dimensions	135
	4.3.1.3	Headquarters-Subsidiary Conflict	136
4.3.2		Interviews	137
	4.3.2.1	Overview	137
	4.3.2.2	The Code List	139
	4.3.2.3	From Individual Codes to Patterns	141
4.4	Scientific Quality Criteria		142
4.4.1		Overview	142
4.4.2		Objectivity	142
4.4.3		Reliability	143
4.4.4		Validity	144

5. Empirical Findings 147

5.1	Introduction		147
5.1.1		The Two Companies	147
	5.1.1.1	Company A, the Strategic Business Unit Autocomp and Autocomp's Subsidiaries	147
	5.1.1.2	Company B, the Division Construc and Construc's Subsidiaries	149
5.1.2		Comments on the Subsidiary Role Dimensions	150
5.1.3		Identifying Perception Gaps	152
	5.1.3.1	Perception Gaps vs. Artefacts	152
	5.1.3.2	Individual Differences	153
	5.1.3.3	Role Behaviour vs. Role Expectations	153

5.1.4	Chapter Overview	154
5.2	The Cases	155
5.2.1	Overview	155
5.2.2	Hungary	156
5.2.2.1	Perceptions of the Role Dimensions	156
5.2.2.2	Implications for the Headquarters-Subsidiary Relationship	161
5.2.2.3	Interpretation According to the Conceptual Framework	162
5.2.3	Poland	165
5.2.3.1	Perceptions of the Role Dimensions	165
5.2.3.2	Implications for the Headquarters-Subsidiary Relationship	168
5.2.3.3	Interpretation According to the Conceptual Framework	168
5.2.4	Turkey	169
5.2.4.1	Perceptions of the Role Dimensions	169
5.2.4.2	Implications for the Headquarters-Subsidiary Relationship	175
5.2.4.3	Interpretation According to the Conceptual Framework	177
5.2.5	Mexico	182
5.2.5.1	Perceptions of the Role Dimensions	182
5.2.5.2	Implications for the Headquarters-Subsidiary Relationship	188
5.2.5.3	Interpretation According to the Conceptual Framework	188
5.2.6	China	189
5.2.6.1	Perceptions of the Role Dimensions	189
5.2.6.2	Implications for the Headquarters-Subsidiary Relationship	194
5.2.6.3	Interpretation According to the Conceptual Framework	195
5.2.7	USA	197
5.2.7.1	Perceptions of the Role Dimensions	197
5.2.7.2	Implications for the Headquarters-Subsidiary Relationship	201
5.2.7.3	Interpretation According to the Conceptual Framework	201
5.3	Perception Gaps Concerning the Subsidiary's Role	203
5.3.1	Subsidiary Role Dimensions in the Present Study	203
5.3.1.1	Overview	203
5.3.1.2	Conceptual and Empirical Review of the Individual Dimensions	204
5.3.1.3	Critical Reflection on the Proposed Subsidiary Role Concept	212
5.3.2	Perception Gaps in the Present Study	214
5.3.2.1	Overview	214
5.3.2.2	Conceptual Structure of the Identified Perception Gaps	215
5.3.2.3	Critical Review of Perception Gaps	218
5.4	Implications of Perception Gaps for the Headquarters-Subsidiary Relationship	219
5.4.1	The Empirical Findings in the Context of the International Business Literature	219
5.4.1.1	Overview	219

- 5.4.1.2 Importance of the Subsidiary's Market ... 219
- 5.4.1.3 Product Scope ... 220
- 5.4.1.4 Subsidiary's Capabilities ... 221
- 5.4.1.5 Knowledge Inflow to the Subsidiary ... 221
- 5.4.1.6 Knowledge Outflow from the Subsidiary ... 222
- 5.4.1.7 Subsidiary's Autonomy and Involvement in Value Chain Activities ... 223
- 5.4.1.8 Conclusion ... 224
- 5.4.2 Fit of the Conceptual Framework in the Light of the Empirical Findings ... 224
  - 5.4.2.1 Overview ... 224
  - 5.4.2.2 Conflict as Implication of Perception Gaps ... 225
  - 5.4.2.3 Role Related Conflict and Further Implications ... 227
  - 5.4.2.4 Critical Review of the Conceptual Framework ... 234
  - 5.4.2.5 Extension of the Conceptual Framework ... 235
  - 5.4.2.6 Conclusion ... 238

6. Discussion ... 240

6.1 Limitations of the Present Study ... 240
- 6.1.1 Scope of the Study ... 240
- 6.1.2 Conceptual Issues ... 241
- 6.1.3 Methodological Issues ... 243

6.2 Implications for the International Business Literature ... 245
- 6.2.1 Knowledge about Subsidiary Roles ... 245
- 6.2.2 Conceptual Contribution ... 246
- 6.2.3 Methodological Implications ... 248

6.3 Avenues for Future Research ... 250
- 6.3.1 Research on Perception Gaps Concerning the Subsidiary's Role ... 250
- 6.3.2 Theoretical Consolidation ... 252
- 6.3.3 Methodological Approaches ... 252

6.4 Managerial Implications ... 253

6.5 Summary ... 256

Appendix ... 257
- Appendix A Questionnaire Results on Disagreement and Interference ... 257
- Appendix B Final Code List ... 263

References ... 267

List of Figures

Figure 1:	Development of the Headquarters-Subsidiary Relationship Literature	10
Figure 2:	The Multinational Corporation as a Network	11
Figure 3:	Bartlett and Ghoshal's Subsidiary Role Typology	23
Figure 4:	Gupta and Govindarajan's Subsidiary Role Typology	27
Figure 5:	Headquarters-Subsidiary Perception Gaps	32
Figure 6:	Overview of the Research Field on Perception Gaps	37
Figure 7:	Basic Paradigms of Organizational Theories According to Burrell and Morgan	55
Figure 8:	Four Views of Organization and Management According to Astley and Van de Ven	56
Figure 9:	Factors Involved in a Role Episode	72
Figure 10:	Organizational Role Theoretical Framework	73
Figure 11:	Elements of a Conflict Situation	75
Figure 12:	Katz and Kahn's Conflict Model	77
Figure 13:	Two Dimensions of Differentiation in Multinational Network Corporations	81
Figure 14:	Application of the Organizational Role Theoretical Framework to Subsidiary Roles	87
Figure 15:	Elements of the Conflict Situation in the Present Study	93
Figure 16:	Proposed Conceptual Framework	100
Figure 17:	Potential Implications of Perception Gaps Concerning Market Importance	104
Figure 18:	Potential Implications of Perception Gaps Concerning Subsidiary Capabilities	106
Figure 19:	Potential Implications of Perception Gaps Concerning Knowledge Inflow	108
Figure 20:	Potential Implications of Perception Gaps Concerning Knowledge Outflow	109
Figure 21:	Perception Gaps Concerning the Subsidiary's Current Role in the Empirical Study	117
Figure 22:	Questions Concerning the Subsidiary's Market	121
Figure 23:	Questions Concerning the Subsidiary's Capabilities	122
Figure 24:	Questions Concerning Knowledge Flows to and from the Subsidiary	124
Figure 25:	Questions Concerning Headquarters-Subsidiary Distribution Conflict	127
Figure 26:	Questions Concerning Headquarters-Subsidiary Process Conflict	128
Figure 27:	Questions Concerning Headquarters-Subsidiary Goal Conflict	129
Figure 28:	Interview Guideline	133
Figure 29:	Sample Chart – Role Perceptions	136
Figure 30:	Sample Chart – Headquarters-Subsidiary Conflict	137
Figure 31:	Components of Data Analysis According to Miles and Huberman	139
Figure 32:	Questionnaire Results for the Role of Autocomp's Hungarian Subsidiary	157
Figure 33:	Questionnaire Results for the Role of Autocomp's Polish Subsidiary	166
Figure 34:	Questionnaire Results for the Role of Autocomp's Turkish Subsidiary	170
Figure 35:	Questionnaire Results for the Role of Autocomp's Mexican Subsidiary	183
Figure 36:	Questionnaire Results for the Role of Autocomp's Chinese Subsidiary	191
Figure 37:	Questionnaire Results for the Role of Construc's US-American Subsidiary	198

Figure 38:	Factors Involved in a Role Episode between Headquarters and Subsidiary	213
Figure 39:	Perceived and Expected Role Behaviour	215
Figure 40:	Constellations of Perception Gaps	216
Figure 41:	Proposed Conceptual Framework	226
Figure 42:	Two-dimensional Taxonomy of Conflict Handling Intentions	236
Figure 43:	Extended Conceptual Framework	238

List of Tables

Table 1:	Comparison of Subsidiary Role Typologies	19
Table 2:	Empirical Studies of Perception Gaps between Headquarters and Subsidiary	36
Table 3:	Typology for Interpersonal Conflict in Organizations	41
Table 4:	Classifications of Organizational Goals	50
Table 5:	Organizational Goal Types in the Present Study	52
Table 6:	Situations Indicating Different Research Strategies	111
Table 7:	Respondents Involved in the Empirical Study	134
Table 8:	Overview of the Analyzed Subsidiaries of Autocomp	149
Table 9:	Perceptions of the Hungarian Subsidiary's Role and their Implications	165
Table 10:	Perceptions of the Polish Subsidiary's Role and their Implications	169
Table 11:	Perceptions of the Turkish Subsidiary's Role and their Implications	181
Table 12:	Perceptions of the Mexican Subsidiary's Role and their Implications	189
Table 13:	Perceptions of the Chinese Subsidiary's Role and their Implications	196
Table 14:	Perceptions of the US-American Subsidiary's Role and their Implications	203
Table 15:	Subsidiary Role Dimensions in the Present Study	211
Table 16:	Implications of Perception Gaps – Dimensions Corresponding to the Role Definition	231
Table 17:	Implications of Perception Gaps – Dimensions not Corresponding to the Role Definition	232
Table 18:	Implications of Perception Gaps – Subsidiary's Should-be Role	233

1. Introduction

1.1 Context

Many contributions in the international business (IB) literature view multinational corporations (MNCs) as intra-organizational networks. MNCs are no longer regarded as hierarchically structured with headquarters as the single centre of resources, power and decision making authority (Lipparini & Fratocchi 1999, p. 656). Terms such as "heterarchy" (Hedlund 1986, p. 9), multifocal "diversified multinational corporation (DMNC)" (Prahalad & Doz 1987, p. 1) and "transnational company" (Bartlett & Ghoshal 1991) were coined in order to describe multinational network corporations (network MNCs) which are often portrayed as resembling a "coalition of interests" (Forsgren 1989, p. 6) rather than a hierarchy. Subsidiaries can play various roles within network MNCs, carry out different activities and focus on diverse steps of the value chain (Bartlett & Ghoshal 1986, 1991; Ghoshal & Nohria 1989). The notion of differentiated subsidiary roles has inspired a considerable amount of conceptual work as well as empirical research (for an overview, see Schmid 2004; Schmid, Bäurle & Kutschker 1998).

One aspect that most authors have neglected is the question of whether headquarters and subsidiary managers perceive a certain subsidiary's role in the same way. A number of factors, such as different experiences of headquarters and subsidiary managers, imperfect flow of information within the MNC and decreasing dependence of subsidiaries on headquarters could be expected to lead to different perceptions of the role on the two sides (Birkinshaw et al. 2000, p. 328; Chini, Ambos & Wehle 2005, p. 146). Although the fact that headquarters and subsidiary managers may perceive certain issues differently has been widely acknowledged (Arvidsson 1999, pp. 32–41; Birkinshaw et al. 2000, p. 322), the possibility that such perception gaps between headquarters and subsidiary managers concerning the subsidiary's role may exist, has received only limited attention in the IB literature (for some exceptions, see Arvidsson 1999; Asakawa 2001; Birkinshaw et al. 2000; Chini, Ambos & Wehle 2005; Denrell, Arvidsson & Zander 2004). This is surprising, as the question of whether or not headquarters and subsidiary managers perceive a foreign subsidiary's role in the same way bears relevance for researchers as well as practitioners.

From a management perspective, perception gaps can lead to suboptimal decisions, idle resources and dissatisfaction at headquarters and subsidiary level (Birkinshaw et al. 2000, pp. 325–326; Denrell, Arvidsson & Zander 2004, p. 1502). The smooth and effective functioning of organizational activity in network MNCs is easier if all units have the same perception of their roles within the network. From a researcher's perspective, one important implication is of methodological nature. In the past, researchers studying subsidiary roles often relied only on headquarters' or only on the subsidiary's point of view (Arvidsson 1999, pp. 32–41). This may have produced results which do not reflect the organizational reality but only a certain party's perspective on it (French & Henning 1966, p. 188; Weigand 1966, p. 83). If headquarters and subsidiary managers (tend to) perceive certain aspects of the subsidiary's role differently, this should be considered in the research process and be incorporated in research findings. Researchers should acknowledge that information provided by one unit may not reflect another unit's view on the same topic (Schmid 2004, p. 249).

A gap has been identified in headquarters-subsidiary relationship research concerning the perception of subsidiary roles (Schmid & Daniel 2007). The present study can be considered a first step in filling this gap. Headquarters and subsidiary managers' perceptions of certain aspects of a subsidiary's role are explicitly compared with each other and consequences of perception gaps are analyzed. The specific goals of the study are presented in the next subsection.

1.2 Goals of the Study

The present study follows two goals.

(1) First, the study is interested in headquarters and subsidiary managers' perceptions of the roles that specific subsidiaries play within the network MNC. Headquarters and subsidiary managers' perspectives on and their respective perceptions of certain aspects of the subsidiaries' roles are compared. The focus of the analysis is on those situations in which headquarters and subsidiary managers perceive a subsidiary's role differently – so-called perception gaps. In particular, potential implications of these perception gaps for the headquarters-subsidiary relationship are analyzed. The main research question can be formulated as follows: What are the implications of perception gaps between headquarters and subsidiary managers concerning the subsidiary's role for the headquarters-subsidiary relationship?

(2) Second, the study intends to contribute to the IB literature on a conceptual level. So far, the subsidiary role literature has been theoretically founded only to a limited extent. Addressing this shortcoming, the present study develops a theoretical framework which can be applied in order to analyze headquarters-subsidiary relationships and, in particular, the

subsidiary role concept. The framework draws on role theoretical considerations which have been rarely acknowledged by the IB literature – although the IB literature frequently refers to the role concept (Schmid, Bäurle & Kutschker 1998, p. 93). The applicability of this framework in the context of the headquarters-subsidiary relationship is theoretically established and empirically tested.

1.3 Outline of the Study

The following overview concludes the introductory chapter 1 that aimed at creating an understanding for the relevance and the aims of the present study. A brief outline of the study's remaining chapters is provided.

Chapter 2 introduces central concepts and thereby establishes the basis for the study. A brief review of the literature on network MNCs serves as a starting point (2.1). While network MNCs are attributed a number of distinct features, from the present study's point of view, subsidiary roles are particularly relevant and are especially highlighted (2.2). Various perspectives taken on the subsidiary role concept in the IB literature are discussed before the present study's approach to subsidiary roles is outlined. Since the main research question is interested in the implications of perception gaps regarding a subsidiary's role, perception gaps are taken into account next (2.3). Following a general introduction to perception gaps and an overview of the small number of contributions focusing on this issue in the IB literature, the present study's understanding of perception gaps is presented. Since headquarters-subsidiary conflict is later suggested as a central implication of perception gaps, it is established as the final component that is necessary in order to develop the conceptual framework (2.4). While the general literature on interpersonal conflict abounds, a limited number of contributions focusing on headquarters-subsidiary conflict can be drawn on. The approach taken to headquarters-subsidiary conflict in the present study is outlined. Chapter 2 concludes with a summary reviewing the presented concepts (2.5).

Chapter 3 resumes the concepts presented in chapter 2 and integrates them into a conceptual framework. The open system approach by Katz and Kahn (Katz & Kahn 1978) serves as a basis for this integration (3.1). The open system approach is briefly described before the role theoretical framework and the conflict model, which are contained in the approach, are depicted in greater detail. After this general presentation, the transferability of the open system approach and its components to network MNCs are established (3.2). It is outlined how the role theoretical framework can be applied to subsidiary roles and in what way the conflict model can be used to describe headquarters-subsidiary conflict. Finally, the research framework for this study is presented (3.3). It is attempted to combine the framework with contributions from the IB literature. On the one hand, ideas are developed regarding the emergence of perception gaps. On the other hand, headquarters-subsidiary conflict is suggested as the main implication of perception gaps and tentative propositions are derived concerning possible conflict issues for the individual role dimensions.

Following this conceptual part of the study, chapter 4 outlines the empirical approach chosen in order to address the goals formulated at the outset. The research design is based on multiple case studies that employ a combination of quantitative and qualitative data (4.1). Data concerning headquarters and subsidiary respondents' perception of subsidiary roles and the implications of perception gaps is collected by standardized questionnaires and semi-structured interviews. Data collection (4.2) as well as data analysis (4.3) methods are described in detail. Chapter 4 concludes with a discussion of scientific quality criteria and their manifestation in the present study (4.4).

The empirical findings of the study are outlined in chapter 5. After a brief introduction to the chapter (5.1), the individual cases are thoroughly described (5.2). Each case description includes a review of headquarters and subsidiary representatives' perceptions of the subsidiary's role, the reported implications of perception gaps and an interpretation of these findings according to the conceptual framework. Following these individual case analyses, cross-sections of the cases are compared. First, the identified perception gaps concerning the subsidiary's role are examined (5.3). Each role dimension's correspondence to the role definition within the conceptual framework and the structure of perception gaps are analyzed. Second, the implications of the perception gaps are taken into account (5.4). In order to evaluate the applicability of the conceptual framework in the context of the IB literature, the empirically identified implications of perception gaps are contrasted with the previously developed ideas concerning potential implications (cp. 3.3). Finally, the fit of the conceptual framework is examined in the light of the empirical findings and an extension of the framework is proposed.

The study concludes with a discussion in chapter 6. The discussion addresses limitations of the study (6.1), its implications for the IB literature (6.2) as well as potential avenues for future research (6.3). Each of these sections deals with issues of content, theory and methodology. Although, the present study has certain limitations in each of these respects, it also contributes to the IB literature with regard to all three issues.

2. Central Concepts

2.1 Multinational Network Corporations

2.1.1 General Characteristics of Multinational Corporations

The literature does not provide a generally accepted definition of MNCs. One of the first definitions was formulated by Lilienthal who describes MNCs as corporations "which have their home in one country but which operate and live under the laws and customs of other countries as well" (Lilienthal 1960, p. 119). This definition is rather open and the nature of foreign activities is not specified. For other authors, in contrast, more specific characteristics are necessary in order to speak of an MNC (see, for instance, Kutschker & Schmid 2008, pp. 242–244 for an overview). Frequently, the existence of a foreign unit is regarded as a prerequisite for an MNC (e.g., Vernon, Wells & Rangan 1996, p. 28). Some authors even require foreign production activities (e.g., Glaum 1996, p. 10; Mucchielli 1998, pp. 18–19). Firms, however, can choose various other forms of foreign activities (cp. Kutschker & Schmid 2008, pp. 846–939 and Root 1998 for overviews): They can export products and services, cooperate with license or franchise partners, create joint ventures, join strategic alliances and establish different kinds of foreign units. Since the present study's interest lies in the relationship between headquarters and foreign subsidiaries, the focus here will be on the last mentioned form of internationalization, i.e., MNCs that own foreign subsidiaries.

Foreign subsidiaries can add considerable complexity to the management of MNCs (Pahlberg 1996a, p. 5). They are located in different countries which may show varying degrees of psychic (O'Grady & Lane 1996; Stöttinger & Schlegelmilch 1998, 2000) and cultural distance (Kogut & Singh 1988) to the firm's home country; in these countries, subsidiaries are involved in local business networks and may develop different ideas and goals from those of headquarters. At the same time, this geographic spread provides a major advantage for MNCs compared to only locally active companies since the subsidiaries' involvement in local business networks in the host country allows the MNC to access diverse sources of knowledge. In addition, MNCs have the potential to combine organization-specific advantages with advantages of different geographic locations through the internal transfer of resources (Ambos & Reitsperger 2004, p. 51; Arvidsson 1999, p. 20; Ensign 1999, p. 292; Gupta & Govindarajan 2000, p. 473).

Traditionally, MNCs were regarded as hierarchically structured entities with headquarters at the top and a number of dependent and homogeneous subsidiaries (Pahlberg 1996a, p. 5;

Paterson & Brock 2002, p. 140). This view not only dominated the academic literature, but was also reflected in the administrative practices of many MNCs (Schmid, Bäurle & Kutschker 1998, p. 2). A "norm of symmetry and uniformity" seemed to be applied in the management of foreign subsidiaries (Bartlett & Ghoshal 1990, p. 241); subsidiaries' responsibilities were confined to their respective market, while headquarters were seen as the single centre of the firm. However, this hierarchical picture of the MNC was challenged by authors who put forth differentiated concepts of distinct types of MNCs. Perlmutter pioneered in 1969 by presenting the non-hierarchical geocentric MNC as one of four organizational types. Starting in the 1980s, concepts that consider the MNC as a network instead of a hierarchy became widely popular (Bartlett & Ghoshal 1991; Harzing 2000; Perlmutter 1969). Among these types, concepts appeared which consider the MNC as a network instead of a hierarchy (e.g., White & Poynter 1989). A change in perspective followed with regard to MNC structure which will be described in the next paragraph (2.1.2) before an overview of network approaches to MNCs will be given (2.1.3).

2.1.2 Towards a Network Model of Multinational Corporations

The indicated shift from a hierarchical model of MNCs to a network model involved a change in perspective with regard to the management of subsidiaries and the headquarters-subsidiary relationship (Birkinshaw 2000; Birkinshaw & Hood 1998a; Kim, Prescott & Kim 2005, pp. 50–53; Paterson & Brock 2002). Generally, four phases through which research in this field has developed and which also reflect developments in organizational practice can be distinguished. The research streams that are associated with these four phases are referred to as (1) the MNC strategy-structure stream, (2) the headquarters-subsidiary relationship stream, (3) the subsidiary role stream and (4) the subsidiary development stream. These streams of research temporally overlap to a considerable extent. Nevertheless, they represent a logical succession starting from a hierarchical towards a network model of MNCs. In the following, it will be described how research that concentrated on issues of subsidiary management and the headquarters-subsidiary relationship has developed.

(1) The beginning of the first phase, the MNC strategy-structure stream, is seen in the 1960s (Paterson & Brock 2002, p. 140) or 1970s (Birkinshaw 2000, p. 5). During this stage, the overall model of MNCs that was proposed by research and that could be found in practice was that of a hierarchy in which headquarters assumed a central position that was distinctly

superior to subsidiaries. In general, this stream of research focused on the connection between strategy and structure of MNCs (Harzing 1999, p. 32). Strategy was seen as under headquarters' control and structure was assumed to change in order to match strategy (Paterson & Brock 2002, pp. 140–141). Studies addressed questions such as why certain structural forms are adopted by MNCs or how an optimal fit between a firm's strategy and structure could be achieved (Daniels, Pitts & Tretter 1984; Egelhoff 1982; Franko 1974; Stopford & Wells 1972). Since the adaptability of the hierarchical model of the MNC is limited, the search for more flexible organizational structures as alternatives to the traditional hierarchy developed into a key concern (Paterson & Brock 2002, p. 140).

(2) Consequently, the newly emerging headquarters-subsidiary relationship stream of research started to shift its focus towards the subsidiary level of analysis (Birkinshaw 2000, p. 5). Particular emphasis was directed at the individual headquarters-subsidiary relationship (Birkinshaw & Hood 1998a, pp. 4–6). Although to a decreasing extent, this research was still dominated by the hierarchical model of the MNC in which subsidiaries are subordinate to headquarters, interact primarily with headquarters and carry out activities that are typically confined to sales and manufacturing (Birkinshaw 2000, pp. 5–6; Birkinshaw & Hood 1998a, p. 4). Nevertheless, this stream of research started to concede that subsidiaries may possess a certain degree of autonomy and may exert influence on decisions made in the MNC (Paterson & Brock 2002, p. 141). It was realized that foreign subsidiaries frequently conducted activities that were equally important as activities carried out at headquarters (Birkinshaw & Hood 1998a, p. 6). Increasing attention was given to the networks and strategies developed by subsidiaries independently of headquarters (Forsgren, Holm & Johanson 1995, p. 488). Rather than communicating exclusively with headquarters, many subsidiaries were engaged in highly developed exchange relationships with subsidiaries in other countries as well as with local business partners (Birkinshaw & Hood 1998a, p. 6). Accordingly, potential heterogeneity among subsidiaries within the same organization was recognized (Paterson & Brock 2002, pp. 141–142). Several authors argued for differentiated control methods, which not only include formal control but also other types of control mechanisms such as management systems or cultural control, to be applied for different subsidiaries (Bartlett & Ghoshal 1986; Brandt & Hulbert 1976, p. 63; De Meyer 1993, pp. 114–115; Ghoshal & Nohria 1989; Herbert 1999, p. 81; Kim & Mauborgne 1993). Furthermore, the benefits of a shared managerial philosophy (Roth & Schweiger 1991, p. 371) and a more cooperative attitude in the headquarters-subsidiary relationship were promoted (Roth & Morrison 1992, p. 733). Consequently, studies that tried to understand how the connection between headquarters and subsidiaries functions were concerned with

facets of the headquarters-subsidiary relationship, such as subsidiary autonomy (e.g., Garnier 1982, 1984; Otterbeck 1981), centralization of decision making (e.g., Gates & Egelhoff 1986; Negandhi & Baliga 1981) or the question of how to integrate a portfolio of subsidiaries in order to maximize their usefulness to the MNC via mechanisms such as coordination and control (e.g., Picard 1980; Prahalad & Doz 1981; Welge 1981b).

(3) While the headquarters-subsidiary relationship stream of research already implied a shift of focus towards the subsidiary level of analysis, the next step involved the explicit acknowledgement of subsidiaries' increased importance within the MNC. This implied a departure from the hierarchical model of the MNC (Birkinshaw & Hood 1998a, p. 6), which was facilitated through the emergence of alternative concepts of the MNC in the mid-1980s, such as Hedlund's heterarchy (Hedlund 1986), Bartlett and Ghoshal's transnational company (Bartlett & Ghoshal 1991) and other network models. Within the network models, subsidiaries were no longer restricted to dyadic relationships with the firm's headquarters but were rather seen as nodes in the larger network (Birkinshaw 2000, p. 6). In particular the acknowledgement that subsidiaries might possess unique resources and may be able to act autonomously implied the idea to allocate different roles within the MNC to the individual subsidiaries (Bartlett & Ghoshal 1986; Paterson & Brock 2002, p. 142). The research stream that focused on subsidiary roles resulted in a large number of subsidiary role typologies which attempted to identify prototypical categories of subsidiaries and to associate them with certain environmental or structural patterns or administrative requirements (particularly important studies in this stream include, for instance, Gupta & Govindarajan 1991; Jarillo & Martinez 1990; White & Poynter 1984).[1] Two specific types of subsidiary roles to which particular attention was paid will be briefly commented on here. The first category consists of subsidiaries that hold so-called World Product Mandates (Paterson & Brock 2002, p. 143; Rugman 1983).[2] A World Product Mandate can be understood as a subsidiary's worldwide responsibility for the development and marketing of a certain product (Crookell 1987, p. 71; Feinberg 2000, p. 155). This concept emerged in Canadian literature and was directed at the benefit of the respective subsidiary as well as of the host country economy (Crookell 1987, p. 71; Feinberg 2000, pp. 165–166; Paterson & Brock 2002, p. 142). The second subsidiary type is the centre of excellence (Kutschker, Schurig & Schmid 2001, 2002). According to Adenfelt and Lagerström, the definition of a centre of excellence commonly entails three dimensions (Adenfelt & Lagerström 2006, p. 385): First, a subsidiary is assumed to have

---

[1] The subsidiary role concept is central for the present study and will be elaborated on in 2.2.
[2] Sometimes the expressions "World Mandate" (Birkinshaw & Morrison 1995, p. 734) or "Product Mandate" (Tavares & Pearce 2002, p. 76; Tavares & Young 2006, p. 583) are used.

developed specific knowledge. Second, this knowledge is recognized as being useful for other units of the MNC. Third, the subsidiary is able and willing to share this knowledge with other units. Centres of excellence can be regarded as a way of rendering unique resources of individual units of the MNC available for the entire MNC (Paterson & Brock 2002, p. 147). They represent an attempt to integrate the advantages of certain locations into the network and utilize them for the entire MNC (Andersson & Forsgren 2000, p. 332).

(4) The last stream of research – referred to as the subsidiary development stream – differs from the streams mentioned so far in that it focuses on a dynamic process instead of a certain state. This line of research is particularly concerned with the questions of how and why the activities of a subsidiary change over time (Birkinshaw 2000, p. 6; Chang & Rosenzweig 1998; Jarillo & Martinez 1990, p. 501; Papanastassiou & Pearce 1994). According to Birkinshaw and Hood, this stream adds an explicit resources and/or capabilities component to the network perspective (Birkinshaw & Hood 1998a, p. 7). It is assumed that over time a subsidiary accumulates valuable capabilities through its network and may thereby enhance its status and extend the scope of its activities. However, the reverse development is also possible when a subsidiary loses some of its former responsibilities (Birkinshaw & Hood 1998c; Galunic & Eisenhardt 1996). While several authors tried to describe subsidiary development processes as changes towards increased integration into the operations of the firm (Delany 1998; Malnight 1995), others attempted to identify specific drivers of subsidiary evolution such as role assignment by headquarters, ambitions of subsidiary management or constraints and opportunities in the subsidiary's local environment (Birkinshaw & Hood 1998c; Malnight 1996; Young & Hood 1994).

An overview of the historical development of the described streams of research is shown in Figure 1.[3]

---

[3] As already alluded to above, this description of the development of the headquarters-subsidiary relationship literature is simplifying in several ways. First, a clear association of each stream to a certain timeframe is hardly possible. Second, the distinction of the individual streams may be criticized because they overlap not only in terms of time, but also in terms of the questions asked and the issues studied. Third, the streams refer to different levels of analysis – e.g., the multinational literature depicted in Figure 1 can be seen as encompassing all the other streams. Nevertheless, the description presented above can give a general idea of the direction into which the headquarters-subsidiary relationship literature developed during the last decades.

```
                                                            Future directions
                                                        Subsidiary development
                                              The subsidiary role stream
                                  The headquarters-subsidiary relationship stream
                      The MNC strategy-structure stream
        Multinational literature
     1950      60       70       80       90      2000       Future
```

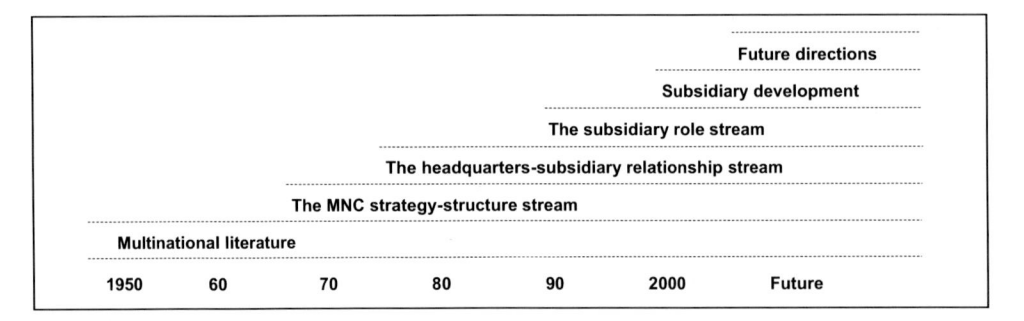

Figure 1:   Development of the Headquarters-Subsidiary Relationship Literature
            Source: Slightly Adapted from Paterson & Brock 2002, p. 140.

Despite the network models' focus on the various relationships in which a subsidiary may be engaged with partners in and outside of the MNC, several authors emphasize that "the subsidiary's most critical relationship was, and still is, with its corporate headquarters" (Birkinshaw & Hood 1998a, p. 6). Although resources and competencies are distributed among different units of the network, the headquarters-subsidiary relationship continues to be crucial since exchange between the individual units needs to be organized and coordinated (Birkinshaw et al. 2000, pp. 321–322; Johnston 2005, p. 3; O'Donnell 2000, p. 543).[4] In order to fulfil this coordinating task, headquarters is required to play a strong central role in network MNCs (Ensign 1999, p. 301; Lipparini & Fratocchi 1999, p. 663). This argumentation justifies the decision taken in the present context to focus on the consequences that perception gaps between headquarters and subsidiary concerning the subsidiary's role may have for the headquarters-subsidiary relationship.

Since the network MNC constitutes the context of the present study, the characteristics of network MNCs will be further described in the following (2.1.3) before the concept of subsidiary roles will be taken into account in more detail (2.2).

2.1.3 Characteristics of Multinational Network Corporations

An MNC can be viewed as both an *intra*-organizational and as part of an *inter*-organizational network (Ensign 1999, p. 292; Schmid, Schurig & Kutschker 2002, p. 45). The intra-organizational perspective focuses on relationships between various units of the same

---

[4] It is acknowledged that the headquarters-subsidiary relationship may not be the most relevant relationship for some units. However, it is assumed that it still is for most units.

organization. One major claim of this perspective is that a clear hierarchical order no longer exists within the MNC. Different units can possess varying degrees of importance and influence at the same time, depending on the issue in question. Interdependent relationships between individual units of the MNC are emphasized (Bartlett & Ghoshal 1991; Doz & Prahalad 1991, p. 147; Ensign 1999, pp. 303–305; Hedlund 1986; White & Poynter 1989, p. 58).

While the intra-organizational perspective reflects on relationships within the MNC, the inter-organizational perspective directs the focus to the relationship between the MNC and its environment. MNCs are no longer considered isolated from their environment, but their social embeddedness is explicitly taken into account (Granovetter 1985). Headquarters as well as subsidiaries can have relationships with various external stakeholders, such as suppliers, customers, competitors, partners, institutions or governments. These relationships not only influence the respective unit but in turn also the entire MNC (Andersson, Forsgren & Holm 2002; Håkansson & Snehota 1995; Schmid, Schurig & Kutschker 2002, p. 45).

Schmid and Kutschker's summary of the intra-organizational and the inter-organizational network perspectives is shown in Figure 2 (Schmid & Kutschker 2003, pp. 163–164).

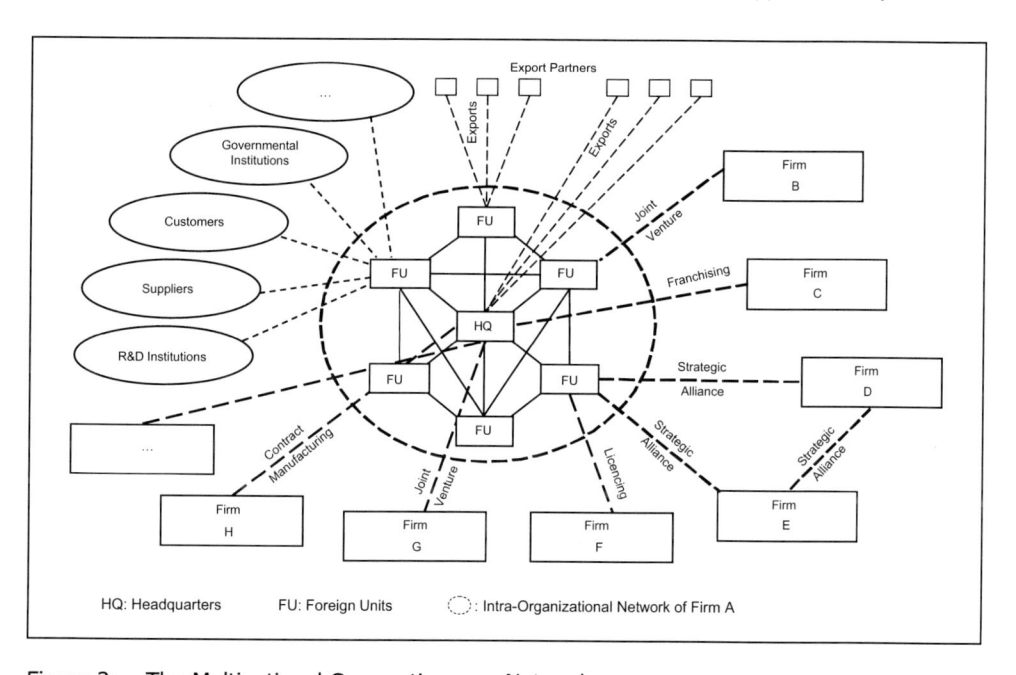

Figure 2:   The Multinational Corporation as a Network
Source: Translation of Schmid & Kutschker 2003, p. 165.

Since the focus is put on the headquarters-subsidiary relationship, this thesis will view MNCs from an intra-organizational network perspective (Schmid & Kutschker 2003, p. 165). Hedlund's "heterarchy" (Hedlund 1986, p. 9), White and Poynter's "horizontal organization" (White & Poynter 1989, p. 55) as well as Prahalad and Doz's multifocal "diversified multinational corporation" (Prahalad & Doz 1987, p. 1) are concepts that have become prominent in this context. In the following paragraphs, central ideas of these network approaches will be summarized.

In heterarchically organized network MNCs, individual subsidiaries can assume more prominent positions than in traditional models of MNCs (Paterson & Brock 2002, p. 142). Horizontal relationships gain importance compared to vertical relationships (White & Poynter 1989, pp. 58–59). Since competencies and capabilities are assumed to be widely dispersed within the MNC, the MNC's units are highly interdependent (Harzing 2000, p. 110; Malnight 1996, p. 43; Tavares & Young 2006, p. 584). Although the degree of interdependence may vary, internationally dispersed organizations can only be successful when the individual units are related to each other through effective communication and coordination (Ensign 1999, pp. 303–305; Hedlund 1986, p. 26; Kobrin 1991, p. 17; Kostova 1998, pp. 308–309; Lipparini & Fratocchi 1999, p. 655; O'Donnell 2000, p. 530). Relationships between headquarters and subsidiaries as well as between individual subsidiaries are characterized by significant reciprocal flows instead of merely sequential, unidirectional flows (Schmid & Kutschker 2003, pp. 163–164). Flows may consist of material resources such as products, capital and people as well as immaterial resources, including information, trust, values, power and knowledge (Randøy & Li 1998, pp. 80–86; Schmid, Schurig & Kutschker 2002, p. 50).

In line with Bartlett and Ghoshal who criticize MNCs for treating all their subsidiaries in the same way, intra-organizational network approaches do not consider subsidiaries to be equal (Bartlett & Ghoshal 1986, p. 88; Birkinshaw & Hood 1998a, p. 6; Paterson & Brock 2002, p. 142). Subsidiaries in network MNCs can adopt highly differentiated roles and fulfil different functions for the entire MNC or for parts of the MNC (Bartlett & Ghoshal 1986, p. 88; Ghoshal & Nohria 1989, p. 323; Schmid 2004, p. 238). Due to their internal resources, their relationships with other units of the MNC or conditions in the local business context in which they are embedded, subsidiaries can even acquire the status of centres of competence or centres of excellence (on centres of excellence, see also Ambos & Reitsperger 2004; Andersson & Forsgren 2000; Frost, Birkinshaw & Ensign 2002; Kutschker, Schurig & Schmid 2002; Schmid 2000; Schmid & Schurig 2003). As a result, (some) subsidiaries can exert considerable influence on decisions and actions of the entire MNC (Schmid & Kutschker 2003, pp. 163–164). Their flexibility and the potential to transfer acquired capabilities across national borders are considered to be central competitive advantages of network MNCs (Kogut 1989, p. 383).

Network approaches seem to correspond increasingly to the reality in MNCs (Harzing 1999, p. 144; Malnight 1996, p. 50; O'Donnell 2000, p. 543; Tavares & Young 2006, p. 587). However, the ideal type that was conceptually formulated has probably not been reached yet (Schmid, Schurig & Kutschker 2002, pp. 65–68). For this thesis, the assumption that subsidiaries can fulfil differentiated roles and functions within the MNC is particularly relevant. The concept of subsidiary roles will be discussed in more detail in 2.2.

2.2 Subsidiary Roles in Multinational Network Corporations

2.2.1 The Subsidiary Role Concept in the International Business Literature

Research on subsidiary roles signifies a turn in the literature on headquarters-subsidiary relationships (Birkinshaw & Hood 1998a, pp. 6–7). The emphasis shifted from headquarters and the control relationship between headquarters and subsidiary towards the subsidiary as a unit of analysis (Paterson & Brock 2002, p. 142). The subsidiary now is considered as an important node within the intra-organizational network of multilateral relationships between headquarters and subsidiaries (Birkinshaw & Hood 1998c, p. 776; see also 2.1.2).[5]

In the IB literature, the term "subsidiary role" is commonly used in relation to the differentiation of subsidiaries in network MNCs. Subsidiaries may be distinguished according to a variety of characteristics. First, they may differ regarding characteristics, such as size or age (Marcati 1989, p. 39), entry motivation or mode of establishment (Ferdows 1997, p. 77; Tavares & Young 2006, p. 585). Subsidiaries can also carry out differentiated tasks and the value chain activities in which they are involved or the geographical scope of these activities can differ (Eckert & Rossmeissl 2007, p. 194). Furthermore, subsidiaries may be

---

[5] Although the role concept has been extensively studied by sociological and socialpsychological research based on role theory, this conceptual knowledge has not been applied in the IB literature. Only the general idea is borrowed. Since role theoretical research is not referred to by this literature, no description of role theory in general will be included in this section on subsidiary roles. However, role theory will be described in relation to the conceptual framework used in the present study in 3.1.3.

differentiated with regard to features such as decision making autonomy (D'Cruz 1986; Taggart 1997a), capabilities (Bartlett & Ghoshal 1986; Benito, Grøgaard & Narula 2003) or their linkages to other units (Nobel & Birkinshaw 1998).

Young and Tavares interpret the subsidiary role concept as a subsidiary's scope of responsibility (Young & Tavares 2004, p. 224).[6] This definition encompasses most, if not all,[7] previous usages of the term subsidiary role and represents a rare instance where the general nature of subsidiary roles is described. In most contributions focusing on subsidiary roles, authors typically consider only the few characteristics according to which they differentiate subsidiaries without defining or commenting on their general understanding of the subsidiary role concept.

In the headquarters-subsidiary relationship, subsidiary roles are usually not explicitly determined but develop in the interaction of several actors and are shaped by complex processes (Birkinshaw & Hood 1998c, p. 775; Dörrenbächer & Geppert 2006, p. 259; Hood & Taggart 1999, p. 515). (1) A subsidiary's role is influenced by headquarters (for instance, via the assignment of a particular role to a subsidiary) as well as by the subsidiary itself (for instance, by efforts to increase its capabilities and to acquire new responsibilities) (Young & Tavares 2004, p. 224). However, when Birkinshaw et al. interpret a subsidiary's role as a "negotiated position that is to some degree understood jointly between HQ [headquarters] and subsidiary managers" (Birkinshaw et al. 2000, p. 324), they neglect the impact of various stakeholders in the local environment, such as suppliers and customers (for instance, by exerting pressure on the subsidiary to adjust to their expectations; regarding the influence of the local environment, see, for example, Benito, Grøgaard & Narula 2003; Eckert & Rossmeissl 2007; Schmid & Schurig 2003). (2) The process through which a subsidiary's role develops can vary according to several characteristics (Schmid, Bäurle & Kutschker 1998, p. 97). First, a role can be deliberately designed in order to fulfil a certain purpose or it may develop randomly due to emergent circumstances (Brock & Barry 2003, p. 552; Schmid

---

[6] While a subsidiary role can be interpreted as a subsidiary's scope of responsibility, a subsidiary initiative is the effort undertaken with the intention to expand this scope of responsibility (Young & Tavares 2004, p. 224). Birkinshaw differentiates subsidiary strategy from subsidiary role. He assumes that the subsidiary role is imposed by headquarters whereas a subsidiary's strategy is defined by subsidiary management (Birkinshaw 2001, p. 389; Birkinshaw & Morrison 1995, p. 733). However, as will be discussed in the following paragraphs, other publications do not support the point of view that a subsidiary role is mainly assigned by headquarters.

[7] For instance, Taggart uses the characteristic "procedural justice" in order to describe subsidiary roles (Taggart 1997a). This attribute does not refer to the subsidiary's scope of responsibility but rather describes the "extent to which the dynamics of a multinational corporation's strategy-making process are judged to be fair by the top managers of its subsidiaries" (Kim & Mauborgne 1993, p. 503).

2003, pp. 284–285). Second, a subsidiary's role can be more or less explicitly defined (Birkinshaw et al. 2000, p. 324). Third, the role may have evolved incrementally in a long-lasting process or revolutionary changes may have led to the present situation (Pahlberg 1996b, p. 22; Tavares & Young 2006, p. 596).

Furthermore, subsidiary roles are not static categories but can evolve over time (see, for instance, the contributions in Birkinshaw & Hood 1998b). Subsidiaries can develop new capabilities, be granted more autonomy or receive responsibility for a larger market. Referring to foreign factories, Ferdows, for instance, emphasizes the potential benefits for MNCs from continuously developing these foreign factories. Depending on the initial role, there is a clear path for upward movement in the factories' strategic role (Ferdows 1989, 1997). However, subsidiaries' capabilities can also deteriorate or fall behind market requirements so that responsibilities can consequently be lost (Birkinshaw 1996; Galunic & Eisenhardt 1996).

Although it is generally assumed that subsidiaries possess one specific role, it may be the case that multiple roles coexist in a subsidiary, in different proportions and in a certain order of importance (Schmid 2004, p. 247; Tavares & Young 2006, p. 596). This may be due to the fact that subsidiaries frequently include distinct business units, have different products and therefore "may exhibit clear traits of one role in a certain business unit, but a distinct strategy concerning another business line" (Tavares & Young 2006, p. 596; cp. also Pearce & Tavares 2002). While this may instigate discussions whether it is justified to refer to a certain subsidiary role, empirical research seems to confirm that a subsidiary can be associated with one predominant (overall) role within the MNC (e.g., Birkinshaw & Morrison 1995; Furu 2001; Gupta & Govindarajan 1994; Harzing & Noorderhaven 2006b; Jarillo & Martinez 1990; Young, Hood & Dunlop 1988).

This short overview illustrates that a subsidiary's role within a network MNC constitutes a complex and multifaceted concept that can be viewed from different perspectives. The variety of factors influencing a subsidiary's role as well as its potentially changing nature (Birkinshaw 1996, p. 467) result in a difficulty to define this role and may lead to perception gaps between headquarters and subsidiary managers concerning the role.[8] Subsidiary role typologies constitute a way by which researchers attempt to structure this wide field.

---

[8] Admittedly, not all aspects of a role may be predisposed to subjective variation to the same degree. Some dimensions such as market scope, product scope and value added scope (White & Poynter 1984) seem considerably more "objective" than, for instance, subsidiary autonomy

2.2.2 Subsidiary Role Typologies

Several researchers tried to reduce the number of possible subsidiary roles to a few prototypes (e.g. Ferdows 1989, 1997; Jarillo & Martinez 1990; White & Poynter 1984; for an overview, see Schmid 2004; Schmid, Bäurle & Kutschker 1998; Schmid & Kutschker 2003). Authors within the IB field typically select two or three dimensions along which subsidiaries can vary and which they consider central with regard to the subsidiary's role. Different authors regard diverse influencing factors as relevant and therefore focus on distinct dimensions. The role types result as a combination of the extreme values of the individual dimensions. Empirical research confirms the assumption that subsidiaries can be differentiated according to their role (e.g., Birkinshaw & Morrison 1995; Furu 2001; Gupta & Govindarajan 1994; Harzing & Noorderhaven 2006b; Jarillo & Martinez 1990; Young, Hood & Dunlop 1988). In Table 1, subsidiary role typologies are summarized which have reached some prominence in the IB literature.

Author/ Authors Year	Dimensions	Roles	Empirical base	Geographic scope of the empirical study
White & Poynter 1984	Market Scope Product Scope Value Added Scope	Miniature Replica Marketing Satellite Rationalized Manufacturer Product Specialist Strategic Independent	More qualitative empirical base About 35 subsidiaries, about 7 in depth	Subsidiaries from Canada (HQ probably in the U.S.)
D'Cruz 1986 I	(Annual Business Plans) (Strategic Plans)	Truncated Business Miniature Replica Mature Non-Strategic Subsidiary Strategically Managed Subsidiary	Personal interviews 47 subsidiaries	Subsidiaries from Canada (HQ probably in the U.S.)
D'Cruz 1986 II	Decision Making Autonomy Extent of Market Involvement	Importer Satellite Business Local Service Business Branch Plant World Product Mandate Globally Rationalized Business	Case study 1 subsidiary	Subsidiary from Canada (HQ in the U.S.)

(Taggart 1997a). However, even dimensions being objective at first sight can be perceived differently.

Author	Criteria	Roles	Methodology	Sample
Bartlett & Ghoshal 1986, 1991	Strategic Importance of Local Environment Competence of the Local Organization	Strategic Leader Contributor Implementer Black Hole	Questionnaire 618 subsidiaries of 66 parent companies	Localization of the subsidiaries not indicated (HQ in North America and Europe)
Marcati 1989	(Level of Coordination) (Dependence from HQs)	Bridgehead Subsidiary Fragmented Subsidiary Connected Subsidiary Loose Subsidiary	Questionnaire 14 subsidiaries	Subsidiaries from the U.S. (HQ in Italy)
Ferdows 1989, 1997	Primary Strategic Reason for the Site Extent of Technical Activities at the Site/Site Competence	Off-Shore Source Server Contributor Outpost Lead	Case studies First 8, then 10 international firms in the electronic industry with their subsidiaries	Subsidiaries mainly from Europe (HQ in North America, Europe and Japan)
Jarillo & Martinez 1990	Degree of Localization Degree of Integration	Autonomous Subsidiary Receptive Subsidiary Active Subsidiary	Structured personal interviews 50 subsidiaries	Subsidiaries from Spain (HQ in North America, Japan and Europe)
Hoffman 1994	MNC Strategy Subsidiary Capabilities Local Environment of the Subsidiary	Partner Contributor Specialist Satellite Independent Interdependent Implementer Isolate	Empirical (secondary) cases only for illustrative purpose 8 subsidiaries	Subsidiaries from countries all over the world (HQ in the U.S., Europe and Japan)
Taggart 1997b I	Degree of Local Responsiveness Degree of Integration	Autonomous Subsidiary Receptive Subsidiary Constrained Independent Quiescent Subsidiary	Questionnaire 171 subsidiaries	Subsidiaries from the UK (localization of HQ not indicated)
Taggart 1997a II	Autonomy Procedural Justice	Vassal Subsidiary Militant Subsidiary Collaborator Subsidiary Partner Subsidiary	Questionnaire 171 subsidiaries	Subsidiaries from the UK (localization of HQ not indicated)
Taggart 1998 III	Coordination of Activities Configuration of Activities	Autarchic Subsidiary Detached Subsidiary Confederate Subsidiary Strategic Auxiliary	Questionnaire 171 subsidiaries	Subsidiaries from the UK (localization of HQ not indicated)

Author	Dimensions	Roles	Method	Sample
Gupta & Govindarajan 1991, 1994	Outflow of Knowledge; Inflow of Knowledge	Local Innovator; Global Innovator; Implementer; Integrated Player	Questionnaire	359 subsidiaries of 79 parent companies. Localization of subsidiares not indicated (HQ in the U.S., Japan and Europe)
Birkinshaw & Morrison 1995	(Market Scope); (Product Scope); (Value Added Scope)	Local Implementer; Specialised Contributor; World Mandate	Questionnaire	115 subsidiaries. Subsidiaries from the U.S., Canada, UK, Germany, France and Japan (localization of HQ not indicated)
Forsgren & Pedersen 1996, 1997	Corporate Embeddedness; External Embeddedness	Independent Centre; External Centre; Internal/Corporate Centre; Strategic Centre	Questionnaire	60 subsidiaries. Subsidiaries from Denmark (HQ worldwide)
Nobel & Birkinshaw 1998	Nature of Activities; Geographic Scope; Linkages to other Entities	Local Adaptor; International Adaptor; International Creator	Questionnaire	110 subsidiaries of 15 parent companies. Subsidiaries from Sweden and outside of Sweden (HQ in Sweden)
Surlemont 1998	Domain of Influence; Scope of Influence	Dormant Centre; Administrative Centre; Strategic Centre of Excellence; Global Headquarters	Questionnaire	Number of subsidiaries not indicated. Subsidiaries from Belgium (HQ worldwide)
Randøy & Li 1998	Outflow of Resources; Inflow of Resources	Resource Independent; Resource Provider; Resource User; Resource Networker	Questionnaire	Aggregated data from 25 industries. Direct investments in the U.S. from all over the world
Benito, Grøgaard & Narula 2003	Scope of Activities; Level of Competence	Miniature Replica; Single-Activity Unit; Multi-Activity Unit; Highly Specialised Unit; Strategic Centre	Questionnaire	728 subsidiaries. Subsidiaries from Denmark, Finland, Norway (HQ worldwide)
Daub 2009; Schmid & Daub 2005	Network Integration; Strategic Relevance	Service Factory; Internal Competence Centre; Support Centre; Specialized Contributor	Case studies	4 subsidiaries. Subsidiaries from Eastern Europe (HQ from Germany)
Tavares & Young 2006	Market Scope; Product Scope; Value Added Scope	Miniature Replica; Rationalized Manufacturer; Product Mandate	Questionnaire	233 subsidiaries. Subsidiaries from Ireland, Portugal, Spain and UK (HQ from Japan and EU)

	Communication Centrality			
Vereecke, Van Dierdonck & De Meyer 2006	Innovation Indegree Innovation Outdegree People Indegree People Outdegree	Isolated Receiver Hosting Network Player Active Network Player	Case studies 8 firms with 4–10 manufacturing plants	Spread of subsidiaries: pan-European or global (HQ in Europe)

Table 1: Comparison of Subsidiary Role Typologies
Source: Extension of Schmid 2004, pp. 242–244.

Despite these numerous attempts to determine the central variables that characterize subsidiaries, no typology has so far met with unanimous approval. In the IB literature, however, subsidiary role typologies have contributed to the change in perspective towards the subsidiary. They highlight the fact that there is not only one type of subsidiary, but many different types depending on the focus chosen (Paterson & Brock 2002, pp. 141–142; Schmid, Bäurle & Kutschker 1998, p. 94). The role typologies, however, are not an end in themselves. First, they "reduce the complexity of multinational organizational reality into a manageable number of related characteristics" (Harzing & Noorderhaven 2006b, p. 196) and thereby make it easier to understand and explain the functioning of multinational companies. Furthermore, by describing meaningful organizational relations, they can be used in a predictive way. For instance, they may be applied in order to establish a relationship between subsidiary roles and ways in which the subsidiaries can be controlled, coordinated and governed accordingly (Gupta & Govindarajan 1991; Johanson, Pahlberg & Thilenius 1996, p. 250; Kim, Prescott & Kim 2005, pp. 50–54). Several caveats, however, are associated with the role typologies. One limitation concerns the selection of the typologies' dimensions. Since authors, in general, do not ground their typologies of subsidiary roles in (organizational) theory, the selection of dimensions seems rather arbitrary. While each typology has a specific focus and takes a certain perspective, there is always a large range of other possible subsidiary role dimensions (Schmid, Bäurle & Kutschker 1998, pp. 95–96).

2.2.3 Approach to Subsidiary Roles in the Present Study

2.2.3.1 Selection of Subsidiary Role Typologies

Young and Tavares describe subsidiary roles as a subsidiary's scope of responsibility (Young & Tavares 2004, p. 224). While this is a rather abstract idea, concrete elements of the role have to be focused on in order to examine the role in an empirical study. Instead of developing an additional subsidiary role typology, the most appropriate of the existing typologies are selected in order to address the questions posed in this thesis.

(1) First, those typologies are discarded which focus on a specific type of subsidiary. This leads to the exclusion of the typologies presented by Ferdows and Vereecke, Van Dierdonck and De Meyer which refer to manufacturing plants (Ferdows 1989, 1997; Vereecke, Van Dierdonck & De Meyer 2006). Furthermore, the typology by Surlemont which concentrates on subsidiaries with world product mandates is removed (Surlemont 1998) as well as the typology by Schmid and Daub which focuses on service offshoring subsidiaries (Daub 2009; Schmid & Daub 2005). The remaining typologies do not specify a certain type of subsidiary.

(2) The second criterion is the impact that a typology has had on IB research in conceptual as well as empirical terms. The most prominent typologies in this respect are the contributions by White and Poynter, Bartlett and Ghoshal and Gupta and Govindarajan (Bartlett & Ghoshal 1986, 1991; Gupta & Govindarajan 1991, 1994; White & Poynter 1984). (a) The typology by White and Poynter represents one of the first typologies of subsidiary roles (White & Poynter 1984). The suggested dimensions market scope, product scope and value added scope were adopted by the authors of other typologies in the following years (Birkinshaw & Morrison 1995; Tavares & Young 2006) and the original typology was subject to empirical tests (Young, Hood & Dunlop 1988). (b) The typology by Bartlett and Ghoshal has to be considered as part of a larger framework that describes a new type of organization – the transnational firm (Bartlett & Ghoshal 1986, 1991). Differentiation of subsidiary roles is one of the central characteristics of the transnational firm, the conceptualization of which represents an important contribution to the network perspective of MNCs. Furthermore, Bartlett and Ghoshal's subsidiary role typology was taken into account in empirical studies of subsidiary roles (Furu 2001). (c) Gupta and Govindarajan presented another central typology that concentrates on intra-corporate knowledge flows (Gupta & Govindarajan 1991, 1994). Since intra-corporate knowledge flows are increasingly recognized as one of the most important sources of competitive advantage (Doz, Santos & Williamson 2001, p. 169; Kogut & Zander 1993, p. 636, 2003, p. 518), Gupta and Govindarajan's typology has been a

prevalent reference in IB research (Harzing & Noorderhaven 2006b, p. 196). Harzing and Noorderhaven tested the typology empirically (Harzing & Noorderhaven 2006b).

(3) Since the aim of the present contribution is the study of the perception of subsidiary roles by headquarters and subsidiary managers, the dimensions of the typology should not be objectively measurable, but their perception should rather depend on subjective interpretation. In other words, this study is not interested in the question of whether managers are able to correctly list all markets for which a subsidiary is responsible; instead, the focus is on the extent to which different managers' ideas of socially constructed variables are identical (see also 2.3). When the dimensions of the remaining three typologies are taken into account, the dimensions "knowledge outflow", "knowledge inflow" and "subsidiary capabilities" can be classified as subjective, since objective measurement of these characteristics is hardly possible (e.g., Arvidsson 1999, pp. 32–41). The dimensions "market scope", "product scope" and "value added scope" concern attributes that in theory could be determined relatively objectively; in practice, however, the dimensions are too complex for a definition to account for all eventualities.[9] Situations for which no rule has been predefined may arise and make it necessary that an actor interprets the situation according to its requirements and his/her previous experiences. Nevertheless, the degree to which these dimensions depend on individual perceptions is assumed considerably lower than the degree to which this is true for knowledge flows and capabilities. For the dimension "market importance", the decision depends on the criteria that determine this importance for a certain MNC. If market importance exclusively depends on the size of a market, measurability is given. If other criteria such as customer demand or quality of suppliers are seen as more relevant, objective measurability is not as apparent. Consequently, particularly

---

[9] The following example, cited after Morecroft et al. 1995, p. 304, from a Harvard Business School case, shows that, in practice, even a dimension such as "market scope" which seems to be quite straightforward, is not always clearly defined and that such lack of definition can lead to problems for the MNC: "Most of the YKK subsidiaries over here engage in exports and YKK also exports from Japan. As a result, at least once or twice a year we find ourselves competing against the export department in Japan for the same customer. It has actually happened that a large customer has tried to play out one YKK subsidiary against the other... Such competition against each other is nonsense. Who loses is the YKK group as a whole. We also confuse our customers, and we are losing face especially if different YKK subsidiaries quote different prices and conditions... The problem is getting bigger every day as the European markets grow closer and closer together. I am not interested in competing against other YKK units. To avoid that, I think every subsidiary should be assigned a certain geographic territory" (Harvard Business School 1977, p. 19).

the dimensions "knowledge inflow", "knowledge outflow" and "subsidiary capabilities" seem interesting for the present study.[10]

Summarizing the three criteria, a decision is taken in favour of the typology by Bartlett and Ghoshal (with the subsidiary role dimensions "subsidiary capabilities" and "strategic importance of the local environment"; Bartlett & Ghoshal 1986, 1991) and the typology by Gupta and Govindarajan (with the subsidiary role dimensions "inflow of knowledge" and "outflow of knowledge"; Gupta & Govindarajan 1991, 1994). Consequently, in the present study, subsidiary roles are conceptualized and operationalized in terms of these four dimensions, although such an approach may be criticized. First, the range of role dimensions provided by the IB literature cannot be considered comprehensive (Schmid, Bäurle & Kutschker 1998, pp. 95–96). It may therefore be questioned whether this collection represents a suitable basis in order to select "the right" or "relevant" subsidiary role dimensions for the present study. Of course, through the selection of four dimensions, the picture of the subsidiary's role is further restricted. It is obvious that a subsidiary's role cannot be reduced to four dimensions. Second, the subsidiary role dimensions that are presented in the literature are commonly not reflected in the managerial practice, i.e., the classification of subsidiaries according to different roles is usually not found in MNCs. Despite these drawbacks, the reference to established dimensions seems to be a viable way for an empirical study of subsidiary roles. On the one hand, individual dimensions have been used in the literature in order to describe subsidiary roles; on the other hand, four characteristics are better manageable than the abstract concept of the subsidiary's role.

2.2.3.2 Differentiation of Subsidiary Roles According to Bartlett and Ghoshal

Bartlett and Ghoshal were among the first authors to promote the advantages that the differentiation of subsidiary roles may have compared to treating all subsidiaries identically (Bartlett & Ghoshal 1986, p. 88).[11] They propose a conceptually developed typology which takes into account strategic considerations as well as organizational circumstances (Schmid, Bäurle & Kutschker 1998, pp. 32–34). They differentiate four subsidiary roles according to

---

[10] It has to be noted that these dimensions are not homogeneous but still contain various "shades of subjectivity". Knowledge flows, for instance, include skills that can hardly be grasped or measured; at the same time, however, they may represent plans and processes that can be clearly defined.

[11] Findings from research on group composition can provide an analogy that confirms this assumption. In line with the proposition of Belbin's team role theory (Belbin 1981; Belbin 1993), it was shown that mixed teams which consist of individuals who fulfil differentiated roles, perform better than teams consisting of individuals who all fulfil the same role (Prichard & Stanton 1999).

the two dimensions "strategic importance of the local environment" and "organizational competence" (Bartlett & Ghoshal 1986, p. 90). Instead of "organizational competence", Bartlett and Ghoshal term the second dimension "level of local resources and capabilities" in a later publication (Bartlett & Ghoshal 1991, p. 106). The typology and the resulting four subsidiary roles are portrayed in Figure 3. In the present study, the focus will be on the dimensions while the prototypical roles are not emphasized. The two dimensions will be discussed in the following paragraphs.

		low	high
Competence of the Local Organization	high	Contributor	Strategic Leader
	low	Implementer	Black Hole
		low	high
		Strategic Importance of the Local Environment	

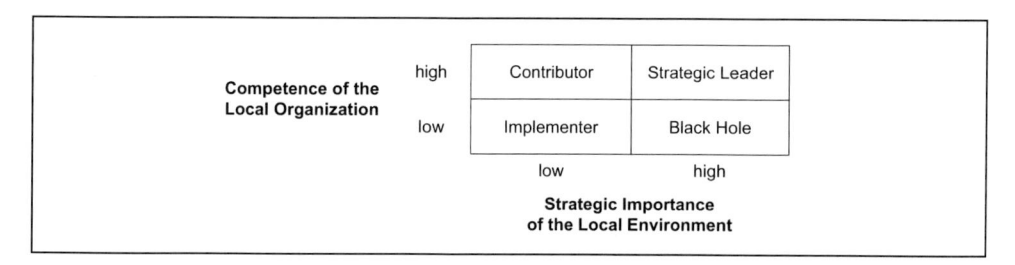

Figure 3: Bartlett and Ghoshal's Subsidiary Role Typology
Source: Bartlett & Ghoshal 1986, p. 90.

Strategic importance of the local environment. Originally, Bartlett and Ghoshal describe an important market in the following way: "A large market is obviously important, and so is a competitor's home market or a market that is particularly sophisticated or technologically advanced" (Bartlett & Ghoshal 1986, p. 90). According to this definition, four indicators of market importance are taken into account: (1) "market size", (2) "competitive intensity", (3) "customer demand" and (4) "technological dynamism". Bartlett and Ghoshal assume that the significance of a certain national environment will strongly influence the strategic importance of the country unit that is active in the respective market (Bartlett & Ghoshal 1991, p. 105).[12] While in their first conceptual publication on the typology, Bartlett and Ghoshal refer to the dimension as "strategic importance of the local environment" (Bartlett & Ghoshal 1986, p. 90), other labels are applied by the authors as well. Although in

---

[12] While an association between the importance of the local market environment and the importance of a specific subsidiary is frequently proposed (e.g. Furu 2001, p. 135), the two concepts are not identical. A subsidiary can as well be important due to other reasons, such as its financial performance, the magnitude of intra-company transactions or the assets fixed in the unit (Leksell & Lindgren 1982, p. 36). Here, however, the focus is on the local market environment in which a subsidiary is located. Regardless of the factors for which a market is considered as important, it can be expected that an important market is of particular interest to an MNC and a subsidiary in such a market will receive a higher degree of attention (Birkinshaw, Bouquet & Ambos 2007, pp. 41–42; Leksell & Lindgren 1982, p. 36).

the conceptual part of their book "Managing Across Borders: The Transnational Solution", Bartlett and Ghoshal use the same term (Bartlett & Ghoshal 1991, p. 105), in the empirical part, they refer to "environmental complexity" instead (Bartlett & Ghoshal 1991, p. 233). In his dissertation, Ghoshal develops a subsidiary role typology that is similar to the one published by Bartlett and Ghoshal (Ghoshal 1986). Here, the respective dimension is referred to as "learning opportunities in the local environment" in the conceptual description (Ghoshal 1986, p. 419) and "learning potential in the local environment" in the empirical part (Ghoshal 1986, p. 437). In two other publications written jointly with Nohria, Ghoshal again refers to "environmental complexity" (Ghoshal & Nohria 1987, pp. 10, 16, 1989, pp. 326, 328, 332). Despite the variation of labels presented by the authors, the present study will speak of "strategic importance of the subsidiary's market". On the one hand, "strategic importance" seems to be the most comprehensive of the abovementioned labels including factors such as market size, competitive intensity and technological dynamism. On the other hand, a subsidiary's market may be detached from the environment in which it is located since this market can exceed country boundaries.

Subsidiary capabilities. While market importance is Bartlett and Ghoshal's "principal strategic consideration" (Bartlett & Ghoshal 1991, p. 105), the second dimension is supposed to reflect organizational issues. Bartlett and Ghoshal suppose that the second dimension, organizational competence, can become evident in any area of the subsidiary, as for instance, in technology, production or marketing. They thereby promote a functional capability definition (Bartlett & Ghoshal 1986, p. 90). However, as with regard to their first dimension, Bartlett and Ghoshal are not consistent in their terminology concerning this second dimension. They not only refer to a subsidiary's capabilities (Bartlett & Ghoshal 1991, pp. 106, 112) but also to its competence (Bartlett & Ghoshal 1986, p. 90, 1991, p. 105) and to the resources it possesses (Bartlett & Ghoshal 1991, pp. 106, 112, 233; Ghoshal 1986, pp. 419, 437; Ghoshal & Nohria 1987, pp. 10, 16, 1989, pp. 326, 328, 332). As Bartlett and Ghoshal use the terms "capabilities", "competence" and "resources" interchangeably, these terms are frequently not clearly distinguished in the business literature. This may be partly attributed to the variety of definitions that have been proposed for any of them (Gouthier & Schmid 2003, pp. 120–122; Schmid & Schurig 2003, p. 757). Resources can be generally defined as "anything which could be thought of as a strength or weakness of a given firm" (Wernerfelt 1984, p. 172). While several classifications for resources have been proposed (e.g., Bamberger & Wrona 1996, pp. 132–134; Grant 1991, p. 119), a general distinction that is frequently referred to is the differentiation between tangible and intangible resources (Schmid & Schurig 2003, pp. 757–758). Since both capabilities and competence can be considered as intangible resources (Bamberger & Wrona 1996, pp. 132–134), the resource concept is broader than either capabilities or competence. For instance, Day defines capabilities as "complex bundles of skills and accumulated knowledge, exercised through organizational processes that enable firms to coordinate activities and make use of their assets" (Day 1994, p. 38). He points out that this definition evades the common distinction between competences as "well-defined routines that are combined with firm-specific assets to enable distinctive functions to be carried out" and capabilities as "the mechanisms and processes by which new competencies are developed" (Day 1994, p. 38). When Bartlett and Ghoshal's description of the four types of subsidiary roles is examined, it becomes apparent that the authors refer to the respective subsidiaries' capabilities and competence but not to their resources (Bartlett & Ghoshal 1986, pp. 90–92). Consequently, in the present context, this narrower conceptualization is followed and the expression "capabilities" is utilized.

In the present study, the functional areas proposed by Benito et al. and Moore are taken into account as fields in which a subsidiary's capabilities may surface (Benito, Grøgaard & Narula 2003, p. 450; Moore 2000, p. 161, 2001, p. 285). However, two changes are made. First, the areas of research and development are combined to one. Second, the area of general management capabilities is added.[13] This results in a focus on the following value chain activities: (1) research and development, (2) production of goods and/or services, (3) marketing and/or sales, (4) logistics and/or distribution, (5) purchasing, (6) human resource management and (7) general management. These seven value chain activities will be referred to in several other sections of this study.

2.2.3.3 Differentiation of Subsidiary Roles According to Gupta and Govindarajan

Gupta and Govindarajan commence their considerations concerning the differentiation of subsidiary roles by conceptualizing the multinational corporation as a network of transactions (Gupta & Govindarajan 1991, p. 770). In general, they mention three types of flows that they consider as relevant – capital, product and knowledge flows. However, they base their typology only on knowledge flows. While some other authors promote a rather restrictive notion of knowledge flow with a strong focus on technical knowledge (Andersson, Björkman

---

[13] General management activities are an additional area of functional activities that is present in Porter's value chain (Porter 1986, pp. 20–21). Since general management activities are frequently argued to be one of the most important resources within a firm (Bamberger & Wrona 2004, p. 43; Lado, Boyd & Wright 1992, pp. 82–84), general management capabilities are included in the present study.

& Forsgren 2005, p. 528), Gupta and Govindarajan's knowledge flow concept is rather broad. They define knowledge flow in the following way:

> "Intracorporate knowledge flow is defined here as the transfer of either expertise (e.g., skills and capabilities) or external market data of strategic value. The type of expertise transferred could refer to input processes (e.g., purchasing skills), throughput processes (e.g., product designs, process designs, and packaging designs), or output processes (e.g., marketing know-how, distribution expertise). Similarly, the transfer of external market data could refer to the transfer of globally relevant information about key customers, competitors, or suppliers. Note that knowledge flow refers to the transfer of either expertise or external market information of global relevance, but not to the transfer of internal administrative information (such as the exchange of monthly financial data)" (Gupta & Govindarajan 1991, p. 773).

With this description, Gupta and Govindarajan provide a rather detailed account of their notion of knowledge flows. Their approach is adopted in the present context. However, when it comes to the specific areas of knowledge flows, slightly different categories are applied than by Gupta and Govindarajan. Gupta and Govindarajan differentiate nine areas of knowledge flows: market data on customers, market data on competitors, product designs, process designs, marketing know-how, distribution know-how, packaging design/technology, purchasing know-how and, finally, management systems and practices (Gupta & Govindarajan 1994, p. 450). These areas refer to knowledge flows that may be associated with different functional areas. In order to obtain a consistent pattern, in the present study, knowledge flows will be structured analogous to the functional areas described in relation to subsidiary capabilities. Consequently, with reference to Benito et al. and Moore (Benito, Grøgaard & Narula 2003, p. 450; Moore 2000, p. 161, 2001, p. 285), knowledge flows concerning the following value chain activities are considered: (1) research and development, (2) production of goods and/or services, (3) marketing and/or sales, (4) logistics and/or distribution, (5) purchasing, (6) human resource management and (7) general management (2.2.3.2).

Gupta and Govindarajan assume that network transactions can be specified according to their magnitude on the one hand and their directionality on the other hand. They use the direction of knowledge flows in order to define the two dimensions of their typology of subsidiary roles. First, knowledge that is received by a certain subsidiary from other organizational units is taken into account and second, knowledge is considered that is provided by the focal subsidiary to other organizational units. Both dimensions are differentiated between low and high. The resulting two-dimensional typology of subsidiary roles is depicted in Figure 4.

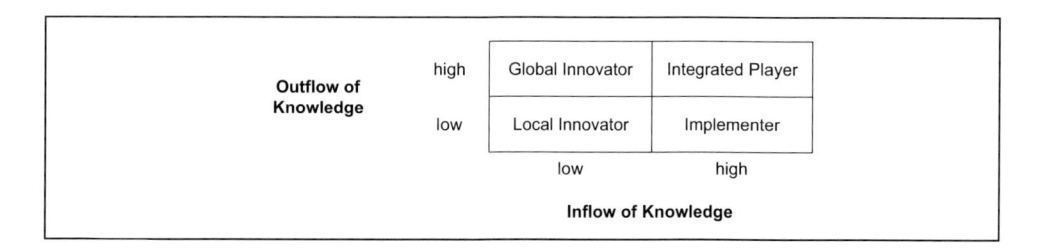

Outflow of Knowledge	high	Global Innovator	Integrated Player
	low	Local Innovator	Implementer
		low	high
		Inflow of Knowledge	

Figure 4:   Gupta and Govindarajan's Subsidiary Role Typology
          Source: Gupta & Govindarajan 1991, p. 774.

2.3 Perception Gaps Concerning Subsidiary Roles

2.3.1 Attributes of Perception Gaps

2.3.1.1   The Subjective Nature of Perception

Perception can be conceived of in two different ways. On the one hand, the term may refer to the process of perception or "perceiving" (Higgins & Bargh 1987, p. 370; Malim 1994, p. 35). From this point of view, perception can be defined as a "set of processes by which we recognize, organize, and make sense of the sensations we receive from environmental stimuli" (Sternberg 2006, p. 111). On the other hand, perception may relate to the result of perceiving, to what is perceived. From that perspective, perception can be considered as the "outcome of individuals' information processing or a consequence of individuals' selective attention, selective comprehension, and judgment" (Waller et al. 2001, p. 586). In the present context, the second approach is followed, since the focus is on the perception that managers have of subsidiary roles rather than the process through which this perception has developed.

While there are different approaches to perception, it is generally accepted that perception does not objectively reflect reality (McClelland 2004, p. 66). Instead, it is always at least to some degree subject to interpretation. Both the process-oriented perspective and the outcome-oriented perspective emphasize this subjective element of perception. The first group of variables which influence perception are subjective factors such as expectations, personal experiences, knowledge, personality characteristics, situational motives or general values (Mezias & Starbuck 2003, p. 4; Zimbardo 1995, p. 162). Second, systematic variations of human perception are due to the use of heuristics and the effect of biases (Tversky & Kahneman 1982). Furthermore, individuals' perceptions may be influenced by environmental factors such as firm or industry characteristics, information availability or culture (for studies of factors leading to different perceptions in a managerial context, see, for example, Sutcliffe & Huber 1998; Waller, Huber & Glick 1995). Consequently, due to these factors, there can be considerable variation in the perception of individuals.

This argumentation may be associated with constructivist approaches in the philosophy of science which consider the existence of objective reality in general as problematic (Flick 2003, p. 151). Radical constructivists deny the existence of objective reality and emphasize the subjective construction of reality. According to this perspective, knowledge can only relate to the organization of experiences in our subjective world (von Glasersfeld 1994, p. 22). Social constructivists do not follow this radical standpoint but focus on the dialectic between individual and objective reality (Berger & Luckmann 1966, p. 57): "Society is a human product. Society is an objective reality. Man is a social product" (Berger & Luckmann 1966, p. 58). In other words, Berger and Luckmann assume that the social world does not exist independently of individuals but is created and influenced by them. On the other hand, individuals experience the social world as real and objectively given. Consequently, the world is seen as possessing subjective as well as objective traits. The present study follows this contention.

2.3.1.2 Perception Gaps vs. Perception Errors

It has been argued that a certain variation among individuals' perceptions is justified for several reasons. However, even if the world is regarded as socially constructed, differences can be discerned in the expected inter-subjective variance of different types of variables. On the one hand, there are variables which may be considered as "objectively measureable", for instance, because they are quantifiable (e.g., Geringer & Herbert 1991, pp. 250–251). They describe objects or issues that can be clearly defined, described or observed and concerning which most individuals would agree in their judgement of the variable. The range of interpretations that would still be considered right or realistic by the majority of individuals is relatively narrow. In case an individual's perception of the object or issue lies outside this range of acceptable interpretations, most observers would rate the perception as wrong. Such a situation is referred to here as perception error. Managers' perception errors were examined by several studies in the management literature. For instance, the accuracy of perceptions which managers have of their organizations and the organizational environment were taken into account (Doty et al. 2006; Mezias & Starbuck 2003; Starbuck & Mezias 1996; Sutcliffe 1994). The studies confirm the prevalence of perception errors concerning organizational as well as environmental properties (variables that were examined include the number of employees, sales growth and industry concentration measured by commonly used indicators).

On the other hand, there are variables for which no generally accepted definition exists, that cannot be observed directly and that depend on individuals' perceptions to a larger extent. These variables are frequently referred to as "socially constructed variables" even by researchers not building on a social constructivist position. Such variables are described as neither "determined by the nature of things" nor "inevitable" (Hacking 1999, pp. 6–7). In other words, these variables are "intersubjectively real because others agree [they are]" (Pouliot 2007, p. 362). Variables such as social time (e.g., Butler 1995; Harvey & Novicevic 2001; Plakoyiannaki & Saren 2006), service orientation (e.g., Lytle & Timmerman 2006) and different types of roles (Wondolleck & Ryan 1999; e.g., gender roles: Perez-Lopez, Lewis & Cash 2001; Young & Hurlic 2007; work roles: Parker 2000, 2007; managerial roles: Chi Cui, Ball & Coyne 2002) are summarized into this category. Such variables contain a certain degree of vagueness by nature and consequently allow some variation in how they are perceived. The range of accepted interpretations for these variables is considerably wider than for variables that are more "objective". Since the individual interpretation cannot be compared to any objective reference, it seems unjustified to speak of perception errors in this case. It is possible, however, to compare the perceptions of different individuals to each other and to refer to "perception gaps" between the subjective representations of different individuals (Arvidsson 1999, pp. 89–118). Perception gaps in this sense were also found in a variety of studies in management literature. Examples include managers' and non-managers' perceptions of the values related to an organization's mission statement (Desmidt & Heene 2007), employees' and customers' perceptions of functional and relational service quality (Peiró, Martínez-Tur & Ramos 2005), managers' and accountants' perceptions of managers' information needs (Pierce & O'Dea 2003) and different parties' perceptions of the authority and responsibilities associated with a certain organizational position (French & Henning 1966; Henning & Moseley 1970; Weigand 1966). These examples constitute instances where both sides look upon the same issue from a different point of view and consequently construct a different picture of reality.

The present study is concerned with inter-individual differences in the perception of variables of the latter kind – in particular, perception gaps regarding a subsidiary's role within the MNC. In the next paragraphs, studies from the IB literature will be presented that focus on perception gaps between headquarters and subsidiary managers concerning subsidiary roles.

2.3.2 Perception Gaps in the International Business Literature

2.3.2.1 Approaches to Perception Gaps

So far, few studies in the IB literature address the phenomenon "perception gaps". Those studies that do focus on perception gaps compare the perceptions of managers working at geographically distant organizational units – namely managers representing headquarters on the one side and managers representing foreign subsidiaries on the other side.[14] Perception gaps are generally defined by IB researchers as situations in which managers who are active in different organizational units hold different opinions or have different perceptions concerning a particular matter (Arvidsson 1999, p. 89; Asakawa 2001, p. 739).

Studies in the IB literature compare the perceptions of headquarters and subsidiary managers regarding issues such as the following: subsidiaries' capabilities (Arvidsson 1999; Denrell, Arvidsson & Zander 2004), subsidiaries' autonomy (Asakawa 2001; Chini, Ambos & Wehle 2005), information sharing between headquarters and subsidiaries (Asakawa 2001; Chini, Ambos & Wehle 2005), subsidiaries' business networks (Holm, Johanson & Thilenius 1995), the marketing process in subsidiaries (Chan & Holbert 2001) and the authority granted to subsidiary-based purchasing managers (Toyne 1978). The contribution by Birkinshaw et al. is the only study that explicitly states its concentration on perception gaps concerning *the subsidiary's role* (Birkinshaw et al. 2000). However, most of the other issues that are studied (e.g., subsidiaries' autonomy and capabilities) have been associated with the subsidiary role concept as well (see 2.2.2). Since the focus of the present study is on perception gaps regarding the subsidiary's role, the contributions related to this issue will be reviewed here. Before the respective studies will be presented (2.3.2.2), further characteristics of perception gaps are described.

The IB literature differentiates several types of perception gaps in terms of various dimensions. (1) Perception gaps may be distinguished according to the hierarchical order of the involved parties. In this regard, Arvidsson describes hierarchical perception gaps that exist between corporate and subsidiary managers and horizontal perception gaps, which emerge between managers from different subsidiaries (Arvidsson 1999, p. 96). In general,

---

[14] The small number of studies addressing this problem is surprising since the fact that headquarters and subsidiary managers may perceive certain issues differently has been widely acknowledged in the IB literature. Cultural differences, differing business environments and varying business partners may contribute to perception gaps. Focusing on the evaluation of capabilities, Arvidsson, for instance, provides an extensive list of studies in which the authors comment on the subjectivity of this evaluation (Arvidsson 1999, pp. 32–41). He concludes that most of the contributions acknowledge the problem of subjectivity but do not draw any consequences.

however, the focus is on the headquarters-subsidiary relationship rather than the relationship between subsidiaries. (2) Second, the directionality of perception gaps may be taken into account. Perception gaps can be distinguished depending on which party perceives a certain attribute to be more or less pronounced. Arvidsson provides a framework for classifying perception gaps concerning subsidiary capabilities as "positive" or "negative" perception gaps (Arvidsson 1999, pp. 102–103). Birkinshaw et al. apply this framework in relation to perceptions of subsidiary roles and change the terminology to "subsidiary role overestimation" versus "HQ role overestimation" since the expressions "positive" and "negative perception gaps" were found to be ambiguous (Birkinshaw et al. 2000, pp. 325–326). The framework by Birkinshaw et al. is presented in Figure 5.[15] Asakawa as well addresses the directionality of perception gaps. He specifies "tense" (Asakawa 2001, p. 739) perception gaps when both partners rate the other more negatively than they rate themselves. In contrast, perception gaps are "relaxed" (Asakawa 2001, p. 739) when both partners rate the other more positively than they rate themselves (for instance, he speaks of a relaxed perception gap when the subsidiary managers view the subsidiary as enjoying more autonomy than headquarters managers do). However, such a classification may be problematic since it involves a clear valuation of the respective attribute. (3) In addition, Asakawa proposes a third dimension on which he distinguishes perception gaps at the level of "perceived reality (as it is)" (Asakawa 2001, p. 739) from perception gaps at the level of "normative expectation (as it ought to be)" (Asakawa 2001, p. 739). Furthermore, the significance of perception gaps can be taken into account (Asakawa 2001, p. 739).

---

[15] A similar framework for the depiction of buyer and seller perceptions of the quality of their relationship was presented by Holmlund and Strandvik. They speak of a "perception configuration map" (Holmlund & Strandvik 1999, p. 689).

```
                    High
                    ┌─────────────────────────────┐
                    │ Subsidiary role        ╱    │
                    │ overestimation       ╱      │
                    │                    ╱        │
                    │                  ╱          │
Subsidiary          │   Small or     ╱            │
perception of the   │   non-existent╱             │
subsidiary role     │   perception╱               │
                    │   gap     ╱                 │
                    │         ╱                   │
                    │       ╱         HQ role     │
                    │     ╱          overestimation│
                    Low ╱                         │
                    └─────────────────────────────┘
                    Low                        High
                    HQ perception of subsidiary role
```

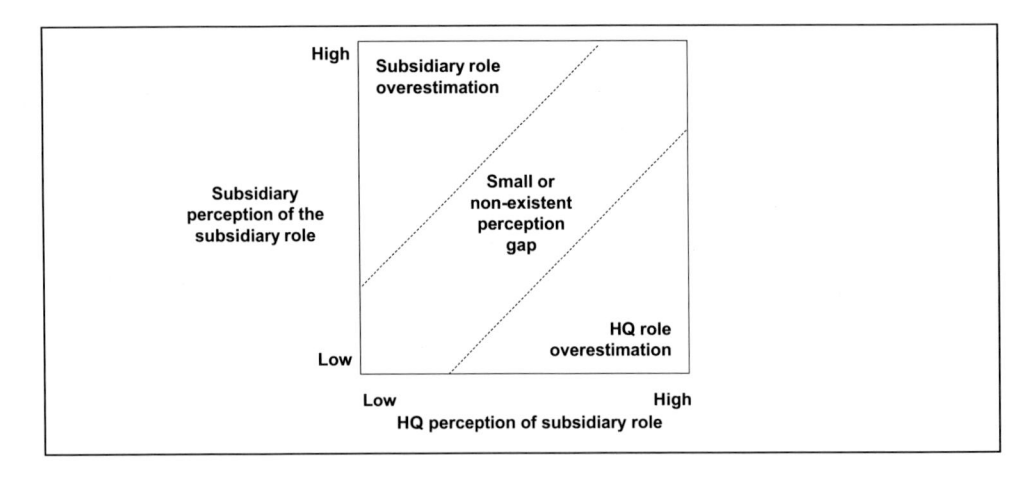

Figure 5:   Headquarters-Subsidiary Perception Gaps
Source: Birkinshaw et al. 2000, p. 326.

2.3.2.2 Contributions on Perception Gaps Concerning Subsidiary Roles

In the following, those studies which address perception gaps between headquarters and subsidiaries concerning subsidiary roles or individual dimensions that have been associated with subsidiary roles will be briefly summarized in chronological order (in similar form, the following review can be found in Schmid & Daniel 2007, pp. 9–13). Particular attention will be given to the perceived issue, factors influencing perception gaps and their consequences. The studies that will be included are (1) Arvidsson 1999, (2) Birkinshaw et al. 2000, (3) Asakawa 2001, (4) Denrell, Arvidsson & Zander 2004 and (5) Chini, Ambos & Wehle 2005.[16]

---

[16]   The decision why several contributions are not included in this review should be explained:
(1) Toyne presented an early study concerned with the differential perceptions that headquarters purchasing managers and subsidiary-based purchasing managers have of the authority granted to the subsidiary-based purchasing manager (Toyne 1978). This study is left aside since it has a strong focus on attributes of an individual manager's position rather than on the overall role of the subsidiary.
(2) The contribution by Holm, Johanson & Thilenius 1995, is not included in this review although the study compares headquarters and subsidiary perspectives. The study compares headquarters and subsidiary managers' assessment of the subsidiary's business network context. The study is not included, since the authors assume that this network context "is a matter of the judgment of the subsidiary managers who are directly engaged in it" (Holm, Johanson & Thilenius 1995, p. 109). This implies that rather than studying perception gaps, this contribution regards the subsidiary's perspective as benchmark and analyzes the correctness of headquarters knowledge about it.
(3) Equally, the contribution by Chan & Holbert 2001 is not included in the literature review. Instead of focusing on subsidiary roles or subsidiary role dimensions, the authors take more detailed aspects of the marketing process in subsidiaries into account. Furthermore, they do not specifically compare perceptions of headquarters and subsidiary managers within the same MNC

Arvidsson (1999). Niklas Arvidsson's PhD thesis provides one of the first examples of a contribution explicitly devoted to the study of headquarters-subsidiary perception gaps regarding role characteristics of the subsidiary. The issue emerged in a research project on knowledge management and knowledge transfer in MNCs in which it was found that headquarters managers and subsidiary managers do not perceive the capabilities that subsidiaries possess in the same way. Arvidsson draws on theories highlighting social perception (Cyert & March 1963; Heider 1958; Kelley 1967) in order to derive possible factors influencing perception gaps. He finally empirically examines the following factors: managers' "access to relevant information", "attention to information" and "interpretation of information" (Arvidsson 1999, pp. 92–93). In Arvidsson's empirical study, selective attention to information is the only one of these variables that shows a significant effect on perception gaps (Arvidsson 1999, p. 189). Arvidsson does not empirically investigate consequences of the perception gaps regarding subsidiary capabilities but (implicitly) assumes that they impede efficient knowledge management.

Birkinshaw, Holm, Thilenius & Arvidsson (2000). Birkinshaw et al. analyze perception gaps concerning the subsidiary's role and confirm their existence (Birkinshaw et al. 2000). While influencing factors on perception gaps are not considered, the authors empirically examine the effects of perception gaps between headquarters and subsidiary managers. A relationship is shown between perception gaps regarding a subsidiary's strategic role and the control headquarters exert over the subsidiary. The more a subsidiary overestimates its strategic role within an MNC, the higher is the level of control headquarters apply; a higher level of control in turn negatively influences the cooperation of the subsidiary and headquarters. No direct link between the perception gap and cooperation is found (Birkinshaw et al. 2000, pp. 336–339).

Asakawa (2001). Asakawa studies perception gaps between headquarters and subsidiary managers concerning the dimensions "subsidiary autonomy" and "information sharing between headquarters and subsidiaries". On the autonomy dimension, he does not identify perception gaps. With regard to information sharing, there is a significant perception gap concerning information being sent from headquarters to the subsidiary but not in the other direction (Asakawa 2001, pp. 742–743). He does not study any influencing factors or consequences but compares the perceived reality ("as it is") of the variables with both sides' normative expectation ("as it ought to be"; Asakawa 2001, p. 739).

---

but contrast the average of a group of headquarters managers in the United States with a group of subsidiary managers in Hong Kong.

Denrell, Arvidsson & Zander (2004). As does Arvidsson, Denrell et al. examine headquarters and subsidiary managers' ratings of subsidiary capabilities. Denrell et al., however, take a broader range of influencing variables into account. First, they consider headquarters managers' knowledge about subsidiaries as well as their experience with the capability in question (Denrell, Arvidsson & Zander 2004, p. 1500). Both of these factors significantly reduce the gap between headquarters managers' perception of subsidiary capability and the subsidiary managers' own rating. The clarity with which a certain capability can be defined, the ease of its evaluation and the question of whether it is tacit or "articulable" were examined as relevant attributes of capabilities. Within the empirical study, however, none of these factors shows a significant influence on perception gaps (Denrell, Arvidsson & Zander 2004, p. 1501). Subsidiary age is the only subsidiary characteristic studied that is significantly related to perception gaps regarding subsidiary capabilities. The younger the subsidiary, the larger the perception gap (Denrell, Arvidsson & Zander 2004, p. 1500). Importance of the subsidiary's market is significant at a level of 0.1 but not at a level of 0.05. The subsidiaries' financial performance has no meaningful influence (Denrell, Arvidsson & Zander 2004, pp. 1500–1501). Two characteristics of the headquarters-subsidiary relationship are analyzed, but neither one exhibits a significant influence: first, the frequency of communication between headquarters and subsidiaries is taken into account; second, cultural distance between headquarters and subsidiary is studied (Denrell, Arvidsson & Zander 2004, pp. 1500–1501). Furthermore, the question of whether a subsidiary is part of a global (compared to a polycentric) firm strategy is considered but does not show a relationship with perception gaps. Possible implications of perception gaps regarding subsidiary capabilities are not empirically examined.

Chini, Ambos & Wehle (2005). Similar to Asakawa (Asakawa 2001), Chini et al. regard subsidiary autonomy and information flow between headquarters and subsidiary. The authors consider industry and country environment as factors influencing the emergence of perception gaps. While the country environment has no influence on perception gaps, different industry environments lead to differing results (Ghoshal & Nohria 1993). Chini et al. detect significantly differing perceptions between headquarters and subsidiary managers concerning subsidiary autonomy in global and transnational but not in multinational environments (Chini, Ambos & Wehle 2005, p. 150). The information flowing from headquarters to subsidiaries is perceived differently only in subsidiaries active in global industries. Conversely, in subsidiaries active in multinational and transnational industries, perception gaps are found for information flowing from the subsidiary to headquarters (Chini, Ambos & Wehle 2005, p. 150). Furthermore, perception gaps are shown to lead to dissatisfaction (Chini, Ambos & Wehle 2005, p. 150). In this respect, the authors do not report any differentiation regarding the individual dimensions.

Table 2 summarizes the studies reported in this section. In addition to the categories introduced before (perceived issues, influencing factors and consequences), an overview of the empirical basis of the relevant publications is provided.

Author(s) Year Issue(s)	Influencing factors	Conse-quences	Methodology, geographical scope	Main findings
Arvidsson 1999 Subsidiary capabilities	Access to information Attention to information Interpretation of information	n/a	Questionnaire: 154 HQ-S pairs Interviews: 63 HQ and S managers 8 MNCs: HQ from Sweden and USA; S worldwide (interviews and questionnaire)	PG between HQ and S managers concerning S capabilities exist Selective attention partly explains PG
Birkinshaw et al. 2000 Subsidiary role	n/a	Level of HQ control of the S Level of HQ-S co-operation	Questionnaire: 89 divisional HQ-S pairs 19 MNC divisions: HQ from Sweden, S from Europe and USA	S managers' overesti-mation of their roles is associated with greater HQ control of the S, which in turn is associated with a lower level of HQ-S cooperation
Asakawa 2001 Subsidiary autonomy Informa-tion sharing	n/a	n/a	Questionnaire: 53 HQ-S pairs Interviews: not specified 10 MNCs: HQ from Japan; S in the UK	PG are more salient in information sharing issues than in autonomy-control issues S seem generally more dissatisfied with both types of issues than HQ
Denrell, Arvidsson & Zander 2004 Subsidiary capabilities	Clarity of definition Ease of evaluation Ease to articulate capability Knowledge of HQ managers Experience of HQ managers Communication frequency Market importance Perceived profitability Subsidiary age Cultural distance Global strategy	n/a	Questionnaire: 171 HQ-S pairs Interviews: 41 HQ and S managers 6 MNCs: HQ from Sweden and USA; S worldwide	Low interrater correlation for capabilities designated as strategic by top management Difference in evaluations is largest for S about which HQ managers know less, for younger S and for S in less important markets

Chini, Ambos & Wehle 2005 Subsidiary autonomy Information sharing	Strategic environment Country	Dissatis-faction	Questionnaire: 79 divisional HQ-S pairs 1 European MNC	Certain strategic environments bear a higher risk for PG concerning information flows between HQ and S and S autonomy Tense PG have a negative effect on managers' satisfaction
Legend	n/a – not applicable (the study does not cover influencing factors or consequences) S – subsidiary/subsidiaries HQ – headquarters PG – perception gap(s)			

Table 2: Empirical Studies of Perception Gaps between Headquarters and Subsidiary
Source: Schmid & Daniel 2007, p. 13.

The contributions summarized in this section represent empirical studies of headquarters-subsidiary perception gaps regarding subsidiary roles within the MNC. Those studies that do not explicitly refer to the concept "subsidiary role" analyze variables, which can as well be found among the dimensions of the subsidiary role typologies and may consequently be assumed to constitute elements of a subsidiary's role[17] ("subsidiary capabilities": Bartlett & Ghoshal 1986, 1991; Benito, Grøgaard & Narula 2003; Hoffman 1994; "subsidiary autonomy": D'Cruz 1986; Taggart 1997a; "information sharing": Gupta & Govindarajan 1991, 1994 examine knowledge flows). Although there may be additional studies focusing on perception gaps between headquarters and subsidiary managers which were not included in this review, Birkinshaw et al.'s statement still seems justified: "While it is widely understood that headquarters and subsidiary managers have different perceptions about the subsidiary's activities, there has been very little research that looks explicitly at this issue" (Birkinshaw et al. 2000, p. 322). This opinion is shared by the present contribution. At the same time, headquarters-subsidiary perception gaps concerning subsidiary roles are considered a highly relevant issue. In the next section, an overview of the research field will be provided.

---

[17] As was mentioned before, defining a subsidiary's role in terms of individual elements such as capabilities or autonomy can, of course, be criticized (Schmid, Bäurle & Kutschker 1998, pp. 95–96). Even if all subsidiary role dimensions listed in Table 1 are taken into account, only a partial representation of a subsidiary's actual role will be attained. However, as discussed in 2.2.3, this method presents an approach to render the concept "subsidiary role" accessible to empirical investigation.

2.3.2.3 Overview of the Research Field

In the next paragraphs, the variables that have been empirically analyzed so far in studies related to the context of headquarters-subsidiary perception gaps concerning subsidiary roles are summarized and structured. A framework can help organize existing research, identify additional factors and position future studies. Figure 6 displays such an integrated framework including perceived issues, influencing factors and consequences of perception gaps.

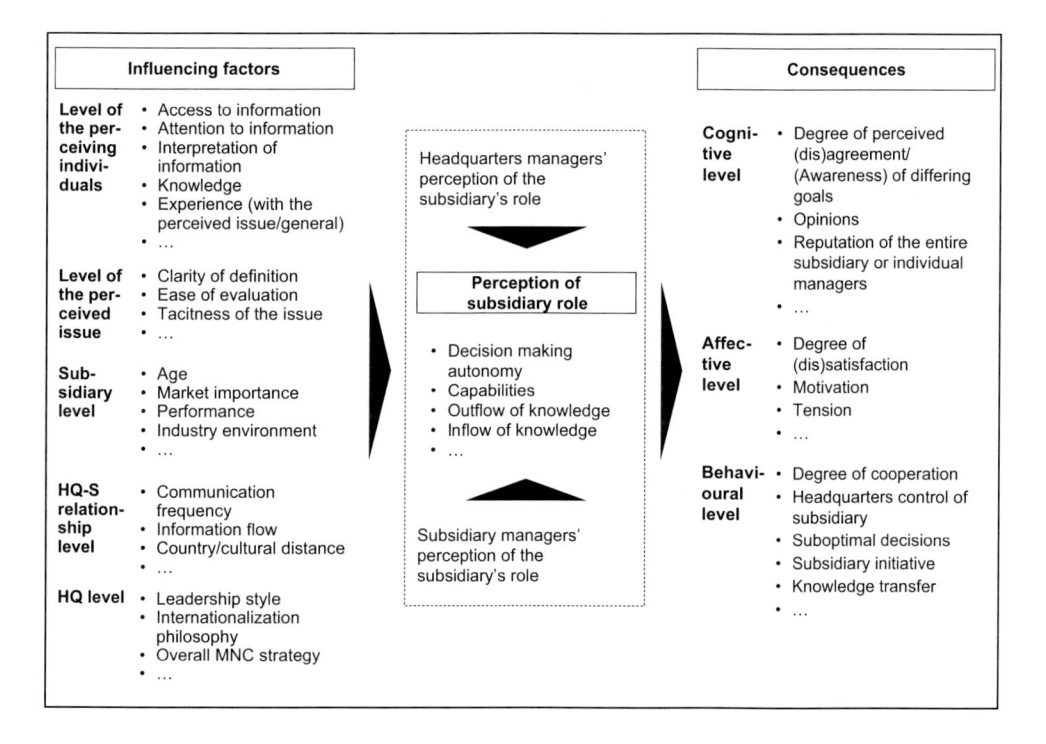

Influencing factors		Consequences	
Level of the perceiving individuals	• Access to information • Attention to information • Interpretation of information • Knowledge • Experience (with the perceived issue/general) • …	**Cognitive level**	• Degree of perceived (dis)agreement/ (Awareness) of differing goals • Opinions • Reputation of the entire subsidiary or individual managers • …
Level of the perceived issue	• Clarity of definition • Ease of evaluation • Tacitness of the issue • …	**Affective level**	• Degree of (dis)satisfaction • Motivation • Tension • …
Subsidiary level	• Age • Market importance • Performance • Industry environment • …	**Behavioural level**	• Degree of cooperation • Headquarters control of subsidiary • Suboptimal decisions • Subsidiary initiative • Knowledge transfer • …
HQ-S relationship level	• Communication frequency • Information flow • Country/cultural distance • …		
HQ level	• Leadership style • Internationalization philosophy • Overall MNC strategy • …		

Central flow: Headquarters managers' perception of the subsidiary's role → **Perception of subsidiary role** (• Decision making autonomy • Capabilities • Outflow of knowledge • Inflow of knowledge • …) ← Subsidiary managers' perception of the subsidiary's role

Figure 6: Overview of the Research Field on Perception Gaps
Source: Adapted from Schmid & Daniel 2007, p. 16.

The examples presented in the framework are merely illustrations of the issues that may be relevant in this context (Schmid & Daniel 2007, pp. 14–17). Additional aspects can enlarge each category. For instance, with regard to influencing factors, at the level of the perceiving individuals, expatriate status, tenure in the present position or personality characteristics may play a role. At the subsidiary level, there may be differences depending on the mode of establishment of the subsidiary, its size or the value chain activities carried out by the subsidiary. Similarly, the list of consequences could be extended, for instance by adding personal dislike at the affective level or an increased frequency of coordination meetings at the behavioural level. By presenting this framework, no complete overview of all aspects of the research field on perception gaps is intended; instead, a structure shall be provided that may be used to integrate previous and future studies in this area and reveal aspects that have not been covered yet.

In the following, the present study will be positioned within this framework and with regard to the approaches to perception gaps found in the IB literature.

2.3.3 Approach to Perception Gaps in the Present Study

First, the context of the present study will be clarified in terms of its position within the framework developed in the previous paragraphs. Starting at the centre of the framework with the issue of perception gaps, subsidiaries' roles within the MNC will be focused on. In particular, four role dimensions that were proposed by researchers will be highlighted: the subsidiary's capabilities, the strategic importance of the subsidiary's market, the extent to which knowledge is being received by the subsidiary from other organizational units and the extent to which the subsidiary provides knowledge to other organizational units (2.2.3). The perceptions of headquarters and subsidiary managers of the subsidiary's position on these four dimensions will be compared.[18] The present contribution will not include the study of factors influencing perception gaps and will start with the question of whether perception gaps exist. Furthermore, emphasis will be placed on potential consequences of perception gaps. In terms of the defining characteristics, perception gaps between headquarters and subsidiary managers constitute hierarchical perception gaps. Regarding directionality, both possible directions of perception gaps are considered. Finally, the focus is on perception gaps at the level of perceived reality, i.e., the subsidiary's current role.

The framework that will be developed in 3.3.3 proposes conflict as the main consequence of perception gaps. Therefore, headquarters-subsidiary conflict will be addressed next before integrating the individual elements presented so far in a conceptual framework (Chapter 3).

---

[18] It is acknowledged that even managers who are active at the same organizational unit may have different perceptions of the same issue (Cronin & Weingart 2007, p. 761; regarding the question of whether it is justified to consider the managers belonging to the same unit as a homogeneous group, see also footnote 72).

2.4 Headquarters-Subsidiary Conflict

2.4.1 General Conflict Literature

Conflict has been studied by researchers throughout the last century from a variety of perspectives and with different foci. In broad terms, intrapersonal and interpersonal conflict can be distinguished. This study will concentrate on interpersonal conflict, which includes conflict between individuals as well as conflict between groups of individuals (e.g., Barki & Hartwick 2004, p. 217).[19] The variety of situations that can be subsumed under the term conflict is countless. Several variables can be taken into account in order to distinguish and describe different types of interpersonal conflict (Grunwald & Redel 1989, pp. 536–537). These variables include, for instance, the parties involved in the conflict (individuals, groups, organizations, nations...), the type of relationship between the parties (hierarchical, lateral...), the context in which the conflict situation takes place (school, organization, family...), the object or issue around which the conflict evolves (goals, processes, values...) or the intensity of the conflict (Grunwald & Redel 1989; Jameson 1999; Rüttinger & Sauer 2000).

Conflict can occur due to various reasons. Wall and Callister distinguish three categories of conflict causes (Wall Jr. & Callister 1995, pp. 517–523). First, conflict may be generated by individual characteristics, such as personality attributes, values or goals. Second, interpersonal factors may lead to conflict; these include communication, behaviours or the relationship structure. Third, Wall and Callister mention "issue characteristics" such as complexity, vagueness and non-divisibility, which render issues more likely to cause conflict. According to Fey and Beamish, the most commonly cited causes of conflict are competition for scarce resources, desire for autonomy, goal divergence and perceptual incongruities (Fey & Beamish 2000, p. 142). However, these variables constitute only a small sample of the potential reasons for conflict. The multitude of possible antecedent conditions and influencing factors can result in very different conflict situations.

---

[19] Intrapersonal conflict is mainly a topic of psychological literature (Gilbert 1998, p. 34; Rahim 1992, p. 97). It has been defined as a situation in which a person is motivated to engage in two or more mutually exclusive activities (Deutsch 1969, p. 7; Reichers 1986, p. 509). Lewin identified three types of intrapersonal conflict: (a) A situation in which a person has to choose between two equally attractive alternatives is called "approach-approach conflict"; (b) he speaks of "approach-avoidance conflict" when an individual has to deal with a situation that implies both positive and negative aspects; (c) the third alternative is "avoidance-avoidance conflict" which occurs when the existing alternatives seem equally unattractive to the person (Lewin 1935; Lewin 1951). This structure of intrapersonal conflict differs considerably from interpersonal conflict which will be the topic of this study.

A general definition of interpersonal conflict needs to look into the common structure of all conflict situations. The question of how to define conflict, however, has not been answered consistently (Barki & Hartwick 2004; Schmidt & Kochan 1972; Thomas 1976, 1992a; Vollmer 2005). Several authors have reviewed the conflict literature and found a great diversity of conflict definitions (for instance, Berkel 1984; Fink 1968; Lewicki, Weiss & Lewin 1992; Putnam & Poole 1987). While most definitions of interpersonal conflict agree that conflict is a process involving two or more parties and some kind of incompatibility or opposition between them, there is considerable disagreement concerning the nature of this incompatibility or opposition (Fink 1968, p. 429). As Wall and Callister state,

> "there is some divergence of opinion as to what the "other" is opposing. Thomas (1976) indicates that the party's "concerns" or "something cared about" (Thomas, 1992b) is opposed. Putnam and Poole (1987) cite other's interference with the party's goods, aims, and values. Donohue and Kolt (1992) refer to needs or interests; whereas, Pruitt and Rubin (1986) discuss aspirations. And Deutsch (1980) talks about "activities"" (Wall Jr. & Callister 1995, p. 517).

Although an element of opposition can be found in most conflict definitions, this opposition may assume very different forms. While some authors refer to mere disagreement (e.g., Amason & Sapienza 1997, p. 495; Anderson & Narus 1990, p. 44), others speak of an awareness of discrepancies (e.g., Sell et al. 2004, p. 46) or behaviour (e.g., Alper, Tjosvold & Law 2000, pp. 627–628; Alter 1990, p. 482). In a review of conflict literature published between 1990 and 2003, Barki and Hartwick find cognitive conditions (e.g., the awareness of incompatible goals), negative affective or emotional states (e.g., anger or tension) and interfering behaviour (e.g., resistance or aggression) as three general themes that summarize the properties underlying most conflict concepts (Barki & Hartwick 2004). Some definitions focus on one or two of the three categories, while according to other authors, all three of them have to be present in order to constitute a conflict situation (e.g., Fisher 1990, p. 6). In an empirical study, Barki and Hartwick find that, taken together, these three categories explain 95% of the variance in individuals' perceptions of interpersonal conflict (Barki & Hartwick 2001). In addition, they notice the differentiation between task content or task process conflict compared to relationship conflict as a common thread of conflict definitions in the literature.[20] Based on these results, they propose a general typology of

---

[20] Applying the terms "subjective" and "objective" conflict potential, Berkel presents a similar differentiation (Berkel 1992, p. 1088). On the subjective side, conflict may be associated with personal attributes of the individuals involved, including personality characteristics, attitudes and motives, knowledge, behaviour and other relationships. On the objective side, Berkel distinguishes conflict regarding values and goals, organizational structure, norms and rules as well as resources.

conflict that takes the two dimensions "interpersonal conflict's properties" and "interpersonal conflict's focus" into account. Table 3 shows the resulting typology.

		Interpersonal conflict's focus	
		Task content or task process	**Interpersonal relationship**
Inter-personal conflict's proper-ties	**Cognition/ disagree-ment**	1 disagreement with the other about what should be done in a task or how a task should be done	2 disagreement with the other's personal values, views, preferences etc.
	Behaviour/ inter-ference	3 preventing the other from doing what they think should be done in a task or how a task should be done	4 preventing the other from doing things unrelated to a task
	Affect/ negative emotion	5 anger and frustration directed to the other about what should be done in a task or how a task should be done	6 anger and frustration directed to the other as a person

Table 3: Typology for Interpersonal Conflict in Organizations
Source: Barki & Hartwick 2004, p. 236.

In another attempt to structure the conflict field, Thomas acknowledges two general approaches to conflict (Thomas 1992a, p. 269). As a first approach, he recognizes more general definitions in the succession of Pondy and his own earlier work (Pondy 1967; Thomas 1976). Thomas defines conflict as "a process which includes the perceptions, emotions, behaviours, and outcomes of the two parties" (Thomas 1976, p. 891). Similarly, Pondy identifies five consecutive stages of a conflict episode: "(1) latent conflict (conditions), (2) perceived conflict (cognition), (3) felt conflict (affect), (4) manifest conflict (behavior), and (5) conflict aftermath (conditions)" (Pondy 1967, p. 300). The second approach Thomas mentions includes literature that follows Schmidt and Kochan. In contrast to the rather broad process models, this literature more narrowly highlights phenomena that are associated with deliberate interference with the other party's goals. Although the dynamic character of occurrences associated with conflict is generally acknowledged, these models define conflict explicitly as behaviour and thereby focus on only one of the process models' stages (Schmidt & Kochan 1972).

Both approaches to conflict can be criticized for different issues. Researchers focusing on one particular aspect of conflict can be accused of disregarding other important facets of the conflict phenomenon (Barki & Hartwick 2004, pp. 232–235). Authors who define conflict more broadly may be reproached for other reasons: First, they often have difficulties clarifying the conceptual relationship between the different dimensions or stages of the conflict episode; second, they frequently do not clearly distinguish conflict from its antecedent conditions (Schmidt & Kochan 1972, p. 360). For instance, some definitions consider interdependence between two parties a defining characteristic of conflict (e.g., Kaufmann & Roessing 2005, p. 237), while other authors maintain that an interdependent relationship rather posits a structural requirement without which conflict cannot emerge (Barki & Hartwick 2001, p. 199, 2004, p. 235; Dorow & Grunwald 1980, pp. 512–513).

The lack of clarity in the conflict field, however, is not restricted to *which* the defining characteristics are, but extends to a debate among researchers concerning the question of *in what way* they have to exist (Vollmer 2005, p. 55). For some authors the mere presence of certain properties (e.g. disagreement, incompatible goals or negative emotion) is sufficient, independent of the involved parties' awareness of their existence (Roth & Nigh 1992, p. 285). Other authors require the perception of these properties by at least one of the parties (Thomas 1976, p. 891).[21] A third group of authors consider the involved parties' expectance that the required constituents of conflict will emerge in the near future as criterion (Berkel 1992, p. 1086; Greenberg & Baron 1997, p. 380). One aspect, however, concerning which researchers agree, is the fact that social organizations will always experience conflict (Aiken & Hage 1968, p. 913; Easterbrook et al. 1993, pp. 9–10). Characteristics as interaction and interdependencies encourage the assumption that "some degree of conflict, though not inevitable in any instinctual sense is endemic to all social systems" (Kabanoff 1985, p. 113). Pondy even proposes a "pure conflict system" as an alternative way of conceptualizing organizations: "Conflict in this alternative model is the very *essence* of what an organization is" (Pondy 1992, p. 259).

Conflict may have functional as well as dysfunctional consequences (Deutsch 1969, 1990; Dorow 1981, p. 685; Gilbert 1998, pp. 39–42; Kabanoff 1985, p. 113; Litterer 1966; Smith 1989, p. 2). While some authors try to associate positive and negative effects with particular patterns of conflict (Jehn & Mannix 2001), others view the way conflict is managed as responsible for functional or dysfunctional consequences (Hignite, Margavio & Chin 2002, p.

---

[21] For instance, it may be considered necessary that the respective parties be aware of the inconsistency of their goals.

316; Kelly 2006, p. 27; Thomas 1976, pp. 891–892). It is frequently assumed that appropriate conflict management can foster the emergence of functional consequences (Alper, Tjosvold & Law 2000, p. 625). Negative consequences of conflict may, for instance, appear in the form of decreased performance (Jehn 1997) or dissatisfaction (De Dreu & Van Vianen 2001, p. B2). On the positive side, conflict may lead to creativity, innovation and change or may help to uncover problems (Alter 1990, p. 482; Berkel 2003, p. 402; Litterer 1966, pp. 179–180; Rahim 2002, p. 211). Different studies confirm positive (e.g., Amason & Schweiger 1997; Jehn 1995) as well as negative (Cox 2003; De Dreu & Weingart 2003; Steensma & Lyles 2000) implications of conflict. Their probability to emerge may differ due to certain circumstances (Mooney, Holahan & Amason 2007; Simons & Peterson 2000). A study by Schwenk offers an interesting insight promoting a differentiated view concerning the effects of conflict (Schwenk 1990): While executives in non-profit organizations state that higher levels of conflict are associated with higher quality of organizational decisions, the reverse relationship is true for executives in for-profit organizations. In summary, a conclusion concerning the consequences of conflict cannot be drawn. Whether the implications of conflict are positive or negative seems to depend strongly on contextual conditions.

2.4.2 Headquarters-Subsidiary Conflict in the International Business Literature

While headquarters-subsidiary conflict is frequently referred to, the subject is rarely addressed in detail in the IB literature (Blazejewski 2006, pp. 69–71). In general, conflict between headquarters and subsidiaries can be considered as a specific form of intergroup conflict (Pahl & Roth 1993, p. 140). Similar concepts studied in the literature are interdepartmental conflict (e.g., Barclay 1991; Ruekert & Walker 1987; Walton & Dutton 1969; Walton, Dutton & Cafferty 1969) or interorganizational conflict (e.g., Alter 1990; Jameson 1999; Vaaland & Håkansson 2003).[22]

---

[22] Although all these concepts refer to conflict between groups, the conflict is enacted by individuals who are members of the respective groups (the relationship between the individual and the collective level is addressed in more detail in 3.2.1.3). The individuals' behaviour in the conflict situation is assumed to be essentially role behaviour (Barclay 1991, p. 146). This means that their behaviour mainly reflects the individuals' roles as representatives of the respective groups (Katz & Kahn 1978, p. 375). In the case of headquarters-subsidiary conflict, the individuals who enact the conflict are assumed to act as representatives of headquarters or of a subsidiary.

Interdependence was mentioned as a necessary precondition for conflict (2.4.1). Consequently, conflict between organizational units can only emerge if the units are interdependent (McCann & Ferry 1979, pp. 116–117; Victor & Blackburn 1987, pp. 487–491). Interdependence can be defined as a "state in which the activities and outcomes of one actor are influenced by the actions of another actor" (O'Donnell 2000, p. 530). A high degree of interdependence can be presumed between units of network MNCs and in particular in the headquarters-subsidiary relationship (Ensign 1999, pp. 303–305). At the same time, it can be expected that "some degree of conflict inevitably accompanies the headquarters-subsidiary relationship" (Roth & Nigh 1992, p. 285). Numerous circumstances may lead to conflict between headquarters and subsidiaries, since headquarters and subsidiary managers can be assumed to have different perspectives on a wide range of issues (Birkinshaw et al. 2000, p. 322; Melewar & Saunders 1998, p. 295). For instance, conflict between headquarters and subsidiary managers may be generated by or revolve around heterogeneous goals (Tasoluk, Yaprak & Calantone 2007; Wright, Madura & Wiant 2002), resource scarcity or resource distribution (Inderst, Muller & Warneryd 2005), heterogeneous beliefs about technology and sociocultural differences (Pahl 1995, pp. 15–22).

In the IB literature, headquarters-subsidiary conflict is frequently associated with Prahalad and Doz's integration-responsiveness framework (Doz & Prahalad 1984; Prahalad & Doz 1987). On the one hand, foreign subsidiaries are expected to be responsive to the local context in which they are active. On the other hand, they are subject to global integration pressures from within the MNC. These contradictory demands imply considerable potential for conflict in the headquarters-subsidiary relationship (Johanson, Pahlberg & Thilenius 1996, p. 253; Pahl & Roth 1993, p. 140; Roth & Nigh 1992, p. 285; Venaik, Midgley & Devinney 2005, pp. 657–658). Prahalad and Doz describe three prototypical positions that subsidiaries can occupy within the integration-responsiveness framework (Prahalad & Doz 1987, pp. 18–26). (1) In businesses characterized by high pressures for local responsiveness and low pressures for global integration, national subsidiaries may act relatively autonomously. (2) In so-called "global businesses", the situation is reversed – the pressures for global integration are high, while the need for local responsiveness is low. In such a case, subsidiaries' strategies are highly integrated and the different units are managed on a worldwide basis. (3) Some businesses demand sensitivity on both dimensions at the same time. These can be met by subsidiaries by following a multifocal strategy. In this situation, subsidiaries will attempt to integrate value chain activities with other units of the MNC, while this effort may be restricted by differences in local demands. A differing degree of interdependence between headquarters and subsidiaries can be expected for each of the three situations (Harzing 2000, pp. 109–110). Consequently, it may be assumed that the potential for headquarters-subsidiary conflict will differ depending on the respective subsidiary strategy. However, in an empirical study, Pahl and Roth could not confirm a relationship between subsidiary strategy and the level of relationship conflict (Pahl & Roth 1993).

According to Gilbert, headquarters-subsidiary conflict in MNCs can be mainly related to structural causes (Gilbert 1998, pp. 53–62). He differentiates five groups of factors that may lead to headquarters-subsidiary conflict. (1) Different degrees of centralization and decentralization are noted. This can be seen in accordance with the abovementioned argumentation building on the integration-responsiveness framework. Conflict in this respect, for instance, evolves around the autonomy that individual units enjoy. (2) Coordination and control may as well lead to conflict. This category of influencing factors is associated with principal-agent issues that address the need to align differentiated interests. (3) Disagreement concerning goals may also result in conflict. Tensions can arise when subsidiaries develop own goals that are not compatible with the goals of the overall system. (4) Conflict may arise due to the distribution of power that enables headquarters to sanction certain behaviours of subsidiaries. Power can also play a role in the form of power over information and resources. (5) Communication processes are the final group of factors considered as conflict potential. The amount of information sent, geographic and temporal distance, distortions and lack of trust are mentioned as influences in this context.

As in other conflict literature, it is assumed that conflict between headquarters and subsidiary may entail positive or functional as well as negative or dysfunctional implications (Johanson, Pahlberg & Thilenius 1996, p. 254; Tasoluk, Yaprak & Calantone 2007). Corresponding to the aforementioned proposition, researchers focusing on the headquarters-subsidiary relationship as well presume that the consequences of conflict can be shaped by appropriate conflict management (Pahl & Roth 1993, p. 148; Tasoluk, Yaprak & Calantone 2007, p. 341). In terms of negative implications, conflict may lead to frustration, impede the achievement of the firm's goals and result in the reduction of overall effectiveness. However, as other relationships, headquarters-subsidiary relationships can, at the same time, benefit from increased creativity, innovation and change that may be activated by conflict (Johanson, Pahlberg & Thilenius 1996, p. 254). Headquarters-subsidiary relationship literature, however, assumes that the negative rather than the positive implications of conflict will usually prevail (Roth & Nigh 1992, p. 286). Such a relationship has been empirically confirmed (Johanson, Pahlberg & Thilenius 1996; Roth & Nigh 1992).

2.4.3 Approach to Headquarters-Subsidiary Conflict in the Present Study

2.4.3.1 Overview

In the present study, headquarters-subsidiary conflict will be defined as observable behaviour of one party preventing or compelling some outcome against the resistance of the other party (Katz & Kahn 1978, p. 613).[23] In terms of Barki and Hartwick's classification, this definition excludes the conflict levels "cognition/disagreement" as well as "affect/negative emotion" and concentrates on the level "behaviour/interference" (Barki & Hartwick 2004, p. 236).[24] Along the second dimension, "interpersonal conflict's focus", the focus will be on "task content or task process conflict". "Interpersonal relationship conflict" will not be taken into account since the focus of the present study is on attributes on the level of organizational units.[25]

While headquarters-subsidiary conflict can be caused by numerous factors (Gilbert 1998, pp. 56–62),[26] the present study examines the implications of perception gaps between headquarters and subsidiary managers concerning subsidiary roles. Depending on which subsidiary role dimension is concerned, conflict regarding different issues may emerge. As was noted above, only task conflict is taken into account in the present context. Even with this focus, a large variety of conflict issues could be imagined in the headquarters-subsidiary relationship. So far, no differentiation of conflict issues that are particularly relevant for headquarters-subsidiary relationships has been presented. Building on the system terminology, in the present study, a differentiation is proposed that distinguishes input, throughput and output issues concerning which conflict may arise. In relation to the headquarters-subsidiary relationship, input, throughput and output are interpreted in the following way: The subsidiary is considered the central system. The subsidiary's processes

---

[23] This definition is formulated based on the theoretical foundation of the present study, which will be described in 3.1.4.
[24] Such a definition is in line with many other studies focusing on inter-organizational conflict. For instance, referring to conflict in international joint ventures (in the following citation "IJV"), Fey states: "Like most of the past IJV conflict literature (Habib 1983, 1987; Hebert, 1994; Tillman, 1990), this study focuses on manifest conflict – that is, the action dimension of conflict. Also, building on Hebert's (1994) definition of conflict, this study defines conflict in an IJV as 'the interaction between parties involved in an IJV, where actions of one party prevent or compel some outcome against the resistance of another party'" (Fey & Beamish 2000, p. 142).
[25] Of course, it is acknowledged that personality characteristics of top managers can play an important role in the headquarters-subsidiary relationship. However, since the present study does not specifically take aspects as personality attributes, personal dislikes and similar aspects into account, the personal relationship between individual managers will not be analyzed here.
[26] March and Simon describe factors that influence the likelihood of conflict between organizational groups in general (March & Simon 1958, p. 121).

and value chain activities are defined as throughput. This includes relationships with suppliers and customers that might as well be considered as input and output in another context. Anything that is transferred from headquarters to the subsidiary is defined as input. Such transfers may concern resource inflows that entail knowledge, financial support or material resources. Finally, transfers from the subsidiary to headquarters are defined as output. While this classification follows system theory, a corresponding differentiation was formulated by Rüttinger and Sauer (Rüttinger 1977, pp. 31–35; Rüttinger & Sauer 2000, p. 19). Their approach will be taken into account here, although their conflict types are not formulated specifically for headquarters-subsidiary conflict. Below, it will be outlined how headquarters-subsidiary conflict is structured according to Rüttinger and Sauer's approach and how the three categories of conflict issues are made accessible for the present study.

2.4.3.2 Conflict Issues

In a publication dating from 1977, Rüttinger distinguishes valuation conflict, assessment conflict and distribution conflict (Rüttinger 1977, pp. 31–35), while in a more recent publication, Rüttinger and Sauer add relationship conflict as a further category (Rüttinger & Sauer 2000, pp. 22–23).[27] (1) Valuation conflict refers to a situation in which the involved parties pursue different goals, because they value the results differently. Consequently, they intend to realize different action plans (Rüttinger & Sauer 2000, pp. 22–23). Instead of "valuation conflict", in the present context, the term "goal conflict" will be used (e.g., Mezias 2002a, p. 277). It can be assumed that in network MNCs, goals will be rather negotiated between headquarters and subsidiaries instead of being entirely dictated by the parent company (Manev 2003, p. 138; Porter 1985, pp. 318–319). While this may lead to an increased degree of commitment to the negotiated goals, there may also be disagreement concerning the "right" goals due to the differing perspectives of headquarters and subsidiary managers. (2) The authors speak of assessment conflict when the actors agree about the goal they want to reach but favour different means in order to reach this goal, because they disagree in their assessment of the effectiveness of these means (Rüttinger & Sauer 2000, pp. 23–24). In the present context, the expression "process conflict" will be applied instead

---

[27] The German expressions used by the authors are "Bewertungskonflikt", "Beurteilungskonflikt", "Verteilungskonflikt" and "Beziehungskonflikt". Particularly the translation of the first two terms is difficult since their meaning is similar. They both refer to a certain value. The major difference is that the first type – "Bewertungskonflikt" – refers to goals while the second type – "Beurteilungskonflikt" – refers to means and processes. In order to be clear, in the present context, the terms "goal conflict" and "process conflict" will be used instead of more literal translations such as "valuation conflict" and "assessment conflict".

of "assessment conflict". (3) Distribution conflict can be described as a situation in which the involved parties compete for something that has a certain value for them. For subsidiaries, this may, for instance be resources (Rüttinger & Sauer 2000, p. 24). MNC subsidiaries commonly depend on headquarters for resources, although this dependence may vary according to the overall strategy of the MNC (Manev 2003, p. 138). Consequently, a certain potential for distribution conflict may be assumed in the headquarters-subsidiary relationship. (4) Relationship conflict might also be referred to as emotional or affective conflict and indicates controversies on a personal level (Rüttinger & Sauer 2000, pp. 24–25). As was argued above, this last category will not be included in the present study.

The reasons for which the differentiation proposed by Rüttinger and Sauer is taken into account are twofold. First, the three categories of goal conflict, process conflict and distribution conflict refer to issues that can be expected to be relevant for any headquarters-subsidiary relationship. At the same time, they are abstract enough to allow for variations in the concrete relationship. Second, each of the three issues finds its counterpart in the theoretical framework of the study (3.2.3). As will be argued, goal conflict can be considered as output conflict, process conflict is associated with throughput conflict and distribution conflict is regarded as input conflict. In the following, the three types of conflict issues, i.e., distribution, processes and goals, will be discussed in relation to headquarters-subsidiary relationships.

Distribution. Whenever subsidiaries depend on headquarters for the distribution of resources, conflict may emerge concerning this distribution (Manev 2003, p. 138). The resource concept has already been briefly discussed earlier in relation to subsidiary capabilities (2.2.3.2). In this context, resources are differentiated according to Bamberger and Wrona in the categories of physical, intangible, financial and organizational resources (Bamberger & Wrona 1996, pp. 132–134). Furthermore, the category of human resources is added. While human resources and the knowledge possessed by the concerned individuals are frequently subsumed under intangible resources (e.g., Chatterjee & Wernerfelt 1991, p. 35), in the present context, this category is stated explicitly, since the transfer of top managers and experts is a relevant issue in the relationships of headquarters and foreign subsidiaries (Au & Fukuda 2002, p. 285; Björkman, Barner-Rasmussen & Li 2004, p. 447; Grant 1991, p. 119; Harzing 2001a, p. 366).

Processes. Conflict concerning processes at the subsidiary can occur with regard to any functional area. As throughout this study, the following value chain activities are taken into account: (1) research and development, (2) production of goods and/or services, (3) marketing and/or sales, (4) logistics and/or distribution, (5) purchasing, (6) human resource management and (7) general management (Benito, Grøgaard & Narula 2003, p. 450; Moore 2000, p. 161, 2001, p. 285). The determination of these functional areas was described in 2.2.3.2.

Goals. A considerable number of scientific contributions have been devoted to the definition and study of organizational goals (see, for instance, the contributions by Perrow 1961, 1967, 1968 and the discussion by Macharzina & Wolf 2005, pp. 205–232). Organizational goals can be defined as "value premises that can serve as inputs to decisions" (Simon 1964, p. 3) or according to Etzioni as a desired future state of affairs, which the organization strives to realize by actively directing organizational resources toward it (Etzioni 1960, p. 257). Although several researchers have differentiated various types of goals, no general typology or taxonomy of organizational goals exists (Bateman, O'Neill & Kenworthy-U'Ren 2002, p. 1135; Connor & Bloomfield 1975, p. 123).[28] For instance, according to Perrow, official and operative goals may be distinguished (Perrow 1961, p. 855). Official goals represent the kind of goals that are determined in an organization's charter or mission statement, are rather general and purposely kept vague. Operative goals, on the other hand, cover the decisions that must be made among alternative ways of achieving the official goals and the priority of the multiple goals pursued by members of the organization. Another differentiation that was proposed by Gross distinguishes output and support goals (Gross 1969, p. 284). Here, output goals constitute those goals that are reflected immediately or in the future through products and services, whereas support goals refer to the organization's adaptation, management, positioning and so on. While the differentiations presented above operate at a rather abstract level, other contributions have attempted to provide more concrete categories of goals (e.g., Bateman, O'Neill & Kenworthy-U'Ren 2002, pp. 1139–1140; England 1967, p. 108; England & Lee 1971, p. 429; Korhonen 2001, p. 430; Messner & Sanvido 2001, p. 396). Types of goals presented by these classifications include financial goals, market goals, organizational efficiency or organizational growth.

In the present study, the goal types referred to by Bateman et al., England as well as Messner and Sanvido will be taken as a starting point for determining which goal categories will be considered (Bateman, O'Neill & Kenworthy-U'Ren 2002, pp. 1139–1140; England 1967, p. 108; Messner & Sanvido 2001, p. 396). Table 4 shows the goal categories promoted by each of these contributions. Bateman et al. as well as Messner and Sanvido empirically

---

[28] While a taxonomy reveals patterns within a set of variables that create interesting, but theoretically unsupported clusters or groups, a typology is developed on the basis of a theory (Kaufman, Wood & Theyel 2000, p. 651; Miller & Friesen 1983, pp. 31–36).

developed their goal types. The classification by England was conceptually derived and empirically tested.

Author(s) Year	Bateman, O'Neill & Kenworthy-U'Ren 2002, pp. 1139–1140	Messner & Sanvido 2001, p. 396	England 1967, p. 108
Goals	Personal goals	Financial	Organizational efficiency
	Financial goals	Market scope	High productivity
	Customer goals	Resource	Profit maximization
	Market goals	Productivity	Organizational growth
	Operations goals	Organization development	Industrial leadership
	Product goals		Organizational stability
	Organizational goals		Employee welfare
	People goals		Social welfare
	Competitive goals		
	Strategy-making goals		

Table 4: Classifications of Organizational Goals

In the following, common categories will be extracted from these three sets of goals. (a) When comparing the three sets of goal types, it becomes clear that "financial goals" appear in all three of them. England's category "profit maximization" is also summarized under this heading. (b) Although with a different focus, each of the sets contains market related goals. Returning to the concept of strategic market importance that was discussed in relation to the respective subsidiary role dimension, it can be argued that issues associated with market, customers and competition may be included in the same category (2.2.3.2). Consequently, Bateman et al.'s "customer goals", "market goals" and "competitive goals", England's "industrial leadership" and Messner and Sanvido's "market scope" will be summarized in the category "market related goals". (c) The third category that can be discerned contains goals related to operations. Hereby, the goal types "(high) productivity", "organizational efficiency" and "operations goals" are covered. (d) Several of the goals are associated with organizational development. This category as well contains "organizational goals", "organizational growth", "strategy-making goals" and "organizational stability". (e) Furthermore, personnel related goals are mentioned. These include "people goals", "personal goals" and "employee welfare" and will be referred to as "personnel development goals".

Some specific categories mentioned in the three sets of goal types are not explicitly pointed out – the category "resources" by Messner and Sanvido may fall into diverse categories from "financial" over "operations" to "personnel development goals". Bateman et al.'s "product goals" originally include the subtypes "core focus" and "diversification", and they may be assumed to fall into the category "market related goals" as well as "organizational development goals". Finally, the category "social welfare" is not included. This goal type is only mentioned by England but not by the other two contributions. In his empirical study, however, England found that this goal category was rated much less important by the responding managers than the other categories (England 1967, p. 108). Therefore, it is left aside in the present context. Table 5 summarizes the five goal categories taken into account in this study and presents some illustrations for each one of them.[29]

---

[29] The five goal categories defined here are also in accordance with the categories included in balanced scorecards. Following Kaplan and Norton, a balanced scorecard contains "financial", "customer", "internal business process" and "learning and growth" issues (e.g., Kaplan & Norton 1992, p. 72; Kaplan & Norton 1996, p. 54; Kaplan & Norton 2007, p. 72). While the first three categories overlap with the structure proposed here, "learning and growth" may be argued to include organizational development and personnel development goals.

Category	Financial Goals	Market Related Goals	Operations Goals	Organizational Development Goals	Personnel Development Goals
Goal types covered	Bateman, O'Neill & Kenworthy-U'Ren 2002, pp. 1139–1140: Financial goals Messner & Sanvido 2001, p. 396: Financial (Resources) England 1967, p. 108: Profit maximization	Bateman, O'Neill & Kenworthy-U'Ren 2002, pp. 1139–1140: Customer goals Market goals Competitive goals (Product goals) Messner & Sanvido 2001, p. 396: Market scope England 1967, p. 108: Industrial leadership	Bateman, O'Neill & Kenworthy-U'Ren 2002, pp. 1139–1140: Operations goals (Product goals) Messner & Sanvido 2001, p. 396: Productivity England 1967, p. 108: Organizational efficiency High productivity	Bateman, O'Neill & Kenworthy-U'Ren 2002, pp. 1139–1140: Organizational goals Strategy-making goals (Resources) Messner & Sanvido 2001, p. 396: England 1967, p. 108: Organization development Organizational growth Organizational stability	Bateman, O'Neill & Kenworthy-U'Ren 2002, pp. 1139–1140: Personal goals People goals Messner & Sanvido 2001, p. 396: (Resources) England 1967, p. 108: Employee welfare
Illustrations	Profit Revenue Cash flow ...	Market share Maintenance of customer base Extension of customer base ...	Productivity Technology Equipment ...	Organizational growth Organizational stability Organizational culture ...	Employee welfare Development and training Motivation Empowerment ...

Table 5:   Organizational Goal Types in the Present Study

2.5 Summary and Conclusions

In the previous sections, concepts were presented that are central for this study. First, MNCs were taken into account (2.1). Network MNCs have gained importance in practice as well as in academic literature compared to hierarchically structured MNCs. They possess several distinct characteristics of which the differentiation of subsidiary roles is of particular relevance in the present context. Consequently, subsidiary roles were considered in more detail (2.2). The use of the subsidiary role concept in the IB literature was reviewed and an extensive list of subsidiary role typologies was presented. Finally, the approach to subsidiary roles chosen in the present study was clarified. While subsidiary roles have received considerable attention in the IB literature, the question of to what extent headquarters and subsidiary managers perceive the role of a certain subsidiary in the same way has been neglected so far. Since the present study aims at addressing this lack of research, the issue of perception gaps concerning subsidiary roles was regarded next (2.3). After describing general attributes of perception gaps, the IB literature in this area was reviewed and the approach to perception gaps chosen in the present study was laid open. Since this study hypothesizes that perception gaps between headquarters and subsidiary managers concerning the subsidiary's role are likely to lead to conflict in the headquarters-subsidiary relationship, the issue of headquarters-subsidiary conflict was taken into account next (2.4). First, a brief overview of the general conflict literature was given. Then, headquarters-subsidiary conflict in the IB literature was considered and, finally, the approach to headquarters-subsidiary conflict that is taken in the present study was presented.

Network MNCs constitute the context for the phenomena addressed in the present study. Although network MNCs have already received substantial attention from empirical research, until now, no comprehensive theoretical basis was proposed for their study. A "theory of the network MNC" is still missing (Ghoshal & Bartlett 1990, p. 621). Similarly, the large body of research on subsidiary roles within network MNCs has not been theoretically grounded so far (Schmid, Bäurle & Kutschker 1998, p. 95). The other two elements presented – perception gaps and headquarters-subsidiary conflict – have not been widely studied. Consequently, an alternative theoretical basis has to be found for the present study. The next chapter is devoted to the development of this conceptual framework. In the first section (3.1), a theoretical framework is proposed that is applied to the context of the present study in the second section (3.2). Finally, the framework is used to derive ideas that will be addressed in the empirical study (3.3).

3. Conceptual Framework

3.1 Open System Approach According to Katz and Kahn

3.1.1 Selecting a Conceptual Approach for the Present Study

3.1.1.1 Categories of Organizational Theories

Organizations can be viewed from a variety of perspectives. Accordingly, a large number of theoretical approaches were formulated in order to explain organizational structures, behaviours or strategies (Ashmos & Huber 1987, p. 607). Two attempts to classify these approaches have received considerable attention in the literature: One was presented by Burrell and Morgan in 1979 and the other by Astley and Van de Ven in 1983. Each of the two approaches yields four categories of organizational theoretical orientations.[30]

Burrell and Morgan first distinguish approaches that conceptualize reality as rather objective or subjective. They use four characteristics in order to distinguish the two extremes: (1) Objective approaches are described by a realist perspective on ontology, a positivist epistemology, a deterministic view on human nature and a nomothetic methodology. (2) Subjective approaches, in contrast, follow a nominalist standpoint regarding ontology, an anti-positivist epistemology, a voluntaristic idea with regard to human nature and an ideographic methodology (Burrell & Morgan 1979, pp. 3–8). The second dimension stretches between two extremes, which the authors call "sociology of regulation" and "sociology of radical change" (Burrell & Morgan 1979, p. 30). The former refers to approaches that are mainly concerned with stability, structure and situations while the latter summarizes approaches that focus on processes and change (Burrell & Morgan 1979, pp. 21–37). These two dimensions and the resulting four categories of organizational theoretical perspectives are depicted in Figure 7.

---

[30] It has to be taken into account that any such attempt is biased through the subjective opinion of the respective researcher(s). First, a decision has to be taken in favour of two dimensions and against others. Second, the four quadrants have to be labelled and theoretical approaches have to be classified in each quadrant.

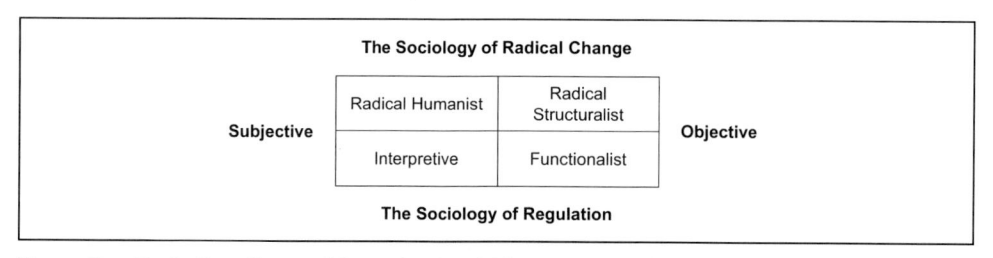

	The Sociology of Radical Change		
Subjective	Radical Humanist	Radical Structuralist	Objective
	Interpretive	Functionalist	
	The Sociology of Regulation		

Figure 7: Basic Paradigms of Organizational Theories According to Burrell and Morgan
Source: Burrell & Morgan 1979, p. 30.

Astley and Van de Ven also describe four general views of organization and management by taking into account two different dimensions (Astley & Van de Ven 1983). On the one hand, they differentiate micro level approaches that focus on individual organizations from macro level approaches, which consider populations and communities of organizations. On the other hand, a distinction is drawn between deterministic and voluntaristic orientations. From the voluntaristic point of view, individuals are the basic unit of analysis. They are regarded as autonomous, proactive and self-directing agents who constitute the main source of change in organizations. In contrast, the deterministic orientation focuses on the structural properties of organizations. Individual behaviour is conceived as determined by structural constraints and mainly reactive in nature. This ensures a certain degree of stability and control within the organization (Astley & Van de Ven 1983, p. 247). Astley and Van de Ven's framework is depicted in Figure 8.

	Natural selection view Schools: Population ecology, industrial economics, economic history. Structure: Environmental competition and carrying capacity predefine niches. Industrial structure is economically and technically determined. Change: A natural evolution of environmental variation, selection and retention. The economic context circumscribes the direction and extent of organizational growth. Behaviour: Random, natural or economic, environmental selection. Manager Role: Inactive.	Collective action view Schools: Human ecology, political economy, pluralism. Structure: Communities or networks of semiautonomous partisan groups that interact to modify or construct their collective environment, rules, options. Organization is collective-action controlling, liberating and expanding individual action. Change: Collective bargaining, conflict, negotiation and compromise through partisan mutual adjustment. Behaviour: Reasonable, collectively constructed and politically negotiated orders. Manager Role: Interactive.
MACRO LEVEL (Populations and communities of organizations)		
MICRO LEVEL (Individual organizations)	System structural view Schools: Systems theory, structural functionalism, contingency theory. Structure: Roles and positions hierarchically arranged to efficiently achieve the function of the system. Change: Divide and integrate roles to adapt subsystems to changes in environment, technology, size and resource needs. Behaviour: Determined, constrained and adaptive. Manager Role: Reactive.	Strategic choice view Schools: Action theory, contemporary decision theory, strategic management. Structure: People and their relationships organized and socialized to serve the choices and purposes of people in power. Change: Environment and structure are enacted and embody the meanings of action of people in power. Behaviour: Constructed, autonomous and enacted. Manager Role: Proactive.
	Deterministic orientation	**Voluntaristic orientation**

Figure 8: Four Views of Organization and Management According to Astley and Van de Ven
Source: Astley & Van de Ven 1983, p. 247.

Both frameworks structure the extensive range of organizational theoretical approaches. When looking for a theoretical perspective that is appropriate for a specific research question, they can provide orientation. By distinguishing between approaches that focus on individual organizations and approaches directed at a group of organizations, the classification by Astley and Van de Ven offers immediate access, since the present study clearly takes individual network MNCs into account. In the following, the classification by Astley and Van de Ven will be utilized in order to narrow the possible range of approaches.

In general terms, the research questions of the present study are concerned with the relationships between headquarters and subsidiaries in MNCs. The focus is on individual MNCs and their internal functioning rather than a group of MNCs. Therefore, the micro level perspective offers itself rather than the macro level perspective. Nevertheless, it should be acknowledged that it would be possible to consider the relationships within a network MNC from a macro level perspective. Doz and Prahalad argue that the network can be seen as a population consisting of the various subunits (Doz & Prahalad 1991, p. 150). In the present context, however, the micro perspective seems more appropriate for the analysis of headquarters-subsidiary relationships in network MNCs. Rather than conceiving of the network MNC as a population of subunits that loosely interact or even compete with each other (e.g., Luo, Slotegraaf & Pan 2006; Tsai 2002), the underlying notion is that of the MNC as an integrated – albeit differentiated – entity. In addition, the focus of the present study is not on the population of subsidiaries within one MNC, but rather on the individual relationships between headquarters and particular subsidiaries. Therefore, it is argued that on the micro vs. macro dimension, the micro perspective corresponds better to the present analysis of network MNC.

Combining the micro level perspective with a deterministic orientation results in a system-structural view of organization and management. Schools that can be summarized in this category are system theory (e.g., Luhmann 1995; von Bertalanffy 1972), structural functionalism (e.g., Parsons 1956a, 1956b) and contingency theory (e.g., Lawrence & Lorsch 1967; Thompson 2004). One common characteristic of these schools is the assumption that relationships between structural elements of organizations can be explained mainly functionally. The internal organizational structure is principally seen as determined by the requirements and demands of the environment. The basic components of the organizational structure are roles that define positions within the structure in terms of responsibilities, behavioural expectations and duties. Individuals are supposed to play these roles and thereby enhance the achievement of organizational goals (Astley & Van de Ven 1983, p. 248).

The second micro level orientation is the strategic choice view that takes a voluntaristic instead of a deterministic standpoint. The major objection that this perspective puts forth against the system-structural orientation concerns the neglect of individuals' influence. The "strategic choice view draws attention to individuals, their interactions, social constructions, autonomy and choices, as opposed to the constraints of their role incumbency and functional interrelationships in the system" (Astley & Van de Ven 1983, p. 249). Schools as action theory, decision theory and strategic management emphasize the subjective influence that actors can exert on organizational life as well as organizational structure. Unlike the deterministic system-structural view, the strategic decision perspective regards the environment and the organizational structure as reflections of individual volition and actions.

When comparing the system-structural view and the strategic choice view regarding their fit for addressing the posed research questions, the former seems to suit this purpose better for several reasons. First, in the present study, the concept of subsidiary roles is particularly central. The functional component of this concept in the context of the network MNC can be reflected by the system-structural point of view. As mentioned, the system-structural perspective assumes that elements within a social organization fulfil certain roles for the entire structure (Astley & Van de Ven 1983, p. 248). Similarly, by taking differentiated roles, subsidiaries within network MNCs are supposed to contribute to the MNC's success (Bartlett & Ghoshal 1986, p. 88; Hedlund 1986, p. 22). Second, the system-structural perspective considers the environment to a higher extent than the strategic choice view. For the development of a network structure in an MNC, environmental conditions play a significant role. Industry characteristics that necessitate both integration and differentiation are assumed to foster the development of the structural traits of heterarchical MNCs (Bartlett 1984; Hedlund 1986, pp. 20–21).[31] Finally, the strategic choice view highlights decisions taken by individuals while such a focus is not intended in the present context. Rather than determined primarily by individual volition, subsidiary roles are assumed to emerge in a complex process from the interaction of various influencing factors (Benito, Grøgaard & Narula 2003; Birkinshaw & Hood 1998c, p. 775; Dörrenbächer & Geppert 2006, p. 259; Eckert & Rossmeissl 2007; Schmid & Schurig 2003). Therefore, in summary, it is argued that the system-structural view seems to be the most appropriate perspective for addressing the questions posed by the present study. In the following, arguments for the selection of one specific theoretical approach out of this category will be given.

3.1.1.2 System Theoretical Approaches to Organizations

Above, it was argued that of the four organizational theoretical views presented by Astley and Van de Ven, the system-structural perspective is considered best suited in order to approach the research questions posed in the present study. Astley and Van de Ven mention system theory (e.g., Luhmann 1995; von Bertalanffy 1972), structural functionalism (e.g., Parsons 1956a, 1956b) and contingency theory (e.g., Lawrence & Lorsch 1967; Thompson 2004) as examples for this category. Each of these three theoretical directions, in turn, contains a large number of different approaches. For the present context, a decision has to be made for one particular approach that can be used as a framework for this study. System

---

[31] Although Hedlund assumes that in the ideal form of the heterarchical MNC, structure may follow strategy, he admits that, in reality, a heterarchical MNC would only develop under certain environmental conditions (Hedlund 1986, pp. 20–21).

theory and in particular an open system perspective[32] is regarded as especially helpful in the present context.[33] In general terms, system theory can be defined as

> "the transdisciplinary study of the abstract organization of phenomena, independent of their substance, type, or spatial or temporal scale of existence. It investigates both the principles common to all complex entities, and the (usually mathematical) models which can be used to describe them" (The Cambridge Dictionary of Philosophy 2001, pp. 898–899, ed. by Audi).

Constituting a rather abstract framework, system theory can be applied to a large variety of phenomena in different disciplines. Particularly in the 1960s and the 1970s, the system paradigm was celebrated as the "major new paradigm" for the study of social organizations (Kast & Rosenzweig 1972, p. 457). Despite this claim, system theory has not received the kind of attention that might have been expected of a "major new paradigm" (Ashmos & Huber 1987, p. 608). Several authors argued that the full potential of system theory in relation to social organizations has not been exploited (Ashmos & Huber 1987, pp. 611–617; Peery Jr. 1972, p. 275). Nevertheless, there are contributions in which system theory with a specific focus on social organizations was elaborated explicitly and comprehensively.

One such application was presented in 1978 by Miller in his contribution on "Living Systems" (Miller 1978). Initially, he defines basic concepts and mechanisms relevant for all kinds of living systems; then, he describes their meaning for specific types of systems ranging from the cell over organs, organisms, groups, organizations and societies to supranational systems.[34] Miller's work constitutes an impressive contribution to system theory. In the same year, Katz and Kahn published another well-known system theoretical approach. In the second edition of their "Social Psychology of the Organization", Katz and Kahn also provide a detailed description of the application of open system theory to social organizations (Katz & Kahn 1978). They first present their general theoretical approach before they describe several models of organizations, problems that may arise in social systems as well as

---

[32] System theory in general can refer to open as well as closed systems (Kast & Rosenzweig 1972, p. 450). While frequently, a general distinction between open and closed systems is suggested (e.g., Ashmos & Huber 1987, p. 608), Kast and Rosenzweig consider open vs. closed a dimension on which systems can take a certain position. All systems taken into account in the present context can be assumed open.

[33] Although system theory is classified here in the system-structural category, it should be noted that not all authors support the view that system approaches do not take the individual decider into account (Ashmos & Huber 1987, p. 617). For instance, Miller includes an elaborate treatment of deciders in his work on living systems (Miller 1978, pp. 548, 642). This shows that the two extremes of the deterministic vs. voluntaristic dimension should be considered the two ends of a continuum rather than two distinct categories. While the system-structural view concedes only limited influence to individual managers, it does not deny their involvement altogether.

[34] According to Miller, "organizations are systems with multiechelon deciders whose components and subsystems may be subsidiary organizations, groups, and (uncommonly) single persons" (Miller 1978, p. 595).

different processes that take place within organizations. Issues that are addressed include role taking, power and authority, decision making, conflict and organizational change.

While system theoretical approaches are considered as system-structural, neither the approach by Katz and Kahn nor Miller's perspective are purely deterministic. In addition to environmental forces, in both cases, the actual structure of systems is assumed to depend to some extent on the characteristics of the entities contained in the system (Katz & Kahn 1978, p. 37; Miller 1978, p. 19). Nevertheless, the deterministic point of view still corresponds better to the open system perspective than the voluntaristic view. Katz and Kahn's explanation is particularly helpful in this respect. They claim that social systems generally emerge from the interaction of individuals. As long as certain environmental demands are met and common goals of the system's members can be reached, the system can take various forms (Katz & Kahn 1978, pp. 41–42). In other words, it is assumed that individual volition can influence the organization within the confines of certain limits set by environmental demands.

From the variety of system theoretical approaches, a decision is made in favour of Katz and Kahn's (1978) open system approach. Katz and Kahn's approach is chosen in particular because it contains two concepts that can be useful with regard to the posed research questions: first, a role theoretical framework that can be applied to subsidiary roles and second, a conflict model that can be used to explain headquarters-subsidiary conflict. These concepts will be described below (3.1.3 and 3.1.4) following an overview of the open system approach (3.1.2).

3.1.2 Overview of the Open System Approach

3.1.2.1 Point of Departure

The open system approach formulated by Katz and Kahn in their classic "Social Psychology of Organizations" (Katz & Kahn 1978)[35] will be applied as theoretical foundation for analyzing headquarters-subsidiary relationships in network MNCs. In this subsection, a short review of the approach will be presented.

---

[35] The "Social Psychology of Organizations" was first published in 1966. The 1966 edition contained a first outline of the open system approach. Twelve years later, the open system framework was published in an extended and more systematic second edition.

Katz and Kahn notice a "problem of levels" (Katz & Kahn 1978, pp. 12 et sqq.) in the social sciences, which as well affects the study of organizations. The problem consists of a confusion of the conceptual level and the phenomenological level. The level of phenomena refers to the description of what can be encountered, observed and measured (i.e., the data), while the conceptual level aims at explaining phenomena through ideas and theories. In the social sciences, the distinction between conceptualization and phenomena is not always clear. For instance, while psychologists and sociologists typically regard events at conceptually different levels, they may rely on the same phenomenological data.

In order to solve this problem, the authors suggest that the study of organizations should take the social system level as its conceptual starting point. At this level, they propose the application of open system theory. According to Katz and Kahn, open system theory can solve the described dichotomy since it permits the combination of both levels (Kast & Rosenzweig 1967, p. 89; Katz & Kahn 1978, p. 15). On the one hand, sociological macro concepts explain the system functioning on a conceptual level. On the other hand, open system theory allows translating these macro concepts into a number of micro concepts that focus on the same area of social behaviour. For instance, the role concept that is part of the system theoretical framework is translated into the phenomena shared values and expectations concerning legitimate behaviour of individuals (Katz & Kahn 1978, p. 15).

3.1.2.2 Characteristics of Open Systems

The definition and identification of organizations is a prerequisite for their study. The clarification of their nature and their boundaries, however, is no easy task. Since common sense approaches to organizations entail a number of problems, Katz and Kahn choose a system theoretic solution. They view organizations as systems that are characteristically defined by their input, their output and the internal functioning. More specifically, they suggest that the organization receives energic input from its environment that is transformed in order to produce a certain output. The energic return from the output is supposed to reactivate the system. The input of energy as well as the conversion of output into renewed energic input presents interactions between the organization and its environment. The authors assume that the boundaries of an organization can be identified by following the energic and informational transactions as they relate to the cycle of input, throughput and output. Behaviour that is not tied to these functions is supposed to lie outside the system (Katz & Kahn 1978, pp. 18–23).

As in system theory in general, the emphasis is on relationships, structure and interdependence of system elements rather than on constant attributes of objects (Katz & Kahn 1978, p. 22). By choosing an open system approach, Katz and Kahn highlight the exchange relationship between system and environment and thereby decidedly distinguish their approach from closed system concepts. The ten characteristics that they attribute to all open systems will briefly be described in the following.[36]

Importation of energy. All open systems import some form of energy from the external environment. Social organizations, for instance, depend on continuous supplies of energy from other institutions, people or the material environment (Katz & Kahn 1978, p. 23).

Throughput. By reorganizing the input, open systems transform the energy available to them. Social organizations may, for example, be occupied with the production of new objects or the training of people (Katz & Kahn 1978, pp. 23–24).

Output. Different kinds of products can be exported into the environment. Examples of organizational outputs include material and immaterial goods or specifically educated people (Katz & Kahn 1978, p. 24).

Systems as cycles of events. Social systems consist of repeated patterns of activities of individuals. The pattern of activities that is related to the exchange of energy within the open system is cyclic in nature. To maintain the pattern requires the renewed inflow of energy. For instance, an industrial firm may use raw materials and human labour to fabricate a product that is sold for money, which in turn is utilized for the purchase of more raw materials and human labour to renew the cycle of activities. Not every repetition of the cycle, however, has to be exactly identical (Katz & Kahn 1978, pp. 24–25).

Negative entropy. A universal law of nature states that all forms of organization are subject to entropy. In the long term, this law applies to open systems as well; they lose their necessary inputs or the ability to transform them and consequently move towards disorganization or death. During their lifetime, however, open systems are able to reverse the process. Due to their capacity to store energy, they can acquire negative entropy (Katz & Kahn 1978, p. 25).[37]

---

[36] Although particularities of social organizations as open systems will be discussed in 3.1.2.3, the examples given here for the characteristics of open systems will also refer to social organizations.
[37] For applications of the concept of entropy in the context of firms, see, e.g., Gabris & Mitchell 1991, pp. 508–509; Smith et al. 1992, p. 66.

Information input, negative feedback and the coding process. In addition to energic materials, open systems receive input that informs them about the environment and their position within the environment. The most basic type of informational input is negative feedback, which helps to correct imbalances within the system. The term "coding" refers to the selective mechanisms of a system by which incoming materials are rejected or accepted and translated for the structure. Certain recruiting standards may, for instance, function as selective mechanisms for individuals who are qualified to work in the organization (Katz & Kahn 1978, p. 26).

Steady state and dynamic homeostasis. A system that is in a steady state is characterized by a continuous flow of energy. As soon as any internal or external factor threatens to disrupt the system, forces emerge that aim at restoring the system as closely as possible to its previous state. Recurring disturbances will lead to anticipatory preparations. The system will not simply restore the prior equilibrium, but will establish a new, more complex and more comprehensive equilibrium. In counteracting entropy, open systems therefore expand. Social systems are inclined to incorporate the external resources that are essential for their survival within their boundaries. While systems initially tend to grow in quantity or size, this will be followed by qualitative changes as supportive subsystems become necessary or as differentiation increases. For instance, the implementation of a more efficient supply management system can enable an organization to handle greater amounts of orders (Katz & Kahn 1978, pp. 26–29).

Differentiation. Open systems develop towards increasing differentiation and elaboration. At the beginning, systems are governed by dynamic interaction of their individual elements. In the course of time, unsystematic patterns are replaced by functions that are more specialized. Fixed conditions of constraint are established that render the system and its parts more efficient. The establishment of separate departments within the firm constitutes an example for differentiation in the context of organizations (Katz & Kahn 1978, p. 29).

Integration and coordination. As differentiation proceeds, processes that hold the system together for unified functioning answer it. While coordination refers to fixed control arrangements, integration stands for the achievement of unification through shared norms and values. Defining a corporate culture and a corporate identity can be seen as examples for value based integration efforts (Katz & Kahn 1978, pp. 29–30).

Equifinality. This concept highlights that "in an open system, the final state (overt response) may be reached from different conditions and in different ways" (Shibutani 1968,

p. 332). A firm of the same size and structure may have emerged from various historical developments (Katz & Kahn 1978, p. 30).[38]

While these ten aspects represent common characteristics of open systems in general, next, the implications of such an open system view for the notion of social organizations will be considered.

3.1.2.3 Social Organizations as Open Systems

Katz and Kahn view general system theory as a skeleton that each discipline has to provide with flesh and blood in order to turn it into a viable model which can support the understanding of phenomena at its respective level of analysis (Katz & Kahn 1978, p. 36). For instance, while both social systems and biological structures can be described by system theory, there are essential differences between them. Katz and Kahn emphasize this distinction and caution against the abundant use of biological metaphors in the study of organizations (cp. Kast & Rosenzweig 1972, pp. 455–456). Most notably, the nature of social systems can be regarded as "socially contrived" (Katz & Kahn 1978, p. 37).

The socially contrived nature of social systems. A central feature that differentiates social systems from biological systems is their lack of anatomy or physical structure. As a cycle of events, a social system has no structure apart from its functioning. In this sense, the nature of social systems can be regarded as "socially contrived" (Katz & Kahn 1978, p. 37). Social systems are human inventions that consist of complex behaviour patterns. They can be devised for a wide range of different objectives and can acquire new and diverse functions in the course of their history (Katz & Kahn 1978, p. 38). The existence of a social system depends on the physical presence of human beings as well as their enactment of the respective patterns of behaviour. Consequently, a core problem of any social system is the variability and instability of human actions. Psychological forces such as attitudes, perceptions, beliefs and motivations hold social systems together. In the absence of any biological restraints, a considerable amount of energy is consumed by social control mechanisms that stabilize social organizations. While certain types of social systems as, for instance, families are biologically based on symbiotic patterns (Katz & Kahn 1978, pp. 38–40), most organizations consist of culturally fabricated role relationships that depend on

---

[38] While Katz and Kahn present equifinality as a general characteristic of open systems, Ashmos and Huber contemplate that this attribute may only apply to systems that have no memory since enduring memories and learning experiences affect the present state of a system (Ashmos & Huber 1987, p. 617).

maintenance by sanctions and rewards. In addition to the enforcement of rules, environmental pressures or task requirements as well as demands arising from shared values and expectations, can reduce the variability of human behaviour (Katz & Kahn 1978, pp. 41–43).

Roles, norms and values as bases of system integration. Social systems are based on the role behaviour of their members, the norms which prescribe these behaviours and the values underlying these norms (Katz & Kahn 1978, p. 44). These three components differ in their degree of abstractness as well as in their justification to sanction behaviour. Roles can be described as specific forms of standardized or institutionalized behaviour that are associated with a certain position (Katz & Kahn 1978, p. 45). The person playing a specific role in a social system is under the demands of this role to act in particular ways. The network of different role behaviours represents the formal structure of an organization. Norms are general expectations all role incumbents encounter. There is agreement among the members of the system that these expectations reflect relevant and appropriate behavioural requirements (Katz & Kahn 1978, p. 386). Values are the most abstract and at the same time, the most basic elements of system integration. They represent generalized ideological justifications from which roles and norms are derived (Katz & Kahn 1978, p. 388). All three mechanisms contribute to the integration of social systems. The integration of smaller organizations may be based to a greater extent on a universal value system; larger organizations will rather depend on normative practices and determined role interdependence. While roles, norms and values describe how individuals are tied into social systems, the understanding of the internal architecture of organizations involves an additional level. A number of subsystems fulfil different tasks within the system.

Generic types of subsystems. Katz and Kahn differentiate five generic types of subsystems that are essential for the functioning of all social systems. First, system maintenance requires two different kinds of energic inputs: Maintenance inputs are needed to sustain the system as such; production inputs have to be processed in order to return a productive outcome. In addition, to ensure successful operation certain internal support functions are needed as well as adjustment in relation to the environment. Finally, the diverse activities have to be coordinated and directed towards a common goal. The five subsystems that fulfil these tasks are briefly described.

(1) The productive subsystem consists of the activities that are concerned with the organization's throughput. Commonly, organizations are classified according to their main

productive process. For instance, systems that are predominantly occupied with the creation of wealth are identified as economic organizations (Katz & Kahn 1978, p. 52).

(2) Organizations typically possess two types of supportive systems that are concerned with the continued provision of production inputs. One is responsible for the procurement of raw materials and the disposal of products and can be considered an extension of the production system into the environment. The other maintains and fosters favourable relations with institutions and structures in the society (Katz & Kahn 1978, p. 52).

(3) The maintenance subsystem on the one hand ensures the availability of human energy and on the other hand ties organizational members into their roles as functioning parts of the system. Functions such as recruitment, socialization, rewarding and sanctioning can be considered tasks of the maintenance subsystem (Katz & Kahn 1978, pp. 52–54).

(4) Since organizations are embedded in a constantly changing environment, adaptive subsystems are needed. These provide devices that can sense relevant changes in the outside world as well as translate them into consequences for the organization. Product research, market research, long-range planning and research and development contribute to the adaptive ability of organizations (Katz & Kahn 1978, pp. 54–55).

(5) The different subsystems and activities within organizations are coordinated, adjusted, controlled and directed by managerial subsystems. The first type of managerial subsystems, regulatory mechanisms, consists of structures that gather and utilize information about the system's energic transactions and provide feedback about the system's output in relation to its input. Authority structures constitute a second type of managerial subsystems. They describe the ways in which decision making and implementation are organized. Irrespective of the mode of decision making applied, decisions are accepted as binding for the members of the system if they were made in the proper manner (Katz & Kahn 1978, pp. 55–59).

While individuals in general may play more than one role (for instance, a production and a maintenance role) and move from one subsystem to another, many systems do not permit the combination of different roles within one individual. Instead, they accentuate the particularities of the different subsystems. Although all subsystems are essential to the organization as a whole, they do not exert the same degree of influence on the total system. There may be one "leading subsystem" (Katz & Kahn 1978, p. 59) that exerts a major influence on the other subsystems and thereby controls the interactions within the overall system.

The organization and its environment. Social systems as open systems have to be seen in their relationship with other social systems. Their classification as systems, subsystems or supersystems depends on the degree of autonomy in terms of their functions and on the point of view of the investigator. For the study of organizations, Katz and Kahn recommend to take first their embeddedness into a supersystem into account, since this defines the limits of variance of the organizations' behaviour (cp. also Montgomery 1998). The subsystems' contributions to the functioning of the system should then be part of a more detailed analytic study (Katz & Kahn 1978, pp. 63–64). Three interrelated concepts that are connected with the relative autonomy of system functioning and with the differentiation of a system from the environment are system openness, system boundaries and system coding. System openness refers to the degree to which the system receives different types of inputs. The specifications concerning the intake of information and energy are referred to as system coding. While all organizations possess formal criteria for the selection or exclusion of inputs, the procedure applied may be more or less rationally developed. Finally, the system boundaries that delineate the barrier between the system and its environment can consist of psychological confines or physical space (Katz & Kahn 1978, pp. 64–66).

After this brief overview of the open system approach according to Katz and Kahn, two concepts that are integrated into the approach will be taken into account in more detail. Both the role theoretical framework and the conflict model developed by Katz and Kahn are considered helpful for the present study.

3.1.3 Role Theoretical Framework

3.1.3.1 Overview of Role Theory

Role theory has long been a popular approach in sociology and social psychology (Biddle 1986, p. 67). In general, role theory attempts to explain individual behaviour in the larger context of groups or society (Jones & Deckro 1993, p. 218; Sarbin & Allen 1968, p. 490). The central idea within role theory is the role concept. Some authors credit the role concept with the achievement to bridge the gap between psychology and sociology, since it takes the level of the individual into account as well as the level of the social system (Dev & Olsen 1989, p. 22).[39] Many authors define roles in relation to a position. A position can be

---

[39] Katz and Kahn provide a particularly colourful depiction of this accomplishment: "Certainly psychologists and sociologists have strung a good deal of intellectual barbed wire along the boundary between their disciplines, with each group implying that there is something slightly

understood as a certain category of persons in a social system (Thomas & Biddle 1966, p. 29). While positions may be used to locate an actor within a system relative to other actors, roles can be seen as the dynamic aspect of the position (Anderson et al. 1998, p. 170). A role involves "function, adaptation, process" (Levinson 1959, p. 172) or "acting" (Parsons 1951, p. 25). Consequently, actors are "usually said to occupy or have a position, but to perform the role or roles that come with the position" (Anderson et al. 1998, p. 170; Jones & Deckro 1993, p. 218).[40]

Role theoretical approaches have been criticized because different authors use varying labels for the same phenomena (Heiss 1981, p. 94). Biddle tries to clarify this diversity by discriminating five main role theoretical perspectives: functional, symbolic interactionist, structural, organizational, and cognitive role theory (Biddle 1986). Although he identifies major differences among these five perspectives, Biddle recognizes common ground in their concern with a triad of concepts: patterned and characteristic social behaviours (which he defines as "roles"), parts or identities that are assumed by social participants ("social positions") and scripts or expectations for behaviour that are understood by all and adhered to by performers ("role expectations") (Biddle 1986, pp. 68–69). Disagreement between researchers commences with their understanding of the role concept. In particular, the relationship between behaviour and expectations and their association with the role concept is unclear. While many authors define roles similar to Biddle as a set of (enduring, regular, desired, expected or prescribed) behaviours that pertain to a particular task, position or social function (e.g., Collins 1982; Dev & Olsen 1989, p. 22; Jones & Deckro 1993, p. 218; Knight & Harland 2005, p. 282), others view the set of shared expectations regarding the behaviour that the occupant of a certain position should show as the role (e.g., Bible & McComas 1963, p. 225; Heiss 1981, p. 95; Jacobson, Charters & Lieberman 1951, p. 19).[41]

Most authors who regard roles as behaviour presume that expectations are the major generators of roles (Biddle 1986, p. 69). However, the opinions concerning the origin and

---

suspect if not superfluous about the level of explanation the other has chosen for its own. On top of this ideological fence sit the social psychologists, striving to look as comfortable as the metaphor will allow. All too often they ease their pain by avoiding the synthesis of sociological and psychological levels of discourse that should be the hallmark of their hyphenated trade. To the extent that choice of concepts can contribute to so complex a synthesis, the concept of role is singularly promising. It is the summation of the requirements with which the system confronts the individual member" (Katz & Kahn 1978, p. 186).

[40] This distinction in wording is cited in order to emphasize the different nature of roles and positions. In the following pages, however, this strict differentiation of verbs being used in association with the two concepts is not followed. The term "occupy" will be used in relation to roles as well as positions.

[41] In the following paragraphs, this person will be referred to as the "role occupant", "role incumbent" or the "focal person" (Abdel-Halim 1981, p. 264; Katz & Kahn 1978, p. 190).

nature of these expectations are diverse. Expectations are, for instance, assumed to represent "norms" (and, consequently, to be prescriptive in nature), "beliefs" (referring to subjective probability) or "preferences" (i.e., personal attitudes) (Biddle 1986, p. 69; Dev & Olsen 1989, p. 24). Other authors view them as comprised of the obligations, duties and privileges that are associated with a social position (Sarbin & Allen 1968). Still another point of view is the presumption that role expectations are negotiated between the focal actor and those who have expectations concerning the role (Knight & Harland 2005, p. 282). Those individuals who have expectations concerning the focal person's role because they occupy interdependent or complementary roles in the social structure are collectively known as the "role set" (Allen & Van de Vliert 1984, p. 8; Solomon et al. 1985, p. 103). The role set consists of the occupants of those roles that are directly linked with the focal person's role (Jones & Deckro 1993, p. 218; Merton 1957, p. 110; Mühlfeld & Reimann 1984, p. 180).

The role expectations held by the members of the role set can be communicated to the role occupant ("sent role") who, in turn, develops a "received role" consisting of his or her perceptions of the totality of sent role expectations regarding the position (Jones & Deckro 1993, p. 218). Role consensus exists when there is agreement among the expectations that are held by various persons (Biddle 1986, p. 76). Several authors argue, however, that complete consensus on role expectations among the occupants of different roles in a social system is rather improbable and is consequently seldom found (Bible & McComas 1963, p. 226; Gross, Mason & McEachern 1958). Instead of role consensus, role conflict and role ambiguity may arise.[42] Role conflict can be defined as a situation in which the role incumbent is faced with incompatible or inconsistent expectations concerning role behaviour (Abdel-Halim 1981, p. 264; Biddle 1986, p. 82; Frost 1983, p. 123; Vora, Kostova & Roth 2007, p. 81). Kahn et al. identify four major types of role conflict (Kahn et al. 1964). (1) They speak of intra-sender conflict when expectations from a single member of the role set are incongruent or contradictory. (2) Inter-sender conflict is identified when two or more members of the role set have incongruent expectations. (3) Inter-role conflict arises when the expectations existing in relation to one role contradict the expectations associated with another role played by the same person. (4) Person-role conflict represents a situation where the expectations of one or more members of the role set are incongruent with the expectations related to the person's subjective role (Chenet, Tynan & Money 1999, p. 140;

---

[42] Role conflict and role ambiguity are among the most frequently studied phenomena related to the role concept. For some examples of studies in the organizational context, see Abdel-Halim 1981; Chenet, Tynan & Money 1999; Currie & Procter 2005; Gong et al. 2001; Grover 1993; House 1970; Jones & Deckro 1993; Lysonski & Johnson 1983; Miles & Perreault Jr. 1980; Pettigrew 1968; Rizzo, House & Lirtzman 1970.

Jones & Deckro 1993, p. 218). Role ambiguity on the other hand occurs when the information available for the performance of a role is insufficient, inadequate or unclear (Abdel-Halim 1981, p. 264; Chenet, Tynan & Money 1999, p. 140; Frost 1983, p. 123).

Following this short overview of general elements of role theory, the role concept that Katz and Kahn present as integrated part of their open system approach will be described.

3.1.3.2 Role Theoretical Framework Within the Open System Approach

Katz and Kahn define social organizations as systems of roles (Katz & Kahn 1978, p. 187).[43] In their terminology, an individual's location within the total set of actions and interactions taking place in the organization is termed the individual's "office", "position" or also his or her "job" (Kahn & Quinn 1970, p. 52; Katz & Kahn 1978, p. 188). Each position within the organization is seen as associated with a set of behaviours expected of any person occupying that position. The behaviours that are expected in connection with a certain social position are considered the "role" (Kahn & Quinn 1970, p. 52; Katz & Kahn 1978, p. 188), while the behavioural demands made of a person in relation to a role are termed "role expectations" (Kahn & Quinn 1970, p. 53; Katz & Kahn 1978, p. 190). Since the role conduct of individuals is always interdependent with the behaviour of individuals in complementary positions, roles are generally defined in relation to other positions in the social structure (Katz & Kahn 1978, p. 189).

The set of people in an organization who are in some way dependent upon the behaviour of an individual occupying a particular role and who consequently have specific expectations regarding his or her behaviour are defined as the "role set" (Katz & Kahn 1978, p. 189). The role set corresponds neither exclusively to formal reporting relations nor to informal relations but can subsume both types of relationships (Kahn & Quinn 1970, p. 53). The expectations held by members of the role set for a certain person will reflect their conception of the occupied office and its requirements modified by their impression of the abilities and the personality of the holder of the position (Katz & Kahn 1978, p. 190). The role expectations according to which the members of the role set evaluate the role occupant's performance tend to be communicated or "sent" to the focal person (Katz & Kahn 1978, p. 190). For the focal person, interactions with members of the role set are a primary source of input into his

---

[43] Katz and Kahn (1978) state that their exposition of the role theoretical framework draws heavily on Kahn et al. 1964 and Kahn & Quinn 1970. These contributions are cited as well in the present context.

or her understanding of the role (Kahn & Quinn 1970, p. 55). Expectations of the role set can be communicated directly or indirectly and more or less completely and accurately (Kahn & Quinn 1970, p. 53). Behaviours by which members of the role set convey their role expectations include explicit descriptions of their expectations, more subtle attempts to influence the role occupant's behaviour or positive or negative reinforcement (Katz & Kahn 1978, pp. 190–192). The role expectations that are actually communicated to the focal person are termed "sent role" (Katz & Kahn 1978, p. 187). The focal person's perceptions and cognitions of what is sent are defined as the "received role" (Katz & Kahn 1978, p. 192).

> "It is the sent role by means of which the organization communicates to each of its members the do's and don'ts associated with his or her office. It is the received role, however, that is the immediate influence on each member's behaviour and the immediate source of his or her motivation for role performance" (Katz & Kahn 1978, p. 193).

These influences which are directly associated with the focal person's formal position within the organization, however, are not the only factors affecting the role occupant's understanding of his or her role (Katz & Kahn 1978, pp. 192–194). Objective, impersonal properties of the situation itself can be a source of influence on role taking as well. In addition, each individual's understanding of a role is influenced by internal motivation, motives, personality traits, cognitive or social abilities as well as other characteristics. Furthermore, a person can be considered to possess his or her own idea of and expectations regarding the role that is associated with a certain position. Within a social organization, a person may even have the opportunity to shape some of the responsibilities of his or her office.

Katz and Kahn's description of role sending and role receiving is based on the four concepts of role expectations, sent role, received role and role behaviour that can be thought of as constituents of a role episode. While the first two components (role expectations and sent role) are related to motivations, cognitions and behaviours of members of the role set, the latter two components (received role and role behaviour), involve motivations, cognitions and behaviours of the focal person (Katz & Kahn 1978, pp. 194–195). On the one hand, the role episode includes the influence of role expectations on role behaviour; on the other hand, there is a feedback loop: "The degree to which a person's behaviour conforms to the expectations of the role set at one point in time will affect the state of those expectations at the next moment" (Katz & Kahn 1978, p. 195). Role playing can therefore be regarded as an ongoing cyclic process. This process does not occur in isolation but is shaped by factors of the individual, interpersonal and organizational context. Figure 9 shows the role episode within this context.

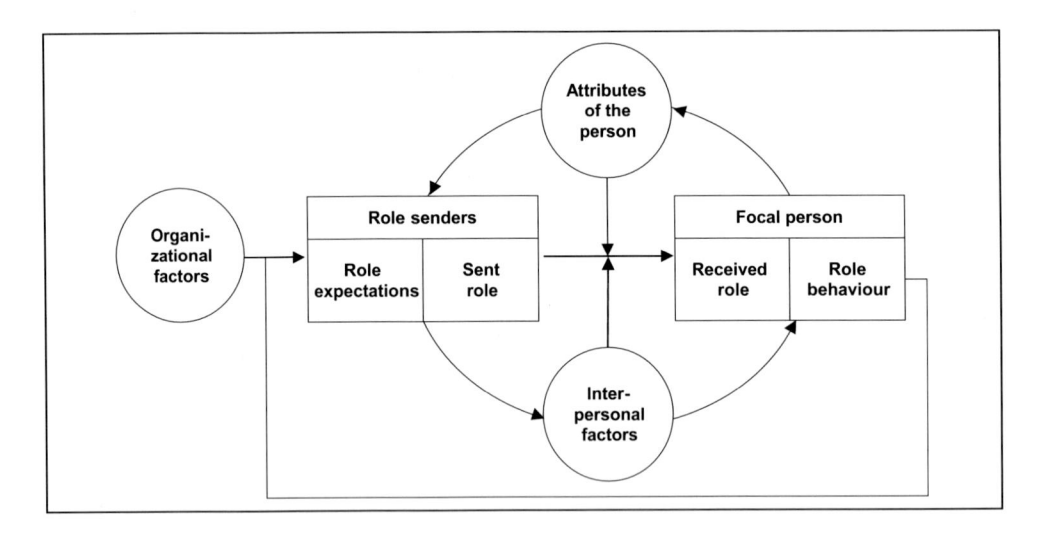

Figure 9: Factors Involved in a Role Episode
Source: Katz & Kahn 1978, p. 196.

While this description of a role episode highlights the focal person's role within the context of a specific organization and in relation to the respective role set, the situation may be more complex. As was mentioned above, expectations held by the focal person may influence the role perception. In addition, the focal person's role concept may be affected by not only group memberships and interpersonal relations that the person has inside the organization. The person may occupy roles in other groups outside the organization that, at times, can even be incompatible with the formal role in the organization. In other instances, additional roles that the person occupies can simply add a different perspective to the formal role in the organization. A depiction of this slightly extended and more detailed description of factors influencing the focal person's role perception and enactment as provided by Kahn and Quinn is portrayed in Figure 10.

```
                    Properties of the focal person:
                    • Personal resources
                    • Reflexive role expectations

┌─────────────────┐   ┌─────────────┐   ┌──────────┐   ┌──────────────┐
│Extra-organizational│→ │Organization │ → │ Role set │ → │ Focal person │
│  environment    │   │             │   │          │   │              │
└─────────────────┘   └─────────────┘   └──────────┘   └──────────────┘
```

- Properties of socio-cultural systems in which the organization participates
- Demands made by external systems for organizational performance
- Resources available to the organization from external systems

Properties of the organization as a whole, e.g., division of labour, pattern of reward and resource allocation

Expectations held for the focal person   Expectations sent to the focal person

Received expectations   Interpreted expectations

Responses:
- Physiological
- Perceptual-cognitive
- Affective
- Coping
- Performance

Group membership and interpersonal relations of the focal person, both inside and outside the organization

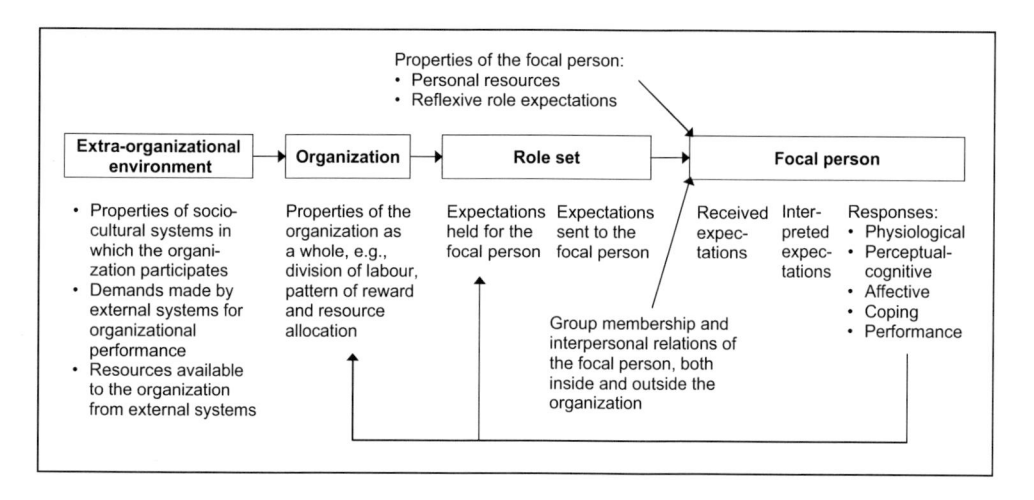

Figure 10: Organizational Role Theoretical Framework
            Source: Kahn & Quinn 1970, p. 55.

As mentioned above, role expectations held by the role set are not always clearly communicated to the person playing a certain role. The role occupant receives the sent expectations and interprets them according to his or her own motives and expectations, taking into account additional roles he or she is occupying in other contexts (Kahn & Quinn 1970, p. 54; Katz & Kahn 1978, pp. 192–194). Based on the resulting understanding of the role, the focal person enacts the role. Considering the different factors influencing the focal person's understanding of the role, it is possible that the role as interpreted by the focal person is not identical with the role as conceived by the members of the role set (Kahn & Quinn 1970, p. 54; Katz & Kahn 1978, p. 203). When the role occupant and the role set have differing understandings of the role, the role occupant's role enactment may not match the expectations of the role set. Such a situation of role dissensus is of particular interest in the present context as it will be interpreted as perception gap in 3.3.[44]

Role theory's assumption that role dissensus generally leads to conflict will be outlined in 3.3.3.1. Since Katz and Kahn's conflict model will be referred to in that context, it will be described in the following paragraphs.

---

[44] The discrepancy of role perceptions between members of the role set and the focal person is referred to here as "role dissensus". This expression is used since none of the role conflict categories defined by Kahn et al. (1964) completely fits (cp. 3.1.3.1). The term "inter-sender conflict" might be applied if the focal person was interpreted as an additional role sender. The term "person-role conflict" could be used in case the focal person's role perception is considered as a "predetermined attribute of the person".

3.1.4 Conflict Model

As an integrated part of their open system approach, Katz and Kahn present a conflict model that explains conflict at an organizational level. The actors within this model are either "total organizations or relatively autonomous subunits of organizations" (Katz & Kahn 1978, p. 612). In comparison to the discussion in the general conflict literature that was reviewed in 2.4.1, Katz and Kahn choose to conceptualize conflict rather narrowly as overt behaviour of which the involved parties are aware. According to Katz and Kahn, "two systems (persons, groups, organizations, nations) are in conflict when they interact directly in such a way that the actions of one tend to prevent or compel some outcome against the resistance of the other" (Katz & Kahn 1978, p. 613). Although Katz and Kahn acknowledge that an analysis of the cognitive and affective levels of conflict can be helpful for fully understanding the conflict phenomenon, they define conflict as behaviour that is observable as a collision of actors (Katz & Kahn 1978, p. 613):

> "If two business firms are engaged in a price war, or a business and labor union are engaged in a strike, it is those actions that constitute conflict as we understand it. Whether a particular instance of such conflict is characterized by real or imagined differences of interest, by great anger or lack of it, by a hostile act or a misunderstood gesture of friendship are appropriate questions to understanding the conflict but not to defining it" (Katz & Kahn 1978, p. 613).

Conflict is seen as a process that consists of a series of episodes that involve an attempted action and a concomitant attempt at resistance. Katz and Kahn view conflict as inherent in the nature of organizations and assume that it may have functional as well as dysfunctional implications (Katz & Kahn 1978, pp. 640–641).[45] Katz and Kahn's model of inter-system conflict will be briefly summarized in the following paragraphs (Katz & Kahn 1978, p. 618 et sqq.). They assume that the conflict process can be subdivided into six categories of variables that describe the process.

Organizational properties. The first of these categories contains organizational properties. The authors assume that systems may possess characteristics, which increase their tendency to engage in conflict. For instance, certain organizational structures or ideologies about conflict may constitute such predisposing organizational properties (Katz & Kahn 1978, pp. 618–619).

Conflict of interest. Subjective as well as objective conflict of interest is relevant for the prediction of conflict behaviour. According to Katz and Kahn, conflict of interest exists when

---

[45] On the issue of conflict in system approaches see also Peery Jr. 1972, pp. 274–275.

the two parties exhibit incompatible properties.[46] Empirical research confirms that the existence of conflict of interest increases the likelihood of conflict behaviour, i.e., manifest conflict (Figure 11). In the context of organizations, conflict can appear in connection with the three general processes of resource attainment, throughput and disposal of output (cp. also Dorow 1978, p. 105). Katz and Kahn mention, however, that overt conflict does not necessarily occur at the point where the incompatibility arises; instead, the overt conflict may surface at a different locus as the conflict of interest (Katz & Kahn 1978, pp. 623–624).[47]

Terminology	Conflict of interest	Conflict behaviour
General description	Existence of incompatibilities concerning a certain issue (latent conflict; conflict potential)	Observable conflictful behaviour (manifest conflict); Conflict issues: input, throughput, output
		...can proliferate to other issues

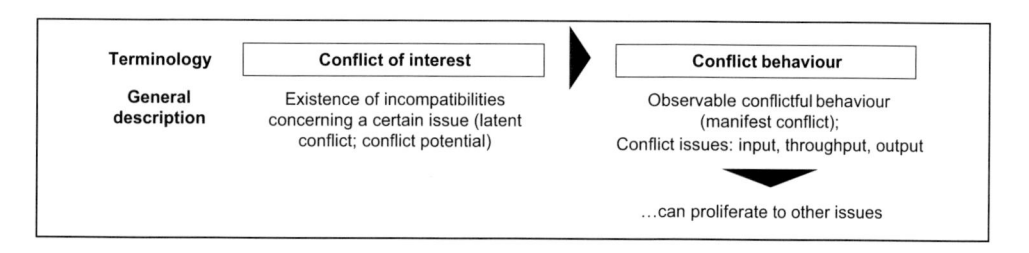

Figure 11: Elements of a Conflict Situation

Role expectations. Conflicts between organizations or organizational units are in general enacted by representatives of the involved parties. Nevertheless, the conflict affects the system as a whole (Vollmer 2005, p. 70). It is the representatives' task to argue for their constituents' interests. Thereby they fulfil what Katz and Kahn refer to as "conflict role" (Katz & Kahn 1978, pp. 626–628). The bearers of conflict roles are exposed to complex expectations – while the opposing party expects them to abide by certain rules as to how the conflict should be enacted, the constituents of their own organization or organizational unit expect them to "win" the conflict for them.

---

[46] In the terminology of other authors, this would be referred to as antecedent conditions of conflict or latent conflict (Pondy 1967, p. 300).
[47] When comparing the terms used in Figure 11 with other contributions in the conflict literature, it becomes apparent that varying labels can be found for identical (or at least similar) phenomena. Authors in the conflict field do not adhere to a consistent terminology and frequently do not even clarify the terms they use (Biddle 1986, p. 68; Heiss 1981, p. 94). In the present context, the term "conflict issues" is applied to describe organizational issues concerning which conflict can generally emerge. If certain conditions arise which involve an increased likelihood of conflict concerning any such issue, this situation is referred to as "conflict of interest". Conflict of interest describes the existence of two parties' incompatible properties (Katz & Kahn 1978, p. 619). Other authors call this constellation "latent conflict" (Pondy 1967, p. 300), "conflict potential" (Berkel 1992, p. 1087) or "conflict causes" (Rüttinger & Sauer 2000, p. 20). Interfering or blocking behaviour which is shown in relation to the conflict of interest is interpreted as the actual conflict (Katz & Kahn 1978, p. 613). Observable conflictful behaviour is referred to as "manifest conflict" by some authors (Pondy 1967, p. 303).

Behavioural predispositions. Another question that deserves consideration is to what extent the behaviour of representatives enacting the conflict depends on behavioural dispositions of the individual. Katz and Kahn discuss empirical results of studies that examine the effect of personality characteristics on individuals' behaviour in conflict situations. Although small effects are detected by some studies in a number of conditions, the main finding seems to be "that situational factors tend to reduce personality effects, and that strong situational factors tend to eliminate personality differences in conflict behavior" (Katz & Kahn 1978, p. 629).

Rules and procedures. Conflicts within and between organizations are generally limited by formal and informal rules and regulations. Experimental confirmation exists that the conflict behaviour exhibited by individuals can be altered by the provision of different rules (Katz & Kahn 1978, pp. 630–634).

Interaction. The final component of the conflict model is the behaviour of the parties enacting the conflict between the two systems. One of the best-established results about conflict interaction is the tendency toward reciprocal or similar behaviours and the resultant escalation of the conflict process. The escalation process, however, not only seems to intensify conflict over the initial issue; the conflict rather tends to proliferate to other issues (Katz & Kahn 1978, p. 635). Experimental research has explored ways by which ongoing conflict may be limited. Of the three initiatives experimentally studied, threats are the least effective, followed by promises. Conditional cooperation or conditional benevolence, which means that a cooperative move is made and at the same time a reciprocal act of cooperation is requested, proved to be most effective (Katz & Kahn 1978, pp. 636–637).

The combination of the individual components in the conflict model by Katz and Kahn is depicted in Figure 12. After describing the model in general terms, its applicability and relevance for the headquarters-subsidiary relationship will be discussed in the following.[48]

---

[48] It should be noted that the model does not explain the concept "role conflict". Role conflict refers to a specific type of conflict that is associated with incongruent expectations related to a certain role (see also 3.1.3.1).

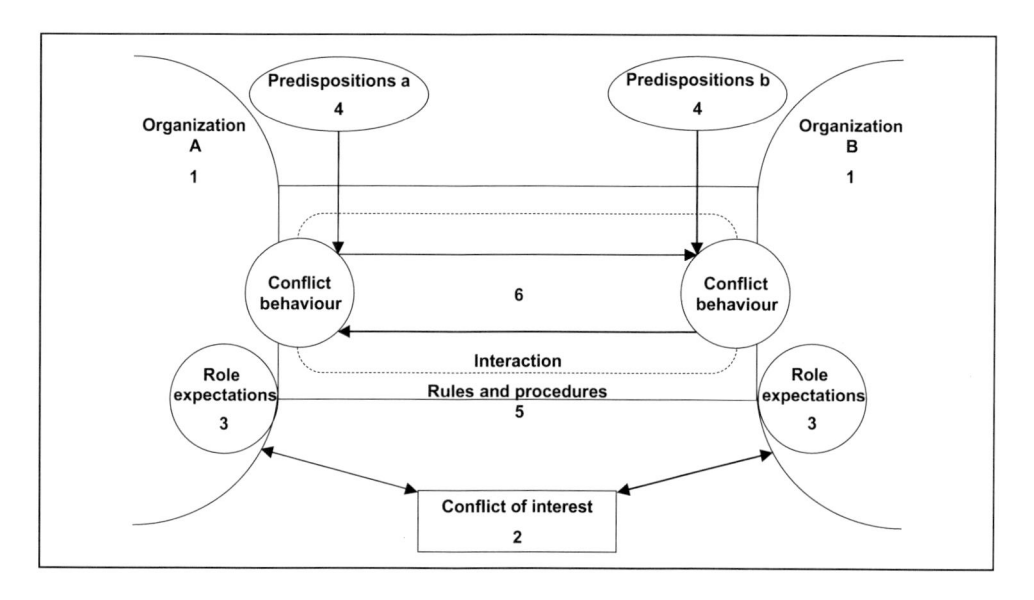

Figure 12: Katz and Kahn's Conflict Model
Source: Katz & Kahn 1978, p. 621.

3.2 Multinational Network Corporations as Open Systems

3.2.1 Applicability of the Open System Approach

3.2.1.1 Parallels Between Network Perspectives and the Open System Approach

Despite their increased popularity, network models of MNCs have not been theoretically grounded so far (Ghoshal & Bartlett 1990, p. 621). A systematic transfer of system theory to network MNCs has not been conducted either.[49] Nevertheless, MNCs were termed open systems before (for instance, Asakawa 2001, p. 737).[50] In the following, several general parallels between open system approaches and network models of MNCs will be outlined.[51]

On an abstract level, Brass et al. describe network perspectives by a "focus on relations rather than attributes, on structured patterns of interaction rather than isolated individual

---

[49] Ashmos and Huber criticize that both organizational theory and the system paradigm missed several opportunities by not referring to each other for decades (Ashmos & Huber 1987, p. 616).
[50] However, the open system approach was used as a frame of reference in other areas of IB research. The study of international joint ventures by Shenkar and Zeira can serve as an example (Shenkar & Zeira 1987). Here, the international joint venture is considered as the open system.
[51] Sydow provides an extensive treatise on organizational networks (Sydow 1992). Among other theoretical approaches, he draws on system theory in order to explain the evolution and organization of organizational networks.

actors" (Brass et al. 2004, p. 795).[52] An almost identical statement was cited in 3.1.2.2 referring to system theory. Both system theory and network perspectives can be considered rather broad in terms of their applicability. This is reflected in their use on multiple levels (Raider & Krackhardt 2002, p. 61). In the case of system theory, Miller (1978) elaborates the specificities for different levels of systems (ranging from cells to supranational systems) in his already mentioned "Living Systems" (see 3.1.1.2). While the same basic principles apply to any of the levels, lower level systems are seen as constituents of higher-level systems. For instance, a cell represents a system on its own, but at the same time, organs and organisms as higher-level systems consist of a large number of cells. The same logic can be applied to network approaches. Here, interpersonal, inter-unit and inter-organizational networks can be differentiated (Brass et al. 2004).

Katz and Kahn formulate their open system approach at the level of the individual organization. Network approaches to MNCs can focus on two different levels, the MNC as an *intra*-organizational network or the MNC as part of an *inter*-organizational network (Schmid, Schurig & Kutschker 2002, p. 45; see also 2.1.3). In the present context, the intra-organizational point of view is considered and the network consisting of different organizational units is examined. Consequently, the focus is on one individual MNC as well. On the one hand, both approaches explain the internal functioning. In both cases, internal differentiation is emphasized as a key characteristic. On the other hand, the relationship with the external environment is considered a vital aspect.

When it comes to the empirical study of network MNCs, the same difficulty arises that Katz and Kahn refer to as "problem of levels" (Katz & Kahn 1978, pp. 12 et sqq.). Conceptual contributions mostly address the level of the entire MNC or organizational units (Bartlett & Ghoshal 1991; Hedlund 1986; Prahalad & Doz 1987; White & Poynter 1989). At the same time, empirical data is usually collected at the level of individual managers. While in the IB literature this issue is commonly not highlighted, Katz and Kahn argue that their open system framework is able to reconcile this problem.

Two of the issues mentioned above will be addressed in more detail in the following paragraphs. First, the parallels between the open system approach and network models of MNCs will be elaborated. Particular demands that network models of MNCs have regarding theoretical approaches and how they may be met by the open system approach will be dealt

---

[52] For a review of general network approaches, see, for instance, Borgatti & Foster 2003.

with (3.2.1.2). Then it will be discussed how the problem of levels is handled in the present context (3.2.1.3).

3.2.1.2 Specific Demands of Multinational Network Corporations

Since a theoretical framework for network MNCs has not been provided yet, the aim is to model characteristic features of network MNCs in terms of Katz and Kahn's open system approach. Doz and Prahalad formulate seven attributes of network MNCs that they understand as prerequisites for the applicability of theoretical approaches to network MNCs (Doz & Prahalad 1991, p. 147).[53] A theory should meet these criteria in order to be able to contribute to the knowledge of network MNCs. In the following, the present study will illustrate the compatibility of Katz and Kahn's open system approach and the network perspective on MNCs along the structure established by Doz and Prahalad.[54]

Structural undeterminacy. Doz and Prahalad assume that any single stable and unidimensional concept of organizational structure will fall short of describing the nature of network MNCs (Doz & Prahalad 1991, p. 146). Even though Katz and Kahn refer to a hierarchical organization when presenting their framework (e.g., Katz & Kahn 1978, p. 331), the concept can be applied to organizations that are structured differently as well. The open system approach as such does not favour a specific type of organizational structure. The principle of equifinality allows for various constellations and development paths (Ashmos & Huber 1987, p. 617; Katz & Kahn 1978, p. 30; Shibutani 1968, p. 332). Furthermore, the possibility of organizational change is explicitly taken into account (Katz & Kahn 1978, pp. 653–749).

Internal differentiation. According to Doz and Prahalad, in order "to be applied to DMNC an organizational theory must therefore incorporate a *differentiated approach to businesses, countries and functions*, and provide enough flexibility for different trade-offs between multiple dimensions to be made" (Doz & Prahalad 1991, p. 146, original emphasis). Internal differentiation is one of the main principles of the open system approach. Specialization of system parts can render the system or organization more efficient (Katz & Kahn 1978, p. 29). On the one hand, formal organizational structure and management processes can be differentiated based on characteristics of the external environment they face, for instance, in

---

[53] Doz and Prahalad speak of DMNCs, i.e., diversified multinational corporations instead of network MNCs (Doz & Prahalad 1991, p. 145). Their conceptualization, however, corresponds to the network models of MNCs.
[54] In their contribution, Doz and Prahalad do not refer to system theory.

diverse countries (Lawrence & Lorsch 1967; Thompson 2004). Differentiation according to characteristics of the external environment is seen as "a direct corollary of the open-systems view of organizations" (Ghoshal & Nohria 1989, p. 324). On the other hand, differentiation can be motivated by the situation within the MNC, i.e., internal power relationships and the distribution of resources (Pfeffer 1981; Pfeffer & Salancik 1978). Within network MNCs, differentiation can be encountered at several levels. While the general differentiation of productive, supportive, maintenance, adaptive and managerial subsystems (Katz & Kahn 1978, pp. 52–59) applies to network MNCs as well, differentiation among subsidiaries can be considered an additional dimension. Each subsidiary may contribute to each of the network MNC's five subsystems. For instance, subsidiary A may play an important role in the productive process of the entire MNC. Still, subsidiary A may only produce a component of the final product and other subsidiaries may be part of the productive subsystem as well. At the same time, subsidiary A may also contribute to the other four subsystems to a certain extent. It may fulfil some activities related to the supportive and adaptive subsystems, play a central part in the maintenance subsystems and be involved in managerial activities to a small extent. Figure 13 illustrates how these two levels of differentiation can relate to each other and to the concept of headquarters and subsidiary roles. However, the depicted relationship with subsidiary roles, especially, is simplifying. As discussed earlier (2.2), a subsidiary's role is assumed also to include less "factual" dimensions such as, for instance, subsidiary autonomy or subsidiary capabilities that are not explicitly considered in this model.[55]

---

[55] The integration of subsidiary role dimensions such as autonomy or capabilities into the graphic model in Figure 13 would have been possible. However, in order to reduce the complexity of the figure this was not realized.

Subsystems	Productive	Supportive	Maintenance	Adaptive	Managerial	
Headquarters	○	○	◯	○	○	Role HQ
Subsidiary A	◯	○	◯	○	○	Role A
Subsidiary B	○	○	○	○	○	Role B
Subsidiary C	◯	○	○	◯	○	Role C
Subsidiary D	○	○	○	○	◯	Role D

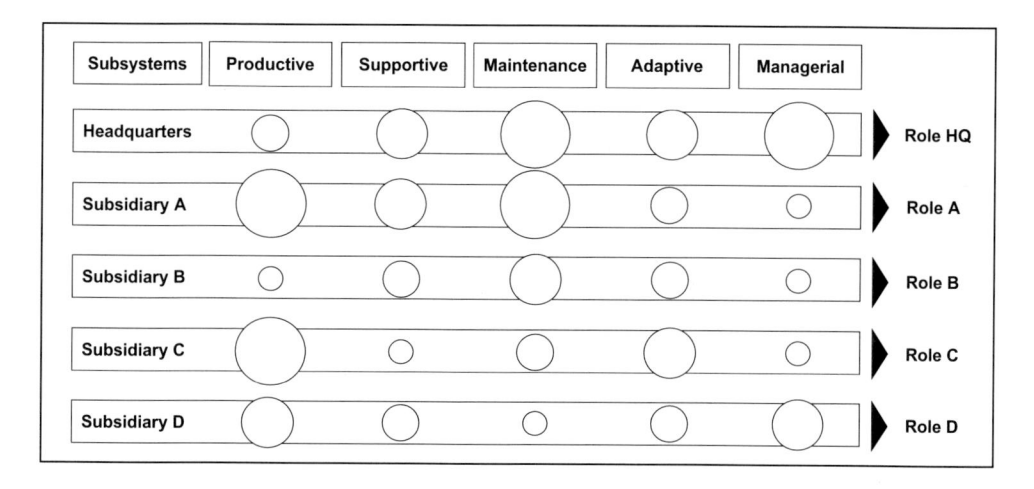

Figure 13: Two Dimensions of Differentiation in Multinational Network Corporations

Integrative optimization. The internal differentiation of the network MNC leads to the emergence of different perspectives and interests (Maynard-Moody & McClintock 1987, p. 135). Consequently, management processes need to account for these potentially conflicting priorities and to "foster varied decision trade-offs" (Doz & Prahalad 1991, p. 147). Differentiation within open systems as well requires that different concerns are reconciled in the decision making process and that compromises are necessary in order to keep the system functioning (Katz & Kahn 1978, p. 481). Katz and Kahn consider issues of decision making primarily in the context of policy formulation (Katz & Kahn 1978, pp. 475–524).

Information intensity. The management of information is viewed as a central management task by Doz and Prahalad since information constitutes a potential source of competitive advantage for network MNCs (Doz & Prahalad 1991, p. 147). Open systems also depend on informative inputs from their environment (Katz & Kahn 1978, p. 26). Relevant information about the environment as well as information processing capabilities are needed in order to achieve optimal adaptation to environmental demands (Chakravarthy 1982, p. 33; Child 1987, p. 35; Hartman, White & Crino 1986, pp. 458–459). Organizations not only have to deal with information efficiently, they also create new knowledge (Nonaka 1994, p. 14). Thereby, information and knowledge become key resources. Interestingly, Gupta and Govindarajan develop a subsidiary role typology for network MNCs based on intra-corporate knowledge flows and differentiate these flows according to system terminology: "The type of expertise transferred could refer to input processes (e.g., purchasing skills), throughput processes (e.g., product designs, process designs, and packaging designs), or output processes (e.g., marketing know-how, distribution expertise)" (Gupta & Govindarajan 1991, p. 773).

Latent linkages. One major advantage of network MNCs compared to more hierarchically structured MNCs is their flexibility that allows them to react rapidly to changed circumstances (Ensign 1999, p. 203). In order to be truly flexible, the organization cannot predefine all potential linkages. Rather, it has to be possible to establish relationships according to emergent needs (Carr, Durant & Downs 2004, p. 87; Doz & Prahalad 1991, p. 147). When describing an open system's adjustment to external circumstances, Katz and Kahn refer to the concepts steady state and dynamic homeostasis (Katz & Kahn 1978, pp. 26–29; see also 3.1.2.2). According to these concepts, the system tries to preserve its character by establishing a new and more complex equilibrium that is as close as possible to its previous state (Katz & Kahn 1978, p. 27). Doz and Prahalad do not specify the issue of to what extent the new relational structure is similar to the preceding one.

Networked organization and "fuzzy boundaries". Both open systems and network MNCs need strong ties with partners in their environment. For Katz and Kahn, relationships between system and environment are essential for the survival of open systems since they need to import energy as well as information for their functioning (Katz & Kahn 1978, p. 23; Porter Liebeskind et al. 1996). They even define a supportive subsystem which is responsible for maintaining favourable relationships with other systems and organizations in the society (Katz & Kahn 1978, pp. 52, 63). Doz and Prahalad speak more specifically of certain types of network partners, i.e., customers and suppliers that have to be incorporated in the organizational network (Doz & Prahalad 1991, p. 147). Due to intense relationships with partners outside of the organization, the organizational boundaries become blurry and the organization or system may sometimes be difficult to define (Katz & Kahn 1978, pp. 20–23).

Learning and continuity. Katz and Kahn describe open systems as cycles of events (Katz & Kahn 1978, p. 24). Although, as a rule, continuity is assumed, the occurrences in each cycle may take a slightly different shape. Such alterations may be caused by changes in the environment or developments within the system and, in general, will increase the system's fit to internal and external demands. While on the one hand, a large number of identical repetitions will lead to lower costs, on the other hand, under certain circumstances innovation and change may be advantageous (Doz & Prahalad 1991, p. 147).

The description of these seven points shows that a considerable degree of correspondence can be discovered between a network perspective on MNCs and Katz and Kahn's open system approach. Consequently, it is concluded that the open system approach may be applied to analyze processes and relations within the network MNC. Admittedly, the system theoretical conceptualization is, in wide parts, quite abstract, so that concrete propositions about the functioning of the MNC are hard to derive (Kast & Rosenzweig 1972, p. 459).[56] However, two concepts that are integrated in the open system framework can be particularly helpful for addressing the research questions posed in this thesis – the role theoretical framework and the conflict model. Before the application of these specific concepts to network MNCs will be elaborated, the issue of the duality of individuals and organizational units will be discussed.

3.2.1.3 Dealing with the Duality of Individuals and Organizational Units

A two-fold "problem of levels" (Katz & Kahn 1978, p. 12 et sqq.) needs to be taken into consideration in the present context. The first difficulty concerns the use of individual level concepts at the level of organizational units. The second issue is associated with the empirical assessment of organizational level concepts by individual level data.

(1) The use of individual level concepts at the level of the organization or organizational units is quite common in organizational theory.[57] However, strictly speaking, neither organizations nor their subsystems "behave" or "act", as is frequently suggested by the conceptual descriptions. Instead, individuals enact any type of organizational behaviour. Decisions are taken and implemented by individuals and relationships between organizational units can be retraced to the interaction of individual representatives of the respective units.

> "There is a danger, nevertheless, in applying the language developed for the psychology of the individual to describe the functioning of a social system. When we speak of organizational goals, organizational choice, organizational learning and decision making, we must restrict our reference to certain leaders or subgroups and not regard the organization as a person" (Katz & Kahn 1978, pp. 480–481).

Despite this word of warning, it was argued that many abstract concepts such as cognition, behaviour, goals or capabilities might be applied not only to individuals but might also be

---

[56] Not all authors, however, share this standpoint. For instance, Ashmos and Huber write: "Despite over half a century of effort, the study of organizations has produced disappointing results; generally findings have low explanatory power and seldom are associated with well-defined domains [...] In contrast to organization theory, the systems paradigm includes precise and widely applicable classification schemes" (Ashmos & Huber 1987, p. 611).

[57] For instance, agency theory in the context of headquarters-subsidiary relationships may be considered: Both headquarters and the subsidiary are viewed as actors who behave in a specific way and who have certain cognitions (e.g., Kim, Prescott & Kim 2005; O'Donnell 2000; Yu, Wong & Chiao 2006).

meaningfully determined at the level of collectives such as groups or organizations (Nonaka 1994, p. 20; Schmid & Schurig 2003, p. 758; Schneider & Angelmar 1993, p. 356). The present study will deal with this controversy as follows. (A) The role concept is an individual level concept that will be used to refer to organizational units. The role concept is borrowed from social psychological role theory and originally refers to an individual's position within a social system (e.g., Sarbin & Allen 1968). Although Katz and Kahn do not explicitly describe organizational units as possible role occupants, a transfer of the role concept to organizational units seems feasible (Anderson et al. 1998, p. 168).[58] As an individual can play a certain role and thereby fulfil a particular function for a social organization, an organizational unit as a collective consisting of several individuals can take such a position as well.[59] (B) In addition to the role concept, the notion of conflict will be applied to the relationship of organizational units and in particular to the headquarters-subsidiary relationship. The idea of different organizational units or departments experiencing conflict in their relationship is already established in the literature (e.g., Alter 1990, p. 482; Barclay 1991; Pahl & Roth 1993; Walton, Dutton & Cafferty 1969). While conflict is, of course, as well enacted by individuals (Barclay 1991, p. 146; Katz & Kahn 1978, p. 375), it may be assumed that conflict between two organizational units is experienced by those members of the units who are not directly involved in the conflict as well (Vollmer 2005, p. 70). Consequently, the term "headquarters-subsidiary conflict" is used. It is concluded that the role concept can be applied to organizational units and the conflict concept may be applied to the headquarters-subsidiary relationship.

While an organizational unit's *behaviour* is conceivable, there are other concepts that are not judged as suitable for use on a collective level. (C) For instance, it seems inappropriate to speak of "an organizational unit's *perception*". The concept perception refers to an individual act and it can hardly be imagined to relate to a collective. Consequently, in order to emphasize the subjective element contained in the act and result of perception, individual perceptions will not be aggregated to statements such as "headquarters' perception of the subsidiary's role". Instead, "headquarters managers' perceptions of the subsidiary's role" are referred to. (D) Based on the same reasoning, role *expectations* will be attributed to individual managers rather than organizational units.

---

[58] Knight and Harland, for instance, apply role theory to entire organizations within the context of business networks (Knight & Harland 2005).

[59] According to Miner, it can be assumed that "much of what is learned about one living system level is also found to hold for higher-order living system levels" (Miner 1984, p. 614).

(2) The issue that Katz and Kahn describe as "problem of levels" is associated with the empirical assessment of concepts which cannot be directly examined but for which phenomena at a different level have to be taken into account. The problem refers to the gap between the conceptual and the phenomenological level and is relevant for the network perspective on MNCs as well as for the open system approach. Both approaches are conceptually located at the level of the organization and its subsystems. Katz and Kahn argue that in their open system approach, individual level data can be used in order to assess system level issues (Katz & Kahn 1978, p. 13). Similarly, in the present context, the assessment of collective attributes such as subsidiary roles or headquarters-subsidiary conflict has to be based on individual data. Individuals who are considered as representatives of the respective units are asked to evaluate a subsidiary's role and the extent to which they find the headquarters-subsidiary relationship is experiencing conflict (Katz & Kahn 1978, p. 374).[60] Top managers of the respective organizational units can be expected to be best suited for this task, since they are directly involved in relations between the different organizational units (Asakawa 2001, p. 740; Böttcher 1996, p. 137).

3.2.2 Subsidiary Roles from a Role Theoretical Perspective

In the present context, the network MNC is considered as a social organization that can be defined as a system of roles according to Katz and Kahn (Katz & Kahn 1978, p. 187). It was argued above that certain individual level concepts can be applied to collectives, such as, for instance, organizational units (Nonaka 1994, p. 20; Schmid & Schurig 2003, p. 758; Schneider & Angelmar 1993). Following this reasoning, the MNC's subsidiaries are interpreted as role bearers in the present context.[61] In the next paragraphs, implications and difficulties of such a transfer will be discussed.

Katz and Kahn define roles as patterns of behaviours that are expected in relation to a social position (Kahn & Quinn 1970, p. 52; Katz & Kahn 1978, p. 188). For subsidiary roles, a comparably widely accepted general definition does not exist. Most authors do not make

---

[60] The key challenge in the empirical study of collective cognitions, behaviours, goals and so on is to combine the individual data in a way that can be assumed to reflect a cross-section or average of characteristics which are then attributed to the group or organization (Breiger 1974; Schneider & Angelmar 1993, pp. 356–361).

[61] As was already noted, the role concept was applied earlier to whole organizations when their role within a business network was analyzed (Anderson et al. 1998; Knight & Harland 2005). Although the connection between subsidiary roles and the sociological role concept had also been noted before (Schmid, Bäurle & Kutschker 1998, p. 93), the subsidiary role literature, surprisingly, never drew on the knowledge gathered by role theoretical research.

their understanding of subsidiary roles explicit and instead describe the role in terms of two or three individual dimensions (see also 2.2). In the present study, subsidiary roles will be conceptualized from an open system perspective. Corresponding to Katz and Kahn's definition, subsidiary roles are understood as patterns of behaviours that are expected in relation to a specific position in the MNC.[62]

Each subsidiary that occupies a certain position within the MNC and plays a specific role that is related to this position can be seen as fulfilling particular functions for the entire MNC or units of the MNC (Bartlett & Ghoshal 1986, p. 88; Hedlund 1986, p. 22). In the same way as roles of individuals, subsidiary roles have to be defined in relation to other interdependent or complementary positions in the social structure (Ensign 1999, pp. 303–305; Katz & Kahn 1978, p. 189; Malnight 1996, p. 43; White & Poynter 1989, p. 58). The units that depend on the subsidiary's role can be understood as the subsidiary's role set. The representatives of these units have certain expectations concerning the subsidiary's enactment of the role (Kahn & Quinn 1970, p. 52). These expectations are communicated to the subsidiary more or less clearly. In addition to the expectations of internal network partners, the subsidiary is confronted with role expectations of external network partners (e.g., Johanson, Pahlberg & Thilenius 1996; Miles & Perreault Jr. 1980, p. 138).

Furthermore, the subsidiary's interpretation of the received role expectations is biased by its managers' motives, their prior expectations or other influencing factors. Consequently, the subsidiary management develops a perception of the subsidiary's role that may differ from the expectations of its network partners (Kahn & Quinn 1970, p. 73; Katz & Kahn 1978, p. 203). Finally, the subsidiary as the role occupant enacts its role according to the role perception prevailing among its top managers (Ammeter et al. 2004, p. 55; Sarbin & Allen 1968, p. 140). This role enactment is being met by the expectations of the subsidiary's network partners and may or may not satisfy these expectations. A schematic overview of the described application of the role theoretical framework to subsidiaries is provided in Figure 14.

---

[62] The definition is formulated on the level of the subsidiary, although individuals representing the subsidiary, of course, enact these behaviours. It may be argued that the individuals representing the subsidiary collectively behave in a certain way and thereby constitute the subsidiary's role behaviour.

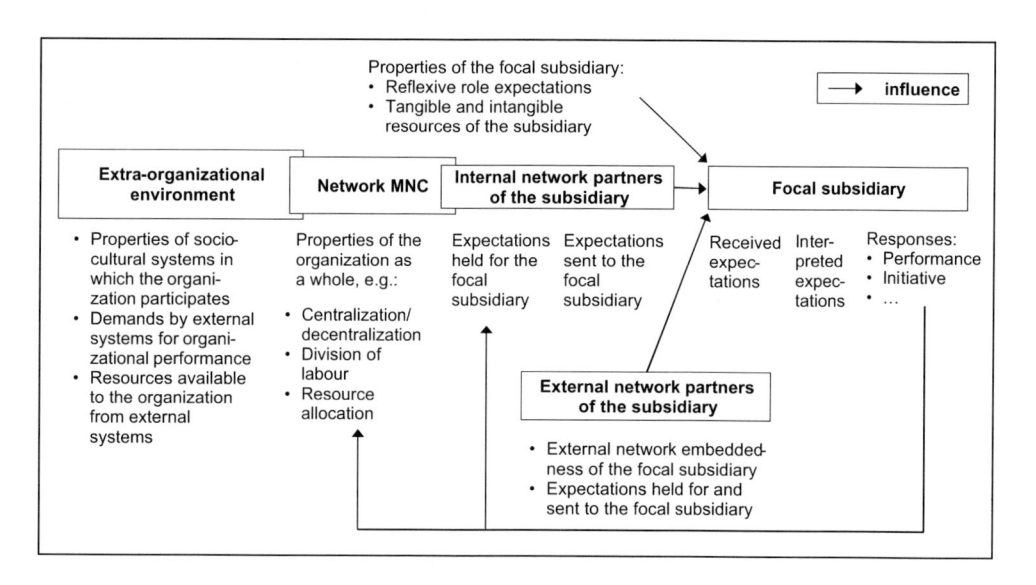

Figure 14: Application of the Organizational Role Theoretical Framework to Subsidiary Roles[63]

Source: Adapted from Kahn & Quinn 1970, p. 55.

Role theory researchers generally assume that a role occupant can play more than one role (Katz & Kahn 1978, p. 53; Witte 1994, p. 31). This is a supposition that is shared by researchers in the IB literature (Schmid 2004, p. 247; Tavares & Young 2006, p. 596). On the one hand, it may be argued that subsidiaries can play different roles in different contexts, in different situations and at different points of time. For instance, a subsidiary may fulfil a particular role within the network of the MNC while playing another role in the context of its local business network (Johanson, Pahlberg & Thilenius 1996, p. 253; Miles & Perreault Jr. 1980, p. 138). On the other hand, it was shown that, even in the context of the MNC, elements of different roles can coexist within one subsidiary (Pearce & Tavares 2002, p. 84).

When subsidiary roles are defined according to the role theoretical framework included in Katz and Kahn's open system approach as patterns of behaviours that are related to a specific position in the MNC, this conceptualization does not fully correspond to the usage of the term subsidiary role in the IB literature.[64] While some of the dimensions, such as

---

[63] The figure was already published in similar form in Schmid & Daniel 2007, p. 18.
[64] As was mentioned above, generally, authors in the IB literature do not formally define the term "subsidiary role". Young and Tavares were cited in 2.2.1 as describing a subsidiary role as a subsidiary's scope of responsibilities (Young & Tavares 2004, p. 224). However, they neither present this statement as a "definition", nor do many other researchers in the field draw on this

"outflow of knowledge", "outflow of resources" or "extent of technical activities" represent attributes that can be interpreted as "behaviour", other dimensions describe aspects of a different nature: "Strategic importance of the subsidiary's market", for instance, refers to the market in which a subsidiary is active rather than the subsidiary itself. "Inflow of knowledge" and "inflow of resources" consider activities that are executed by other organizational units instead of by the subsidiary itself. "Procedural justice" addresses the "extent to which the dynamics of a multinational corporation's strategy-making process are judged to be fair by the top managers of its subsidiaries" (Kim & Mauborgne 1993, p. 503) but does not imply any behavioural consequences for the subsidiary.[65] Due to this differentiated fit of the proposed definition, the possibilities to apply this definition to the four dimensions that are selected for the present study has to be considered in more detail.

In the present context, the subsidiary role dimensions of "knowledge inflow", "knowledge outflow", "subsidiary capabilities" and "strategic importance of the subsidiary's market" are taken into account. (1) As mentioned above, "knowledge outflow" can be understood as related to subsidiary behaviour. It refers to expertise, skills, processes, information or solutions that a subsidiary provides to other organizational units. In this case, the respective role expectations consist of demands with which the subsidiary is confronted concerning the type and amount of knowledge to be sent to specific other organizational units. (2) The second dimension, "knowledge inflow", is more difficult to interpret as an element of a subsidiary's role when viewed from Katz and Kahn's perspective. Rather than behaviour of the subsidiary, knowledge inflow primarily refers to behaviour that is expected of other organizational units in relation to the focal subsidiary. It may be argued that a subsidiary that receives large amounts of knowledge from other units will be expected to use this knowledge for the benefit of the entire MNC. As noted earlier, knowledge transfer is costly and will only be engaged in when a specific goal is aimed at (Davenport, De Long & Beers 1998, p. 46; Szulanski 1996, pp. 29–30), for instance, changes in a subsidiary's behaviour. Consequently, the dimension knowledge inflow can be interpreted as exerting an indirect influence on the subsidiary's role in Katz and Kahn's understanding. (3) The third dimension, "strategic importance of the subsidiary's market", can be more easily associated with a subsidiary's position than its role. Due to the close relationship between the concepts role and position, however, the dimension strategic importance of the subsidiary's market can be

---

"description". It is possible to relate this "scope of responsibilities" to the "pattern of behaviours" named by Katz and Kahn (1978, p. 188).

[65] This assortment of dimensions can be attributed to the lack of theoretical basis of the literature on subsidiary roles. Since no integrative foundation has been used in the various contributions, a consistent line in the different approaches is missing.

expected to have a strong influence on a subsidiary's role in terms of expected behaviour. A subsidiary that is located, for instance, in an extremely important environment could be imagined to play various roles. The specific role will depend, among other influencing factors, on the particular attributes that contribute to a certain environment's strategic importance. For instance, in case of a very large market, the subsidiary located in this market might be expected to reach a particularly high turnover. If the market is important due to its technological dynamism, the subsidiary will rather be expected to strive to get access to the latest technological developments. The relationship between the dimension strategic market importance and the respective subsidiary's behaviour can therefore be indirectly established. (4) Finally, "subsidiary capabilities" are considered. Subsidiary capabilities directly influence a subsidiary's behaviour. They can be considered prerequisites that enable a subsidiary to fulfil the requirements of a certain role (Luo 2002, p. 194). Their existence may also influence expectations that other units have concerning a subsidiary (for instance, a unit with outstanding capabilities will be confronted with higher expectations than a unit that is considered average). In this sense, a subsidiary's capabilities will affect the expectations regarding a subsidiary's behaviour and thereby its role.

In summary, Katz and Kahn's role definition can therefore be applied to the subsidiary role concept of the present study, although the relationships are not altogether straightforward. In the following, the final component of the conceptual framework is presented – headquarters-subsidiary conflict viewed from an open system perspective.

3.2.3 Headquarters-Subsidiary Conflict from an Open System Perspective

In the following, the conflict model by Katz and Kahn will be transferred to headquarters-subsidiary conflict. Since Katz and Kahn conceptualize their conflict model for "total organizations or relatively autonomous subunits of organizations" (Katz & Kahn 1978, p. 612), the applicability of the model for the present context is assumed. Headquarters and the focal subsidiary are seen as organizations A and B in Katz and Kahn's conflict model (Figure 12).[66] The six categories of variables that determine the conflict process will be related to headquarters-subsidiary conflict below.

---

[66] This interpretation may be criticized for several reasons. First, the particular quality that characterizes the headquarters-subsidiary relationship even in network MNCs can be emphasized. Nevertheless, since Katz and Kahn do not confine the applicability of their model to conflict

Organizational properties. Two aspects will be highlighted with regard to organizational properties. First, the high degree of interdependence between individual units that is a central property of network MNCs is taken into account. This interdependence provides a prerequisite for conflict within network MNCs. Despite the increased weight of relationships between subsidiaries, it has been argued that the headquarters-subsidiary relationship remains central (Birkinshaw et al. 2000, pp. 321–322; Birkinshaw & Hood 1998a, p. 6; Ensign 1999, p. 301; Lipparini & Fratocchi 1999, p. 663; O'Donnell 2000, p. 543) The strong interdependence between headquarters and subsidiary is one reason why some researchers argue that the headquarters-subsidiary relationship is prone to experience conflict (e.g., Doz & Prahalad 1981; Johanson, Pahlberg & Thilenius 1996, p. 254; Roth & Nigh 1992, p. 285). Second, a subsidiary is engaged in relationships with numerous internal and external partners other than headquarters. Particularly, the embeddedness within its local business network exposes the subsidiary to expectations that are potentially incompatible with headquarters' expectations (e.g., Andersson & Forsgren 2002; Johanson, Pahlberg & Thilenius 1996, p. 253; Mezias 2002b, p. 232). On the one hand, incompatible expectations may lead to role conflict for the subsidiary since it is supposed to satisfy different demands at the same time (Pahlberg 1996b, p. 12). On the other hand, relationships with important external partners, the acquisition of knowledge from the local environment and specific experiences gained over time may influence subsidiary managers' perceptions of the subsidiary's role within the MNC. The subsidiary managers' role perceptions can thereby develop in a different direction from headquarters managers' perceptions.

Conflict of interest. Incompatibilities between headquarters and subsidiaries within MNCs can arise concerning various issues as, for instance, decision making power or distribution of resources (Scholl 2004, p. 547). Applying the general distinction between input, throughput and output to the headquarters-subsidiary relationship, the following examples can be imagined: From the subsidiary's viewpoint, conflict concerning the input may refer to resources received from headquarters (e.g., Inderst, Muller & Warneryd 2005). Conflict with regard to the throughput may refer to production methods or decision making autonomy (e.g., Chan & Holbert 2001), and output conflict may refer to a certain expectancy concerning market position or sales volume (e.g., Scharfstein & Stein 2000). In the present

---

between specific types of organizational units, it will be used to describe headquarters-subsidiary conflict here. Furthermore, the fact that the embeddedness of headquarters and the subsidiary in the larger network MNC is neglected in the model may be highlighted as a shortcoming, since the headquarters-subsidiary relationship can be influenced by relationships to other organizational units. In the present context, however, it seems necessary to isolate the headquarters-subsidiary relationship in order to reduce the complexity of the analysis. It is acknowledged that this procedure may be simplifying in some respects.

study, perception gaps between headquarters and subsidiary managers are examined as antecedent conditions of conflict. Differing perceptions of the subsidiary's role within the MNC are interpreted as conflict of interest.

Role expectations. It was argued above that individuals who act as representatives of the involved groups enact intergroup conflict (3.1.4). The group representatives enacting the conflict fulfil a so-called "conflict role" that is associated with specific expectations. When considering conflict at the level of the headquarters-subsidiary relationship, the individuals occupying the conflict role, in general, will be top managers of headquarters or the subsidiary.[67] The other unit members will expect the outcome of the conflict interaction to be in accordance with the subsidiary role perception that prevails in the unit.

Behavioural predispositions. On the one side, experimental studies on behaviour in general conflict situations reveal only limited influence of personality characteristics on variations in the individuals' conflict behaviour. On the other side, studies of top managers' personality characteristics, motives or ambitions and their implications are rare. Those studies that exist focus on the effect of top managers' personality characteristics on their immediate leadership behaviour in their own unit (e.g., Gupta, Govindarajan & Malhotra 1996; Peterson et al. 2003). So far, the influence of top managers' characteristics on their conduct in situations of headquarters-subsidiary conflict has not been examined.

Rules and regulations. The headquarters-subsidiary relationship is regulated by laws, corporate governance regulations, statutes or intra-organizational arrangements. These rules may influence the occurrence and the development of headquarters-subsidiary conflict in various ways. For instance, different foreign units may be related to headquarters by different governance structures (e.g., Kiel, Hendry & Nicholson 2006; Kim, Prescott & Kim 2005). In case a subsidiary is legally independent of the parent company, there may be higher conflict potential than when the parent company directly manages the foreign unit. Furthermore, many MNCs position top managers from headquarters in the boards of their foreign subsidiaries in order to exert a certain degree of control (e.g., Harzing 2001a). This may be a possibility to reduce conflict between headquarters and subsidiary.

---

[67] Top managers of foreign subsidiaries occupy a priori difficult positions since they are expected to bridge the (geographic) gap between the subsidiary's local operations and headquarters. This task is termed as "boundary spanning" by several studies in the IB literature (e.g., Au & Fukuda 2002; Chung, Gibbons & Schoch 2006; Friedman & Podolny 1992; Gong et al. 2001; Lysonski & Johnson 1983; Shenkar & Zeira 1992). Furthermore, in such a situation, subsidiary managers have to deal with "dual identification" (Vora & Kostova 2007, p. 327; Vora, Kostova & Roth 2007, p. 595).

Interaction. Unlike other areas of the headquarters-subsidiary relationship such as, for instance, issues of coordination and control,[68] the dynamics at work in headquarters-subsidiary conflict have not been widely studied. Comparably, more studies examine conflict in the relationship between organizations not related through a parent-subsidiary bond (e.g., Anderson & Narus 1990; Vaaland & Håkansson 2003) or conflict in the relationship between functional departments within the same organization (e.g., Barclay 1991; Ruekert & Walker 1987; Walton & Dutton 1969).[69] Consequently, little is known about the interactions and mechanisms that can be expected in headquarters-subsidiary conflict.

The preceding paragraphs show how the conflict model by Katz and Kahn can be transferred to the headquarters-subsidiary relationship. This approach to conflict is followed in the present context. Headquarters-subsidiary conflict is conceptualized as observable behaviour of one party preventing or compelling some outcome against the resistance of the other party (Katz & Kahn 1978, p. 613). Differing perceptions of headquarters and subsidiary managers concerning the subsidiary's role are interpreted as conflict of interest according to Katz and Kahn's model. Interfering behaviour arising due to this conflict of interest constitutes the conflict behaviour or manifest conflict. Initially, the conflict can be expected to be related to issues that are close to the subsidiary's role. As Katz and Kahn claim, however, from such rather confined issues, conflict can spread to other issues (Katz & Kahn 1978, p. 635; cp. also Dorow 1978, p. 144). Figure 15 gives an overview of the relationships of the elements of the conflict situation in the present study.

---

[68] For overviews of the literature on coordination and control, see, for instance, Harzing 1999, pp. 16–30; Martinez & Jarillo 1991; Wolf 1994, p. 116.

[69] These relationships, however, differ from the headquarters-subsidiary relationship in important characteristics. For instance, headquarters-subsidiary relationships can be considered as vertical relationships while the relationship between different functional departments is horizontal (Gilbert 1998, p. 56). Furthermore, as mentioned above, the headquarters-subsidiary relationship is governed by specific rules and regulations.

Terminology	Conflict of interest	Conflict behaviour
General description	Existence of incompatibilities concerning a certain issue (latent conflict; conflict potential)	Observable conflictful behaviour (manifest conflict); Conflict issues: input, throughput, output
Interpretation in the present context	Perception gap concerning subsidiary's role and related incompatible expectations	Interfering behaviour concerning the subsidiary role; Conflict issues: distribution, processes, goals
		...can proliferate to other issues

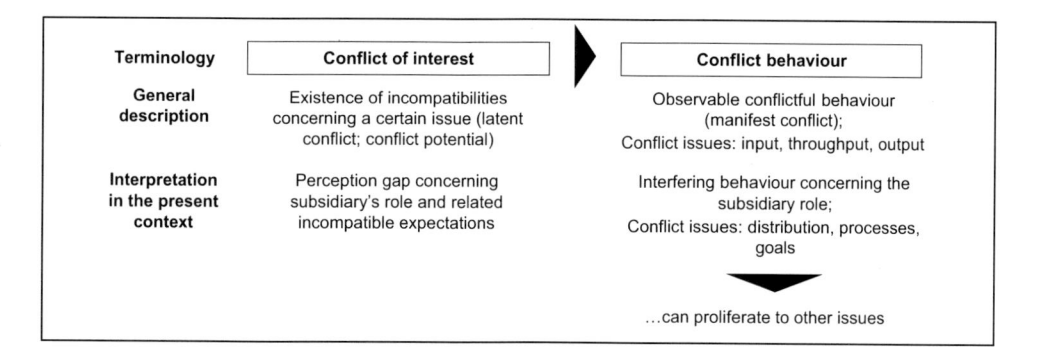

Figure 15: Elements of the Conflict Situation in the Present Study

In 2.4.3.2, conflict issues were classified as linked with goal, processes and distribution (Rüttinger & Sauer 2000, pp. 19–24). These categories can be associated with the differentiation of conflict issues as input related, throughput related or output related by Katz and Kahn (Katz & Kahn 1978, p. 623). (1) When the subsidiary is considered as the focal system, conflicts concerning subsidiary goals can be regarded as output conflict since they refer to the results that are expected from the subsidiary in different respects (Parsons 1960, p. 17; Thompson & McEwen 1958, pp. 24–25). (2) Input conflict can be seen in connection with distribution issues. In order to fulfil their role, subsidiaries may require certain inputs from headquarters or other units that are distributed among several units (e.g., Inderst, Muller & Warneryd 2005). (3) Throughput conflict refers to the internal functioning of a unit and can consequently be linked to conflict issues concerning internal processes at the subsidiary (e.g., Chan & Holbert 2001).[70]

3.3 Research Framework

3.3.1 Overview

In the previous paragraphs, Katz and Kahn's open system approach was described (3.1) and its applicability to network models of MNCs was established (3.2). In the following will be discussed in how far the presented framework is able to provide answers concerning the

---

[70] As was argued in 2.4.3.2, the category relationship conflict that was added by Rüttinger and Sauer to their initial set of conflict types is not taken into account (Rüttinger 1977, pp. 31–35; Rüttinger & Sauer 2000, pp. 19–24). This category does not have a counterpart in Katz and Kahn's model either.

specific research questions posed in this study. First, arguments will be presented for the assumption that perception gaps concerning the subsidiary's role within the MNC can be found in a considerable number of headquarters-subsidiary relationships. It will be examined whether perception gaps concerning all four selected subsidiary role dimensions can be expected (3.3.2). Next, the framework's assumptions regarding consequences of perception gaps will be outlined (3.3.3). In general, the framework proposes that perception gaps concerning the subsidiary's role will lead to headquarters-subsidiary conflict (3.3.3.1). Finally, conceptual and empirical contributions from the IB literature will be drawn on in order to differentiate this proposition in the context of MNCs and to illustrate potential pathways via which perception gaps concerning the four subsidiary role dimensions might result in conflict (3.3.3.2 to 3.3.3.5).

3.3.2 Likelihood of Perception Gaps

3.3.2.1 Perception Gaps Concerning the Subsidiary's Overall Role

In the present context, a subsidiary's role is defined as a set of behaviours that is related to the position that a subsidiary occupies within the MNC (Katz & Kahn 1978, p. 188). Subsidiary managers as well as headquarters managers each have a certain idea of this set of behaviours. In role theoretical terms, the subsidiary is conceptualized as the role occupant (Katz & Kahn 1978, p. 190), while headquarters represent a member of the subsidiary's role set (Jones & Deckro 1993, p. 218; Merton 1957, p. 110). As role theory concedes, role occupant and members of the role set may have different perceptions of the role occupant's role and consequently differing expectations regarding the related role behaviours (Kahn & Quinn 1970, p. 73). Such differences may occur due to different reasons. Transferred to the context of the present study, several arguments can be found as well for the assumption that perception gaps between headquarters and subsidiary managers concerning a subsidiary's role may appear. The diverse influences and expectations which affect the role occupant's role perception are primarily responsible for the emergence of these gaps (Kahn & Quinn 1970, pp. 70–75).

Internal role set. The first source of role expectations is the subsidiary's internal role set. Members of this role set are those units within the MNC that are in some way interdependent with the focal subsidiary (Allen & Van de Vliert 1984, p. 8; Solomon et al. 1985, p. 103). In the present context, the most prominent member of the subsidiary's role set is headquarters. Subsidiary managers may learn about headquarters managers' expectations regarding the subsidiary's role in different ways. On the one hand, headquarters managers can unmistakably state their expectations regarding the subsidiary's role. However, subsidiary roles are usually neither explicitly defined nor clearly communicated (Birkinshaw & Hood 1998c, p. 775; Dörrenbächer & Geppert 2006, p. 259; Hood & Taggart 1999, p. 515). On the other hand, they may indirectly convey their expectations in the course of interactions with subsidiary managers. In this case, subsidiary managers might not recognize their sent expectations or they may be misinterpreted. In addition, the flow of information within the MNC may be less than perfect, so that certain signals that are sent do not reach the receiver in the intended form or way (Birkinshaw et al. 2000, p. 328; Chini, Ambos & Wehle 2005, p. 146). Consequently, since direct communication and interaction are the main sources for subsidiary managers to learn about headquarters managers' expectations (Ammeter et al. 2004, p. 55; Kahn & Quinn 1970, p. 55), subsidiary managers may not possess a clear picture of headquarters managers' point of view.

Focal subsidiary. Second, not only headquarters managers but also subsidiary managers have their own ideas regarding the subsidiary's role (Kahn & Quinn 1970, p. 73). Taking a subsidiary perspective, their point of view may differ from headquarters managers' perspective due to biases, differing experiences, specific motives and ambitions (Birkinshaw et al. 2000, p. 328; Chini, Ambos & Wehle 2005, p. 146). Particularly when headquarters managers view a subsidiary as occupying a less demanding role (e.g., the "Implementer" role as described by Bartlett & Ghoshal 1986, p. 90), subsidiary managers may not be willing to see their unit in the same role.[71] They may be convinced of their subsidiary's higher competence or the importance of their market and try to enhance their position within the MNC in terms of reputation or responsibilities (Birkinshaw 1996, pp. 477–483; Birkinshaw, Hood & Young 2005, p. 230).

External role set. The third source of role expectations are members of the subsidiary's external role set who may have completely different expectations than the subsidiary's internal partners (Johanson, Pahlberg & Thilenius 1996, p. 253; Miles & Perreault Jr. 1980, p. 138). While for headquarters managers the emphasis lies on subsidiaries' integration in the network MNC, the subsidiary is exposed to pressures of local responsiveness in interaction with business partners in the host country (Doz & Prahalad 1984; Prahalad & Doz 1987). Particularly, in network MNCs, subsidiaries' dependence on headquarters is decreased

---

[71] Bartlett and Ghoshal assume that relegating foreign subsidiaries to mere implementers of headquarters' directives on the one hand risks underutilizing the firm's worldwide assets and capabilities; on the other hand, such behaviour will demotivate subsidiary managers or even make them feel disenfranchised (Bartlett & Ghoshal 1986, p. 88; Bartlett & Ghoshal 1991, p. 112).

markedly (O'Donnell 2000, p. 530). Consequently, when subsidiaries possess considerable autonomy, are strongly integrated in their own local business network and are exposed to the expectations of partners from within this network, this may lead to perception gaps between headquarters and subsidiary managers (Birkinshaw 1997, p. 215; Holm, Johanson & Thilenius 1995, pp. 115–116).

These arguments justify the expectation that perception gaps between headquarters and subsidiary managers concerning subsidiary roles will be found in a considerable number of headquarters-subsidiary relationships.[72] It is not assumed that headquarters and subsidiary managers will exhibit opposing perceptions in all cases; rather, a certain degree of variability in terms of the level of perceptual agreement is expected. In the present study, subsidiary roles are conceptualized in terms of the four dimensions "subsidiary capabilities", "strategic importance of the subsidiary's market" (Bartlett & Ghoshal 1986, 1991), "knowledge inflow" and "knowledge outflow" (Gupta & Govindarajan 1991, 1994). While it was argued above that perception gaps between headquarters and subsidiary managers concerning subsidiary roles can be expected on a general level, there may be differences with regard to these four individual dimensions. In the following, arguments will be reviewed that pertain to the perceptions of the four subsidiary role dimensions.

3.3.2.2 Perception Gaps Concerning the Importance of the Subsidiary's Market

The first subsidiary role dimension that is considered is the importance of the subsidiary's market. A priori, headquarters and subsidiary managers have very different perspectives on the subsidiary's market – headquarters managers are supposed to coordinate the MNC's dispersed units and play a central role in developing the overall MNC strategy (Ensign 1999, p. 301). Therefore, they need to be able to compare the different units' markets with each

---

[72] It is implicitly expected that top managers who are active in the same organizational unit are more likely to have similar perceptions of a subsidiary's role than top managers who represent different organizational units are (with regard to subsidiary capabilities, Arvidsson shows in an empirical study that evaluations by managers within the same unit are in most cases more similar than the evaluations by managers who are active in different units; Arvidsson 1999, pp. 177–178). Top managers within the same unit share the same internal and external environment and have frequent opportunities to exchange their opinions in formal as well as informal meetings. In comparison, top managers within differing units have considerably less personal contact and do not necessarily know the internal and external environment of the other unit very well (Harzing & Noorderhaven 2006a, p. 168). Consequently, it is expected that the perceptions of a certain subsidiary's role may differ more strongly among top managers who are active in different organizational units. Relative homogeneity concerning their perception of a certain subsidiary's role is expected among the top managers of the same organizational unit. Of course, this assumption needs empirical confirmation.

other. Subsidiary managers, on the other side, have to focus on their respective market. Due to a subsidiary's more intense involvement in its market, subsidiary managers know much more about the market than headquarters managers. They may see opportunities that are not perceived by headquarters managers (Birkinshaw, Hood & Young 2005, p. 228; Prashantham & McNaughton 2006, p. 450) and may therefore attribute a differing strategic importance to their subsidiary's market than headquarters managers.

3.3.2.3 Perception Gaps Concerning the Subsidiary's Capabilities

Second, subsidiary capabilities are considered. It is relatively well established that the evaluation of subsidiary capabilities provides significant difficulties. Arvidsson presents an extensive list of studies that comment on the subjective element inherent in the evaluations of subsidiary capabilities (Arvidsson 1999, pp. 34–38). In his own study, he finds perception gaps between headquarters and subsidiary managers regarding subsidiaries' marketing capabilities. Denrell et al. (2004) as well discover low interrater reliability when headquarters and subsidiary managers' assessments of different types of subsidiary capabilities are compared. Other studies reveal that a large proportion of subsidiary managers feel that the R&D capabilities of their subsidiary are not recognized (Holm & Pedersen 2000b, p. 146). In the light of these results, it is expected that the present study will replicate the finding that perception gaps between headquarters and subsidiary managers concerning a subsidiary's capabilities frequently exist. While both headquarters and subsidiary managers may perceive a subsidiary as more capable, it is assumed that subsidiary managers are more likely to overestimate their unit's capabilities. The tendency that group members consistently rate their group higher than other groups is empirically confirmed (Ferguson & Kelley 1964, p. 223; Weigand 1966, p. 81).

3.3.2.4 Perception Gaps Concerning Knowledge Flows

Finally, the subsidiary role dimensions of "knowledge inflow" and "knowledge outflow" are taken into account. Gupta and Govindarajan conceptualize knowledge flows as a function of the factors "value of the source unit's knowledge stock", "motivational disposition of the source unit", "existence and richness of transmission channels", "motivational disposition of the target unit" and "absorptive capacity of the target unit" (Gupta & Govindarajan 2000, p. 475). Placing the focus on the process of knowledge transfer, Szulanski proposes the four knowledge transfer stages initiation, implementation, ramp-up[73] and integration (Szulanski 1996, pp. 28–29). Both perspectives open up a variety of possibilities for imperfect knowledge flow between two organizational units (Szulanski & Cappetta 2003, pp. 518–521). The motivational disposition of the source unit is a predisposition for the outflow of knowledge. However, even if the intention to transfer knowledge is present, other barriers may impede successful transfer (Delios & Beamish 2001, p. 1029). For instance, cultural differences can pose such an obstacle (Javidan et al. 2005, p. 59). In addition, the target unit may not use the received knowledge, for example, because it does not know how to use it (what might be referred to as a lack of absorptive capacity)[74] or because the knowledge is not applicable to the receiving unit's environment (Delios & Beamish 2001, p. 1029; Minbaeva et al. 2003, p. 587).

In addition to the benefit of the MNC, it can be assumed that each unit focuses on the maximization of its own benefits in knowledge exchange interactions (Lin, Geng & Whinston 2005, p. 199). Since knowledge can be considered a valuable resource, each unit will be rather reluctant to share it (Davenport, De Long & Beers 1998, p. 52; Hansen, Mors & Løvås 2005, p. 790) and aim at receiving at least the same amount of knowledge that it provides to other units (Schulz 2001, p. 666, 2003, p. 447), unless specific incentives are offered by the organization in order to encourage knowledge sharing (Zhao & Luo 2005, p. 82).

The studies by Asakawa and Chini et al. examine perception gaps between headquarters and subsidiary managers concerning information sharing between headquarters and subsidiary (Asakawa 2001; Chini, Ambos & Wehle 2005). Asakawa argues that the increased degree of environmental uncertainty in the consequence of internationalization may lead to confusion concerning the appropriate level of information to be shared between headquarters and subsidiary (Asakawa 2001, p. 738). In his study, headquarters managers and managers in R&D subsidiaries differ in their perception of information being sent from headquarters to the subsidiary but not in the other direction (Asakawa 2001, pp. 742–743). Chini et al. find significant perceptual differences regarding information flows in both directions, although not in all examined industries (Chini, Ambos & Wehle 2005, p. 150).

---

[73] According to Szulanski, ramp-up refers to the stage in which the recipient starts using the transferred knowledge, identifies and resolves unexpected problems that occur and gradually improves performance (Szulanski 1996, p. 29).

[74] For more details on the concept absorptive capacity, see, for instance, Cohen & Levinthal 1990; Lane, Koka & Pathak 2006; Lane & Lubatkin 1998.

3.3.2.5 Summary

Summarizing the arguments presented above, perception gaps between headquarters and subsidiary seem to be likely regarding all four subsidiary role dimensions. However, the existence of a perception gap in a headquarters-subsidiary relationship provides merely a prerequisite to address the main research question of the present study. The study is interested in the consequences that perception gaps between headquarters and subsidiary managers regarding the subsidiary's role within the MNC have for the headquarters-subsidiary relationship. Therefore, in the following, attention will be shifted to potential consequences of perception gaps.

3.3.3 Consequences of Perception Gaps

3.3.3.1 Conflict as General Consequence Proposed by the Conceptual Framework

The focus in this section is on situations in which headquarters and subsidiary managers perceive the subsidiary's role differently. This situation – referred to here as perception gap concerning the subsidiary's role – can be interpreted as conflict of interest according to Katz and Kahn (Katz & Kahn 1978, pp. 623–624). Empirical research confirms that overt conflict or conflictful behaviour is more likely to emerge when conflict of interest is present (Katz & Kahn 1978, pp. 623–624). Following Katz and Kahn's reasoning, it can be argued that conflict of interest regarding a subsidiary's role will increase the probability of overt conflict between headquarters and subsidiary. However, this logic building on conflict of interest is very general and a priori applies to any relatively important and, at the same time, incompatible issue existing in the relationship between two interdependent parties. Role theory provides additional and more specific arguments why conflict of interest, or a perception gap, concerning a subsidiary's role is bound to result in conflict between headquarters and subsidiary. When the role occupant and members of the role set perceive the role occupant's role differently, this situation can be referred to as "role dissensus" (e.g., Floyd & Lane 2000, p. 164; Toffler 1981, p. 401). It has been argued that such inconsistencies within a role system may decrease the efficiency of the interaction between role occupant and members of the role set (Solomon et al. 1985, p. 105). In particular, role theory expects that role dissensus will lead to conflict:

> "Role theory is clear in its implications regarding the consequences of role dissensus. If it is not removed, the interaction is unlikely to proceed smoothly and satisfactorily. If there are important differences in the participants' roles, their behaviours will not mesh and cooperative action will be difficult to achieve. What actor views as the correct response

to his behaviour will not be the behaviour suggested to other by his role definition. In addition, mutual dislike is likely to develop because each will feel that the other is not behaving properly. In fact, just the knowledge that one's interaction partner sees things differently may be sufficient to cause a significant degree of enmity" (Heiss 1981, pp. 120–121).

Role dissensus is first a perceptual or cognitive concept. However, perceptions and cognitions are central drivers for human actions and as such are also the basis of role behaviour (Deutsch 1969, p. 14; Fisher 1990, p. 6; Grinyer & Spender 1979, p. 130; Mantere 2008, p. 294; March & Simon 1958, pp. 127–129). In the case of the subsidiary's role, a certain role perception will entail corresponding role expectations. When headquarters and subsidiary managers develop differing role expectations, then, one party's behaviour will not match the other party's expectations (Bartlett & Ghoshal 1986, p. 88).[75] Behaviour that is inconsistent with the other side's expectations may be interpreted as interference or blocking by the other party. Empirical research confirms that behaviour that is considered as interference, blocking or otherwise conflictful will evoke conflictful behaviour in response (Katz & Kahn 1978, p. 635).[76] Similar reasoning can be found in the literature on international joint ventures where the fact that perceptual differences often result in conflict has been discussed as well (see, e.g., Fey & Beamish 2000, p. 143). Figure 16 summarizes the arguments presented above.

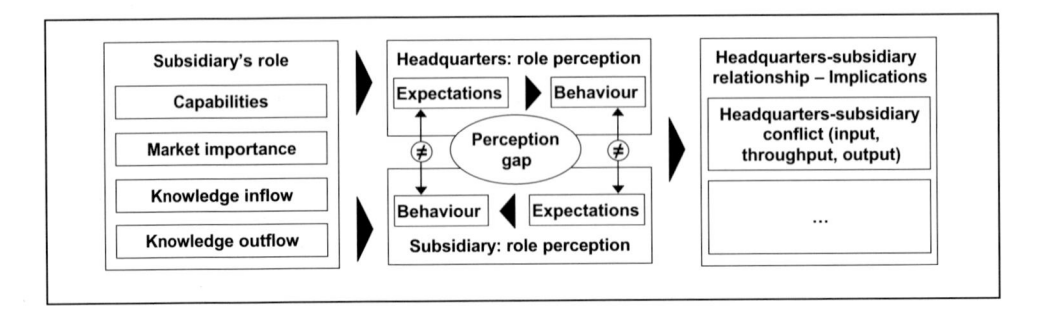

Figure 16: Proposed Conceptual Framework

---

[75] Bartlett and Ghoshal found empirical evidence that differing perceptions and expectations at headquarters and subsidiary lead to conflict: "As strategy implementation proceeded, we observed country managers struggling to retain their freedom, flexibility, and effectiveness, while their counterparts at the center worked to maintain their control and legitimacy as administrators of the global strategy. Its not surprising that relationships between center and the periphery became strained and even adversarial" (Bartlett & Ghoshal 1986, p. 88).

[76] It should again be emphasized that conflict (i.e., in the present context, interference or blocking behaviour) is not assumed to be necessarily negative. Rather, it may as well lead to positive consequences as changes or innovation (Alter 1990, p. 482; Berkel 2003, p. 402; Litterer 1966, pp. 179–180; Rahim 2002, p. 211).

As outlined in 2.4.3.2, the potential conflict issues are differentiated in three types: input or distribution conflict, throughput or process conflict and output or goal conflict. Katz and Kahn state that overt conflict does not necessarily occur "at the point of the essential incompatibility [...]. The locus of the overt conflict might presumably be chosen for reasons of strategy, left to chance, or might develop out of competitive activities in the area of incompatibility" (Katz & Kahn 1978, pp. 623–624). While this statement cautions to keep in mind that the connection between conflict of interest and overt conflict is probably not always straightforward, it is not assumed that both issues are entirely unrelated. Consequently, in the following paragraphs, some ideas will be presented regarding pathways along which conflict of interest, i.e., a perception gap concerning a subsidiary's role, might affect the headquarters-subsidiary relationship.

It is not intended to provide a comprehensive list of perception gaps' consequences. Rather, the following argumentation wants to show how Katz and Kahn's framework can be combined with contributions from the IB literature in order to suggest potential effects of perception gaps. The basic idea can be described as follows: The IB literature formulates various assumptions concerning characteristics of the headquarters-subsidiary relationship depending on the subsidiary role or individual subsidiary role dimensions. These relationships between a subsidiary's role and the headquarters-subsidiary relationship are conceptually derived or empirically established. In the terms of the framework presented above, it follows that the subsidiary's role is associated with specific behaviours and specific expectations – both on headquarters' and the subsidiary's side. Thereby, the framework brings in an additional dimension that allows drawing further conclusions: When differing perceptions of the subsidiary's role exist among headquarters and subsidiary managers, it can be assumed that the behaviours of the one side will probably not match the other side's expectations. According to the conceptual framework, this is likely to result in headquarters-subsidiary conflict. Depending on where the conflictful behaviour is expected, input, throughput or output conflict is proposed to emerge.

3.3.3.2 Perception Gaps Concerning the Importance of the Subsidiary's Market

In the following, perception gaps concerning the strategic importance of the subsidiary's market are focused on. In general, two situations may emerge that can be referred to as perception gaps. On the one hand, subsidiary managers may perceive a subsidiary as more capable than headquarters managers. On the other hand, the reverse situation is conceivable (Arvidsson 1999, pp. 102–103; Birkinshaw et al. 2000, p. 326). In order to be able to present a clear argumentation, the following reasoning will be based on the simplifying assumption that either subsidiary managers perceive high market importance and headquarters managers perceive low market importance or vice versa. While the presented argumentation concentrates on the extreme cases, it is acknowledged, however, that in reality, many constellations in between can occur.[77]

Distribution/input conflict. First, input into the subsidiary in the form of resources is taken into account. In this respect, it proves helpful to take a look at Bartlett and Ghoshal's explanations concerning their subsidiary role typology in which market importance constitutes one dimension besides subsidiary capabilities (Bartlett & Ghoshal 1986, 1991). In accordance with other authors in the IB literature, Bartlett and Ghoshal assume that an MNC's investment in a subsidiary should increase with increasing market importance as well as with increasing capabilities (Bartlett & Ghoshal 1991, pp. 105–111). Despite the expected interaction effect between subsidiary capabilities and market importance, a trend can be predicted for each individual dimension. When subsidiary managers perceive their market as more important than headquarters managers do, they will probably expect more resource inflows from headquarters than are provided. While subsidiary managers consider a higher degree of resource inflows necessary in order to utilize the market's opportunities, headquarters managers will not be disposed to invest more in a subsidiary in a market that is not as important from their point of view as from subsidiary managers' perspective (Furu 2001, p. 138; Luo 2003, pp. 293–294). For instance, subsidiary managers may put forward initiatives and propose potential investment projects to headquarters managers that will probably be turned down when headquarters managers do not share their opinion regarding the market's importance (Birkinshaw 2000, pp. 35–37). When subsidiary managers' efforts to direct headquarters managers' attention to their market are unsuccessful, distribution conflict will follow (Birkinshaw, Bouquet & Ambos 2006, p. 6). Conversely, headquarters managers are expected to tend to support a subsidiary in an important market through the provision of financial as well as non-financial resources (Birkinshaw, Bouquet & Ambos 2006, p. 6; Furu 2001, p. 138; Luo 2003, pp. 293–294). Distribution conflict is consequently unlikely when headquarters managers perceive the subsidiary's market as more important than subsidiary managers do.

Process/throughput conflict. A subsidiary that is responsible for a strategically important market should be particularly responsive to the requirements of this market. Responsiveness

---

[77] The same dichotomized argumentation will be presented in relation to the other subsidiary role dimensions; i.e., it will be implicitly assumed that headquarters and subsidiary managers possess either high or low perceptions of each dimension while intermediate positions are neglected.

generally implies higher subsidiary autonomy (Taggart & Hood 1999, p. 233). When headquarters does not regard the subsidiary's market as important as subsidiary managers do, they may not consider a high degree of responsiveness by the subsidiary required. Instead, they may aim at a close integration of the subsidiary's processes into the MNC and may not be willing to grant the subsidiary much autonomy (Taggart 1999). Subsidiary managers, in contrast, may consider a higher degree of autonomy necessary in order to be able to respond to the requirements of the market. Such a situation may result in process conflict. However, at the same time, it might be claimed that headquarters managers who do not judge a subsidiary's market as strategically important will grant the subsidiary a considerable degree of autonomy. In this case, process conflict would be unlikely. When headquarters managers perceive the subsidiary's market as more important than subsidiary managers do, the reverse argumentation is possible: Headquarters managers are presumed to grant subsidiary managers a relatively high degree of autonomy regarding the processes at the subsidiary (Holtbrügge 2005, p. 573).[78] If this reasoning is followed, they are not expected to interfere with the processes at the subsidiary and process conflict is not supposed to occur. However, here as well, the reasoning can be turned around: Headquarters managers who consider a subsidiary's market as strategically very important may aim at a high level of control over the respective subsidiary's processes. The resulting lack of autonomy on the subsidiary's side might lead to process conflict. In summary, in both situations, argumentation for and against process conflict can be found.

Goal/output conflict. Furthermore, perception gaps concerning the strategic importance of a subsidiary's market will affect the subsidiary's market related goals. First, the situation is taken into account when subsidiary managers consider the market in which their subsidiary is active as more important than headquarters managers do. In this case, they will be very eager to utilize their position within this important market and set their own goals rather high. In addition, they will try to bring the potential which they perceive in their market to headquarters managers' attention (Birkinshaw, Bouquet & Ambos 2007, pp. 41–42). This situation does not present an immediate reason for goal conflict. On the other hand, when headquarters managers consider a market as very important, it is their goal to be present within this market through a capable and successful subsidiary (Bartlett & Ghoshal 1991, pp. 105–111). In case subsidiary managers regard the market as less important, they will conceive of headquarters managers' plans as too ambitious, for instance, because they do

---

[78] It has to be mentioned that although he conceptually derives this connection, Holtbrügge finds no relationship between the importance of a subsidiary's market and the extent to which it is controlled by headquarters in an empirical study (Holtbrügge 2005, p. 573).

not agree with the market potential perceived at headquarters. Influences on the other goal types are also possible – financial goals may be touched when headquarters managers judge the earnings potential of a market higher than subsidiary managers do. Furthermore, headquarters managers may expect certain adaptations in operations, organization and personnel that reflect the importance of the market and which subsidiary managers do not consider necessary. Due to these reasons, goal conflict is anticipated.

Figure 17 provides an overview of the described implications of perception gaps concerning the importance of a subsidiary's market.

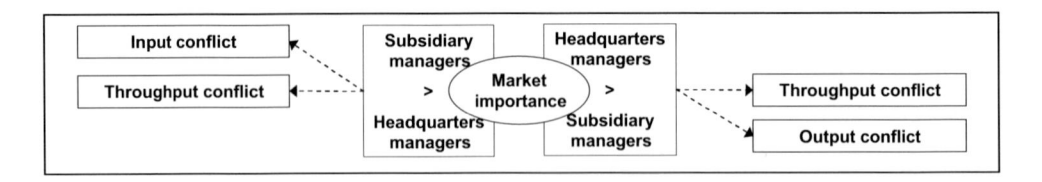

Figure 17: Potential Implications of Perception Gaps Concerning Market Importance

3.3.3.3 Perception Gaps Concerning the Subsidiary's Capabilities

Distribution/input conflict. Bartlett and Ghoshal's reasoning for a positive relationship between subsidiary capabilities and headquarters investment in the respective subsidiary was presented above (Bartlett & Ghoshal 1991, pp. 105–111). Their argumentation implies that a higher degree of capabilities tends to be associated with a higher degree of investment (Lusk 1972, p. 567). Such a relationship has been empirically confirmed for financial and non-financial investments (Furu 2001, p. 143). This can be supposed to apply to financial, physical, intangible, human as well as organizational resources. According to the proposed conceptual framework, it may be assumed that differing perceptions of the subsidiary's position in terms of capabilities may lead to differing expectations concerning the distribution of resources. Subsidiary managers who perceive their subsidiary as more capable than headquarters managers do may feel deprived of due recognition from headquarters' side in the form of various types of resources that would allow utilizing the subsidiary's capabilities to their full extent. This situation may result in distribution conflict in relation to any of the proposed resource types. In the reverse situation, when headquarters managers regard a subsidiary as more capable than subsidiary managers, subsidiary managers will not expect to obtain more resources from headquarters than they receive. Therefore, distribution conflict is less likely when headquarters managers perceive a subsidiary as more capable than subsidiary managers do.

Process/throughput conflict. Empirical research shows that headquarters managers who perceive a subsidiary as insufficiently capable are likely to interfere with the subsidiary's processes (Tasoluk, Yaprak & Calantone 2007, p. 337). Headquarters managers may attempt to change processes at the subsidiary or interfere with the subsidiary's practices in its market. When subsidiary managers, at the same time, rate their subsidiary's capabilities rather high, they will attempt to resist headquarters' interference, so that process conflict arises.[79] In contrast, when headquarters managers perceive a subsidiary as more capable in a particular function than subsidiary managers do, this is probably associated with the judgement that the related processes at the subsidiary are satisfactory. Headquarters managers are supposed to be less inclined to see a need for improvement of the subsidiary's processes. This proposition is backed by the finding that more capable subsidiaries are likely to enjoy higher autonomy than less capable subsidiaries are (Young & Tavares 2004, p. 217). Since the transfer of best practices is costly and difficult due to the "stickiness" of knowledge (Davenport, De Long & Beers 1998, p. 46; Szulanski 1996, pp. 29–30; Teece 1977, p. 242), the probability that headquarters managers will attempt to introduce new processes to a capable subsidiary against subsidiary managers' resistance is rather low. A reason for conflict regarding processes at the subsidiary is consequently not detected.

Goal/output conflict. Finally, attention is directed to the subsidiary's goals. Depending on its perceived capabilities, certain goals will be regarded realistic for a subsidiary (Delios & Beamish 2001, p. 1029). When subsidiary managers judge their subsidiary more capable than headquarters managers do, it might be assumed that subsidiary managers will consider the goals set by headquarters as easy to reach (Luo 2002, p. 194). However, at the same time, it is possible that subsidiary managers who perceive their subsidiary as very capable might try to pursue their own goals that may not be fully aligned with headquarters goals, thereby paving the way for goal conflict. If headquarters managers perceive higher capabilities than subsidiary managers do, they will aim at higher goals and will expect better results than subsidiary managers will. Therefore, subsidiary managers who do not consider their subsidiary as capable as headquarters managers do will judge the goals that headquarters managers have in mind as too ambitious. Consequently, goal conflict may follow concerning any of the proposed goal types.

---

[79] As argued before, subsidiary capabilities can be observed in relation to processes in various functional areas – R&D, production, marketing, logistics and so on (Benito, Grøgaard & Narula 2003, p. 450; Moore 2000, p. 161; Moore 2001, p. 285; Porter 1986, pp. 20–21). Conflict is expected to emerge in the functional area in which the perception gap exists (i.e., when headquarters and subsidiary managers judge the subsidiary's marketing capabilities differently, conflict is expected to occur within the marketing function).

Figure 18 summarizes the potential pathways outlined above via which perception gaps concerning a subsidiary's capabilities may result in different types of headquarters-subsidiary conflict. The role dimension "knowledge inflow" will be focused on next.

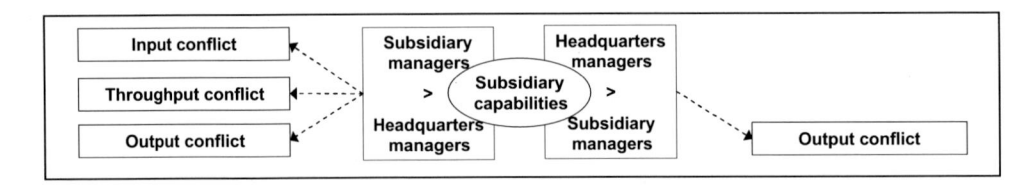

Figure 18: Potential Implications of Perception Gaps Concerning Subsidiary Capabilities

3.3.3.4 Perception Gaps Concerning Knowledge Inflow

Distribution/input conflict. The third subsidiary role dimension taken into account is the inflow of knowledge into a subsidiary. Knowledge flows directed towards a subsidiary may consist, for instance, of best practices or other types of knowledge from other units. Best practices are identified in particularly successful units and are transferred to other units with the goal to enhance their performance (Szulanski 1996, p. 27). Other types of knowledge, such as market data on customers and competitors as well aim at improving the receiving unit's opportunities (Delios & Beamish 2001, p. 1029). Consequently, knowledge inflow from headquarters can be directly classified as distribution of resources to a subsidiary. When subsidiary managers judge the knowledge inflow into the subsidiary as being larger than headquarters managers do, they feel that the subsidiary is sufficiently involved in knowledge exchange processes within the MNC. Distribution conflict concerning knowledge resources is therefore unlikely. No conclusion can be drawn about distribution conflict regarding other types of resources. When subsidiary managers perceive less knowledge inflow than headquarters managers do, distribution conflict concerning knowledge resources may occur particularly in the case where subsidiary managers expect more knowledge resources to be provided (Luo & Zhao 2004, p. 98). At the same time, they may demand the inflow of other types of resources as compensation.

Process/throughput conflict. Knowledge can be transferred to a subsidiary for different reasons. On the one hand, it may be provided in order to improve the focal subsidiary's knowledge base. Thereby, the subsidiary may gain advantages when it comes to designing its internal and external operations. On the other hand, for example, processes may be transferred to the subsidiary with the clear order to implement them. This might be the case when the aim is to standardize processes across units. Harzing and Noorderhaven hypothesize and empirically confirm a negative relationship between the amount of knowledge inflow into a subsidiary and the unit's autonomy (Harzing & Noorderhaven 2006b, p. 200). Although this result was gained by asking subsidiary managers, the interpretation is possible that knowledge is provided to subsidiaries with the intention to influence their processes. Consequently, when subsidiary managers perceive that a large amount of knowledge is provided to the subsidiary, this may be interpreted as interference with the processes implemented at the subsidiary (Taggart 1997a, p. 52). Particularly when subsidiary managers perceive continued requests put forth by headquarters managers aiming at the "implementation of 'yet another program'" (Kostova 1999, p. 308), this may lead to frustration and the refusal to comply.[80] The consequence may be process conflict. If subsidiary managers perceive less knowledge inflow than headquarters managers do, they may judge the knowledge as insufficient to apply it and do not adjust their processes accordingly (Kostova 1999, p. 308). At the same time, headquarters managers perceive a large amount of knowledge and information being provided to the subsidiary, and they expect subsidiary managers to apply this knowledge to the subsidiary's processes and practices. This implies process conflict when headquarters managers miss the expected changes at the subsidiary.

Goal/output conflict. In an empirical study, Monteiro et al. show that both knowledge inflow to and knowledge outflow from a subsidiary are significantly correlated with the performance of the subsidiary (Monteiro, Arvidsson & Birkinshaw 2004, p. B6).[81] As mentioned above, knowledge flows are generally directed towards a subsidiary in order to enhance the subsidiary's opportunities and its performance. When subsidiary managers perceive more knowledge inflow into the subsidiary than headquarters managers do, they will consider their subsidiary as being integrated into the network of organizational units and taking part in knowledge exchange processes. They can be assumed to regard their subsidiary as being equipped for relatively high performance (Luo 2003, p. 294; Monteiro, Arvidsson & Birkinshaw 2004, p. B6). Consequently, no rationale for goal conflict can be found. However, a subsidiary that receives a large amount of knowledge from headquarters or from other units will be expected to show good results (Luo 2003, p. 294). When subsidiary managers do not perceive the same amount of knowledge inflow as headquarters

---

[80] Such a reaction may also be seen in relation to the so-called "Not Invented Here" syndrome (Szulanski 1996, p. 31).
[81] It has to be noted, however, that in this study, knowledge flow measures were collected from subsidiary managers while subsidiary performance was indicated by headquarters respondents (Monteiro, Arvidsson & Birkinshaw 2004, pp. B4–B5).

managers do, they may not consider the goals that headquarters managers have in mind for the subsidiary attainable. This situation may result in goal conflict.

A summary of the abovementioned considerations is provided in Figure 19.

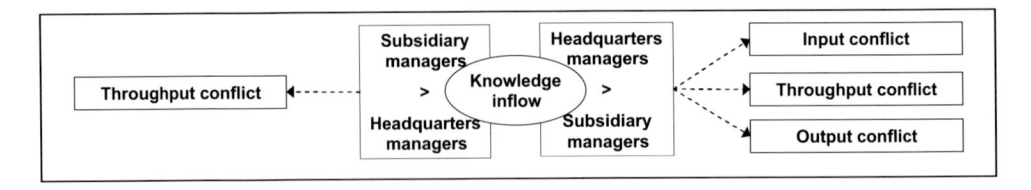

Figure 19: Potential Implications of Perception Gaps Concerning Knowledge Inflow

3.3.3.5 Perception Gaps Concerning Knowledge Outflow

Distribution/input conflict. When headquarters managers conceive of the knowledge that is created by a subsidiary and transferred to other organizational units as an important contribution to the MNC, they are expected to provide the subsidiary with the necessary resources to support the knowledge creation taking place at the subsidiary. Subsidiary managers who perceive that their subsidiary provides a large amount of knowledge to other organizational units will expect a corresponding recognition or approval (Bartlett & Ghoshal 1991, p. 109). Such recognition can take, for instance, the form of financial resources being transferred in order to show that the knowledge generation taking place at the subsidiary for the entire MNC is valued. In addition, a unit's knowledge sharing in one field could be reciprocated by the provision of knowledge to the subsidiary in another field. If such recognition is not granted, distribution conflict may be the result. In case headquarters managers rate the knowledge outflow from a subsidiary higher than subsidiary managers do, it is supposed that headquarters will provide the subsidiary with an amount of resources with which subsidiary managers are content. Consequently, no distribution conflict is expected.

Process/throughput conflict. As long as headquarters managers are satisfied with the outflow from the subsidiary, process conflict is unlikely. Gupta and Govindarajan assume that higher expected outflow of knowledge is associated with a higher need for autonomy and a higher degree of decentralization (Gupta & Govindarajan 1991, pp. 783–785). When headquarters managers perceive less knowledge outflow from the subsidiary than subsidiary managers do, they may demand a heightened involvement of the subsidiary in knowledge exchange processes within the MNC. On the one hand, this may imply sharing knowledge that exists at the subsidiary; on the other hand, the subsidiary may also be expected to adjust its processes to organizational guidelines. Consequently, process conflict may follow. On the other hand, headquarters managers who view the creation of knowledge by a subsidiary positively are not supposed to interfere with the processes at the subsidiary. Process conflict is therefore not anticipated.

Goal/output conflict. According to Monteiro et al.'s study, high knowledge outflow from a subsidiary as perceived by subsidiary managers is associated with high subsidiary performance as perceived by headquarters managers (Monteiro, Arvidsson & Birkinshaw 2004, p. B6). As the authors interpret this result as a positive relationship between knowledge outflow and performance of the subsidiary, in the present context, the meaning may be viewed in the following way: When the managers of a subsidiary are convinced that their subsidiary transfers a considerable amount of knowledge to other organizational units, chances are that headquarters managers judge the subsidiary's performance as rather high and as achieving the subsidiary's goals. When headquarters managers do not perceive the same amount of knowledge outflow from the subsidiary, although they expect it, goal conflict is anticipated. Gupta and Govindarajan propose that with increasing knowledge outflow from a unit, headquarters managers will rely more strongly on behaviour control (processes) and less on output control (goals) (Gupta & Govindarajan 1991, p. 783). When headquarters managers have the impression that a subsidiary provides more knowledge to other units than subsidiary managers do, they will focus less on goals than on processes (Chung, Gibbons & Schoch 1999, p. 650). In addition, headquarters managers may interpret high knowledge outflow from a subsidiary as a significant contribution to the MNC so that their focus on other goals decreases. Therefore, no foundation for goal conflict exists.

Figure 20 summarizes the potential pathways outlined above via which perception gaps concerning the knowledge outflow from a subsidiary might result in different types of headquarters-subsidiary conflict.

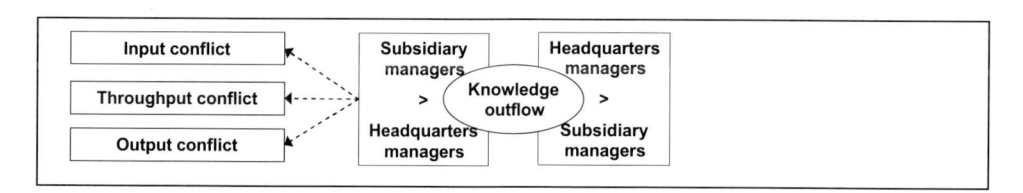

Figure 20: Potential Implications of Perception Gaps Concerning Knowledge Outflow

3.3.4 Summary

In the previous paragraphs, the theoretical framework that was developed based on Katz and Kahn's open system approach (3.1) and conceptual and empirical results from the IB literature were combined in order to propose potential consequences of perception gaps. The theoretical framework generally suggests that perception gaps concerning a subsidiary's role will lead to headquarters-subsidiary conflict. As the previous discussion showed, the IB literature provides substance for this general proposition. It was attempted to establish differentiated relationships between perception gaps regarding four subsidiary role dimensions and diverse types of conflict. Arguments were presented that perception gaps concerning all four considered subsidiary role dimensions may lead to conflict. Furthermore, the differentiation of input, throughput and output conflict proved helpful in order to structure the different types of conflict that may result from perception gaps in the headquarters-subsidiary relationship. As Katz and Kahn mention, however, the way from conflict of interest to overt conflict may take various directions (Katz & Kahn 1978, pp. 623–624). Accordingly, no claim is made that the described relationships constitute a comprehensive picture of the potential consequences of perception gaps concerning the subsidiary's role. Rather, the presented relations can only comprise a sample of the range of potential connections and are meant to illustrate some ideas about the implications of perception gaps.

In summary, the study of the main research question concerning the consequences of perception gaps will require an empirical approach that is open to the discovery of additional pathways via which perception gaps concerning a subsidiary's role may lead to headquarters-subsidiary conflict. The empirical approach that is chosen in the present study will be described in the next chapter.

4. Empirical Study

4.1 Research Design

4.1.1 Rationale for a Case Study Approach

The research design can be understood as a logical plan that states how the research questions will be addressed by the data that will be empirically collected. It provides a framework that guides the researcher from the research problem through the process of collecting, analyzing and interpreting observations (Ghauri & Grønhaug 2005, p. 56; Yin 2003, pp. 19–20). The research design should be influenced by the objective of the study, the theoretical framework and the nature of the research problem (Zalan & Lewis 2004, p. 512). Furthermore, the availability of temporal, personal and material resources should be taken into account. The research design should specify aspects such as the selection of empirical material, the methodological procedures and the degree of standardization and control (Flick 2004, pp. 146–147).

In order to answer the questions posed in relation to a particular research problem, a variety of methods or research strategies can be applied (Creswell 2003, p. 20; Yin 2003, pp. 3–4). Yin describes three conditions that influence which research strategy is most appropriate in a specific situation: (a) the type of the research question posed, (b) the extent of control a researcher has over behavioural events and (c) the degree of focus on contemporary as opposed to historical events (Yin 2003, p. 5). Table 6 summarizes these three conditions and the proposed research strategies for each situation.

Strategy	Form of Research Question	Requires Control of Behavioural Events?	Focuses on Contemporary Events?
Experiment	how, why?	yes	yes
Survey	who, what, where, how many, how much?	no	yes
Archival analysis	who, what, where, how many, how much?	no	yes/no
History	how, why?	no	no
Case study	how, why?	no	yes

Table 6: Situations Indicating Different Research Strategies
Source: Yin 2003, p. 5.

In the present context, a case study approach seems particularly appropriate.[82] Case studies are recommended when *how* or *why* questions are to be answered, when the researcher has little or no control over the behavioural events involved and when the focus is on contemporary events that cannot be studied outside their real-life context (Lee 1999, p. 58; Yin 2003, p. 5). Moreover, case studies are well suited "when a phenomenon is broad and complex, where the existing body of knowledge is insufficient to permit the posing of causal questions" (Bonoma 1985, p. 207), when a process should be explored (Creswell 2003, p. 106) and when the boundaries between phenomenon and context are not clearly evident (Yin 2003, p. 13). Case studies allow the researcher to retain the holistic and meaningful characteristics of events (Yin 2003, p. 2). "The case study inquiry copes with the technically distinctive situation in which there will be many more variables of interest than data points and as one result relies on multiple sources of evidence, with data needing to converge in a triangulating fashion, and as another result benefits from the prior development of theoretical propositions to guide data collection and analysis" (Yin 2003, pp. 13–14).

These criteria correspond to the situation of the present study. The main research interest focuses on the consequences of perception gaps between headquarters and subsidiary managers concerning the subsidiary's role for the headquarters-subsidiary relationship. The question of how such perception gaps affect the headquarters-subsidiary relationship has to be studied in the real-life context of a company and the researcher's control over the related events can be considered minimal. The phenomena of interest are highly complex and unclearly defined. The knowledge of how different parties' perceptions of the subsidiary's role affect the headquarters-subsidiary relationship is very limited and does not allow theoretically grounded and differentiated causal hypotheses. Consequently, the processes that are initiated by perceptual differences between headquarters and subsidiary managers concerning the subsidiary's role shall be explored through a case study approach.[83]

Case studies can be applied to reach different goals. On the one hand, case studies may be used to provide a "thick description" (Geertz 1973, pp. 3–30) of a certain phenomenon. On the other hand, case studies can be helpful in order to generate, refine or test theory

---

[82] While the case study is frequently categorized as a "method", it is more appropriate to consider it a "research strategy" (Hartley 2004, p. 323; Titscher et al. 2000, p. 43). As Stake puts it: "Case study is not a methodological choice but a choice of what is to be studied. By whatever methods, we choose to study the case" (Stake 2000, p. 435).

[83] In 2.3.2.2, several studies are reviewed that also analyzed perception gaps regarding the subsidiary's role. Rather than conducting case studies, these contributions relied on surveys. These surveys generally examine the relationships between few predetermined variables while the present study takes a broader and more open approach. In order to be able to shed light on the phenomenon perception gaps and its consequences, in depth case studies are considered appropriate.

(Eisenhardt 1989, p. 535; Keating 1995, p. 69). The specific feature that gives the case study its particular value in this respect is the "intensity of the study of the object, individual, group, organization, culture, incident or situation" (Ghauri & Grønhaug 2005, p. 115). In the present study, two goals are aimed at. (1) The main research question concerns the potential consequences of perception gaps. The theoretical framework that was developed based on Katz and Kahn's open system approach (Katz & Kahn 1978) proposes that headquarters-subsidiary conflict can be expected as a consequence of perception gaps. However, it cannot be assumed that conflict is the only implication of perception gaps. Therefore, the focus of the present study will not be restricted to headquarters-subsidiary conflict as potential consequence; instead, the approach will be rather open for further empirically observed implications of perception gaps. In relation to this first goal, the case studies will, consequently, serve exploratory purposes. (2) At the same time, the applicability of the role theoretical framework to the analysis of headquarters-subsidiary relationships is examined. This is the second goal of the present study. The empirical analysis should reveal in how far the developed theoretical framework is able to represent the headquarters-subsidiary relationship and the consequences of perception gaps realistically and comprehensively (Keating 1995, pp. 69, 74–75). This is in line with suggestions for the use of case studies in the literature, which state "that case studies are likely to be most valuable where they are clear about their initial theoretical position and where they consciously attempt to develop their own theoretical modifications, however tentatively" (Otley & Berry 1998, p. 107). In relation to this second goal, the case studies will, therefore, be used in order to examine whether the role theoretical framework developed on the basis of Katz and Kahn is appropriate for the study of subsidiary roles.

4.1.2 Overview of the Case Study Design

4.1.2.1 Unit of Analysis

An important part of case study research is the description, definition and justification of the unit of analysis (Ford & Chan 2003, p. 16; Lee 1999, pp. 59–60; Yin 1993, p. 10; Zalan & Lewis 2004, p. 527). In the present context, it is most appropriate to define the headquarters-subsidiary relationship as a unit of analysis. Although the subsidiary's role is not only relevant for the headquarters-subsidiary relationship but in the larger context of the network MNC, it was argued above that the relationship with headquarters is usually the most significant relationship for subsidiaries within the MNC (Ensign 1999, p. 301; Lipparini &

Fratocchi 1999, p. 663; O'Donnell 2000, p. 543). On the one hand, the perceptions of headquarters and subsidiary managers regarding the subsidiary's role are analyzed. On the other hand, consequences of differing perceptions on both sides for the headquarters-subsidiary relationship are examined. Therefore, the headquarters-subsidiary relationship is determined as a unit of analysis.

In general, single and multiple case designs can be distinguished (Yin 2003, p. 40). No general guideline exists concerning how many cases should be taken into account in a specific case study research design (Ghauri & Grønhaug 2005, p. 119; Yin 2003, p. 51). Due to the in-depth nature of case studies, the number of cases involved is usually rather small (Lee 1999, p. 59). However, single case designs are only recommended under specific circumstances for critical, unique, representative, revelatory or longitudinal cases (Yin 2003, pp. 40–42). When the consequences of perception gaps concerning the subsidiary's role are taken into account, it is assumed that each headquarters-subsidiary relationship can highlight different aspects of the related phenomena. Different headquarters-subsidiary relationships can be supposed, for instance, to show different types of perception gaps; however, even the same types of perception gaps may differ in their implications depending on the respective circumstances. Therefore, a multiple case design including several headquarters-subsidiary relationships seems most promising in the present context.

4.1.2.2 Case Selection

The applicability of the theoretical framework is not assumed restricted to certain industry environments or companies of a specific type or size. Rather, it should be relevant for any headquarters-subsidiary relationship within network MNCs. Consequently, other criteria are drawn on regarding the selection of cases. In general, case selection is guided by the research interest of the respective study (Maxwell 1996, pp. 69–73; Merkens 2004, p. 165). Since headquarters-subsidiary relationships are determined as a unit of analysis, suitable headquarters-subsidiary relationships have to be sampled. From a conceptual perspective, these headquarters-subsidiary relationships have to be situated in network MNCs. This is necessary because the research focus is on the perception of subsidiary roles and the idea that subsidiaries take differentiated roles is mainly relevant for subsidiaries in network MNCs (Silverman 2000, pp. 106–107). As was outlined in 2.1.3, however, the ideal type of a network MNC is still unlikely to be found in reality (Kutschker & Schmid 2008, p. 544; Schmid, Schurig & Kutschker 2002, pp. 65–68). Nevertheless, the companies included in the present analysis possess several features that are characteristic of network MNCs – for instance, direct lateral relationships between subsidiaries involving knowledge exchange, interdependent flows between headquarters and subsidiaries, differentiated roles and the subsidiaries' involvement in decision making processes.[84] For the present study, smaller and medium-sized firms are targeted since the structures linking their individual units with each other are likely to be less complex than in large MNCs. Furthermore, they are supposed to own shorter and faster communication lines, to be more flexible and to allow easier access to overall or in-depth information (Ghauri & Grønhaug 2005). In order to facilitate personal access to the respective companies, firms with German headquarters were given preference (Merkens 2004, p. 166).

Suitable firms were contacted by mail. A letter of intent and a description of the project goals were addressed to the CEO of the selected companies. Two companies signalled interest in the research topic and decided to participate in the study. In the following, these companies will be referred to as Company A and Company B. In personal meetings, the author and top managers of the two companies jointly determined appropriate cases (i.e., headquarters-subsidiary relationships). In both companies, one strategic business unit (SBU) or division was to participate in the study. The SBU selected by Company A will be referred to as "Autocomp" in the following; the participating division of Company B will be referred to as "Construc". Rather than group headquarters, divisional or SBU headquarters were consequently defined as headquarters level for the study in both companies.[85] Foreign subsidiaries were defined as "any operational unit controlled by the MNC and situated outside the home country" (Birkinshaw 1997, p. 207). Only fully owned subsidiaries were considered for the present study since shared ownership would add further complexities from both a theoretical and an empirical perspective. Mode of establishment of the subsidiary, on the other hand, was not considered a relevant selection criterion. While the extent to which perception gaps concerning the subsidiary's role exist may differ for subsidiaries created through a greenfield investment or an acquisition, consequences of perception gaps can be analyzed in both types of subsidiaries. However, in order to assume an established headquarters-subsidiary relationship, selected subsidiaries should have been

---

[84] Still, the companies cannot be regarded as fulfilling all requirements mentioned in relation to network MNCs. For the present study, the central prerequisite is the differentiation of subsidiary roles. This condition is clarified on establishing contact with a company.

[85] In a study of headquarters-subsidiary relationships, Johanson et al. argue for the legitimacy of such a decision in the following way: "An MNC may have various HQs on several levels of the firm. In this analysis, HQ refers to the division HQ – the managerial level directly above the subsidiary level. Corporate HQ seldom have the direct managerial contact with single subsidiaries that a divisional HQ usually has. The division HQs are also more directly involved in the ongoing operations of the firm and thus have operational responsibility for the strategic function" (Johanson, Pahlberg & Thilenius 1996, p. 257).

part of the MNC for at least one year (Johanson, Pahlberg & Thilenius 1996, p. 257). Within the relationship, the subsidiaries should possess considerable autonomy but still be strongly linked to headquarters.

In Autocomp, five subsidiaries were included in the analysis. Construc initially selected three subsidiaries; however, only one of them could be retained for the study as no perception gaps regarding the subsidiary's role were identified in the other two. Although such a process of elimination may be suspected of introducing some kind of bias in the sample, it is necessary due to the focus of the present study. Since the goal is to analyze the implications of perception gaps, it makes sense to examine only those cases in which perception gaps exist (on case selection, cp. Yin 2003, p. 37). This procedure leads to a total number of six cases.[86] While there are ongoing discussions concerning the number of cases that should be included in a case study based research project, there is no definite answer to this question (Ghauri & Grønhaug 2005, p. 119; Yin 2003, p. 37). Six cases allow for some variation concerning subsidiary characteristics and perception gaps in the headquarters-subsidiary relationship.

4.1.2.3 Types of Data

While case studies are frequently associated with qualitative research (e.g., Creswell 2003, p. 183), such a classification is too narrow. Case studies can draw on various sources of data that may be quantitative as well as qualitative (e.g., Ghauri & Grønhaug 2005, p. 116; Yin 2003, p. 15). Case studies may utilize data collected through interviews, observation, archives, reports or questionnaires (Bonoma 1985, p. 203; Eisenhardt 1989, p. 534; Ghauri & Grønhaug 2005, pp. 114–115). The present study takes advantage of this possibility and uses different types of data – both qualitative and quantitative. The perception of the subsidiary's role as well as potential consequences of perception gaps are evaluated by questionnaire and interview data. The convergence between different kinds of data can be considered as one possibility to confirm the collected assessments (Abernethy et al. 1999, p. 16).

In the present study, the data collection procedure for each case consists of two steps: First, a questionnaire is applied that quantitatively assesses headquarters and subsidiary managers' perceptions of the subsidiary's role as well as the extent to which conflict

---

[86] The two firms and the six subsidiaries will be described in more detail in 5.1.1.

concerning different issues is experienced. Second, semi-structured interviews are conducted that are mainly concerned with the consequences of the identified perception gaps. The issue of data collection will be addressed in more detail in 4.2.

4.1.3 Operationalization of the Conceptual Framework

The present study's main research question addresses the implications of perception gaps between headquarters and subsidiary managers regarding the subsidiary's role within the MNC. In 2.3.3, it was determined that the focus is on the subsidiary's current role (as-is role) rather than its should-be role. In the conceptual framework, which was introduced in 3.3.3.1, the subsidiary's current role is best represented by the role behaviour shown by the subsidiary. Consequently, the focus of the empirical study is on the subsidiary's behaviour in terms of the role dimensions analyzed. Headquarters and subsidiary managers' perceptions of this behaviour are compared in order to identify gaps between them (Figure 21 illustrates this focus within the conceptual framework).

Despite this focus on the subsidiary's behaviour, neither headquarters' behaviour nor headquarters and subsidiary managers' expectations in this context can be neglected due to the complex interrelationships between them.[87] Particularly the expectations held by headquarters and subsidiary managers regarding the subsidiary's role behaviour will be highlighted when the consequences of the identified perception gaps are interpreted (5.4.2).

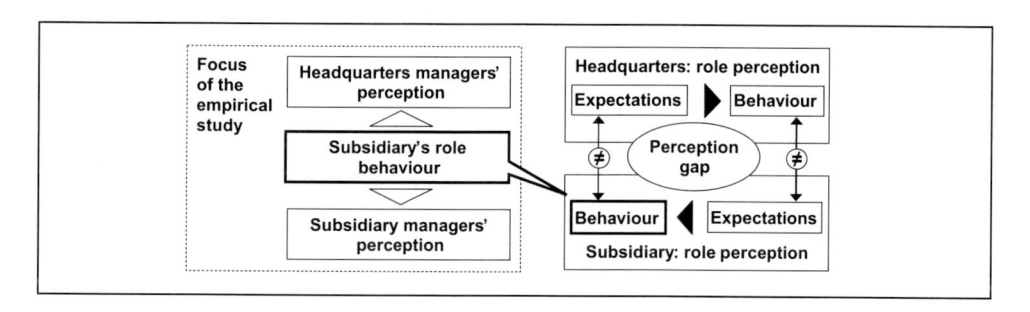

Figure 21: Perception Gaps Concerning the Subsidiary's Current Role in the Empirical Study

---

[87] The depiction of these interrelationships in Figure 21 is certainly simplifying. For instance, the perception of specific behaviours may also influence the expectations held and vice versa. At the same time, the expectations do not only influence the behaviour, but also the other way round.

It might be assumed that the subsidiary's current behaviour can be objectively documented and that therefore there should be no perception gaps between headquarters and subsidiary managers regarding this behaviour. However, differing perspectives, expectations and predispositions can result in differing perceptions of the same behaviour. For instance, headquarters managers may not be aware of some of the subsidiary's behaviours; the degree of certain behaviours may be considered as too much or too little; or the quality of specific actions may be judged differently.

4.2 Data Collection

4.2.1 Questionnaire

4.2.1.1 Goals

The initial step of data collection consists of a questionnaire that is designed to assess headquarters and subsidiary managers' perceptions of the subsidiary's role and to identify perception gaps between the two sides.[88] Since the involved parties are not necessarily aware of perception gaps in their relationship, they cannot be asked directly to indicate their existence. Instead, both sides are asked independently for their perceptions of the subsidiary's role.[89] In addition, the questionnaire is used to obtain a first impression of the conflict that is experienced in the headquarters-subsidiary relationship. Headquarters-subsidiary conflict in the three conflict areas determined in 2.4.3.2 is assessed.[90] The assessment of conflict at this stage opens the opportunity to take up the respective results in the following interviews. Since conflict is considered difficult to identify, especially when it is caused by a representational gap (Cronin & Weingart 2007, p. 769), this dual strategy seems promising.

---

[88] The use of a standardized questionnaire to obtain assessments of a subsidiary's role follows the tradition of a considerable number of studies concerned with subsidiary roles (e.g., Benito, Grøgaard & Narula 2003; Papanastassiou & Pearce 1997; Tavares & Young 2006).

[89] Several authors discuss the general necessity to consider both the headquarters and the subsidiary managers' perspective, especially when complex notions such as the subsidiary's role or headquarters-subsidiary conflict are concerned (e.g., Marschan-Piekkari et al. 2004, p. 254; van de Ven & Ferry 1980, p. 411; Young & Tavares 2004, p. 231).

[90] Due to the relatively small sample size, the case study approach does not allow a statistical analysis of relationships between the identified perception gaps and headquarters-subsidiary conflict.

4.2.1.2 Procedure

As was argued in 3.2.1.3, top managers are considered the most suitable representatives of organizational units (Asakawa 2001, p. 740; Böttcher 1996, p. 137). Therefore, the questionnaire was answered by members of headquarters' and the subsidiaries' top management. If possible, more than one opinion was collected from each unit in order not to mistake an individual's perception for the perception prevailing in the entire unit (Lee 1999, p. 154). The study's sponsors in both firms' headquarters indicated the persons that should be contacted as representatives of the various units.

In each subsidiary, two to three members of the unit's top management team were identified as respondents. At headquarters level, the situation differed for Autocomp and Construc. In Autocomp, the top management is differentiated functionally: Each member of the top management team is responsible for a specific function for all subsidiaries. Consequently, it was decided that all top management team members should participate in the study and answer the questionnaire for all five included subsidiaries. Despite the functionally differentiated responsibility of the top management team, the entire questionnaire was to be answered by all seven respondents. Construc's top management, on the other hand, is characterized by a regional differentiation, i.e., each manager is responsible for the subsidiaries in a certain geographic area. Here, it was determined that the headquarters representatives should only assess the subsidiaries within their area of responsibility. Since the three initially selected subsidiaries are located in different regions, three representatives of headquarters each evaluated one subsidiary.[91]

The headquarters level sponsors informed the respondents about the MNCs' support of the study. Then, the link for the online questionnaire was sent to the respondents by the author. One reminder was sent to all respondents after three weeks. A second reminder was sent to respondents of those units in which not all persons had answered (since the questionnaire was anonymous, personal identification of the missing respondents was not possible). The decision in favour of an online questionnaire was made because online (web-based) questionnaires provide several advantages compared to the traditional paper and pencil format.[92] These advantages include automated data collection, higher data quality, increased flexibility of the presented questions, lower costs, faster delivery and quicker responses

---

[91] Although only one subsidiary could be included in the final analysis, representatives of all three selected subsidiaries answered the questionnaire and interviews were conducted with headquarters representatives of all three subsidiaries. Only after these steps, was it clear that two of the headquarters-subsidiary relationships did not represent appropriate cases for the present study.
[92] The questionnaire was hosted by the site www.unipark.de.

(Kwak & Radler 2002; Lumsden & Morgan 2005).[93] On the other hand, most problems associated with online questionnaires can be ruled out through the procedure chosen in the present study. For instance, coverage error (which is "the result of not allowing all members of the survey population to have an equal or known chance of being sampled for participation in the survey", Dillman 2007, p. 11) was not relevant as the link to the questionnaire was directly mailed to the individual respondents. It could be presumed that all respondents have internet access and receive their e-mail on a daily basis. In order to keep the non-response rate low, prospective respondents were addressed personally, and they received one or two reminders.

4.2.1.3 Operationalization of the Subsidiary Role Dimensions

Strategic importance of the subsidiary's market. Although Bartlett and Ghoshal empirically study their role typology, they do not provide a detailed description of how they assess the two dimensions (for the conceptual description of the subsidiary role dimensions, see 2.2.3.2). In the empirical part of their book "Managing Across Borders: The Transnational Solution", Bartlett and Ghoshal mention the variables "competitive intensity" and "technological dynamism" with regard to the "subsidiary's environmental context" (Bartlett & Ghoshal 1991, p. 232). In his dissertation, Ghoshal analyzes the variables "competitive intensity", "technological sophistication" and "sourcing implications" (Ghoshal 1986, p. 534). Correlation analysis confirms that these indicators are significantly related to each other (Ghoshal 1986, p. 434). Turning back to Bartlett and Ghoshal's conceptual definition of market importance, the indicators mentioned are (1) market size, (2) competitive intensity, (3) customer demand and (4) technological dynamism (Bartlett & Ghoshal 1986, p. 90). Since the authors' methodology remains unclear in their publications, in the present study, this definition of a strategically important market is chosen as a starting point for operationalization and the four listed indicators are taken into account.[94] While

---

[93] For instance, the flexibility of online questionnaires is used in the following way: Regarding a certain subsidiary, respondents are initially asked to indicate which value chain activities are carried out at the subsidiary. In the following questions concerning subsidiary capabilities, knowledge flows and process conflict, only those questions that pertain to the value chain activities, which were indicated before, are presented to the respondents.

[94] In the literature as well, similar indicators are considered with regard to strategic market importance. Denrell et al., for instance, assess "market importance" through the indicators "strategic importance" and "competitive intensity" (Denrell, Arvidsson & Zander 2004, p. 1497). For this approach, they refer to Ghoshal's dissertation. Other authors refer to "customer demand" and "quality of suppliers" (Furu 2001, p. 141) or "market growth" and "industry concentration" (Kuester, Homburg & Robertson 1999, p. 99) in relation to the importance of a subsidiary's local environment.

Bartlett and Ghoshal link these indicators to the country market in which the subsidiary is located, it was argued in 2.2.3.2 that subsidiaries in network MNCs may not only be responsible for their local country market, but also for a larger geographical area. Therefore, the questions posed do not refer to the subsidiary's local environment, but to the market for which the subsidiary is responsible. Figure 22 shows the specific questions contained in the questionnaire.[95]

---

1. Subsidiary's Market

The following questions assess your opinion about characteristics of your subsidiary's market. Please indicate for each characteristic to what extent it applies to the market for which your subsidiary is responsible on a scale ranging from "not at all" to "to a very high extent".

	not at all						to a very high extent
Market volume (e.g., size, number of customers)	○	○	○	○	○	○	○
Competitive intensity (e.g., number of (major) competitors, substitute products)	○	○	○	○	○	○	○
Technological dynamism (e.g., number of innovations and patents)	○	○	○	○	○	○	○
Customer demand intensity (e.g., level of information, sophistication)	○	○	○	○	○	○	○

Figure 22: Questions Concerning the Subsidiary's Market

Subsidiary capabilities. Capabilities are highly specific in their relation to a particular firm and its organizational processes. As was noted before, Bartlett and Ghoshal define capabilities with regard to certain functional areas (Bartlett & Ghoshal 1986, p. 90; see 2.2.3.2). While they do not describe their operationalization of this dimension in their publication "Managing Across Borders: The Transnational Solution" (Bartlett & Ghoshal 1991),[96] in Ghoshal's dissertation, respondents are asked to indicate the overall level of "technological and managerial capabilities" at the respective subsidiary on a scale ranging from 1 ("low resources and capabilities") to 5 ("high resources and capabilities") (Ghoshal 1986, p. 538). In accordance with Bartlett and Ghoshal's functional definition of capabilities, many empirical studies of organizational capabilities as well apply a functional approach (e.g., Amit & Schoemaker 1993, p. 35; Hall 1993, p. 610). Respondents are asked to rate the capabilities of an organization or unit in different functional areas. Typically, the areas of research, development, production, marketing, sales, logistics, distribution and purchasing are included (e.g., Holm & Pedersen 2000a, p. 23). Some authors additionally consider

---

[95] The presented questions display the version for subsidiary managers. The questions for headquarters managers were slightly adapted.
[96] They merely state that "direct indicators" were used (Bartlett & Ghoshal 1991, p. 232).

human resource management (e.g., Benito, Grøgaard & Narula 2003, p. 450; Moore 2000, p. 161, 2001, p. 285).[97] As was outlined above (2.2.3.2), the following value chain activities are taken into account in the present study: (1) research and development, (2) production of goods and/or services, (3) marketing and/or sales, (4) logistics and/or distribution, (5) purchasing, (6) human resource management and (7) general management. Commonly, respondents are asked to rate the respective capabilities on a Likert-type scale (e.g., Roth & Morrison 1992, p. 725). Scales typically range from "very weak" to "very strong" or "far below average" to "far above average" (e.g., Birkinshaw & Hood 2000, p. 150; Moore & Heeler 1998, pp. 8–9; Schmid & Schurig 2003, p. 767). The questions posed in the present study are shown in Figure 23.

---

2. Subsidiary's capabilities

The following questions refer to your subsidiary's capabilities in each of the activities it carries out. Please indicate for each activity how capable your subsidiary is on a scale ranging from "not at all capable" to "capable to a very high extent".

	not at all capable						capable to a very high extent
Research and/or development	○	○	○	○	○	○	○
Production of goods and/or services	○	○	○	○	○	○	○
Marketing and/or sales	○	○	○	○	○	○	○
Logistics and/or distribution	○	○	○	○	○	○	○
Purchasing	○	○	○	○	○	○	○
Human resource management	○	○	○	○	○	○	○
General management	○	○	○	○	○	○	○

Figure 23: Questions Concerning the Subsidiary's Capabilities[98]

Knowledge inflow and knowledge outflow. While their 1991 publication is purely conceptual, Gupta and Govindarajan later describe a survey instrument that can be used to classify subsidiaries according to their typology (Gupta & Govindarajan 1994, 2000). In their study, the head of each subsidiary completes the instrument. For both knowledge inflow and

---

[97] While this presents a general approach that may be applied to study any firm, the questions could also be tailored to the conditions present in a certain firm. For instance, Denrell et al. cooperated with top managers from each firm they included in their study in order to formulate capability items which fit the respective firm (Denrell, Arvidsson & Zander 2004). This has the advantages that respondents are likely to share a common understanding of the meaning of the items used and that the capabilities studied are relevant for the firm.

[98] At the beginning of the questionnaire, the respondents are asked to indicate which activities are carried out by the subsidiary. The subsequent questions regarding the subsidiary's capabilities as well as knowledge flows are only posed for those functional areas in which the subsidiary is involved according to the respective respondent.

knowledge outflow, they differentiate flows involving the parent corporation and flows between peer subsidiaries (Gupta & Govindarajan 1994, p. 450). This leads to four knowledge flow contexts. For each of these knowledge flow contexts, nine types of knowledge that might be exchanged between units are taken into account. Respondents are asked to rate on a seven-point-scale (ranging from "not at all" to "a very great deal") the extent of knowledge flow in which the focal subsidiary is engaged concerning "(1) market data on customers; (2) market data on competitors; (3) product designs; (4) process designs; (5) marketing know-how; (6) distribution know-how; (7) packaging design/technology; (8) purchasing know-how; (9) management systems and practices" (Gupta & Govindarajan 1994, p. 450). Responses are first aggregated across the nine items for each of the four knowledge flow contexts by averaging the nine values. Then knowledge outflows to parent and peers are combined into one outflow measure. Equally, one composite measure of knowledge inflow into the subsidiary from the parent and from peer subsidiaries is obtained. In a later study, Gupta and Govindarajan combine the aspects "market data on customers", "market data on competitors" and "marketing know-how" into the category "marketing know-how" (Gupta & Govindarajan 2000, p. 483).

In the present study, the four knowledge flow contexts are taken into account separately as well. The headquarters and subsidiary respondents are asked to indicate the extent of knowledge inflow/outflow to/from the focal subsidiary from/to headquarters or peer subsidiaries. The flow of knowledge is again rated on a seven-point Likert scale. In the present study, the areas of knowledge are slightly adapted from Gupta and Govindarajan's original instrument. In accordance with other authors assessing knowledge flows within MNCs, the knowledge areas are formulated more similarly to the seven value chain activities taken into account as areas of subsidiary capabilities (e.g., Björkman, Barner-Rasmussen & Li 2004, p. 448; Chung, Gibbons & Schoch 1999, p. 656; Harzing & Noorderhaven 2006b, p. 203). The questions posed are shown in Figure 24.

3. Knowledge flows

The next pages are concerned with knowledge flows. Knowledge flows refer to the transfer of expertise, skills, solutions or strategically important market data between organizational units. First, the knowledge which is received by your subsidiary from other units is taken into account (3.1 Knowledge inflow). Then, the knowledge is regarded which is provided by your subsidiary to other organizational units (3.2. Knowledge outflow).

3.1 Knowledge inflow

The following questions are concerned with knowledge that your subsidiary receives from other organizational units. First, knowledge is taken into account which your subsidiary receives from headquarters. Then knowledge inflows from other subsidiaries are considered.
Please indicate the extent to which your subsidiary receives knowledge in each of the following areas on a scale ranging from "not at all" to "to a very high extent".

Knowledge inflow from headquarters/other subsidiaries [author comment: this set of questions is posed for headquarters and subsidiaries respectively]

	not at all						to a very high extent
Research and/or development	O	O	O	O	O	O	O
Production of goods and/or services	O	O	O	O	O	O	O
Marketing and/or sales	O	O	O	O	O	O	O
Logistics and/or distribution	O	O	O	O	O	O	O
Purchasing	O	O	O	O	O	O	O
Human resource management	O	O	O	O	O	O	O
General management	O	O	O	O	O	O	O

3.2 Knowledge outflow

The following questions are concerned with knowledge that your subsidiary provides to other organizational units. First, knowledge is taken into account which your subsidiary provides to headquarters. Then knowledge outflows to other subsidiaries are considered.
Please indicate the extent to which your subsidiary provides knowledge in each of the following areas on a scale ranging from "not at all" to "to a very high extent".

Knowledge outflow to headquarters/other subsidiaries [author comment: this set of questions is posed for headquarters and subsidiaries respectively]

	not at all						to a very high extent
Research and/or development	O	O	O	O	O	O	O
Production of goods and/or services	O	O	O	O	O	O	O
Marketing and/or sales	O	O	O	O	O	O	O
Logistics and/or distribution	O	O	O	O	O	O	O
Purchasing	O	O	O	O	O	O	O
Human resource management	O	O	O	O	O	O	O
General management	O	O	O	O	O	O	O

Figure 24: Questions Concerning Knowledge Flows to and from the Subsidiary

4.2.1.4 Operationalization of Headquarters-Subsidiary Conflict

Empirical literature on headquarters-subsidiary conflict is rather rare (for some exceptions, see the studies by Johanson, Pahlberg & Thilenius 1996; Pahl 1995; Pahl & Roth 1993; Roth & Nigh 1992). In the existing studies, operationalizations of conflict on a cognitive level prevail. For instance, Johanson et al. operationalize headquarters-subsidiary conflict in a questionnaire based survey by the following two statements: "division HQ and subsidiary's interests are usually identical when it concerns marketing" and "division HQ and subsidiary's interests are usually identical when it concerns production" (Johanson, Pahlberg & Thilenius 1996, p. 259). Roth and Nigh as well as Pahl and Roth assess conflict in terms of disagreement "1) over the goals and priorities of the subsidiary, 2) regarding specific ways work is done or services are provided, and 3) about the specific terms of the relationship between the subsidiary and headquarters" (Pahl 1995; Pahl & Roth 1993, p. 150; Roth & Nigh 1992, p. 289).

While these operationalizations focus on cognitive aspects as disagreement or fit of interests (Barki & Hartwick 2004, p. 236), in the present study, headquarters-subsidiary conflict is defined according to Katz and Kahn as observable behaviour of one party preventing or compelling some outcome against the resistance of the other party (Katz & Kahn 1978, p. 613). Although not in relation to headquarters-subsidiary relationships, behavioural or manifest conflict was studied in the context of other relationships. For instance, Barclay addressed manifest conflict in interdepartmental relationships (Barclay 1991, pp. 150–151). Similarly to Walton et al., he refers to variables such as interference between the respective departments, the question of whether the information presented by each of the departments is accurate and the degree of cooperation between the concerned departments (Barclay 1991, p. 157; Walton, Dutton & Cafferty 1969, p. 526). Other authors as well take the behavioural dimension of conflict into account as dimension of intergroup conflict and, for instance, ask for blocking or preventing behaviour that is observed by either side (Barki & Hartwick 2004, p. 225; van de Ven & Ferry 1980, p. 411) or the degree of mutual assistance between the groups (Rahim 1983, p. 194).

Although in the present study, conflict is conceptualized as observable behaviour, disagreement and incompatibility on a cognitive level are also relevant. In Katz and Kahn's conflict model, incompatible issues occurring in the relationship of interdependent parties are regarded as conflict of interest. It was argued above that perception gaps concerning the subsidiary's role can as well be conceptualized as conflict of interest (3.2.3). In order to be able to observe the relationship between conflict of interest and manifest conflict regarding the same issue, both levels are assessed. While these considerations refer to the level at which headquarters-subsidiary conflict is observed, in the following, the issues on which the conflict focuses will be addressed.

The studies concerned with headquarters-subsidiary conflict take value chain activities, such as marketing or production, into account (Johanson, Pahlberg & Thilenius 1996, p. 259) or goals, processes and the headquarters-subsidiary relationship on a more general level (Pahl & Roth 1993, p. 150; Roth & Nigh 1992, p. 289). While each of these studies select some issues, a systematic typology of conflict issues relevant for the headquarters-subsidiary relationship has not been presented. As was outlined above (2.4.3.2), in the present context, the classification of conflict issues presented by Rüttinger and Sauer is applied, and the categories goal conflict, process conflict and distribution conflict are taken into account (Rüttinger 1977, pp. 31–35; Rüttinger & Sauer 2000, p. 19). For each of the issues two different levels are addressed. First, the questionnaire asks for disagreement between headquarters and subsidiary concerning the respective aspect. This reflects the perception of "conflict of interest", which is considered to increase the likelihood of actual conflict that manifests itself in observable behaviour (Katz & Kahn 1978, pp. 623–624). Second, the questionnaire asks for interference concerning the three categories.

Distribution conflict. Distribution conflict is taken into account with regard to different types of resources. The covered resource categories are financial, physical, intangible, organizational and human resources (Bamberger & Wrona 1996, pp. 132–134; Chatterjee & Wernerfelt 1991, p. 35; Grant 1991, p. 119). The different resource categories are addressed in 2.2.3.2 and 2.4.3.2. The questions regarding distribution conflict included in the questionnaire are presented in Figure 25.

> **4. Distribution of resources**
>
> The following questions refer to situations in which headquarters and your subsidiary disagree or interfere with each other regarding the distribution of resources to your subsidiary. Please indicate the frequency with which headquarters and your subsidiary experience each situation on a scale that ranges from "never" to "very frequently".
>
> How often do your subsidiary and headquarters **disagree** concerning the distribution of the following types of resources?
>
> | | never | | | | | | very frequently |
> |---|---|---|---|---|---|---|---|
> | Financial resources | ○ | ○ | ○ | ○ | ○ | ○ | ○ |
> | Physical resources (e.g., materials, goods, assets) | ○ | ○ | ○ | ○ | ○ | ○ | ○ |
> | Intangible resources (e.g., know-how, patents) | ○ | ○ | ○ | ○ | ○ | ○ | ○ |
> | Organizational resources (e.g., systems, processes) | ○ | ○ | ○ | ○ | ○ | ○ | ○ |
> | Human resources (e.g., top managers, experts) | ○ | ○ | ○ | ○ | ○ | ○ | ○ |
>
> How often is there **interference** between headquarters and your subsidiary concerning the distribution of the following types of resources?
>
> | | never | | | | | | very frequently |
> |---|---|---|---|---|---|---|---|
> | Financial resources | ○ | ○ | ○ | ○ | ○ | ○ | ○ |
> | Physical resources (e.g., materials, goods, assets) | ○ | ○ | ○ | ○ | ○ | ○ | ○ |
> | Intangible resources (e.g., know-how, patents) | ○ | ○ | ○ | ○ | ○ | ○ | ○ |
> | Organizational resources (e.g., systems, processes) | ○ | ○ | ○ | ○ | ○ | ○ | ○ |
> | Human resources (e.g., top managers, experts) | ○ | ○ | ○ | ○ | ○ | ○ | ○ |

Figure 25: Questions Concerning Headquarters-Subsidiary Distribution Conflict

Process conflict. The areas within which process conflict is examined correspond to the value functions considered as areas of capabilities and knowledge flows. The following value chain activities are included: research and/or development, production of goods and/or services, marketing and/or sales, logistics and/or distribution, purchasing, human resource management and general management. The selection of the functional areas is discussed in 2.2.3.2 (Benito, Grøgaard & Narula 2003, p. 450; Lado, Boyd & Wright 1992, pp. 82–84; Moore 2000, p. 161, 2001, p. 285; Porter 1986, pp. 20–21). Figure 26 portrays the questions concerning process conflict between headquarters and subsidiary.

5. Processes at the subsidiary

The following questions refer to situations in which headquarters and your subsidiary disagree or interfere with each other regarding processes at your subsidiary. Please indicate the frequency with which headquarters and your subsidiary experience each situation on a scale that ranges from "never" to "very frequently".

How often do your subsidiary and headquarters **disagree** concerning the execution of the following processes at your subsidiary?

	never						very frequently
Research and/or development	○	○	○	○	○	○	○
Production of goods and/or services	○	○	○	○	○	○	○
Marketing and/or sales	○	○	○	○	○	○	○
Logistics and/or distribution	○	○	○	○	○	○	○
Purchasing	○	○	○	○	○	○	○
Human resource management	○	○	○	○	○	○	○
General management	○	○	○	○	○	○	○

How often is there **interference** between headquarters and your subsidiary concerning the execution of the following processes at your subsidiary?

	never						very frequently
Research and/or development	○	○	○	○	○	○	○
Production of goods and/or services	○	○	○	○	○	○	○
Marketing and/or sales	○	○	○	○	○	○	○
Logistics and/or distribution	○	○	○	○	○	○	○
Purchasing	○	○	○	○	○	○	○
Human resource management	○	○	○	○	○	○	○
General management	○	○	○	○	○	○	○

Figure 26: Questions Concerning Headquarters-Subsidiary Process Conflict

Goal conflict. The goals that are taken into account in the present study have been determined on the basis of the goal typologies by Bateman et al., England and Messner and Sanvido (Bateman, O'Neill & Kenworthy-U'Ren 2002, pp. 1139–1140; England 1967, p. 108; Messner & Sanvido 2001, p. 396; see 2.4.3.2). The goal types that are considered are financial goals, market related goals, production related goals, organizational development goals and personnel development goals. With regard to these goals, participants are asked to respond to the questions displayed in Figure 27.

6. Goals of the subsidiary

The following questions refer to situations in which headquarters and your subsidiary disagree or interfere with each other regarding your subsidiary's goals. Please indicate the frequency with which headquarters and your subsidiary experience each situation on a scale that ranges from "never" to "very frequently".

How often do your subsidiary and headquarters **disagree** concerning the following types of goals of your subsidiary?

	never						very frequently
Financial goals (e.g., profit, revenue, cash flow)	○	○	○	○	○	○	○
Market related goals (e.g., market share, maintain/extend customer base)	○	○	○	○	○	○	○
Operations related goals (e.g., productivity, quality, procurement)	○	○	○	○	○	○	○
Organizational development goals (e.g., organizational growth, stability, culture)	○	○	○	○	○	○	○
Personnel development goals (e.g., training, retention, motivation, empowerment)	○	○	○	○	○	○	○

How often is there **interference** between headquarters and your subsidiary concerning the following types of goals of your subsidiary?

	never						very frequently
Financial goals (e.g., profit, revenue, cash flow)	○	○	○	○	○	○	○
Market related goals (e.g., market share, maintain/extend customer base)	○	○	○	○	○	○	○
Operations related goals (e.g., productivity, quality, procurement)	○	○	○	○	○	○	○
Organizational development goals (e.g., organizational growth, stability, culture)	○	○	○	○	○	○	○
Personnel development goals (e.g., training, retention, motivation, empowerment)	○	○	○	○	○	○	○

Figure 27: Questions Concerning Headquarters-Subsidiary Goal Conflict

4.2.2 Interviews

4.2.2.1 Goals

The interviews as the second step of the empirical study serve two purposes: On the one hand, the perception gaps regarding the subsidiary's role that are detected in the questionnaire study are examined more closely. On the other hand, consequences of the perception gaps for the headquarters-subsidiary relationship are addressed.

First, headquarters and subsidiary managers are asked to explain the rationale behind their evaluations of the subsidiary role dimensions. This should provide a clearer picture of the criteria that influence the evaluation of a subsidiary on a certain role dimension and reveal whether headquarters and subsidiary managers refer to the same characteristics when answering the questionnaire. Only when headquarters and subsidiary managers understand the posed questions identically and assess the same characteristics of the subsidiary, can perception gaps be identified.[99]

Second, this part of the research design addresses the main research question and examines the consequences of perception gaps. On the one side, respondents are openly asked for their opinions concerning consequences of the identified perception gaps. On the other side, the results of the questionnaire covering conflict are taken into account and respondents are asked for causes of the conflict indicated in the questionnaire. This is seen as another possibility to examine whether the conflict that is experienced by headquarters and the subsidiary can be traced back to the existence of perception gaps concerning the subsidiary's role.[100]

4.2.2.2 Procedure

Semi-structured interviews with representatives of headquarters and the subsidiaries seem an appropriate means to reach the abovementioned aims. Such interviews are particularly suitable for exploratory and inductive purposes (Daniels & Cannice 2004, p. 186; Ghauri & Grønhaug 2005, p. 133) and they are recommended when there is only a small number of possible respondents (Daniels & Cannice 2004, p. 186). Semi-structured interviews allow taking the respondent's perspective on the research topic and understanding how and why a certain perception has developed (King 1994, p. 14). Thereby, they enable the researcher to gain a more accurate picture of the respondent's position and ideas. In particular, in the case of complicated or sensitive issues, interviews allow the researcher to ask for further elaboration of answers and attitudes (Ghauri & Grønhaug 2005, p. 133). In the present

---

[99] An example can clarify this issue: A question may ask for "the subsidiary's strategic decision making autonomy". When answering this question, headquarters managers may rate the subsidiary's autonomy rather low since the subsidiary managers are not authorized to decide on questions such as product range or pricing autonomously. At the same time, subsidiary managers may rate the subsidiary's autonomy rather high because they have in mind that they, for instance, can freely choose their suppliers or logistics partners. In such a case, the different values should not be interpreted as a perception gap between headquarters and subsidiary managers, but should rather be attributed to the ambivalence of the question.

[100] The simultaneous existence of perception gaps concerning the subsidiary's role within the MNC and headquarters-subsidiary conflict is not sufficient to confirm a relationship between the two variables. Generally, in order to designate one variable as the "cause" of another, the two variables have to vary concomitantly, the first variable has to precede the effect in terms of time order, and alternative causes have to be ruled out (Ghauri & Grønhaug 2005, pp. 60–61). A theoretical explanation of the relationship may support the hypothesized direction (Cook & Campbell 1979, pp. 22–23). In the context of case studies, it can be attempted to establish a "chain of evidence" between two variables (Yin 2003, pp. 105–106). This is the goal of the semi-structured interviews.

context, the interviews can provide insights that are more detailed into headquarters and subsidiary managers' perception of the subsidiary's role and the four role dimensions. Furthermore, the open-ended questions are appropriate for exploring the respondents' opinions concerning the consequences of perception gaps (Marshall & Rossman 1989, p. 82).

Interviews are conducted only after the questionnaire results for the respective units have been analyzed, since the interview questions are based on and refer to the results of the questionnaire. As the questionnaire results reflect the opinion of several managers of each unit, one interviewee is judged sufficient in most units. Since the position of managing director is the position that allows the most comprehensive overview of the subsidiary's operations and activities, an interview with the managing director(s) of a subsidiary seems most promising in the majority of cases (see, e.g., Kvale 1996, p. 102 on the "law of diminishing returns"). In general, the main respondents from headquarters as well as from the subsidiaries are determined by the headquarters-based sponsors of the study and asked to participate in the interviews.[101]

Overall, the advantages of personal face-to-face interviews outweigh the advantages of telephone interviews (Shuy 2001). Personal interviews are assumed, for instance, to lead to more accurate responses (owing to contextual naturalness), to possess a greater likelihood of self-generated answers, to be more effective with complex issues and to be preferable when speaking about sensitive topics (Shuy 2001, pp. 541–544). In contrast, the advantages of telephone interviews mainly comprise greater standardization, cost efficiency and speed (Shuy 2001, pp. 540–541). In the present study, personal interviews were conducted whenever they could be arranged onsite at the German headquarters. Interviews with subsidiary managers located abroad were conducted via telephone, especially due to budget restrictions.

4.2.2.3 Interview Guideline

Semi-structured interviews are characterized by the use of an interview guideline that consists of open questions. An interview guideline is essential as it helps to direct the interview process (Wilkinson & Young 2004, p. 211). The interviewer addresses all of the stated issues in the course of the interview without necessarily insisting on a certain order. Both sequence and wording of the questions are adapted to the respondent and the context

---

[101] The opportunity to talk to the "right person" (Yeung 1995, p. 329) is mentioned in the literature as a distinct advantage of qualitative personal interviews.

of the specific interview (Patton 1990, pp. 280–284). While this allows the interviewer to pursue matters of interest as they arise in the conversation (Lee 1999, p. 62), it demands a skilled and cautious interviewer who possesses a complete understanding of the research problem and the information being sought (Ghauri & Grønhaug 2005, p. 133). The author of the present study conducts all interviews, so that sufficient awareness of the research problem can be assumed.

In the present study, the interview initially focuses on the respondent's perception of a certain subsidiary's role within the MNC and especially, the four selected role dimensions. Particular attention is paid to those issues concerning which the questionnaire results show a perception gap between headquarters and subsidiary managers. First, a more detailed description of the respondent's idea of the respective subsidiary role dimension is obtained. This also serves as a basis to determine whether the perception gap that is identified by the questionnaire constitutes a "real" perception gap or whether it is an artefact of the questionnaire.[102] Then, the respondent is asked for the implications of the perception gap that he or she conceives of in the headquarters-subsidiary relationship. Although the theoretical framework suggests that perception gaps concerning the subsidiary's role lead to conflict, this question is posed openly in order not to restrict the respondent's answer or to direct him or her in a certain direction.

After the respondent stated his or her opinion regarding the consequences of perception gaps, the questionnaire results pertaining to headquarters-subsidiary conflict are taken into account. In a case where the questionnaire reveals that the headquarters-subsidiary relationship experiences conflict in a certain area, the respondent is asked for additional information. First, he or she is asked to describe the particular conflict situations. Then, the interviewee is asked for his or her opinion regarding the reasons for the emergence of conflict.[103] The interview guideline used in the present study is displayed in Figure 28.

---

[102] In the concrete interview situation, it may not be possible to definitively answer the question whether the perception gap is real. For instance, if a representative of the subsidiary is interviewed before any headquarters representatives were interviewed, no comparison is possible. In such a case, the questionnaire rating of the interviewee is confirmed, and, for the time of the interview, it is assumed that the respondents of the other unit referred to the same characteristics when answering the questionnaire.

[103] It is acknowledged that conflict between headquarters and subsidiary managers can be caused by multiple factors and that perception gaps are only one of them. Using the qualitative interviews, an attempt is made to disentangle the consequences of perception gaps from other influences.

Interview Guideline

Prerequisite: Perception gaps exist in the headquarters-subsidiary relationship concerning at least one subsidiary role dimension (→ dimension X)

Goals:
(A) Confirm the HQ/S assessment of dimension X
(B) Explore potential consequences of the pg concerning dimension X
(C) Probe for HQ-S conflict as potential consequence of the PG concerning dimension X and note other reasons for HQ-S conflict

Introduction to the interview
- First of all, thank you very much for answering the questionnaire that I sent you
- After analyzing the responses which I received, I would like to talk with you about the results of the questionnaire and your interpretation of these results

Show diagrams with results.
- On these diagrams, HQ and S managers' evaluation of each of the subsidiary's characteristics are compared
- I am particularly interested in those cases in which the evaluations of HQ and S managers differ from each other
- In the following, I would like to talk with you about those cases in particular

Approach
- Ask the following questions for each subsidiary for each dimension with a significant PG.
- Proceed through the four dimensions one after the other and talk about differing results.

(A) Confirm the HQ/S assessment of dimension x
- The results of the questionnaire indicate that HQ and S managers differ in their evaluation of dimension X
- Could you explain to me the reasons behind HQ/S managers' evaluation of dimension X?

(B) Explore the potential consequences of the PG concerning dimension X
- Would you have expected that HQ and S managers evaluate this characteristic of the subsidiary differently?
    - If yes: • What are the reasons for you to expect such a difference?
        - Does this difference in evaluation show in the cooperation of HQ and Subs A?
            - If yes: (1) In what ways does this difference show in your cooperation?
                (2) Can you describe the processes set off by this difference in evaluation?
                (3) What are the results of this difference in evaluation?
            - If no: Why do you think that this difference does not show in your cooperation?

(C) Reasons for HQ-S conflict
- The results of the questionnaire indicate that the headquarters-subsidiary relationship experiences conflict concerning Y
- Could you describe to me what HQ-S conflict concerning Y looks like?
- What do you think are the reasons for HQ-S conflict concerning Y?

Figure 28: Interview Guideline

4.2.3 Respondents

Table 7 provides a list of the respondents who participated in the present study. The overview reveals those respondents who filled in the questionnaire and those who were interviewed. All but two managers replied to the questionnaire – one of them was not originally selected by the company representatives and one could not fill in the questionnaire due to time reasons. Interviews were conducted with fewer persons. In general, interviews were scheduled with all representatives of both companies' headquarters management.

Additionally, each subsidiary's general manager was targeted as interviewee. As an exception two top managers representing the Hungarian subsidiary were interviewed, because technical and commercial responsibilities are divided between them. Furthermore, no more interviews were conducted with representatives of two of Construc's subsidiaries. Neither the questionnaire nor the interviews with headquarters representatives indicated the existence of perception gaps in these cases.

Company	Unit	Country	Respondent	Nationality	Questionnaire	Interview
Autocomp	HQ	Germany	Managing Director	German	✓	✓
Autocomp	HQ	Germany	Managing Director	German	✓	✓
Autocomp	HQ	Germany	Head of Sales	German	✓	✓
Autocomp	HQ	Germany	Head of Process Engineering	German	✓	✓
Autocomp	HQ	Germany	Head of Strategic Purchasing	German	✓	✓
Autocomp	HQ	Germany	Head of R&D	German	✓	✓
Autocomp	HQ	Germany	Head of Quality and Environment	German	✓	✓
Autocomp	S	China	Plant Manager	German		✓
Autocomp	S	China	General Manager	Chinese	✓	
Autocomp	S	China	Sales Manager	Chinese	✓	
Autocomp	S	Hungary	General Manager	German	✓	✓
Autocomp	S	Hungary	General Manager Finance	German	✓	✓
Autocomp	S	Hungary	Team Leader	Hungarian	✓	
Autocomp	S	Mexico	Managing Director	German	✓	✓
Autocomp	S	Mexico	Plant Operations Manager	Mexican	✓	
Autocomp	S	Mexico	Sales and Engineering Director	American	✓	
Autocomp	S	Poland	General Manager	German	✓	✓
Autocomp	S	Poland	Customer Service Manager	Polish	✓	
Autocomp	S	Poland	Logistics & Customs Manager	Polish	✓	
Autocomp	S	Turkey	General Manager	Turkish		✓
Autocomp	S	Turkey	Customer Service Manager	Turkish	✓	
Autocomp	S	Turkey	Commercial Manager	Turkish	✓	
Contruc	HQ	Germany	Divisional Director	German	✓	✓
Contruc	HQ	Germany	Managing Director	German	✓	✓
Contruc	HQ	Germany	Director	German	✓	✓
Contruc	S	Romania	Managing Director	Romanian	✓	
Contruc	S	Romania	Financial Manager	Romanian	✓	
Contruc	S	UAE	Managing Director	Pakistani	✓	
Contruc	S	UAE	Branch Manager	Arabian	✓	
Contruc	S	UAE	Branch Manager	Arabian	✓	
Contruc	S	USA	President	US-American	✓	✓
Contruc	S	USA	Vice President	US-American	✓	
Contruc	S	USA	Workshop Manager	US-American	✓	

Table 7: Respondents Involved in the Empirical Study

4.3 Data Analysis

4.3.1 Questionnaire

4.3.1.1 Overview

The questionnaire yields numerical data. Due to the small sample size, the data is not analyzed statistically, but it mainly serves descriptive purposes. Each person's responses to the individual questions are coded as numbers ranging from one to seven for the subsidiary role dimensions and as numbers ranging from one to six for the questions pertaining to conflict. The values of those questions that are related to the same subsidiary role dimension or the same conflict area are not combined into one value, but each question is considered individually. For instance, in the case of subsidiary capabilities, perceptions of the capabilities in each value chain activity are taken into account separately. Since significant perception gaps may emerge in a specific functional area, this seems more appropriate than focusing on the subsidiary's overall capabilities. The same reasoning can be applied to the other subsidiary role dimensions and the conflict areas.[104]

Responses for each question are aggregated at the level of organizational units by calculating the average of each unit's representatives. As discussed in 3.2.1.3, considering the average of individual values as group value is not without problems. Nevertheless, in the present study, the numerical average may serve as a basis for discussion with individual respondents in the interviews. The interviews give the representatives the opportunity to position themselves in relation to the average value.

4.3.1.2 Subsidiary Role Dimensions

The focus regarding the perceptions of the four subsidiary role dimensions is on perception gaps. On the one hand, the difference between the two values is calculated. On the other hand, the two values are contrasted in graphical form. The resulting charts provide the basis for the discussion in the subsequent interviews. Within the charts, the following information is summarized: (1) Which subsidiary is concerned? (2) How many respondents were contacted? (3) How many responses were received? (4) Which subsidiary role dimension is depicted? (5) What are the individual questions concerned with? (6) What is the scale? (7)

---

[104] Subsidiary role typologies generally do not take such a differentiated perspective. However, there is criticism emphasizing that subsidiaries may play different "roles" in different functional areas (Schmid 2004, p. 247).

What is the average rating of headquarters respondents? (8) What is the average rating of subsidiary respondents? (9) Respondents are asked at the beginning of the questionnaire whether particular value chain activities are carried out at a subsidiary. The circled "n/a" and "1" indicate when none or only one respondent of a unit answered this question in the affirmative and consequently replied to questions concerning this activity. (10) Furthermore, differences between headquarters and subsidiary managers' evaluations by two or more scale points are explicitly noted. A sample chart is depicted in Figure 29. The legends relate the information on the chart to the ten aspects listed above.

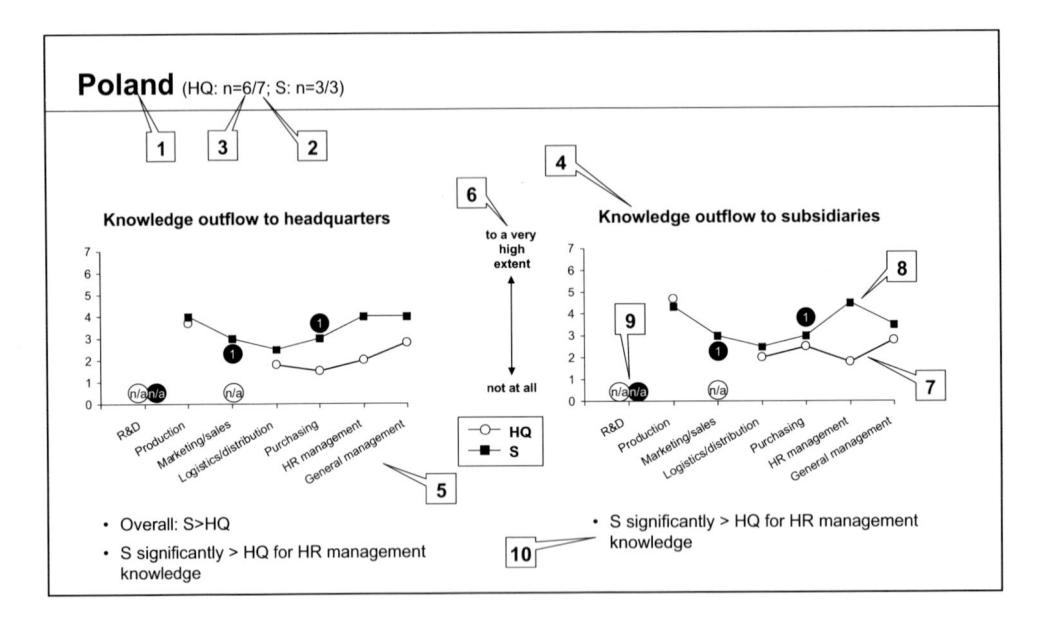

Figure 29: Sample Chart – Role Perceptions

4.3.1.3 Headquarters-Subsidiary Conflict

While for the questions pertaining to the subsidiary role dimensions the comparison between headquarters and subsidiary respondents is central, in the case of the questions asking for headquarters-subsidiary conflict, the absolute values indicated by headquarters and subsidiary respondents are particularly interesting.[105] The values indicate the frequency with which the respondents experience conflict with the other party. These values are also summarized in charts that are presented to the interviewees. The following information is

---

[105] Differences in the degree to which headquarters and subsidiary respondents experience conflict were not specifically searched for. However, the emerging differences show that the same situation may be experienced differently by the involved parties and will be addressed in 5.2.

contained in the charts: (1) Which subsidiary is concerned? (2) How many respondents were contacted? (3) How many responses were received? (4) Which conflict area is depicted? (5) What are the individual questions concerned with? (6) What is the scale? (7) What is the average of headquarters respondents? (8) What is the average of subsidiary respondents? (9) Whenever the average within one unit was closer to "very frequently" than to "never" (i.e., when the average value was equal to or exceeded 3.5), this was explicitly noted on the chart. A sample chart is depicted in Figure 30. The indicated numbers relate the chart to the information listed above.

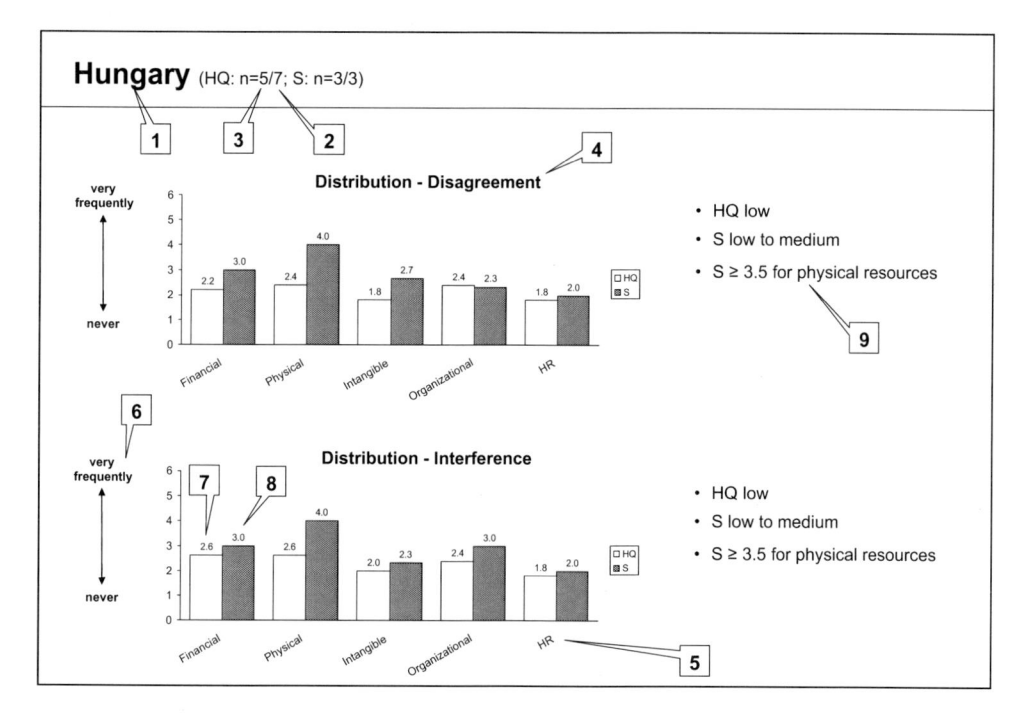

Figure 30: Sample Chart – Headquarters-Subsidiary Conflict

4.3.2 Interviews

4.3.2.1 Overview

Guidelines for qualitative research suggest that interviews should be tape-recorded to ensure that their content is exactly retained (Bogdan & Biklen 1992, p. 128; Patton 1990, pp. 349–351; Silverman 2000, pp. 148–151). In the present study, most interviewees did not object to the interviews being recorded. Whenever recordings were obtained, they were fully transcribed following the interviews. While there are highly complex rule systems determining exactly which features of conversational behaviour (verbal, prosodic, paralinguistic, extralinguistic) should be transcribed in what way, it is recommended that "only those features of conversational behaviour should be transcribed which will actually be analysed" (Kowal & O'Connell 2004, p. 251). Since for the present study, the content of the interviews is most relevant, only the verbal features of the interviews are transcribed while other aspects such as prosodic, paralinguistic and extralinguistic characteristics are neglected (on interview transcripts, see also Kvale 1988). In those cases in which interviewees do not want the interview to be voice recorded, notes are taken during the interview that are written out in full and filled in from memory immediately afterwards (King 1994, p. 25). Consequently, written text is obtained in the form of content-focused transcripts or interview notes that represent the raw data for further analysis (Schilling 2006, p. 30).[106]

According to Miles and Huberman, qualitative data analysis consists of three components that constitute concurrent flows of activity: data reduction, data display and conclusion drawing and verification (Miles & Huberman 1994, pp. 10–12). (1) Data reduction refers to the process of selecting, focusing, simplifying, abstracting, and transforming the data that appears in field notes or transcriptions (Miles & Huberman 1994, p. 10). Activities such as writing summaries, coding and clustering chunks of data or identifying themes may be carried out in order to reduce data. (2) Data display, the second major analysis activity, involves the organized and condensed assembly of information that permits conclusion drawing (Miles & Huberman 1994, p. 11). Particularly, when qualitative data are displayed as extended text that is poorly structured and bulky, the goal is to find better forms of data displays such as, for instance, matrices, graphs, charts and networks that make information more immediately accessible. (3) The third concurrent stream of activity is conclusion drawing and verification (Miles & Huberman 1994, p. 11). Here, the analyst notes regularities, patterns, explanations, possible configurations and propositions. At the same time, these conclusions have to be tested continuously for their plausibility and their "confirmability" as the analysis proceeds. Miles and Huberman present these three components as interwoven activities that can be represented as the interactive, cyclical process displayed in Figure 31. The interactive nature of qualitative data analysis is furthermore emphasized in the recommendation to commence data analysis before "retiring from the field" (Miles & Huberman 1994, p. 50; see also Maxwell 1996, p. 77).

---

[106] This procedure is in line with Miles and Huberman's assumptions about "data": "We are focusing on *words* as the basic medium, and are assuming that the words involved have been *refined* from raw notes or tape recordings into a text that is clear to the reader or analyst" (Miles & Huberman 1994, p. 51, emphasis in the original).

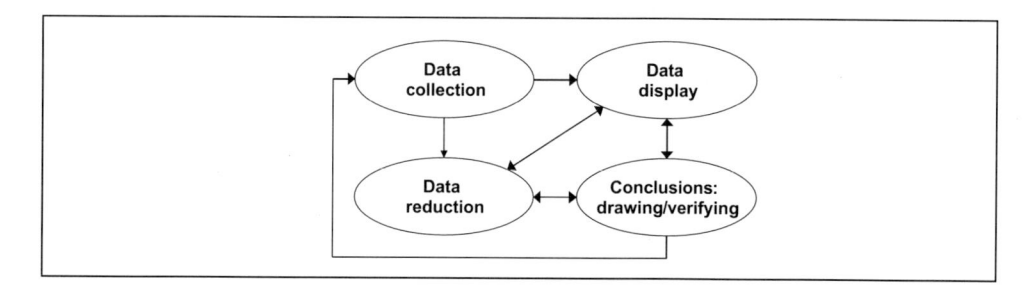

Figure 31: Components of Data Analysis According to Miles and Huberman
Source: Miles & Huberman 1994, p. 12.

In the present study, mainly coding and clustering chunks of text achieve data reduction. The emerging categories are laid out in charts or structured in tables. These displays of data are continuously reorganized and refined as new data is collected. Any iteration of this process is associated with slightly altered conclusions concerning the meaning of the data. Although data reduction, data display and conclusion drawing interplay in the process of data analysis, they will be addressed separately. First, it will be discussed how the present study handles the reduction of data – the construction of a code list that is applied for coding the text material is described (4.3.2.2); the final code list is presented in Appendix B. In 4.3.2.3, it will be attempted to give an impression of the iterative process of data analysis by describing how the codes are used in order to reach conclusions eventually about the data. Both the final data displays in the form of various tables and the conclusions drawn from the data analysis will be reported in the results section (5.3 and 5.4).

4.3.2.2 The Code List

In the present study, the coding of texts obtained in the form of interview transcriptions and notes serves as the first step of data reduction. According to Miles and Huberman, codes are tags or labels for assigning units of meaning to the descriptive or inferential information compiled during a study. Codes are usually attached to "chunks" of varying size – words, phrases, sentences or whole paragraphs. They can take the form of a straightforward category label or a more complex one (e.g., a metaphor) (Miles & Huberman 1994, p. 55). Three important features of codes can be noted (Miles & Huberman 1994, pp. 57–58): First, they can refer to different levels, ranging from merely descriptive to inferential. Second, they can be defined at different times of the analysis, before the actual start or during the course of the analysis. The third and most important characteristic is that codes are astringent, which means that they are able to pull together material from different sources. This feature makes them useful in order to retrieve and organize chunks of data that are related to the same subject for further analysis.

Codes can be developed inductively from the analyzed material or deductively from the theoretical framework on which a study is based (Mayring 1997, pp. 74–76). Even if a code list is developed based on the conceptual framework, the research questions or certain propositions, the process of qualitative analysis should allow for the emergence of additional codes from the data (Miles & Huberman 1994, p. 55). Thereby, the analysis can achieve a synthesis of theory guided investigation and empirical openness (Gläser & Laudel 1999, p. 3). Miles and Huberman describe the process of code development in the following way:

> "For all approaches to coding – predefined, accounting-scheme guided, or postdefined – codes will change and develop as field experience continues. Researchers with start lists know that codes will change; there is more going on out there than our initial frames have dreamed of, and few field researchers are foolish enough to avoid looking for these things. Furthermore, some codes do not work; others decay. No field material fits them, or the way they slice up the phenomenon is not the way the phenomenon appears empirically. [...] Other codes flourish, sometimes too much so. Too many segments get the same code, thus creating the familiar problem of bulk. This problem calls for breaking down codes into subcodes. [...] Still other codes emerge progressively during data collection" (Miles & Huberman 1994, pp. 61–62).[107]

In the present study, the conceptual framework introduced in Chapter 3 is used as a starting point for the development of codes. Taking the research questions into account, codes are devised in the following areas: (1) Each aspect concerning the four subsidiary role dimensions is considered by an individual code. (2) The existence of a perception gap between headquarters and subsidiary managers as well as the directionality of the gap are recorded in codes. (3) The three conflict areas and the individual aspects concerning when they may exist obtain codes. (4) Finally, the country in which the subsidiary is located is coded in order to make it easier to retrieve information related to the same case.

In addition to these conceptually based codes, several codes emerge during data analysis. Whenever it appears to be advisable to take an additional code into account, this code is

---

[107] Although Miles and Huberman do not associate their strategy of qualitative data analysis with content analysis (they categorize content analysis as a "more linguistically oriented [approach]", Miles & Huberman 1994, p. 14), researchers describing or applying content analysis frequently refer to Miles and Huberman (e.g., Morin 2001, p. 106; Sashittal & Jassawalla 1998, p. 534). While elaborate content analytic methods and procedures exist (e.g., Mayring 1997), the use of the term "content analysis" by many researchers is not very restrictive. "Content analysis" is frequently applied to refer to any activity that is directed at the analysis of communicative statements, messages or texts (Mostyn 1985, p. 115; Patton 1990, p. 381).

included in the code list and the interviews that were coded earlier are searched for instances where this new code is appropriate. (5) Although conflict is defined as a behavioural phenomenon in the present study (interference), implications of perception gaps which can be identified at a cognitive and an emotional level are as well coded. (6) A number of respondents comment on potential causes of perception gaps between headquarters and subsidiary managers. Although not directly related to the research questions, these comments are also acknowledged by codes since they are considered potentially useful for evaluating the overall fit of the theoretical framework. (7) Furthermore, several respondents observe methodological aspects of the research setting that are also provided with appropriate codes. Appendix B presents the final code list and the definitions of the individual codes. In the present study, the software ATLAS.ti is used as an aid for the coding and retrieval process.

4.3.2.3 From Individual Codes to Patterns

After codes have been attached to the appropriate passages of the interview transcripts and the interview notes, the codes are used to retrieve specific information from the text systematically.[108] In a first step, each case is examined separately before all six cases are compared with each other (cp. Miles & Huberman 1994). The major goal of the individual case analysis is the examination of the consequences of the perception gaps identified in relation to the case. The text analysis considers one case after another and examines each subsidiary role dimension separately. Therefore, coded chunks that refer to a specific subsidiary and a specific subsidiary role dimension are retrieved subsequently. The retrieved passages are then further structured and condensed. When headquarters and subsidiary respondents' comments seem to allow the interpretation that a perception gap exists regarding a certain dimension, the context of this perception gap is examined in more detail. In particular, hints at potential implications of the perception gap for the headquarters-subsidiary relationship are sought. As soon as a comprehensive picture of the perception gaps regarding a specific dimension and their implications has been gained, the respondents' statements concerning disagreement and interference between headquarters and subsidiary are analyzed. If these descriptions provide hints that relate the reported occasions of conflict

---

[108] Miles and Huberman emphasize that "not every piece of notes must be coded" (Miles & Huberman 1994, p. 65). It is reasonable to assume that parts of the interviews may not be related to the research questions.

to the identified perception gaps, this information is incorporated in the case analysis. This procedure is applied for all subsidiary role dimensions in relation to all analyzed cases.

Following the within case analyses, the perception gaps identified in relation to all cases and their implications are brought together and investigated from different angles. In particular, the perception gaps are structured according to the different subsidiary role dimensions. The initial goal is a common sense understanding of the perception gaps pertaining to the different role dimensions and their implications. In a next step, it is attempted to relate the framework developed in the conceptual part of the study with these instances. The analysis process involves several loops and a number of dead ends. Not every iteration and pathway will be described here. Rather, the results of the process will be presented in the section displaying the empirical findings.

4.4 Scientific Quality Criteria

4.4.1 Overview

While there are established criteria for evaluating the quality of quantitative research methods, qualitative research still struggles to determine equally accepted criteria. Although a number of attempts were made to define new criteria that are suitable specifically for qualitative research (Lincoln & Guba 1985; Mayring 2002; Steinke 1999, 2004), several researchers argue that the criteria applied in quantitative research may be used in qualitative research as well (e.g., Brühl & Buch 2006; Kirk & Miller 1986). The present study follows the latter opinion. Since the transferability of the quantitative criteria can be shown, and the criteria validity, reliability and objectivity are firmly established, it seems advantageous to refer to the same guidelines in different types of empirical research. Objectivity and reliability are primarily associated with the applied research methods, while validity can concern the research methods as well as the research design. In the following, the three criteria will be discussed in relation to the present study.

4.4.2 Objectivity

Qualitative research is by definition not objective, since it involves an "interpretive, naturalistic approach to the world" (Denzin & Lincoln 2000, p. 3). As a quality criterion, objectivity is supposed to ensure that research results are not distorted by the individual researcher, but that the same results could be gained by another researcher using the same methods (Lamnek 2005, pp. 252–255). Bortz and Döring refer to this requirement as "intersubjective verifiability" (Bortz & Döring 2002, p. 36). A common recommendation for qualitative researchers in this context is transparency (Knoblauch 2004). Transparency can be reached through full documentation and disclosure of all steps and procedures applied (Andersen & Skaates 2004, pp. 480–481; Bryman 2004, p. 285; Zalan & Lewis 2004).

The present study tries to satisfy the criterion of objectivity by a highly transparent description of the processes of data collection and data analysis. In order to serve this purpose, the questionnaire (4.2.1), the interview guideline (4.2.2) and the sampling procedure are laid open (4.1.2.2). In terms of data analysis, transcripts are prepared of all interviews that are provided to two scientific examiners evaluating the study. Furthermore, the process through which the interviews are analyzed is described in considerable detail (4.3.2), and the final code list is presented (Appendix B). The empirical findings concerning the individual cases are described thoroughly (5.2), and any conclusions drawn in the between-case analysis remain in close contact to the previous case descriptions (5.3 and 5.4). Overall, the present study's transparency is assumed sufficiently high, thereby complying with the objectivity criterion.

4.4.3 Reliability

In quantitative research, the reliability of a test is defined as the degree of accuracy with which the test measures a certain characteristic (Bortz & Döring 2002, p. 195). A perfectly reliable test measures the respective characteristic without any measurement error and yields exactly the same value in repeated applications (Schnell, Hill & Esser 2005, p. 151). In practice, however, even for standardized tests, this ideal case is unlikely (Bortz & Döring 2002, p. 195). The idea of reliability may be related to several aspects of qualitative research. First, the process of data collection can be considered. In order to increase the reliability of information collected on a certain case, multiple respondents can be referred to (Lee 1999, p. 155). This recommendation is followed in the present study, as several respondents are included in both the questionnaire and the interview study for each case.

Second, reliability can be considered in the context of data analysis. In the present study, particularly the interpretation of text material is concerned. Reliability requires that repeated interpretations of the same material result in the same findings (Brühl & Buch 2006, p. 26). Thereby, the question of reliability concerns, first, the coding of the interview transcripts and the interview notes and, second, the conclusions that are drawn from the coded material. In terms of reliability of the coding procedure, inter-coder reliability is frequently taken into account, i.e., two individuals code the same material according to the same coding scheme and the degree to which they agree in their ratings is analyzed afterwards. Since the author is the only coder in the present study, a different procedure is chosen and "intra-coder reliability" is referred to instead (Schnell, Hill & Esser 2005, p. 405). A large part of the material is coded a second time by the author at least six weeks after the interviews were coded for the first time and the correspondence of the outcomes is compared. The resulting reliability coefficient is 0.90 which can be considered as high (Bortz & Döring 2002, p. 199; Schnell, Hill & Esser 2005, p. 153). While this provides a measurable value that indicates the reliability of the coding procedure, the reliability of the conclusions that are drawn from the coded material cannot be expressed as clearly. It is supposed that the reliability of interpretations may be increased when preconceptions of the researcher are explicated (Andersen & Skaates 2004, pp. 480–481; Lamnek 2005, p. 170; Wrona 2006, p. 207). In the present study, the conceptual framework explicates the author's anticipations and is assumed thereby to contribute to the reliability of the interpretations of the coded interview material.

4.4.4 Validity

As was outlined above, validity may refer to the research methods or to the research design. In the following, both perspectives will be discussed.

Validity of the research methods. The validity of a research method or a test indicates its ability to measure what it claims to measure (Bortz & Döring 2002, p. 199). In the context of qualitative research, validity is frequently associated with trustworthiness (Lincoln & Guba 1985, p. 290), while another perspective understands validity in terms of the truth of conclusions (Brühl & Buch 2006, p. 31). Several strategies are proposed in order to increase the validity of qualitative research through the establishment of interpersonal consensus (Bortz & Döring 2002, pp. 328–329). Two of these strategies are applied in the present study. (1) The first strategy is known as "triangulation", which refers to the collection of information from various perspectives by complementary methods. Triangulation is supposed to reduce the risk of distortions or biases that may be associated with each individual method or perspective (Bryman 1992, pp. 63–66; Cox & Hassard 2005; Maxwell 1996, pp. 75–76; Patton 1990, pp. 464–472). In the present context, the paired use of a questionnaire and interviews in order to detect and confirm perception gaps helps to balance the advantages and disadvantages of both methods. Furthermore, several managers comment on each headquarters-subsidiary relationship, so that none of the cases is evaluated based on a single perspective. (2) The second strategy, known as "communicative validation", makes use of the possibility to ask the respondents for confirmation of the empirical findings (Lamnek 2005, pp. 155–156). In the present study, the empirical findings are presented to the respondents and feedback is requested. The overall positive feedback affirms the validity of the conclusions that are attained through the applied research methods.

Validity of the research design. Design validity concerns the question of whether a specific research design is appropriate in order to answer the research questions that are posed. In general, internal and external validity are distinguished. (1) Internal validity addresses the degree to which differing conclusions can be drawn from the same study (Bortz & Döring 2002, pp. 56–57). In quantitative research, this includes the appropriate operationalization of constructs and the control of confounding variables (Cook & Campbell 1979, p. 67). Internal validity is difficult to substantiate in qualitative research (Brühl & Buch 2006, p. 34). Yin suggests four "tactics" on which case studies may draw in order to test for internal validity: pattern-matching, explanation-building, addressing rival explanations and the use of logic models (Yin 2003, p. 34). In the present study, the second strategy, explanation-building, is applied. As recommended by Yin, an initial theoretical proposition is presented that is tested against the empirical findings of the study and finally extended (Yin 2003, pp. 120–122). While one deviating case might already question the validity of the explanation (Seale 1999, pp. 83–85; Silverman 2000, p. 107), the cases analyzed in the present study correspond to the developed framework. This finding supports the assumption that the conclusions drawn are internally valid. (2) External validity, in contrast, concerns the question of to what extent the results of a study are meaningful beyond the confines of the study, i.e., to which degree the findings can be generalized (Bortz & Döring 2002, p. 57). Several methods were proposed in order to evaluate the external validity of qualitative research findings (Brühl & Buch 2006, p. 34). These include theoretical sampling, the creation of prototypes and ecological validation (Wrona 2006, p. 206). In terms of ecological validity, case studies have a distinct advantage compared to other research strategies – while experiments are frequently criticized for their artificial settings, the natural setting is a specific strength of case studies (Hammersley 1992, pp. 43–45).[109] In the present study, the

---

[109] However, in order to allow the transfer of the conclusions from one study to other contexts, it is necessary to provide a detailed description of the conditions under which the findings are obtained (Geertz 1973, pp. 3–30; Seale 1999, p. 108).

phenomena of interest are studied in their natural environment, i.e., in network MNCs.[110] This ensures the ecological validity of the empirical findings. Furthermore, a theoretical foundation also contributes to the external validity of case study research. Gomm et al. outline that "the aim in research directed towards drawing conclusions on the basis of theoretical inference is to identify a set of relationships among variables that are universal, in the sense of occurring everywhere that specified conditions hold, other things being equal" (Gomm, Hammersley & Foster 2000a, p. 103). This is considered true for experimental research as well as for case studies. Both experiments and case studies have to be replicated in order to substantiate their findings (Eisenhardt 1989, p. 542; Eisenhardt & Graebner 2007, p. 25; Gomm, Hammersley & Foster 2000a, p. 103; Yin 2003, pp. 47, 52). In case study research, each of a small number of cases should be individually considered as a comprehensive test of the proposed theory or conceptual framework rather than part of a representative sample (Yin 2003, pp. 10, 37). Instead of statistical generalization, Yin presents the concept of "analytic generalization", which builds on this logic (Yin 2003, p. 10). These suggestions are followed in the present study. The examined cases are certainly not representative for all headquarters-subsidiary relationships. However, despite their differences, all cases correspond to the conceptual framework in terms of their structure. This finding strongly supports the proposition that the developed conceptual framework is applicable to a larger population of headquarters-subsidiary relationships.

---

[110] For the question to what extent the companies included can be considered network MNCs, see 4.1.2.2.

5. Empirical Findings

5.1 Introduction

5.1.1 The Two Companies

5.1.1.1 Company A, the Strategic Business Unit Autocomp and Autocomp's Subsidiaries

Company A is a German-based firm that is active as a supplier of components for various industries ranging from telecommunications to aviation. Worldwide, Company A employed roughly 37,000 people in 2007. Turnover was 2.4 billion €. Subsidiaries of Company A are located in numerous countries on four continents. Company A is structured in more than 20 strategic business units (SBU) that are closely related in their businesses. The SBU included in the present study mainly delivers to customers in the automotive industry, and it will be referred to as Autocomp in the context of this study. Representing the company's largest SBU, Autocomp has about 1,500 employees; its contribution to Company A's turnover is disproportionately higher. Autocomp comprises SBU headquarters and six foreign subsidiaries, of which five participated in the present study. The subsidiaries are located in Hungary, Poland, Turkey, Mexico and China.[111] In the following, the division of labour and responsibilities between SBU headquarters and the involved subsidiaries will be described.

The subsidiaries' major function is production. They are responsible for mass-producing the largest part of Autocomp's products while German headquarters specializes on custom-made production. Autocomp's business focuses on few large customers who are serviced through key accounts at headquarters.

Marketing and sales are therefore carried out centrally at Autocomp's headquarters in Germany, whereas the subsidiaries' function is generally limited to customer service. However, there are several exceptions to this strategy. The Chinese subsidiary is to some extent involved in marketing and sales, which is mainly attributed to the considerable geographic distance as well as to the large cultural differences. The Mexican subsidiary as well is involved in marketing and sales.[112] The Turkish subsidiary is the only subsidiary possessing distinct partial responsibilities in terms of marketing and sales. The subsidiary sells to "local" customers relatively independently, i.e., to customers that are located and

---

[111] The Slovakian subsidiary is not included in the study.
[112] The sales office of the Mexican subsidiary is located geographically separate from the production site in Detroit in the USA in order to be closer to the customers.

active in the areas Turkey, India, the Middle East and Africa. So-called "global" customers with worldwide activities and plants in the region are handled by central sales at headquarters. In all cases in which the subsidiary is involved in sales processes, contracts either are still made by headquarters or have to be approved by headquarters before being closed.

Purchasing of raw and primary material is as well carried out centrally at Autocomp's headquarters. The Mexican subsidiary carries out a large part of its purchasing independently but still relies on headquarters for entering the main contracts. The Turkish subsidiary also purchases part of its raw material independently. As in sales, contracts have to be approved by headquarters.

In terms of R&D, two centres exist: One centre is located at the level of group headquarters. The second centre at Autocomp's headquarters was only recently installed. None of the subsidiaries has its own "classical" R&D function. However, those subsidiaries that do not produce for the European market have to conform to differing standards. For this reason, the Mexican and the Chinese subsidiaries have a small product management function that may be viewed as carrying out "applied R&D".

Each subsidiary is responsible for managing its logistics and distribution as well as its human resources, although there are central offices at group headquarters in order to support the subsidiaries. Certain functions, such as IT and accounting, are organizationally located at group headquarters for all subsidiaries. Table 8 summarizes the subsidiaries' functions, their mode of establishment and the year in which they were established.

Unit	China	Hungary	Mexico	Poland	Turkey
Mode of establishment	"Joint Venture"[113]	Greenfield	Greenfield	Greenfield	Acquisition
Year of establishment	2003	1997	1989	1999	1999
R&D	○	○	○	○	○
Production	●	●	●	●	●
Marketing/ sales	◐	○	◐	○	◐
Logistics/ distribution	●	●	●	●	●
Purchasing	◐	○	◐	◐	◐
HR management	●	●	●	●	●
General management	●	●	●	●	●
Legend	●	Function is carried out by the unit with full responsibility			
	◐	Subsidiary has distinct responsibilities in some areas of the function			
	◐	Subsidiary supports headquarters in the function			
	○	HQ is fully responsible for the function			

Table 8: Overview of the Analyzed Subsidiaries of Autocomp

5.1.1.2 Company B, the Division Construc and Construc's Subsidiaries

Company B is a German-based firm that is active in the construction industry. Worldwide, Company B employs roughly 7,000 people. Turnover was 1.2 billion € in 2007. Company B is comprised of three divisions that are closely related in their businesses. The division included in the present study has about 3,700 employees and is responsible for about 38% of the group's turnover, amounting to 460 million € in 2007. It will be called Construc in the following. Construc consists of headquarters and more than 30 subsidiaries worldwide.

In comparison to Autocomp, Construc's subsidiaries are expected to be more independent in terms of their processes. They generally carry out the entire range of value chain activities except for R&D, which is organizationally located at Construc's headquarters. The subsidiaries' strategy is developed in close cooperation with headquarters in accordance with

---

[113] The Chinese subsidiary was founded in cooperation with another SBU of Company A. The two units not only shared the same building, but also many support functions. The top management of the unit reported to the second SBU. One year before the study, the decision was taken to separate the two subsidiaries in terms of location as well as with regard to management.

the framework that is provided by Construc's overall strategy. Subsidiaries mainly serve their local or regional markets and cooperate in projects that are more complex or when specific capabilities are required. Local staff is hired for all levels of the subsidiaries.

Originally, three of Construc's subsidiaries were to be included in the study, but as perception gaps were identified only between headquarters and one of them, only one was analyzed further.[114] The subsidiary is located in the United States, and it was acquired in 1994. Before the acquisition, the unit had been an independent regionally active construction company. As the other subsidiaries, the US-subsidiary is expected to function rather autonomously. In Construc, two headquarters representatives were interviewed onsite at headquarters and one person in a neutral setting. One representative of the US-American subsidiary was interviewed via telephone.

5.1.2 Comments on the Subsidiary Role Dimensions

In the conceptual part, the four subsidiary role dimensions of "strategic importance of the subsidiary's market", "subsidiary capabilities", "knowledge inflow to the subsidiary" and "knowledge outflow from the subsidiary" are selected for the present study (2.2.3). The questionnaire focuses on these dimensions. The interviews, however, reveal several other characteristics of the subsidiary's role that are perceived differently by subsidiary and headquarters representatives. These features will be addressed in the following.

Product scope. First, the subsidiary's product scope is mentioned as an additional issue and is taken into account in the analysis. Product scope refers to the "latitude exercised by a subsidiary's business with regard to product line extensions and new product areas" (White & Poynter 1984, p. 59). The subsidiary's product scope is one of three role dimensions in the typology presented by White and Poynter (White & Poynter 1984).[115] In the present study, this dimension is relevant primarily as a component of the subsidiary's should-be role. Although headquarters and the subsidiary representatives generally agree on the products

---

[114] Construc selected the subsidiaries in the USA, Romania and the UAE.
[115] The typology was resumed and applied in similar form by Birkinshaw and Morrison as well as by Tavares and Young (Birkinshaw & Morrison 1995; Tavares & Young 2006; see also Schmid, Bäurle & Kutschker 1998, pp. 19–21). The two other dimensions in the typology are the subsidiary's market scope and value added scope. The subsidiary's market is taken into account as well in the present study, although not the aspect market scope specifically. The dimension value added scope is also considered through the subsidiary's involvement in value chain activities which will be referred to below.

that are currently produced by the subsidiary, they have different opinions concerning necessary future developments in two cases (Hungarian subsidiary: 5.2.2; Turkish subsidiary: 5.2.4).

Involvement in value chain activities. The second additional dimension is concerned with the subsidiary's involvement in value chain activities. In their typology, White and Poynter define the dimension value added scope as the "range of ways a subsidiary adds value" (White & Poynter 1984, p. 59). In the present study, however, it became clear that the location of a subsidiary on the range between no involvement in an activity and full responsibility for an activity has to be differentiated in various shades. Although it may be agreed that responsibility for a certain function is centralized at headquarters, headquarters and the subsidiary can still have different opinions concerning the extent to which a subsidiary is involved in the function. Consequently, involvement in value chain activities is defined here as the range of value chain activities in which a subsidiary is involved and the extent to which it is involved. In the cases presented in the following, this involvement includes, for instance, the subsidiary bringing in suggestions for the improvement of processes and the participation of subsidiary managers in negotiations. The dimension involvement in value chain activities is relevant in two cases (Hungarian subsidiary: 5.2.2; Turkish subsidiary: 5.2.4).

Autonomy. Autonomy was taken into account in subsidiary role typologies proposed in the literature before (D'Cruz 1986; Taggart 1997a). Subsidiary autonomy has been approached from many different perspectives and has been defined in various ways (e.g., O'Donnell 2000, p. 528; Taggart 1997a, p. 55; Venaik, Midgley & Devinney 2005, p. 659). In general, autonomy can be defined as concerning "the constrained freedom or independence available to or acquired by a subsidiary, which enables it to take certain decisions on its own behalf" (Young & Tavares 2004, p. 228). The question of to what degree the subsidiary is free to take certain decisions plays a central role in two of the cases analyzed in the present study (Turkish subsidiary: 5.2.4; Mexican subsidiary: 5.2.5).

Knowledge flows. Finally, it is necessary to comment on the respondents' understanding of the dimensions reflecting knowledge flows. In the questionnaire, knowledge flows are defined in accordance with Gupta and Govindarajan as transfer of expertise, skills, solutions or strategically important market data between organizational units – a definition that implicitly excludes internal administrative information (Gupta & Govindarajan 1991, p.

773).[116] In the interviews, however, several respondents do not adhere to this definition but expose varying interpretations. While some respondents use a wide definition of knowledge, including aspects of the subsidiary's reporting to headquarters, others apply a narrow notion that is limited to expertise, skills and solutions and even exclude strategically important market data. A third interpretation relates knowledge inflow from headquarters to the subsidiary to the transfer of instructions, orders and guidelines prescribing the design of processes in the subsidiary. Since the period between filling in the questionnaire and the interviews ranged between one to three months for the individual respondents, it is not confirmed that the respondents had exactly the same idea in mind during the interviews as when answering the questionnaire.

In general, respondents of Company A prefer the term "information" instead of "knowledge". At the same time, this appears to be the more fitting term for many of the transfers that are referred to (cp. footnote 116). As information seems immediately relevant for the respondents, they are not asked to confine their statements to knowledge flows in the strict sense of the definition.[117] For the analysis, however, knowledge flows have to be distinguished from information transfers in order to obtain the subsidiary role dimension defined by Gupta and Govindarajan.

5.1.3 Identifying Perception Gaps

5.1.3.1 Perception Gaps vs. Artefacts

The present study follows a two-step design in order to identify perception gaps and to determine their implications for the headquarters-subsidiary relationship. The perception gaps are primarily uncovered by the questionnaire and confirmed in the course of the interviews. This method turned out very expedient for the following reasons. There are some

---

[116] Although it is more concrete, Gupta and Govindarajan's knowledge definition corresponds to a frequently used distinction of knowledge and information. Knowledge is thereby defined as "information in context, together with an understanding of how to use it" (Brooking 1999, p. 5). This understanding differentiates knowledge from information through its relation to human action (Nonaka 1994, p. 15). It thereby refers to aspects of "know-how" and "know-why" (Gurteen 1998, p. 5). It has to be acknowledged that this definition leaves some ambiguity and does not distinguish knowledge and information clearly (cp. Bick 2004, p. 13). Nevertheless, in the present context, it will be attempted to determine whether respondents' statements match Gupta and Govindarajan's definition and distinguish those transfers as information that does not imply an action component for the recipient.

[117] Information flows are, for instance, relevant in the dimension "involvement in value chain activities" that was referred to above.

cases where the questionnaire results show large gaps between headquarters and subsidiary respondents' ratings, which the interviews expose as artefacts of the questionnaire. This may be caused, for instance, by the fact that respondents interpret the questions differently and refer to slightly different issues in relation to the same question. Whenever both headquarters and subsidiary respondents attribute a difference that appears in the questionnaire results to reasons other than differing perceptions, the difference is not considered as a perception gap in the analysis. In contrast, differences that are not very sizable according to the questionnaire results appear relevant from the respondents' point of view. Consequently, in the analysis, some perception gaps will be described that cannot be traced back to questionnaire results.

5.1.3.2 Individual Differences

As was mentioned above, it cannot be assumed that all respondents who represent the same unit share exactly the same perception of a certain subsidiary's role (3.2.1.3). This is reflected by the results of the questionnaire study: In few instances, the respondents of one unit fully agree in their ratings. Most of the time, the ratings within one unit vary slightly with occasional larger deviations. However, there are several instances where the individual ratings cover the entire range of the answer scale. Since the numbers of respondents within the same units in the present study are too low for statistical analysis of variance (Bortz & Döring 2002, p. 613), the variance between the individual responses is examined more subjectively. In particular, whenever a perception gap appears in the averaged questionnaire results, the individual responses obtained from headquarters and subsidiary representatives are compared. When in the following case descriptions no particular reference is made to individual differences within one unit, they are judged as insignificant. The gap is considered as pertaining to differing perceptions of the two units when the individual ratings allow such an interpretation.

5.1.3.3 Role Behaviour vs. Role Expectations

In the conceptual part of this study, roles are defined according to Katz and Kahn as patterns of behaviour that are expected in connection with a certain social position (Kahn & Quinn 1970, p. 52; Katz & Kahn 1978, p. 188). The ideas that each party has about a subsidiary's role manifest themselves in two ways. (1) They can be stated in the form of expectations concerning the behaviour that is anticipated from a role occupant. These expectations were introduced as role expectations above (Kahn & Quinn 1970, p. 53; Katz & Kahn 1978, p. 190). (2) They may also surface in the form of behaviours that are shown in relation to the role. The subsidiary's behaviours can be regarded as role enactment – which is central in the present context – while other parties' behaviours express their attitudes towards the subsidiary's role.

Although Katz and Kahn's definition of roles as expected behaviour patterns suggests a close association of role expectations and role behaviours, the empirical findings of this study necessitate the separate consideration of behaviours and expectations as they do not match in several cases.[118] Since the subsidiary's current role is the present study's chief interest (2.3.3), the behaviour that a subsidiary presently shows in relation to a certain role dimension is particularly highlighted (4.1.3). Headquarters and subsidiary respondents' perceptions of the subsidiary's role enactment will be classified as "perceived role behaviour". Both parties' expectations concerning the way the subsidiary should enact its role will be reported separately as "role expectations".[119]

5.1.4 Chapter Overview

The remainder of chapter 5 is structured in the following way. First, the analyzed cases will be described in detail (5.2). After these individual case descriptions, the cases will be brought together and their structures will be compared (5.3 and 5.4). The subsidiary role dimensions taken into account will be reviewed in the light of the conceptual framework and the empirical findings (5.3.1) before perception gaps regarding these dimensions will be analyzed (5.3.2). Finally, the implications of these perception gaps will be examined. The empirical findings are contrasted with the propositions derived (5.4.1; cp. 3.3.3 for the

---

[118] If the perceived role behaviour and the role expectations of one party do not match, the behaviour that *would* correspond to the role expectations can be interpreted as the subsidiary's should-be role (Asakawa 2001, p. 739). A similar differentiation is referred to by Schmid, Bäurle and Kutschker who distinguish the subsidiary's real role and its ideal role (Schmid, Bäurle & Kutschker 1998, p. 93). The real role is defined as the role that is actually played by the subsidiary whereas the ideal role rather represents a (normative) desirable concept. In the present study, the terms "as-is role" and "should-be role" are chosen instead of "real" and "ideal role", since the expression "ideal" might be understood as referring to an idea that is detached from reality and not related to the situation of the focal subsidiary.

[119] At this point, it becomes clear again that there is no "one role", but that different aspects of a role and different perspectives on a role have to be taken into account. This issue will be discussed in more detail in 5.3.2.

propositions) before an in-depth analysis of the implications is provided from the proposed theoretical standpoint (5.4.2).

5.2 The Cases

5.2.1 Overview

The six cases are described consecutively. The case descriptions are structured in the following way. (1) The questionnaire results depicting headquarters and the subsidiary respondents' assessments of the four subsidiary role dimensions serve as a starting point.[120] The questionnaire results are combined with the responses obtained in the interviews in order to distinguish perception gaps and artefacts. Differences between headquarters and subsidiary respondents' replies are explained for each subsidiary role dimension. (2) Subsequently, the confirmed perception gaps are resumed and their implications for the headquarters-subsidiary relationship are elaborated. All circumstances are considered as "implications of perception gaps" that appear as consequences of a situation where headquarters and subsidiary managers perceive the subsidiary's role differently. (3) Finally, the findings are interpreted from the perspective of the proposed conceptual framework. Thereby, it is attempted to relate the identified perception gaps concerning the subsidiary's role and the reported implications of these perception gaps to Katz and Kahn's role concept and their definition of conflict. From Katz and Kahn's conceptual standpoint, a certain role perception implies specific expectations regarding the role bearer. These expectations prompt the involved parties to engage in behaviour corresponding to their respective role perception. When the involved parties' role perceptions do not match, it is assumed that the behaviour shown by one party is likely to be perceived as conflictful by the other party. Conflict in terms of Katz and Kahn is defined as observable behaviour of one party preventing or compelling some outcome against the resistance of the other party (Katz & Kahn 1978, p. 613). The implications of each perception gap will be disentangled and compared to this definition.

In the conceptual part of the study, a differentiation of conflict types was introduced that established distribution conflict, process conflict and goal conflict as an analogy to the

---

[120] The results of the questionnaire concerning disagreement and interference between headquarters and the subsidiary are displayed in Appendix A.

categories input, throughput and output in the system terminology (2.4.3.2).[121] In the following case descriptions, each conflict that is identified will be classified according to this differentiation. The classification will be indicated in the summarizing tables included in the reports but will not be elaborated in the text. Since the three categories were used above in order to structure the field of the IB literature in terms of potential implications of perception gaps (3.3.3), they will be referred to again when the empirical findings of the present study will be compared with these previously developed ideas (5.4.1). References to the interviews are included in the form of a capitalized letter indicating the company and a number that marks the interview, e.g., "A1".

5.2.2 Hungary

5.2.2.1 Perceptions of the Role Dimensions

The results of the questionnaire reflecting headquarters and the Hungarian subsidiary managers' perceptions of the Hungarian subsidiary's role are displayed in Figure 32.[122] Although one subsidiary respondent indicates in the questionnaire that marketing and sales are carried out by the subsidiary, headquarters and subsidiary representatives agree in the interviews that the subsidiary's activities in this area do not exceed a customer service function (A9). Similarly, although several subsidiary and headquarters respondents indicate that the subsidiary is active in purchasing, both sides point out that the subsidiary is not involved in strategic purchasing processes, but only in operative purchasing on a minor scale (A10).

---

[121] Input, throughput and output relate to the headquarters-subsidiary relationship in the following way: The subsidiary is considered the central system. Consequently, the subsidiary's processes and value chain activities are defined as throughput. This includes relationships with suppliers and customers that might as well be considered as input and output in another context. Anything that is transferred from headquarters to the subsidiary is defined as input. Such transfers may concern resource inflows that entail knowledge, financial support or material resources. Finally, transfers from the subsidiary to headquarters are defined as output.

[122] A detailed description of the structure of the result charts is provided in 4.3.1.2.

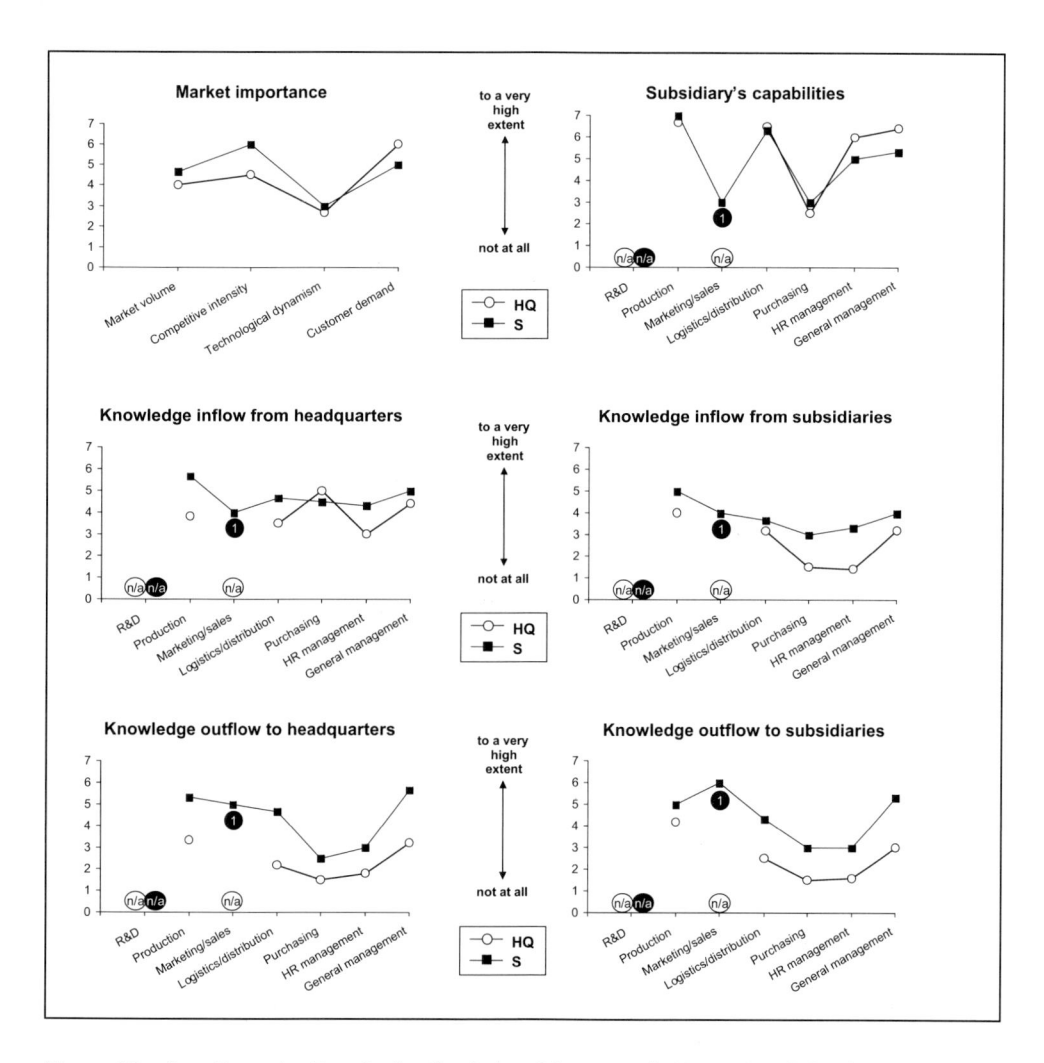

Figure 32: Questionnaire Results for the Role of Autocomp's Hungarian Subsidiary

Market importance. In terms of market importance, headquarters and subsidiary respondents' ratings are similar. The only difference emerges in terms of competitive intensity.[123] A closer look at the questionnaire results reveals that half of the headquarters respondents rate the competitive intensity in the subsidiary's market as high as the subsidiary, while the other half rate the competitive intensity rather low. The picture is

---

[123] The difference regarding the competitive intensity in the subsidiary's market is found in several other cases as well and is generally attributed to the fact that the subsidiary managers are likely to experience considerable pressure in the subsidiary's market, while headquarters' perspective is more distanced (A4, A9, A10).

repeated in the interviews: Some respondents argue for a higher rating (A1) whereas others confirm the lower rating (A3, A6). Since the subsidiary respondents confirm their high rating in the interviews (A9, A10), a perception gap seems to exist between part of the headquarters respondents and the Hungarian subsidiary managers in this respect.

Product scope. The perception gap related to the dimension product scope concerns the subsidiary's future. In terms of the current situation, headquarters and subsidiary respondents agree that the subsidiary's momentary product scope is very lean and focuses on few commodity products (A1, A6). While headquarters representatives do not intend to change this situation in the near future, subsidiary respondents emphasize their conviction that an extension of the subsidiary's product portfolio is required (A9, A10). On the one hand, this is regarded necessary in order to improve the subsidiary's future development possibilities. On the other hand, they conceive of developments in the market that they consider important to acknowledge for Autocomp in total (A10). Consequently, there is a perception gap between headquarters and subsidiary representatives concerning the subsidiary's should-be product scope.

Subsidiary capabilities. The questionnaire does not reveal any large perceptual differences between headquarters and subsidiary respondents regarding the subsidiary's capabilities. This impression is confirmed by the interviews.

Knowledge inflow from headquarters. The questionnaire results reveal a gap in terms of inflow of production knowledge from headquarters to the subsidiary. The subsidiary's rating is higher than headquarters' is. Except for one respondent, all headquarters representatives rate the knowledge inflow that the subsidiary receives from headquarters lower than subsidiary respondents do. The interviews, however, expose the difference as an artefact of the questionnaire; subsidiary and headquarters respondents consistently explain the ratings in the following way: Inflow of production knowledge from headquarters to the subsidiary is low in the subsidiary's day-to-day operations (A1, A9). Within a certain framework, the subsidiary manages its production rather autonomously since the subsidiary's production is very specialized and its capabilities in this area are high (A1, A9). However, when new products or materials are introduced or when new machines are installed, the entire knowledge is transferred from headquarters to the subsidiary (A9). Both sides agree that, depending on which perspective is taken, a higher or a lower rating of knowledge inflow from headquarters to the subsidiary is justified.

Knowledge inflow from subsidiaries. The Hungarian subsidiary's assessment of knowledge inflow from other subsidiaries is overall higher than headquarters' rating. The differences are most pronounced for purchasing and HR management knowledge. For both of these functions, the ratings of all headquarters respondents are extremely low while the subsidiary respondents' ratings are higher. In the interviews, the subsidiary respondents state that they have a very close relationship with their Polish sister and that there is considerable knowledge exchange concerning various issues, while informal exchange and knowledge sharing with other subsidiaries is rare (A10). Institutionalized knowledge exchange between subsidiaries exists only in the production area – so far between the subsidiaries in Hungary, Poland, Turkey and (recently) Mexico; the Chinese subsidiary is expected to join this circle in the near future (A4, A9). In summary, however, subsidiary representatives admit that their questionnaire ratings in the areas of purchasing and HR management knowledge are probably too high and that headquarters' assessment is more realistic (A10).[124] Consequently, no perception gap is identified regarding knowledge inflow from subsidiaries.

Knowledge outflow to headquarters. The Hungarian subsidiary's rating of knowledge outflow to headquarters is overall higher than headquarters' judgement. However, the flows that are mentioned by subsidiary respondents in the interviews rather relate to the category labelled as "information" above, referring mainly to the large amount of required reporting (5.1.2).[125] Subsidiary respondents do not back up their comparatively high ratings with specific examples of knowledge that is transferred from the subsidiary to headquarters, but rather concede that knowledge outflow in terms of this study's definition does not take place to the indicated extent (A9). Headquarters respondents, however, admit that the Hungarian subsidiary has developed and now possesses a considerable amount of knowledge in various areas (A7).[126] Nevertheless, at present, transfer of this knowledge to headquarters does not take place and is not encouraged by Autocomp's strategy (A7). In summary, the perception gap concerning knowledge outflow to headquarters does not persist.

Knowledge outflow to subsidiaries. As for the categories knowledge outflow to headquarters and knowledge inflow from subsidiaries, subsidiary respondents do not retain

---

[124] Nevertheless, headquarters representatives concede that they do not notice all contacts between subsidiaries, which might explain their generally low ratings of knowledge flows between subsidiaries (A1, A4).
[125] When information flow is considered, headquarters respondents agree with the Hungarian subsidiary's high rating (A2).
[126] Headquarters managers admit that they are probably frequently not aware of the full extent of knowledge existing at the subsidiaries (A4).

their higher assessments in the interviews. Consequently, no perception gap is determined regarding knowledge outflow to subsidiaries.

Involvement in value chain activities. A perception gap is identified regarding the subsidiary's involvement in value chain activities between the subsidiary and the representatives of some departments at headquarters, in particular, representatives of highly centralized functions.[127] Headquarters managers perceive the Hungarian subsidiary as an extended workbench (A3, A5), the task of which is only to produce (A3). This perception corresponds to Autocomp's organization according to which functions, such as marketing and sales, purchasing or finance are carried out centrally without participation of the Hungarian subsidiary (A1, A3, A6). Subsidiary respondents, however, perceive at least some involvement in various centralized functions (A9). Some examples may illustrate the perception gap. (1) Organizationally, the subsidiary does not carry out marketing and sales activities; the subsidiary does, however, meet customers and, for instance, show them the production site. While the subsidiary representatives interpret these activities as marketing and sales related, headquarters managers appear to consider them production related. (2) The finance function is organizationally located at group headquarters. As the central finance department works for all units, each subsidiary is affected by its work in financial issues. The Hungarian subsidiary possesses specific expertise concerning finance through former experiences of one of the managing directors and regards it as part of the subsidiary's role to contribute to Autocomp's benefit through suggestions for improvement (A2, A9). However, the central finance department does not seem to share the subsidiary's idea concerning the unit's involvement in finance activities.[128] (3) Finally, the purchasing function is taken into account. While the subsidiary respondents agree with headquarters respondents that the subsidiary does not carry out purchasing activities, there seems to be disagreement concerning the subsidiary's should-be involvement in the function. At the moment, the subsidiary receives relatively little information and is mainly confronted with final agreements and contracts (A10). At present, the subsidiary managers cannot exert any influence and have no opportunity to introduce the subsidiary's needs and specific requirements into these processes (A10). From the subsidiary's perspective, it would be necessary that input from the subsidiary be taken into account in the process in order to ensure that certain

---

[127] It should be noted that the perception gap only exists between the subsidiary and part of headquarters (cp. A1 vs. A3, A5). In the following, when headquarters is referred to, those representatives are meant who perceive the subsidiary's role differently.

[128] It has to be noted that no representative of the central finance department participated in the present study. Consequently, the description of the situation is solely based on subsidiary managers' statements and to some extent on headquarters' general management.

requirements are met in agreements with suppliers. Headquarters, however, does not perceive a need to involve the subsidiary in purchasing processes.

Overall, subsidiary respondents consider the subsidiary as an eye-level partner to headquarters (A9, A10), while the attitude shown by headquarters management reflects a rather hierarchical idea of the headquarters-subsidiary relationship (A5, A10).[129] In summary, a perception gap between headquarters and subsidiary representatives concerning the subsidiary's involvement in value chain activities seems to exist.

5.2.2.2 Implications for the Headquarters-Subsidiary Relationship[130]

Market importance. For the perception gap concerning competitive intensity in the subsidiary's market, no specific implications are identified (A4, A5, A10). Nevertheless, headquarters respondents admit, in this context, that the pressure on the subsidiaries is generally very high and that this pressure leads to tensions between headquarters and subsidiaries (A3). However, the conflicts that result from the increased sensitivity cannot be traced back to the differing perception of the competitive intensity (A3).

Product scope. While subsidiary representatives consider an extension of the subsidiary's product portfolio necessary, headquarters representatives do not show support for their ambitions. So far, headquarters rejected the subsidiary's proposals and refused to provide investments for new products to the subsidiary. The final consequence of this situation is that the subsidiary's product scope has not been extended (A9, A10).

Involvement in value chain activities. The differing perceptions of headquarters and subsidiary representatives regarding the subsidiary's involvement in value chain activities have several implications for the headquarters-subsidiary relationship. The abovementioned examples will be resumed here. (1) The first instance concerns the subsidiary's involvement in marketing and sales activities. The following situation is mentioned as an implication of this perception gap: When the subsidiary is visited by a customer, subsidiary representatives expect to be informed by the responsible person at central sales about recent issues and the

---

[129] Provocatively, subsidiary representatives point out that they could as well take the reverse perspective in which the central departments are perceived as mere service providers carrying out the subsidiary's orders (A9, A10).
[130] As defined in 5.2.1, all circumstances are considered as "implications of perception gaps" that appear as consequences of a situation where headquarters and subsidiary managers perceive the subsidiary's role differently.

current developments in the relationship with the customer in order to enter the meeting with the customer equipped with this additional knowledge (A10). However, central sales representatives generally do not actively provide this information to the subsidiary (A10).[131] (2) The differing perceptions of the Hungarian subsidiary's involvement in the finance function results in the following situation that is described by subsidiary respondents: Subsidiary managers occasionally suggest possibilities to save costs and to improve financial returns for Autocomp. These suggestions are frequently not even replied to; sometimes, brief statements, such as "board decision" serve as a basis to explain immediate rejection (A9). (3) Finally, the subsidiary's should-be involvement in purchasing processes is taken into account. The subsidiary management is not content with the present situation and regards changes necessary because the current lack of involvement of the subsidiary in purchasing processes had, for instance, the following implication: In accordance with an agreement made by central purchasing, the subsidiary received primary material from a supplier in a form that cannot be stored at the site. After the first incident, the subsidiary made it clear that this condition leads to problems at the subsidiary. The incident, however, happened again several times with the same people being responsible (A9, A10).

In addition to the behavioural implications pointed out above, the differing perceptions of the subsidiary's role in the headquarters-subsidiary relationship lead to frustration and dissatisfaction among subsidiary managers (A9). On the one hand, the subsidiary managers do not feel they are taken seriously when suggesting improvements concerning Autocomp or the entire group (A9); on the other hand, they do not conceive of promising perspectives for the subsidiary's future development (A9, A10).

5.2.2.3 Interpretation According to the Conceptual Framework

In the following, the identified perception gaps and their implications are regarded in the light of the proposed conceptual framework.[132]

Market importance. The first perception gap concerns the competitive intensity of the subsidiary's market. Referring to market importance or competitive intensity as aspects of

---

[131] Subsidiary respondents emphasize that this issue is not true for all representatives of central sales, but only part of them. There are large differences depending on the person; while cooperation is very good with some representatives, it is not with others (A10).

[132] The conceptual framework is displayed in Figure 16. It clarifies the relationships between headquarters and subsidiary managers' perceptions of the subsidiary's role, the corresponding behaviours and expectations as well as perception gaps and their consequences.

the subsidiary's role contradicts the definition of roles according to Katz and Kahn. The focus of these issues is on characteristics of a specific market rather than a subsidiary's behaviour pattern. Although it is possible that managers have specific expectations concerning the behaviour of a subsidiary in a particularly important or unimportant market, no such expectations are explicated in the present case. As neither specific behaviours nor behavioural expectations are associated with the higher or lower perception of competitive intensity in the present case, no implications of the perception gap are identified either.

Product scope. Second, the perception gap regarding the subsidiary's should-be product scope is taken into account. Headquarters and the subsidiary managers' perceptions of this dimension are associated with clear behavioural expectations on both sides. While headquarters management expects the subsidiary to produce the current product portfolio and no additional products, the subsidiary representatives see the subsidiary's future role in the production of an extended portfolio. However, in order to play this role, the subsidiary depends on an investment commitment by headquarters. Since the headquarters management does not share the subsidiary managers' perception of the subsidiary's should-be role, the investment is not provided. From the subsidiary's perspective, headquarters' rejection of the subsidiary's investment proposals prevents the wished-for extension of the product portfolio. Consequently, the situation can be interpreted as conflict according to Katz and Kahn. Headquarters' conflictful behaviour inhibits the subsidiary's transition from its current role to its envisioned should-be role.

Involvement in value chain activities. While the subsidiary managers consider active contributions to various functions as part of the subsidiary's role, headquarters representatives do not expect such contributions and act accordingly. (1) The subsidiary managers regard the subsidiary as to some extent involved in marketing and sales and expect headquarters to support this involvement by providing information on customer relationships. Since headquarters representatives do not perceive the subsidiary's involvement in this function, they do not provide the expected information. Thereby, headquarters prevents the subsidiary from optimally fulfilling its role and acts conflictful from the subsidiary's perspective. (2) Second, while the subsidiary managers expect that their suggestions regarding finance are taken seriously, headquarters managers do not anticipate any involvement of the subsidiary in this respect and generally do not consider the subsidiary's proposals. Subsidiary representatives experience headquarters' rejections as conflictful; the outcome that is prevented is the implementation of the subsidiary's suggestions.[133] (3) No perception gap exists between headquarters and subsidiary regarding the subsidiary's current involvement in the purchasing function, but concerning its should-be involvement. Nevertheless, conflict arises from this situation: The prospected outcome from the subsidiary's perspective is the realization of the envisioned role. The fact that headquarters does not support the implementation of the subsidiary's imagined role prevents the realization of this outcome and is interpreted as conflictful behaviour.[134]

While the implications mentioned so far could be interpreted as conflict according to Katz and Kahn, the perception gap also leads to dissatisfaction and frustration of the subsidiary managers, as they do not feel they are taken seriously. Although Katz and Kahn state that conflict may have affective implications, they do not consider emotions as part of the conflict itself. This issue was already mentioned (3.1.4) and will be addressed in more detail later (5.4.2). Table 9 summarizes the empirical findings for the presented case. The structure of the table corresponds to the categories proposed by the conceptual framework. Gaps between headquarters and subsidiary are highlighted through italics.

Unit	Market importance					
	Perception		Role expectation	Implications		
	Dimension	Role behaviour		Conflictful behaviour	Outcome	Further implications
HQ	low market importance (competitive intensity, part of HQ)	-	-	-	-	-
S	high market importance (competitive intensity)	-	-	-	-	-

---

[133] It should be noted here that the situation is described from the subsidiary's rather than from headquarters' perspective. The emerging conflict is experienced by the subsidiary but not by headquarters. In the present context, no judgement about headquarters' behaviour is intended. From headquarters' perspective, understandable reasons may explain the described behaviour.

[134] Again, the account describes the subsidiary's perspective rather than headquarters' point of view. This situation may also be attributable to specific conditions at headquarters that might provide good reasons for headquarters' behaviour.

Unit	Product scope					
	Perception		Role expectation	Implications		
	Dimension	Role behaviour		Conflictful behaviour	Outcome	Further implications
HQ	limited product scope	subsidiary focuses on narrow product portfolio	same as as-is role	rejects the subsidiary's investment proposals → input conflict	prevented: extension of product portfolio	-
S	limited product scope	subsidiary focuses on narrow product portfolio	subsidiary produces an extended portfolio of products	-	-	-

Unit	Involvement in value chain activities					
	Perception		Role expectation	Implications		
	Dimension	Role behaviour		Conflictful behaviour	Outcome	Further implications
HQ	limited involvement in value chain activities (marketing and sales, finance, part of HQ)	subsidiary focuses on production and is not involved in other value chain activities ("extended workbench")	same as as-is role	does not provide subsidiary with current information (e.g., sales) → input conflict	prevented: subsidiary meets customers with latest information on customer relationship	-
				subsidiary's suggestions for finance function neglected → output conflict	prevented: realization of suggestions	
				does not consult subsidiary when entering supplier/ customer agreements → throughput conflict	prevented: consideration of the subsidiary's needs in contracts with suppliers	
S	some involvement in value chain activities (marketing and sales, finance)	subsidiary is at least to some extent involved in other functions (marketing and sales, finance)	subsidiary is actively involved in other value chain activities as well (purchasing)	-	-	subsidiary managers are dissatisfied as they do not feel taken seriously
				-	-	
				-	-	

Table 9: Perceptions of the Hungarian Subsidiary's Role and their Implications

5.2.3 Poland

5.2.3.1 Perceptions of the Role Dimensions

The Polish subsidiary respondents' and headquarters respondents' perceptions of the considered subsidiary role dimensions are depicted in Figure 33. Overall, the relationship of the Polish subsidiary with headquarters appears to be the case with the strongest consent between headquarters and subsidiary representatives concerning the subsidiary's role. Very few disagreements are reported. Headquarters as well as subsidiary respondents argue that this is probably due to the extremely close and frequent communication between the top management of both units (A4, A7, A12). In the questionnaire, one subsidiary respondent indicates that the subsidiary has a marketing and sales function. As the Hungarian subsidiary, however, the Polish subsidiary only carries out customer service activities. In terms of purchasing activities, one subsidiary respondent and two headquarters respondents indicate that the subsidiary is active in purchasing. Headquarters management confirms that the subsidiary does possess a purchasing function although central purchasing carries out most activities for the subsidiary (A5).

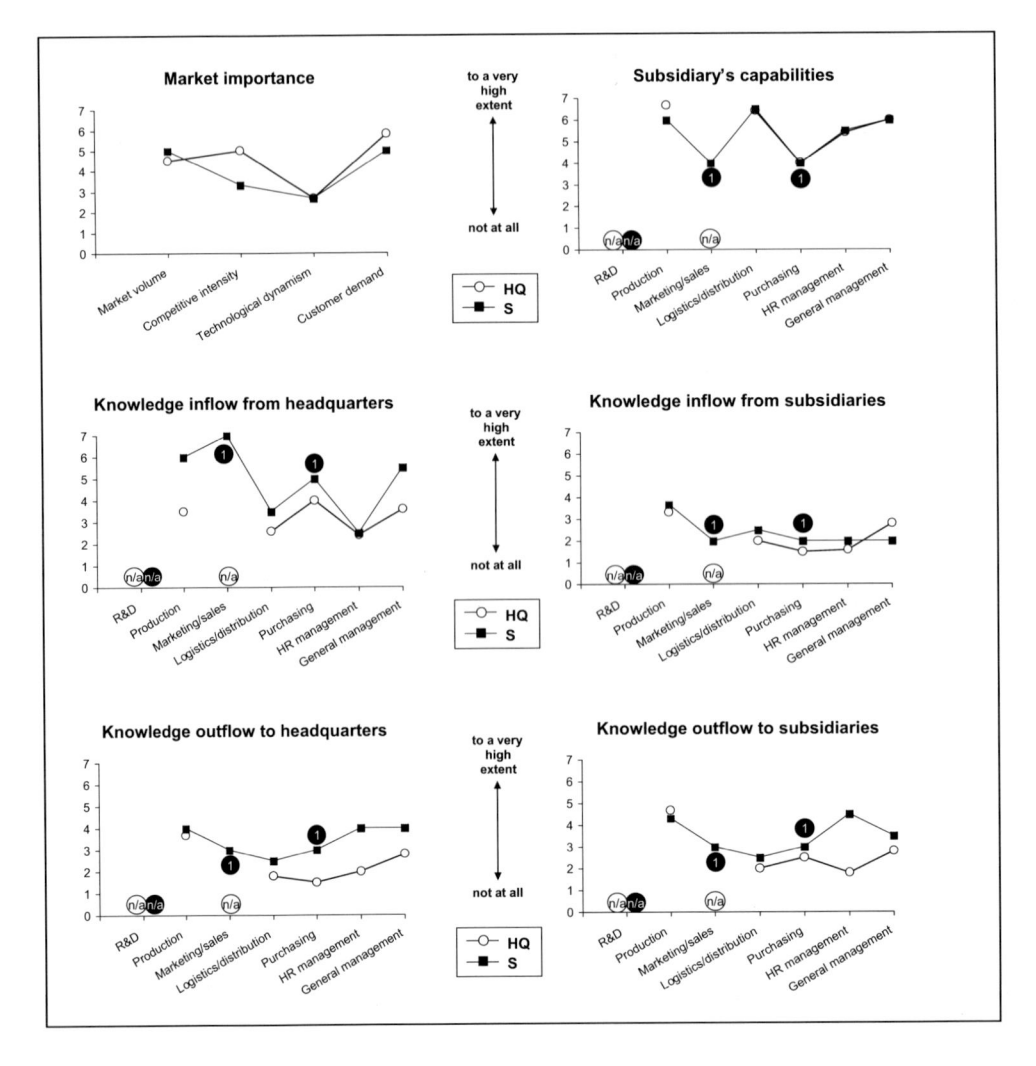

Figure 33: Questionnaire Results for the Role of Autocomp's Polish Subsidiary

Market importance. The present case is the only case included in the analysis in which the subsidiary's rating of competitive intensity is lower than headquarters' rating. However, the respondents do not consider the difference meaningful.

Subsidiary capabilities. Headquarters and subsidiary respondents assess the subsidiary's capabilities almost identically in all areas.

Knowledge inflow from headquarters. In terms of knowledge inflow from headquarters, a relatively large gap appears in the questionnaire results concerning production knowledge: The subsidiary respondents consistently indicate that knowledge inflow from headquarters is very high, while all headquarters respondents' assessments are considerably lower. Headquarters as well as subsidiary representatives' explanations of the gap resemble the interpretation of the situation in the Hungarian subsidiary – a high rating of production knowledge inflow is justified when the overall framework is taken into account (A1). The rating should be lower when inflow regarding the subsidiary's day-to-day operations is concerned (A1).[135] Consequently, no perception gap is identified concerning inflow of production knowledge from headquarters to the Polish subsidiary.

Knowledge inflow from subsidiaries. Headquarters and subsidiary respondents' ratings of the knowledge inflow from other subsidiaries are very similar.

Knowledge outflow to headquarters. The area HR management constitutes the largest difference in this category. In the questionnaire, subsidiary respondents rate the outflow of knowledge regarding HR management consistently higher than headquarters respondents do. Both headquarters and subsidiary representatives justify their respective ratings in the interviews (A6, A12). The background of the higher rating on the subsidiary's side is the following: Shortly before the questionnaire was distributed, a personnel manager with overall responsibility for Autocomp was installed at the Polish subsidiary (A1, A12). The decision was taken at the level of group headquarters and finally communicated to Autocomp's headquarters (A6). The personnel manager fulfils several central tasks for Autocomp and in this context provides HR management knowledge to headquarters and to other subsidiaries (A1, A2). While subsidiary managers already perceive a relatively large amount of knowledge outflow in the HR area, most headquarters representatives have not yet noticed any effect

---

[135] When information is considered instead of knowledge, according to subsidiary respondents the rating should also be very high. The subsidiary management states that any information which is needed can be obtained – also because the responsible persons at headquarters are personally known to the subsidiary management (A12).

(A6).[136] Consequently, a perception gap exists between headquarters and subsidiary representatives concerning the outflow of HR management knowledge from the Polish subsidiary to headquarters.

Knowledge outflow to subsidiaries. The situation outlined above as well applies to knowledge outflow to other subsidiaries – representatives of the Polish subsidiary perceive a higher outflow of HR related knowledge to other subsidiaries while headquarters respondents do not perceive such knowledge outflow.

5.2.3.2 Implications for the Headquarters-Subsidiary Relationship

Knowledge outflow to headquarters and knowledge outflow to subsidiaries. As pointed out, the installation of a personnel manager at the Polish subsidiary who is responsible for the entire SBU caused subsidiary respondents to rate the knowledge outflow concerning HR from the Polish subsidiary higher than headquarters respondents did. Most headquarters respondents have no clear idea of the tasks related to the position and so far have not perceived any effect (A6). Since headquarters representatives have no specific expectations regarding such effects either, the perception gap does not seem to have any implications (A6). This lack of consequences may also be related to the short period that passed since the new position was created.

5.2.3.3 Interpretation According to the Conceptual Framework

Knowledge outflow to headquarters and knowledge outflow to subsidiaries. Headquarters and subsidiary representatives differ in their perceptions of the Polish subsidiary's transfer of HR management knowledge to headquarters and other subsidiaries. Since both sides expect exactly the behaviour that they perceive, neither side's expectations remain unfulfilled, and the perception gap does not have any implications.

---

[136] In the interviews, most headquarters respondents are not immediately aware of the new function and do not actively refer to the newly installed function (e.g., A3).

Unit	Knowledge outflow					
	Perception		Role expectation	Implications		
	Dimension	Role behaviour		Conflictful behaviour	Outcome	Further implications
HQ	low knowledge outflow (HR management)	subsidiary transfers little knowledge concerning HR management to headquarters and other subsidiaries	same as as-is role	-	-	-
S	high knowledge outflow (HR management)	subsidiary transfers a considerable amount of knowledge concerning HR management to headquarters and other subsidiaries	same as as-is role	-	-	-

Table 10: Perceptions of the Polish Subsidiary's Role and their Implications

5.2.4 Turkey

5.2.4.1 Perceptions of the Role Dimensions

The questionnaire results pertaining to the role of the Turkish subsidiary are presented in Figure 34. The Turkish subsidiary was acquired in 1999 from another group. Initially, Autocomp's goal was to integrate the subsidiary into the network to the same extent as the other subsidiaries (A1). These integration plans mainly affected the highly centralized function of marketing and sales as well as purchasing. However, the subsidiary had enjoyed a relatively high degree of freedom before the acquisition (A3) and refused to completely abandon its activities in marketing and sales and in purchasing. Finally, the subsidiary received partial responsibility in both areas (A1, A3, A4, A13). In particular, the subsidiary is responsible for marketing and sales to so-called local customers in the regions of Turkey, India, the Middle East and Africa and for purchasing part of its raw material.

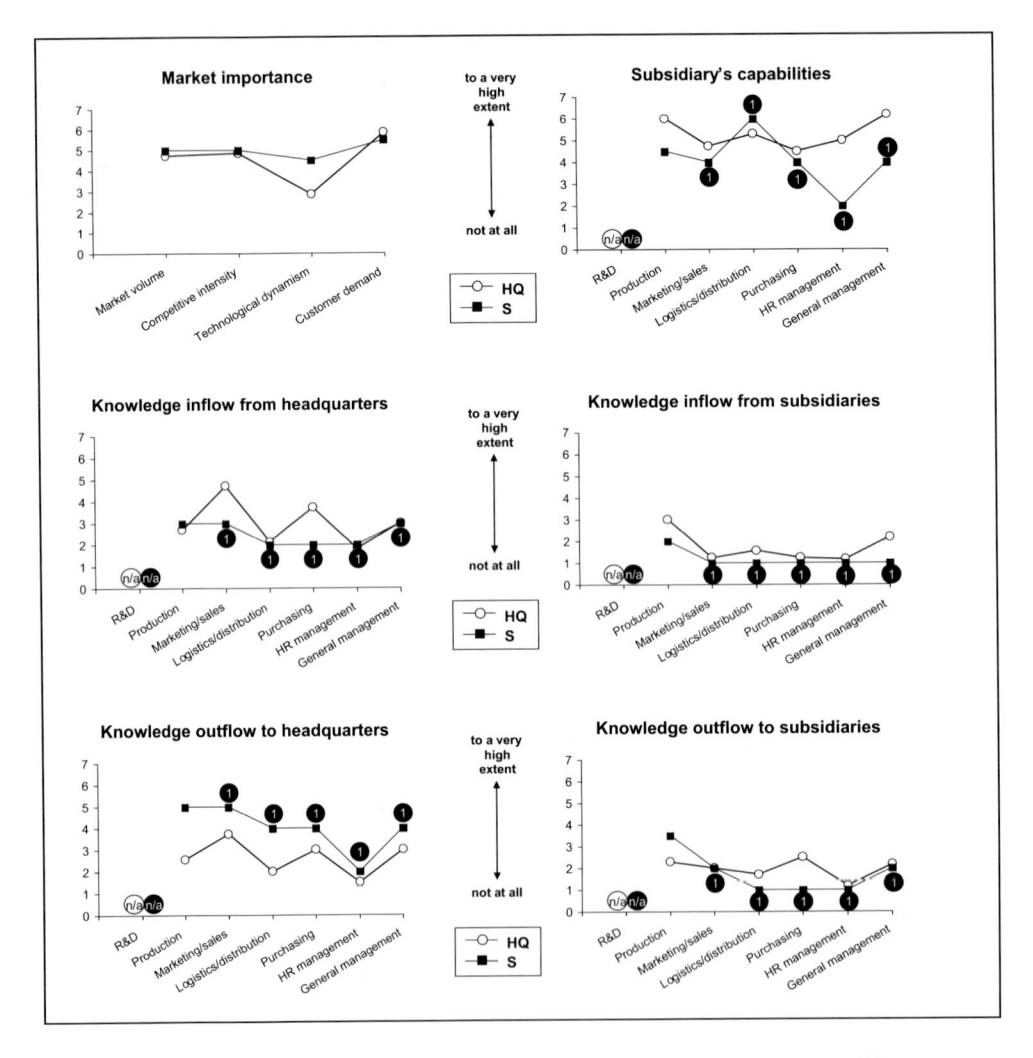

Figure 34: Questionnaire Results for the Role of Autocomp's Turkish Subsidiary[137]

Market importance. Overall, the Turkish subsidiary's market is not attributed very high strategic importance by headquarters (A1). From headquarters' perspective, developments in the past years did not demand any extensions of the Turkish subsidiary; neither is the market considered a future growth market (A1). With regard to market importance, the questionnaire hints at a perception gap concerning technological dynamism; this perception

---

[137] Only two of the three subsidiary managers addressed for their opinion answered the questionnaire. One of them indicated that the subsidiary is only active in production and consequently did not fill in the questions for the other value chain activities.

gap, however, is not confirmed in the interviews. Instead, a perception gap related to competitive intensity is determined in the interviews (A13). (1) While headquarters perceives the technological dynamism in the Turkish subsidiary's market at the same level as for all other subsidiaries, the Turkish subsidiary judges this dimension higher. Headquarters respondents confirm their low ratings in the interviews and mention that the low technological dynamism is not specific for the Turkish market, but rather for Autocomp's products (A6). Adaptations are rare and minimal (A1) as customers demand stability and reliability rather than innovation (A6). The higher rating of technological dynamism on the subsidiary's side is not confirmed in the interviews. No perception gap is identified concerning the subsidiary role dimension technological dynamism. (2) Although not reflected by the questionnaire results, the management of the Turkish subsidiary is convinced that headquarters representatives underestimate the competitive intensity of the subsidiary's market (A13). From the subsidiary's perspective, considerable effort is necessary in order to persist in the competition. Headquarters representatives, however, do not judge the competitive pressure on the subsidiary higher than on the average subsidiary. Consequently, they do not perceive the necessity to take any specific measures.

Product scope. As the representatives of the Hungarian subsidiary, the Turkish subsidiary's representatives think that the subsidiary's product scope should be extended. The subsidiary management perceives unused opportunities in the subsidiary's market that should be exploited (A1, A3).[138] Headquarters managers, however, do not share the subsidiary's judgement, so that a perception gap is identified regarding the subsidiary's should-be product scope (A1, A3, A4).

Subsidiary's capabilities. Except for logistics and distribution capabilities, the subsidiary's capability ratings are consistently lower than headquarters' ratings. In no other case, does this appear in such an extreme way.[139] In the present case, headquarters as well as subsidiary representatives interpret the Turkish subsidiary's low self-rating as unnecessary modesty (A4, A6, A13). On the contrary, the Turkish subsidiary is considered highly capable. The result surprises headquarters respondents, since in their daily cooperation, the subsidiary management seems to be fully aware of the subsidiary's capabilities (A4).

---

[138] The subsidiary's activities in searching for new market opportunities may be seen in relation to efforts to encounter the competition in the subsidiary's market.
[139] However, it has to be taken into account that all ratings were given by one subsidiary representative only – except for the rating for production capabilities.

Consequently, the questionnaire results represent an artefact rather than an actual perception gap.

Knowledge inflow from headquarters. No other subsidiary judges the knowledge inflow from headquarters or from other subsidiaries as low as the Turkish subsidiary does in any knowledge category. Neither does headquarters rate its overall knowledge transfer to any other subsidiary lower. Headquarters' and the subsidiary's ratings of knowledge inflow from headquarters differ regarding the areas of marketing and sales and purchasing. In both areas, one headquarters respondent rates the knowledge inflow at the same level as the subsidiary, while all other headquarters respondents consistently indicate a higher knowledge transfer to the subsidiary. (1) In the interviews, headquarters representatives confirm that a relatively large amount of marketing and sales knowledge is transferred to the subsidiary from headquarters (A1). Although they admit that the subsidiary is very active in marketing and sales, they stress the dominance of key account customers in Autocomp's business (A1, A2). Marketing and sales concepts for these key account customers are designed and managed by headquarters and transferred to the Turkish subsidiary (A1); furthermore, the subsidiary receives information on the key account customers from central sales (A1). Headquarters respondents suppose that the subsidiary's knowledge inflow assessment is rather low because subsidiary representatives want to emphasize their own contribution in comparison to the support received from headquarters (A1, A3, A4, A7). They presume that subsidiary representatives thereby express the opinion that they do not depend on knowledge inflow from headquarters (A5). From the subsidiary's perspective, however, only little knowledge inflow concerning marketing and sales from headquarters is perceived (A13). In contrast to headquarters respondents' presumption, the subsidiary management indicates that a higher inflow from headquarters concerning key account customers would be helpful for the subsidiary's activities (A13). Hence, a perception gap exists between headquarters and subsidiary regarding inflow of marketing and sales knowledge from headquarters to the Turkish subsidiary. (2) The subsidiary is responsible for buying part of its raw material from local suppliers that offer very competitive prices (A3, A5). Contracts are finalized by the subsidiary in cooperation with central sales representatives (A5, A13). However, each side seems to perceive the part that it plays in the process as more pronounced (A5, A13). As in the marketing and sales area, headquarters respondents rate the transfer of knowledge to the subsidiary from central sales higher than the subsidiary management does and confirm this perception in the interviews (A5). Headquarters representatives assume that the results reflect the subsidiary managers' perception that the subsidiary's contribution in the purchasing area is higher than headquarters' contribution (A1, A3, A4) and that support by headquarters is not considered necessary from the subsidiary's perspective (A5). According to the subsidiary management, however, headquarters' knowledge transfer is actually low (A13). The subsidiary would appreciate receiving more purchasing knowledge and information on new suppliers or new prices from central sales (A13). A perception gap is identified concerning the knowledge inflow to the subsidiary from headquarters in the purchasing area.

Knowledge inflow from subsidiaries. Knowledge inflow to the Turkish subsidiary from other subsidiaries is consistently judged low. The only exception is production knowledge, which is perceived higher by both headquarters and subsidiary representatives. The higher rating of production knowledge can be attributed to the formalized working group in this area (A4, A6). Overall, headquarters and subsidiary managers perceive knowledge inflow to the Turkish subsidiary from other subsidiaries identically.

Knowledge outflow to headquarters. The subsidiary's questionnaire ratings of knowledge outflow to headquarters are overall slightly higher than headquarters' ratings. Differences are most pronounced for production knowledge as well as logistics and distribution knowledge. (1) When the questionnaire results on production are taken into account, one headquarters respondent judges the subsidiary's knowledge transfer to headquarters at the same level as the subsidiary, while the remaining headquarters respondents rate the knowledge outflow considerably lower. The subsidiary's relatively high rating of outflow of production knowledge to headquarters is confirmed in the interviews (A13). Although the large amount of reporting to headquarters seems to have influenced the subsidiary's rating, actual production knowledge – concerning, for instance, improvements of the production process – is also referred to by the subsidiary management (A13). On headquarters' side, a relatively high level of information flow from the subsidiary is attested (A1). Transfer of actual production knowledge, however, is neither expected by headquarters representatives nor perceived, since the subsidiary produces commodity products that do not require specific capabilities or knowledge (A2, A6). The situation is interpreted as a perception gap between headquarters and subsidiary. (2) Only one subsidiary respondent assesses the logistics and distribution function. This single respondent's rating is higher than the rating of any headquarters respondent. However, neither headquarters nor subsidiary representatives provide an explanation for the subsidiary's high questionnaire rating (A1, A2, A6).

Knowledge outflow to subsidiaries. The largest difference in headquarters and subsidiary respondents' questionnaire replies concerning knowledge outflow to other subsidiaries is related to purchasing knowledge. The subsidiary's low rating is explained by the lack of purchasing activities at other subsidiaries (A13). On headquarters' side, most respondents perceive a rather low amount of knowledge outflow from the Turkish subsidiary to other subsidiaries. However, one respondent rates the outflow of purchasing knowledge from the subsidiary considerably higher, as he perceives the subsidiary promoting its suppliers to the entire SBU network (A5). As the higher rating on headquarters' side essentially depends on this one respondents' high rating, the difference is not interpreted as a perception gap between headquarters and subsidiary.

Autonomy. Although not part of the questionnaire, the subsidiary role dimension autonomy plays a role in this case. It is important to note that headquarters respondents emphasize that the situation described in the following has changed; the perception gap concerning the Turkish subsidiary's autonomy no longer exists according to headquarters respondents. They claim to have found a solution and reached common understanding with the subsidiary (A1, A5). Before being acquired by Autocomp, the Turkish subsidiary possessed considerable autonomy in its former group (A1). At the time of the acquisition, Autocomp's management aimed at integrating the new subsidiary into its network to the same extent as the other subsidiaries (A1). From headquarters' perspective, this integration implied significant cuts in the subsidiary's autonomy in such areas as marketing and sales or purchasing. However, the Turkish subsidiary management did not consider the change in ownership as changing the subsidiary's autonomy. Consequently, a perception gap emerged between headquarters and subsidiary in terms of the subsidiary's autonomy.

Involvement in value chain activities. According to headquarters respondents, the perception gap concerning the subsidiary's autonomy was resolved or at least decreased significantly (A1). Nevertheless, in some aspects, the differing perceptions of the subsidiary's involvement in value chain activities can be seen as a continuation of the earlier perception gap. This issue appears most relevant in the marketing and sales function. Even though the subsidiary management now accepts that headquarters has central responsibility for this function, it still desires that the subsidiary be more strongly involved in the respective processes (A13). For the subsidiary management, the subsidiary's ideal role entails, for instance, a more active part in negotiations with customers: It would be considered beneficial if subsidiary representatives were allowed to participate in negotiations also with those of the subsidiary's customers that belong to a global key account. Headquarters respondents, however, do not consider such involvement necessary (A3). Consequently, a perception gap exists between headquarters and the subsidiary that concerns the subsidiary's should-be involvement in marketing and sales activities.

5.2.4.2 Implications for the Headquarters-Subsidiary Relationship

Market importance. In order to persist in the competition, the subsidiary shows efforts to fulfil requests of customers for products that are not part of Autocomp's regular product portfolio (A3, A4). In this respect, the subsidiary frequently needs feedback from headquarters regarding the feasibility or certification of the respective products before being able to respond to the customers' requests (A3, A4). From headquarters' perspective, however, this is not always first priority (A3).[140] Certification processes are generally time-consuming and determining the feasibility of products may take quite long (A3, A4). Since the competitive intensity and the pressure on the subsidiary are considered lower from headquarters' perspective, the subsidiary management is perceived as too impatient in this process (A3). From the subsidiary's perspective, headquarters' reaction to the requests is often not as fast as hoped for and may hinder the subsidiary's acquisition of customers and orders (A3, A4).

Product scope. Since the subsidiary management perceives various market opportunities for new products, it started several initiatives to convince headquarters to extend the subsidiary's product portfolio (A1, A3, A4). Therefore, detailed information on new products is sent to headquarters (A1) and investments are proposed (A4). So far, however, the subsidiary's investment proposals were rejected by headquarters (A1, A4). On the one hand, headquarters management does not share the subsidiary's judgement concerning market opportunities (A1, A3). On the other hand, some of the subsidiary's proposals conflicted with other SBUs' product portfolios and were not supported in order to maintain a clear separation between SBUs (A4).

Knowledge inflow from headquarters. The perception gaps regarding inflow of marketing and sales knowledge and purchasing knowledge from headquarters to the Turkish subsidiary do not show any implications for the headquarters-subsidiary relationship.

---

[140] For instance, because the prospective amount to be sold is comparatively small (A3).

Knowledge outflow to headquarters. No consequences are attributed to the perception gap concerning outflow of production knowledge to headquarters.

Autonomy. The perception gap regarding the Turkish subsidiary's autonomy was particularly pronounced in highly centralized functions such as marketing and sales or purchasing. (1) The subsidiary management had been very active in marketing and sales and was not willing to give up its numerous personal contacts to customers and its influence on marketing and sales processes (A5). As direct relationships with customers were sustained, this behaviour was perceived as interference by headquarters management (A1, A5). Conflicts resulted as both parties maintained their ground. Only recent discussions have led to convergence of the two parties, according to headquarters respondents. Considering that the acquisition took place nine years before, it can be assumed that mutual understanding and concessions did not come easily. By now, a solution has been found that seems to accommodate both parties: On the one side, the subsidiary management accepted that key account customers are handled by the central sales department at headquarters (A1, A13). On the other side, the subsidiary received sales responsibility for local customers in the sales areas of Turkey, India, the Middle East and Africa. First, this allows the subsidiary to maintain at least some of its business relationships. Second, headquarters management realized that the subsidiary's sales qualities offer considerable potential and can be used as a resource for Autocomp (A1).[141] Nevertheless, contracts have to be approved by headquarters before being signed by the subsidiary management. Although the subsidiary management acknowledges that Autocomp's customer structure demands a key account organization that is centred at headquarters, there are still requests that the subsidiary should be more strongly involved in marketing and sales processes (A6, A13). This will be outlined in relation to the dimension involvement in value chain activities. (2) Purchasing represents a second function in which the subsidiary management initially judged the subsidiary's autonomy higher than was envisioned by headquarters representatives. Here as well, the differing ideas led to conflict when the subsidiary attempted to go its own way (A5). The subsidiary management had many personal contacts with suppliers that it did not intend to give up (A5). Assuming that the subsidiary could still act autonomously, raw material was ordered repeatedly without the central purchasing department's knowledge (A1). This not only undermined the central purchasing department's authority, but also was problematic because it concerned transactions requiring consent ("zustimmungspflichtige Geschäfte")

---

[141] According to headquarters respondents, the subsidiary's managing director has very good access to customers and visits them frequently. He takes in a lot of information concerning market movements, competitors' actions and customers' plans and transfers it to headquarters (A1).

(A1, A2). Headquarters was compelled to interfere on several occasions (A1, A5). Finally, a similar solution was found as in the marketing and sales area: The subsidiary was made responsible for buying some of its raw materials and can thereby use existing personal contacts and the favourable conditions offered by the local suppliers. However, as in the marketing and sales area, contracts cannot be entered into entirely autonomously, but have to be approved by headquarters. Headquarters respondents maintain that this mutually agreed on regulation contributed to the resolution of existing differences (A1).

Involvement in value chain activities. Although the subsidiary management acknowledges the necessity of a key account organization, the subsidiary's involvement in negotiations with customers to whom it delivers would be considered advantageous (A6, A13). Subsidiary representatives are convinced that they not only know the subsidiary's market best, but that they also know best how to handle customers in their culture (A13). The subsidiary management has been attested remarkable perseverance in sales negotiations (A6) which it misses in the central sales team (A13). In the ideal case, the subsidiary management envisions headquarters' central sales representatives and subsidiary representatives combining and coordinating their knowledge before meeting the customer together as a team (A13). At the moment, this is not the case and not intended by headquarters. Recently, one of the Turkish subsidiary's long time customers – the relationship of the subsidiary with the customer exceeded the subsidiary's membership in Autocomp by about ten years – decided to turn to one of Autocomp's competitors (A1, A5). For the subsidiary, this means a loss of about 40% of its production capacities. While this is not stated by the subsidiary, headquarters respondents allude to considerable arguments and discussions that followed this incident, since the subsidiary management blames this development on headquarters' sales methods and the subsidiary's exclusion from the process (A5, A13).

5.2.4.3 Interpretation According to the Conceptual Framework

Market importance. As was outlined in relation to the Hungarian subsidiary, the dimension market importance does not correspond to the role definition by Katz and Kahn who view roles as patterns of behaviour. Nevertheless, in the case involving the Turkish subsidiary, respondents mention expectations that indirectly relate the dimension market importance to behavioural implications. The subsidiary representatives experience more pressure from competition in the market than headquarters managers do. While both headquarters and subsidiary representatives consider it part of the subsidiary's role to react effectively to this competition, the effort that is necessary to reach this goal is judged differently. From the subsidiary's perspective, appropriate behaviour by the subsidiary entails, for instance, quick responses to customers' requests concerning products that are new to the subsidiary. Headquarters management does not share the subsidiary representatives' opinion and does not expect extremely fast reactions to customers' requests. From the subsidiary's perspective, headquarters' slow responses are perceived as conflictful as they do not support, but rather inhibit, the subsidiary's goal to promptly react to customers.[142]

Product scope. Headquarters and the Turkish subsidiary management perceive the subsidiary's should-be product scope differently. The subsidiary managers suggested several new product investments to headquarters in order to realize an extension of its portfolio and expected headquarters to support these efforts. So far, however, headquarters has rejected the subsidiary's proposals and the subsidiary's product portfolio has remained unchanged according to headquarters managers' expectations. From the subsidiary's perspective, headquarters' behaviour can be interpreted as conflictful according to Katz and Kahn.

Knowledge inflow from headquarters. The subsidiary representatives perceive less knowledge inflow from headquarters in the areas of marketing and sales and purchasing than headquarters respondents do. From Katz and Kahn's perspective, knowledge that is being sent to the subsidiary does not constitute a characteristic of the subsidiary's role. Rather than behaviour that is shown by the subsidiary, the knowledge inflow depends on headquarters' behaviour. The subsidiary's role may be affected by knowledge inflow to the subsidiary if the role involves the application of the received knowledge. In the present case, however, there are no expectations of this kind. The subsidiary does not seem to need the knowledge inflow in order to fulfil its role and headquarters does not intend to change the subsidiary's behaviour with this knowledge transfer. Since there are no specific behavioural expectations attached to the knowledge transfer, the differing perceptions do not show any particular implications.

---

[142] It may be questioned whether the interpretation of the observed situation as a perception gap regarding the subsidiary's role in terms of the definition is justified. It is acknowledged that headquarters management and subsidiary management agree regarding their general expectations of the subsidiary's function to act successfully in the existing competition. They disagree, however, with regard to the behaviour that is necessary in order to persist in the competition and thereby fulfil this function. This disagreement can be interpreted as a perception gap concerning the subsidiary's role.

Knowledge outflow to headquarters. In the present case, a perception gap exists regarding knowledge outflow from the subsidiary to headquarters. However, at the same time, headquarters representatives do not expect the creation and transfer of knowledge concerning production part of the Turkish subsidiary's role. Since neither side's expectations are disappointed, there are no implications for the headquarters-subsidiary relationship, although a perception gap is identified.

Autonomy. Shortly after the acquisition, the subsidiary perceived a higher degree of autonomy than headquarters. While headquarters management expected the subsidiary to refer to headquarters in relation to decisions that were to be taken in marketing and sales or in purchasing, the subsidiary assumed that such decisions could be made independently. (1) When the subsidiary management continued to maintain direct relationships with customers, this behaviour interfered with headquarters representatives' idea of the subsidiary's role; headquarters managers did not expect the subsidiary to retain direct customer relationships and perceived the subsidiary's behaviour as conflictful. The outcome that was prevented from headquarters' perspective was the clear global key account organization. (2) When the subsidiary purchased raw material without notifying the central purchasing department, this as well conflicted with headquarters' role expectations. Since it prevented the subsidiary's imagined integration in Autocomp's organizational structure, this situation can also be interpreted as headquarters-subsidiary conflict according to the conceptual framework.

Involvement in value chain activities. The subsidiary management considers a higher degree of involvement in marketing and sales activities to be the logical consequence of its better knowledge of customers and the region's culture. The subsidiary representatives' idea about this involvement implies the subsidiary's participation in sales negotiations with customers to whom the subsidiary delivers. Headquarters management does not agree with this perspective and does not intend to involve the subsidiary in global key account relationships. Although the perception gap concerns the should-be role rather than the current role, conflict arises from the situation: Headquarters' refusal to involve the subsidiary in negotiations with customers belonging to a global key account represents conflictful behaviour as it prevents the subsidiary from playing its envisioned should-be role.

The conceptual analysis of the relationship between Autocomp's headquarters and the Turkish subsidiary is summarized in the following table.

Market importance

Unit	Perception		Role expectation	Implications		
	Dimension	Role behaviour		Conflictful behaviour	Outcome	Further implications
HQ	low market importance (competitive intensity)	subsidiary takes all means to persist in the competition → moderate effort necessary	same as as-is role	reacts relatively slowly to subsidiary's requests concerning feasibility and certification of new products → **input conflict**	prevented: subsidiary's fast reaction to potential customers' requests	-
S	high market importance (competitive intensity)	subsidiary takes all means to persist in the competition → high effort necessary	(support by headquarters necessary)	-	-	-

Product scope

Unit	Perception		Role expectation	Implications		
	Dimension	Role behaviour		Conflictful behaviour	Outcome	Further implications
HQ	limited product scope	subsidiary focuses on narrow product portfolio	same as as-is role	rejects the subsidiary's investment proposals → **input conflict**	prevented: extension of product portfolio	-
S	limited product scope	subsidiary focuses on narrow product portfolio	subsidiary produces an extended portfolio of products	-	-	-

Knowledge inflow

Unit	Perception		Role expectation	Implications		
	Dimension	Role behaviour		Conflictful behaviour	Outcome	Further implications
HQ	high knowledge inflow (marketing and sales, purchasing)	-	-	-	-	-
S	low knowledge inflow (marketing and sales, purchasing)	-	-	-	-	-

Unit	Knowledge outflow					
	Perception		Role expectation	Implications		
	Dimension	Role behaviour		Conflictful behaviour	Outcome	Further implications
HQ	low knowledge outflow (production)	subsidiary transfers little knowledge concerning production to headquarters	same as as-is role	-	-	-
S	high knowledge outflow (production)	subsidiary transfers a considerable amount of knowledge concerning production to headquarters	same as as-is role	-	-	-

Unit	Autonomy (past)					
	Perception		Role expectation	Implications		
	Dimension	Role behaviour		Conflictful behaviour	Outcome	Further implications
HQ	low degree of autonomy (marketing and sales, purchasing)	subsidiary takes unauthorized decisions concerning its marketing and sales or purchasing activities	decisions in marketing and sales or purchasing are taken by headquarters	sustains direct relationships with customers → throughput conflict	prevented: subsidiary's integration in the centralized marketing and sales organization (key account organization)	headquarters' responsibility for global key account customers is accepted; subsidiary obtained regional sales responsibility
S	high degree of autonomy (marketing and sales, purchasing)	subsidiary rightfully takes decisions concerning its marketing and sales or purchasing activities	same as as-is role	purchases raw material without central sales' knowledge → throughput conflict	prevented: subsidiary's integration in the centralized purchasing organization (transactions requiring consent)	subsidiary obtained responsibility for purchasing part of its raw material

Unit	Involvement in value chain activities					
	Perception		Role expectation	Implications		
	Dimension	Role behaviour		Conflictful behaviour	Outcome	Further implications
HQ	limited involvement in value chain activities (marketing and sales)	subsidiary is involved in marketing and sales to local, but not to global customers	same as as-is role	does not involve the subsidiary in sales negotiations → throughput conflict	prevented: subsidiary's contribution to marketing and sales processes	loss of a long-time customer of the subsidiary (causality unclear)
S	high involvement in value chain activities (marketing and sales)	subsidiary is involved in marketing and sales to local, but not to global customers	subsidiary is involved in marketing and sales activities for all of its customers	-	-	-

Table 11: Perceptions of the Turkish Subsidiary's Role and their Implications

5.2.5 Mexico

5.2.5.1 Perceptions of the Role Dimensions

The questionnaire results displaying headquarters and the Mexican subsidiary respondents' perceptions of the subsidiary role dimensions are presented in Figure 35. The Mexican subsidiary was established in 1989, and it is thereby Autocomp's oldest foreign unit. After several years, it became clear that the geographic distance and time difference from headquarters require more local involvement in sales activities (A1). A small sales office was established in 1998, located in the USA close to Autocomp's customers in the automotive industry. The sales office works 100% for the Mexican subsidiary and is therefore considered part of the foreign unit (A6). In terms of financial performance, the Mexican subsidiary is the foreign unit that worries headquarters most (A6, A7). Despite a market share of about 20% in North America, the subsidiary's results have disappointed headquarters for years (A1, A5). The reasons for the bad results, however, are only partly ascribed to the subsidiary and are seen as market related to the largest extent (A1, A2, A6). Nevertheless, headquarters attempted to initiate internal improvements in the subsidiary (A5). In the year before the study, Autocomp's experts in several areas, such as marketing and production, visited the subsidiary. The goal of this visit was to evaluate administration and production processes and to initiate improvements if necessary (e-mail communication). Shortly before the study, the subsidiary's managing director was replaced (A5, A11).

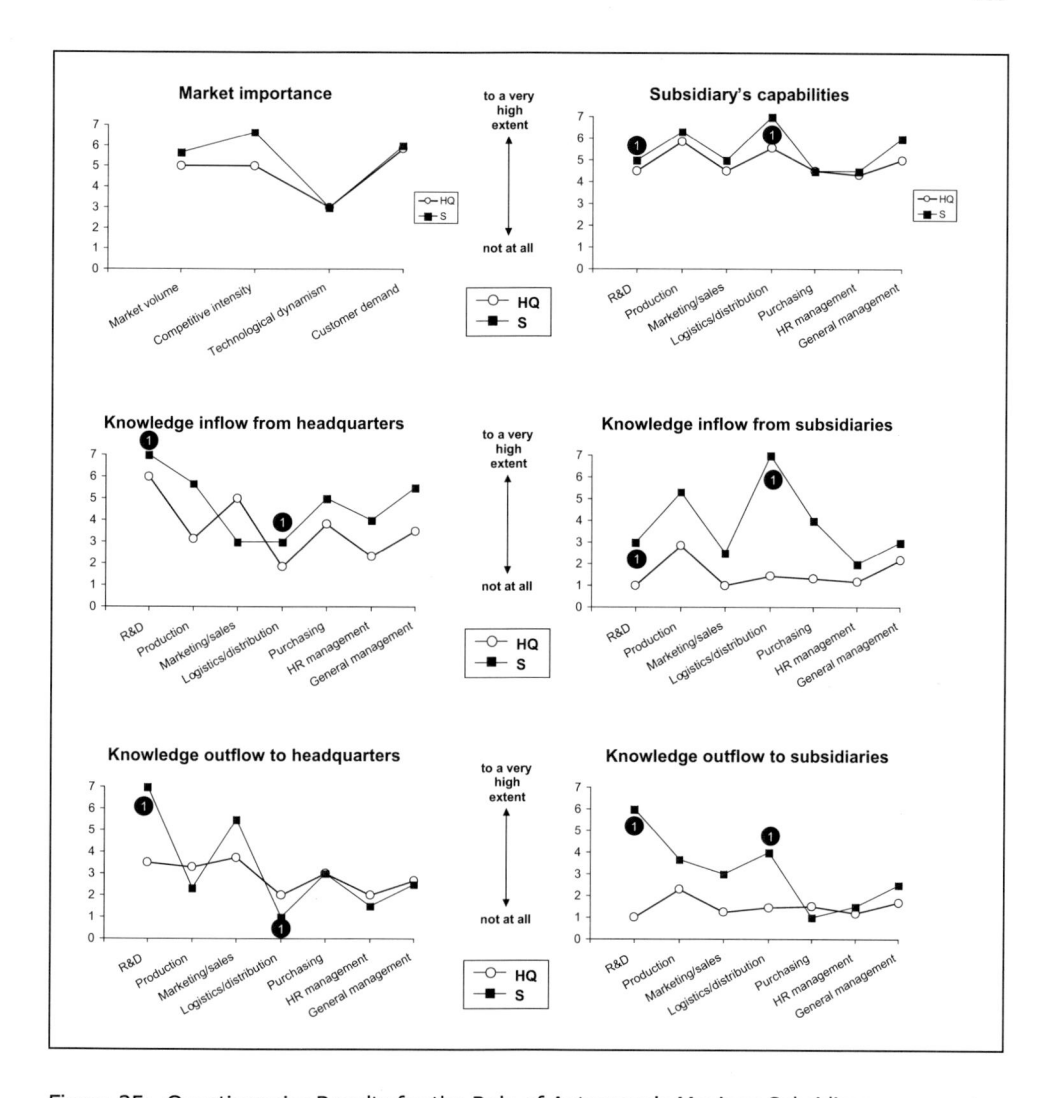

Figure 35: Questionnaire Results for the Role of Autocomp's Mexican Subsidiary

Market importance. As in several other cases, subsidiary respondents rate the competitive intensity in the subsidiary's market higher than headquarters respondents do. About half of the headquarters respondents rate the competitive intensity in the Mexican subsidiary's market as high as the subsidiary does; others rate it slightly lower. From the subsidiary's side, the high rating is confirmed in the interview (A11). Some headquarters respondents explain the difference in the questionnaire results in the same way as in the other cases – the subsidiary's perspective is likely to result in a more intense perception of the competition in the market while headquarters representatives view the market from a larger distance

(A5, A6). However, several other headquarters respondents admit that the competition in the American market (for which the subsidiary is responsible) is currently quite intense in comparison with other subsidiary's markets (A1, A3). Overall, no significant perception gap appears between headquarters and the Mexican subsidiary.

Subsidiary's capabilities. Headquarters and subsidiary respondents rate the subsidiary's capabilities similarly; no perception gaps are indicated in this regard. In contrast to the questionnaire results, in the interviews, several headquarters respondents attribute the subsidiary rather low capabilities in the marketing and sales area (A1, A2, A7). A survey that Autocomp conducted in relation to the abovementioned improvement project revealed, for instance, that the responsible managers possessed very little knowledge of their customers. However, the perception gap could not be clearly determined and will not be considered below.

Knowledge inflow from headquarters. (1) While headquarters respondents rate the inflow of production knowledge to the Mexican subsidiary low to medium, subsidiary respondents rate it high in the questionnaire. In the interviews, headquarters respondents state that the subsidiary is generally rather autonomous in terms of production (A1). The subsidiary receives a lot of knowledge and support from headquarters, when new processes are introduced or new machines are installed, but hardly any further input concerning the day-to-day operations (A1). The fact that headquarters sent a production specialist from one of the other subsidiaries for several weeks as a consultant to the Mexican subsidiary in order to transfer production knowledge and implement improvements in the production process may have led subsidiary respondents to rate the inflow of production knowledge from headquarters higher (A4, A5). The subsidiary management explains the situation in the same way: A high rating is justified on special occasions but not as an indication of a continuous inflow of knowledge (A11). Consequently, no perception gap exists concerning the inflow of production knowledge from headquarters to the subsidiary. (2) In the questionnaire, one headquarters respondent rates the inflow of marketing and sales knowledge to the subsidiary equally to the subsidiary; the remaining headquarters respondents judge the knowledge inflow higher. In the interviews, the low rating concerning the inflow of marketing and sales knowledge is confirmed by the subsidiary management (A11). A marketing and sales meeting for the American market that took place shortly before the study revealed that the central marketing and sales department possesses a lot of knowledge that could be of use for the marketing and sales team at the subsidiary (A11). While headquarters representatives think that much of this knowledge is provided to the subsidiary, the knowledge does not reach the right people at the subsidiary and is consequently not acknowledged there (A11). However, the subsidiary management concedes that the discrepancy was discovered and changes were initiated. Consequently, a medium value between headquarters' and the subsidiary's rating is considered most appropriate. No perception gap is determined.

Knowledge inflow from subsidiaries. Although the subsidiary's assessments are in general higher than headquarters' ratings, the respondents do not consider the difference remarkable. Only the functions of production and logistics and distribution will be explained since they constitute the largest differences. (1) Headquarters representatives state that production is the value chain activity where the knowledge exchange between the Mexican subsidiary and other subsidiaries is highest (A1, A3, A6). Nevertheless, only one headquarters respondent rates the inflow of production knowledge from other subsidiaries to the Mexican subsidiary at the same level as subsidiary respondents; the other respondents provide considerably lower ratings. From the subsidiary's side, the argumentation resembles the dimension inflow of production knowledge from headquarters (A11). Since the production expert who was sent to the Mexican subsidiary by headquarters came from another subsidiary, the knowledge inflow in this context may also be seen as knowledge inflow from other subsidiaries (A4). (2) In terms of logistics and distribution, headquarters respondents cannot imagine any knowledge inflow to the Mexican subsidiary from other subsidiaries (A1). In the interview, the subsidiary management agrees with headquarters representatives that the high rating obtained from a single respondent is not realistic (A11). Overall, no meaningful perception gap regarding knowledge inflow from subsidiaries is identified.

Knowledge outflow to headquarters. (1) In the questionnaire, only two headquarters representatives and one subsidiary representative indicate that R&D activities are carried out at the subsidiary. Just as the other foreign units, the subsidiary does not possess a "classical" R&D function and does not carry out basic research. New products and materials are developed exclusively by headquarters, while the subsidiary has only a product management function (A1, A2, A7). However, several headquarters respondents admit that the subsidiary's activities concerning applied research represent an extension of R&D (A1) and may be conceived of as "on the verge of R&D" (A3, A7). After the development of products by headquarters' central R&D, the subsidiary adapts them and makes them fit for mass production that complies with the standards required by the market (A1, A3, A4, A6). The Mexican subsidiary informs headquarters about product adjustments that are necessary for the American market (A1, A4, A6). Nevertheless, the subsidiary management neither thinks that the subsidiary does carry out R&D activities (A11) nor that knowledge in that area is transferred to headquarters or other subsidiaries (A11). Consequently, the perception gap is not confirmed. (2) On average, the subsidiary management judges the marketing and sales knowledge that it transfers to headquarters higher than the headquarters' side does. However, the questionnaire responses are inconsistent on both sides. On the subsidiary's side, they range from medium to high, while on the headquarters' side, they range from low to high. In the interviews, headquarters respondents' argumentation differs depending on the definition of knowledge:[143] While the subsidiary's outflow of marketing and sales knowledge in terms of concepts, methods or approaches to headquarters is judged low by headquarters respondents (A2, A3), there appears to be agreement among headquarters representatives that the subsidiary does send a lot of data concerning customers and market developments to headquarters (A1, A3). In the interview, the subsidiary management considers the subsidiary's outflow of knowledge in the marketing and sales as low as headquarters respondents do (A11). In summary, the perception gap concerning knowledge outflow from the Mexican subsidiary to headquarters in the marketing and sales area that is indicated by the questionnaire results is not confirmed by the interviews.

Knowledge outflow to subsidiaries. (1) Outflow of R&D knowledge to other subsidiaries is judged in the same way by the respondents as knowledge outflow to headquarters (A1, A2, A3, A7, A11). As there is no classical R&D function at the subsidiary, knowledge outflow in that area is consistently judged low in the interviews (A1). A certain influence is acknowledged in the sense that products that were adjusted or modified in the Mexican subsidiary are applied in other subsidiaries as well, but the extremely high assessment from a single respondent seems unjustified (A4). (2) The questionnaire results indicate that the subsidiary representatives rate the outflow of marketing and sales knowledge to other subsidiaries higher than headquarters representatives do. In the interviews, headquarters respondents confirm their low questionnaire rating and state that no knowledge outflow from the Mexican subsidiary to other subsidiaries is perceived (A1, A3, A6). The subsidiary management agrees that the knowledge outflow concerning marketing and sales from the subsidiary is generally low (A11). (3) The high rating of outflow of logistics and distribution knowledge to other subsidiaries by a single subsidiary respondent cannot be explained by

---

[143] As was mentioned above (5.1.2), some headquarters respondents seem to have included "important market and customer data" in their interpretation of knowledge (as was indicated in the definition on the questionnaire), while others left out such data from their understanding of knowledge flow.

headquarters nor by the subsidiary management (A5, A11). Consequently, none of the perception gaps suggested by the questionnaire results concerning knowledge outflow to other subsidiaries are confirmed by the interviews.

Autonomy. While headquarters and subsidiary respondents agree that the subsidiary's involvement in marketing and sales processes is currently low to medium and that more local activity in this area is necessary (A3, A11), they do not have the same idea regarding the degree of autonomy that the subsidiary should have in the future. However, with regard to the present situation, neither headquarters nor the subsidiary managers seem to be satisfied. Headquarters representatives state that the subsidiary acts too independently and does not necessarily fulfil central sales' requests and comply with orders (A3). This encourages the opinion that the subsidiary does not carry out its responsibilities in the marketing and sales area satisfactorily (A1, A7). From the subsidiary's perspective, headquarters tries to control the unit too closely in terms of marketing and sales (A11) and interferes in many issues that should better be carried out locally without headquarters' involvement (A11). Headquarters management and subsidiary management agree that the subsidiary's role in this respect has to change. Headquarters' central sales department appears to envision the subsidiary's role in marketing and sales as closely controlled by headquarters (A11). The subsidiary is seen as a provider of current information on customers and market developments and as an implementer of headquarters' instructions that carries out market research studies or similar activities in order to support headquarters' marketing and sales decisions (A3). Consequently, headquarters' idea does not entail an autonomous part for the subsidiary. Although the subsidiary management agrees with headquarters representatives that a key account organization managed by headquarters is necessary and that strategic decisions have to be taken or at least approved by headquarters (A3, A11), the managers do not see the subsidiary in a subordinate and merely executing role. They expect, for instance, to receive more information from central sales concerning current developments in negotiations with customers (A3). Furthermore, the subsidiary managers would like to be more strongly involved in the sales process; they would like to bring in their own ideas and to take certain decisions independently (A3, A4, A11). A higher degree of autonomy is considered beneficial from the subsidiary's perspective due to the large geographic distance and the time difference. It would allow the subsidiary to act more immediately. In summary, a perception gap between headquarters and the subsidiary regarding the subsidiary's should-be autonomy is confirmed.

5.2.5.2 Implications for the Headquarters-Subsidiary Relationship

Autonomy. The identified perception gap regarding the Mexican subsidiary's autonomy concerns the subsidiary's should-be role. So far, neither party could realize the should-be role that it envisions for the subsidiary. However, the discontent with the current situation that is experienced on both sides already motivated some action: Shortly before the study, a sales meeting took place for the American market that was supposed to clarify expectations. The decision was taken that the US sales office should be expanded. However, it cannot be determined yet whether the subsidiary's autonomy has changed.

5.2.5.3 Interpretation According to the Conceptual Framework

Autonomy. Headquarters representatives and the Mexican subsidiary management have differing ideas of and consequently differing expectations regarding the subsidiary's should-be autonomy in marketing and sales activities. Headquarters' idea of a subsidiary that implements the decisions taken by central sales and provides the requested market data is opposed by the subsidiary's idea of more autonomy and active involvement in marketing and sales processes. In their future role, subsidiary managers want to bring in and realize their own ideas as well. While headquarters tries to reach its goal by close supervision and control of the subsidiary, the subsidiary requests that headquarters withdraw from local management to some extent. The conflict that is perceived from the subsidiary's side is headquarters' continued involvement in local decisions. Thereby, headquarters prevents the subsidiary from more immediate customer and market development. At the same time, conflict is experienced on headquarters' side because the subsidiary does not comply with instructions. By this behaviour, the subsidiary does not realize the measure intended by headquarters. The conflict identified on both sides is related to the fact that headquarters inhibits the subsidiary from playing its envisioned should-be role and vice versa. This perception gap regarding the subsidiary's should-be autonomy is displayed in Table 12.

	Autonomy					
Unit	Perception		Role expectation	Implications		
	Dimension	Role behaviour		Conflictful behaviour	Outcome	Further implications
HQ	low degree of autonomy (marketing and sales)	subsidiary contributes little in the marketing and sales area	subsidiary carries out headquarters' instructions and provides market data	is too involved in local decisions ("micro-management") → throughput conflict	prevented: subsidiary managers taking decisions and bringing in their own ideas	decision to increase number of people in the sales office
S	low degree of autonomy (marketing and sales)	subsidiary contributes little in the marketing and sales area	subsidiary takes certain decisions concerning marketing and sales independently	does not comply with headquarters' instructions → throughput conflict	prevented: realization of measures intended by headquarters management	-

Table 12: Perceptions of the Mexican Subsidiary's Role and their Implications

5.2.6 China

5.2.6.1 Perceptions of the Role Dimensions

For several years, Autocomp's Chinese subsidiary was part of a joint unit with a subsidiary of another SBU of Company A. The two units not only shared the same building, but also many support functions. The top management of the unit reported to the other SBU's headquarters. One year before the study, the decision was made to separate the two subsidiaries in terms of location and to install a distinct general management function for each of the two subsidiaries. At the time of the study, the new managing director of Autocomp's Chinese subsidiary started his work at the plant's new location.

In terms of the subsidiary's overall role, headquarters' strategy for the subsidiary's role is not clear in every aspect. This concerns the subsidiary's current role as well as its should-be role (A7, A8). In terms of the subsidiary's current role, the separation of responsibilities for specific value chain activities does not seem finally determined and unambiguously communicated.[144] At the same time, no clear picture can be discerned of the prospected role the subsidiary should play in the future (A7, A8). Overall, the relationship between headquarters and the Chinese subsidiary seems to be the most conflictful case included in the present study. This picture is conveyed by the questionnaire results as well as by the

---

[144] Different respondents described several issues differently. This is taken as a sign that the situation is not entirely clear. For instance, one headquarters respondent stated that the direct market access takes place almost exclusively through the Chinese subsidiary (A6). Other headquarters respondents state that the Chinese subsidiary has hardly any direct contact with customers (A1).

interviews. However, at least according to the questionnaire results that are presented in Figure 36, perception gaps between headquarters and subsidiary concerning the subsidiary's role do not immediately appear as the major cause for the conflicts. In the interviews, the Chinese culture, the large geographical distance and the organization as combined unit were cited as main reasons for many of the conflicts. Headquarters' side hopes that the physical separation of the subsidiary from the other SBU and the installation of a general management level for the subsidiary will solve many conflicts. In particular, this step is supposed to make it easier to manage the subsidiary (A1). In the following, the identified perception gaps as well as their implications will be described.

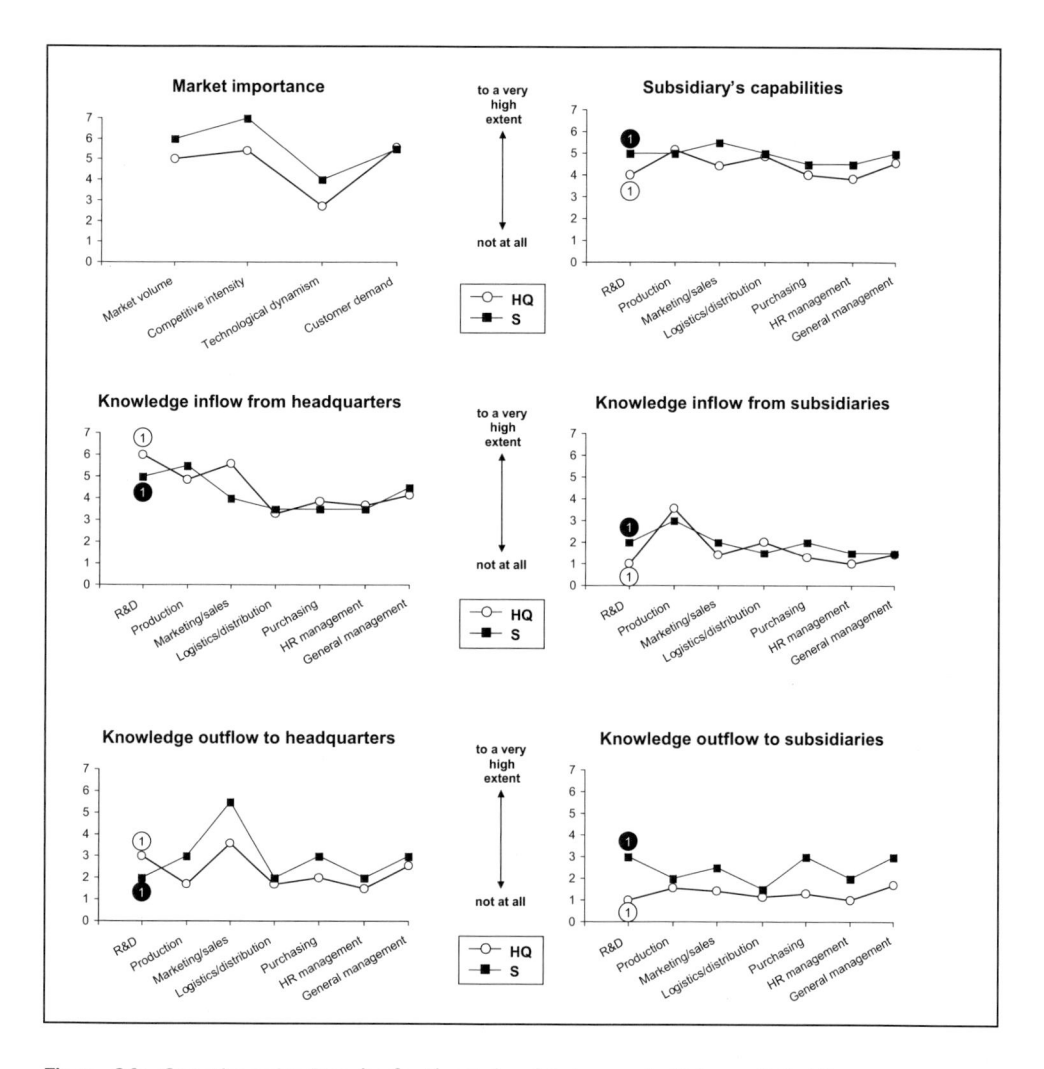

Figure 36: Questionnaire Results for the Role of Autocomp's Chinese Subsidiary

Market importance. According to the questionnaire results, the Chinese subsidiary judges the competitive intensity in its market higher than headquarters does. In comparison with the other subsidiaries' markets, headquarters respondents as well rate the competitive intensity of the Chinese market higher in the questionnaire but, on average, only by one scale point above the lowest rated subsidiary's market (Hungary). In the interviews, headquarters respondents attribute the Chinese subsidiary's market a relatively high competitive intensity so that no perception gap is identified between headquarters and subsidiary concerning competitive intensity (A3, A6).

Subsidiary's capabilities. The Chinese subsidiary's capabilities are judged similarly by headquarters and subsidiary respondents.

Knowledge inflow from headquarters. Headquarters and subsidiary respondents overall rate knowledge inflow from headquarters to the Chinese subsidiary similarly. There is one difference, however, concerning the knowledge inflow in the marketing and sales area: Headquarters respondents indicate a higher amount of knowledge transfer to the subsidiary than subsidiary respondents do. In this context, it has to be noted that the ratings of headquarters respondents are relatively consistent, whereas the value on the subsidiary's side consists of one very high and one very low rating. However, the perception gap is confirmed in the interviews. Furthermore, the interviews hint at a similar situation not only in the marketing and sales function but in other areas as well (A1, A8). The fact that headquarters respondents perceive more knowledge transfer to the subsidiary than the subsidiary representatives do is associated with different expectations regarding the type of knowledge (or information) that is required and that should be transferred (A8). Headquarters representatives are not fully aware of the subsidiary's expectations and lack understanding of why knowledge (or information) is needed in a specific form (A8).[145] Headquarters is convinced to communicate a lot and to transfer a considerable amount of knowledge (and information) to the subsidiary (A1, A6, A8); however, since the transferred knowledge does not match the subsidiary's expectations, it does not "arrive" there or may even be considered useless (A1, A8). Consequently, a perception gap is identified: Headquarters respondents perceive a higher amount of knowledge inflow to the subsidiary than the subsidiary representatives do.

Knowledge inflow from subsidiaries. Headquarters and subsidiary respondents judge the knowledge inflow from other subsidiaries to the Chinese subsidiary similarly. Overall, both sides' ratings of the knowledge inflow from other subsidiaries are rather low (A4). The highest rating concerns production knowledge, but even here, the Chinese subsidiary is not yet integrated in the subsidiaries' working group on production issues due to the large geographic distance (A4, A9).

Knowledge outflow to headquarters. The questionnaire results concerning the outflow of knowledge from the Chinese subsidiary resemble the results for inflow of knowledge from

---

[145] The same statement is true for the converse situation: On the subsidiary's side, there is no understanding of headquarters' requirements. This is relevant for knowledge flows from the subsidiary to headquarters.

headquarters to the Chinese subsidiary: The major difference appears in the marketing and sales function. The subsidiary's ratings indicate a higher outflow of knowledge than headquarters ratings do (A6). In the questionnaire, one headquarters respondent assesses the inflow of marketing and sales knowledge from the Chinese subsidiary at the same level as the subsidiary, while the remaining headquarters representatives judge the outflow lower. The difference seems to be associated with the differing expectations of headquarters and subsidiary respondents with regard to the type of knowledge to be sent (A1, A8). Headquarters respondents concede that the Chinese subsidiary transfers a lot of information on the Chinese market to headquarters (A1, A2, A3).[146] However, they are not fully content with the received information (or knowledge) in terms of type, amount, structure and processing (A1, A6). Furthermore, it is even considered difficult to receive satisfying and correct responses from the Chinese subsidiary when specific questions are being asked (A3). In summary, a perception gap is identified concerning the knowledge outflow from the subsidiary to headquarters in the marketing and sales area.

Knowledge outflow to subsidiaries. Knowledge outflow to other subsidiaries is generally judged very low from headquarters' side. This is associated with the large geographic distance and time difference between the Chinese subsidiary and the other subsidiaries (A4). The largest gap appears for knowledge outflow regarding R&D. However, the ratings stem from a single respondent on both sides. In the interviews, headquarters representatives state that the Chinese subsidiary does not carry out classical R&D activities but merely possesses a product management function that is only in the process of being built (A2, A6). The subsidiary's activities are confined to product adaptations and modifications for the Asian market (A6). In that context, some R&D related knowledge transfer from the product management may be noted in direction to headquarters, but not to other subsidiaries (A6).[147] Since the subsidiary management does not confirm the higher rating of R&D knowledge outflow to other subsidiaries in the interviews, no perception gap is identified in this area.

Culture. As was mentioned above, the relationship between Autocomp's headquarters and the Chinese subsidiary experiences frequent conflicts. Many of these conflicts seem to be rooted in the cultural differences between China and Germany. As the identified perception

---

[146] Headquarters respondents emphasize that this information should not be understood as knowledge (A3).
[147] This is due to various reasons: First, there is not much R&D in China at the moment. Second, the other subsidiaries have to comply with differing (mostly European) standards. Third, any transfer of technology from the Chinese subsidiary involves headquarters as a hub (A6).

gaps also seem to be associated with these cultural differences, a brief summary will be provided of repeatedly mentioned issues that appear to be relevant for the present case. (1) Different expectations lead to communication problems between headquarters and the subsidiary (A3, A4, A8). This is seen as one cause for the perception gaps concerning knowledge inflow to the subsidiary from headquarters and knowledge outflow from the subsidiary to headquarters (A8). (2) A second issue concerns the German thoroughness that does not match the Chinese mindset (A3). While Germans try to plan every detail in advance and check any eventuality, the Chinese managers are perceived as acting very quickly and also expecting faster reactions from headquarters (A3). (3) The lack of a clear leadership structure for the subsidiary in China collides with the hierarchical orientation of the Chinese culture (A2). It is difficult to communicate orders and instructions at the same hierarchical level; generally, instructions should be communicated from a higher level (A1). These three issues concern only a small selection of the cultural differences between Germans and Chinese. However, these aspects are actively mentioned by the respondents in the present study.[148]

5.2.6.2 Implications for the Headquarters-Subsidiary Relationship

Knowledge inflow from headquarters. Subsidiary representatives do not perceive a high level of knowledge inflow, since they cannot use much of the knowledge that is being transferred (A8). At the same time, headquarters representatives have the impression that a large amount of knowledge and information is being provided to the subsidiary that is not applied or implemented by the subsidiary. Since the subsidiary does not apply the knowledge that is transferred, it is judged incapable or unwilling to assume responsibility of the respective activities. This motivates headquarters to take back responsibilities that were initially provided to the subsidiary (A8). As the subsidiary does not fulfil many of headquarters' expectations in different areas, headquarters tries to control the subsidiary closely (A1, A4, A5). Headquarters managers mention, for instance, that processes at the subsidiary only function when headquarters representatives are physically present in China in order to ensure that the procedures are carried out correctly (A1, A3, A4). Instead of trying to develop the organization of the Chinese subsidiary (A6, A7) and to manage the subsidiary by setting objectives, processes and steps are prescribed in detail by headquarters (A8).

---

[148] For a more comprehensive comparison of the Chinese and the German culture, see, for instance, Thomas & Schenk 2001.

Although the Chinese employees and managers do not necessarily mind receiving detailed instructions (and thereby giving back responsibilities to headquarters) (A8), this situation is problematic. In order to give detailed instructions regarding processes at the subsidiary, a high level of knowledge of the local conditions is required that headquarters does not possess (A8).[149] Since headquarters does not create an understanding at the subsidiary why certain things are needed, instructions and requests are frequently perceived as arbitrary (A8). Furthermore, the large geographic distance makes close control of the subsidiary difficult (A8). Finally, this situation leads to dissatisfaction and frustration on both sides (A8).

Knowledge outflow to headquarters. Managers on the subsidiary's side as well have the impression to transfer a lot of knowledge (or information) to headquarters – particularly in the marketing and sales area, while headquarters management does not perceive this knowledge (or information) transfer. Headquarters representatives admit that expectations with which the subsidiary is faced are very high, although they are aware that the subsidiary hardly has the possibility to fulfil these expectations due to time restrictions and lack of expertise (A1). Nevertheless, in the time before the study, pressure on the sales department in China was high. Despite headquarters' decision to strengthen the marketing and sales function in the Chinese subsidiary through the new general manager and additional support staff, the manager principally responsible for marketing and sales in China left the company during the research project (A2).

5.2.6.3 Interpretation According to the Conceptual Framework

Knowledge inflow from headquarters. The subsidiary perceives less knowledge inflow than headquarters does. As was mentioned above, knowledge inflow to the subsidiary cannot be immediately interpreted as a role characteristic that corresponds to Katz and Kahn's framework. Nevertheless, the knowledge transfer to the Chinese subsidiary is associated with specific behavioural expectations that concern the subsidiary's behaviour. The Chinese subsidiary is expected to apply the transferred knowledge and thereby adjust its processes and activities to headquarters representatives' expectations. When the subsidiary does not fulfil these expectations, this behaviour is perceived as conflictful from headquarters' point of view. The outcome that is prevented from headquarters' perspective is the improvement and adjustment of the subsidiary's processes and activities.

---

[149] This lack of knowledge about the local conditions is partly attributed to the fact that headquarters representatives rarely visit the Chinese subsidiary (A6, A7).

Knowledge outflow to headquarters. The transfer of a considerable amount of knowledge to headquarters is conceived as part of the subsidiary's role. While the subsidiary respondents indicate that a large amount of knowledge is transferred to headquarters, headquarters representatives rate the outflow of knowledge from the subsidiary significantly lower. The outflow that reaches headquarters from the subsidiary does not fulfil the goal to inform headquarters sufficiently about important developments concerning customers in the Asian market. The subsidiary's behaviour does consequently not match headquarters management's expectations concerning this role dimension and is experienced as conflictful.

The described implications are summarized in Table 13.

	Knowledge inflow					
	Perception		Role expectation	Implications		
Unit	Dimension	Role behaviour		Conflictful behaviour	Outcome	Further implications
HQ	high knowledge inflow (marketing and sales)	subsidiary does not apply the knowledge that it receives from headquarters	subsidiary applies all knowledge that is transferred and adjusts its processes	-	-	takes back responsibilities from the subsidiary; dissatisfaction
S	low knowledge inflow (marketing and sales)	subsidiary applies all knowledge that it receives from headquarters	same as as-is role	does not apply the knowledge transferred by headquarters → throughput conflict	prevented: adjustment of activities and processes	is perceived as unwilling or incapable; dissatisfaction

	Knowledge outflow					
	Perception		Role expectation	Implications		
Unit	Dimension	Role behaviour		Conflictful behaviour	Outcome	Further implications
HQ	low knowledge outflow (marketing and sales)	subsidiary transfers little knowledge concerning customers and market developments	subsidiary transfers much knowledge concerning customers and market developments	-	-	cannot use the knowledge sent by the subsidiary; exerts a lot of pressure on the subsidiary; strengthens sales function through new general manager and support staff; dissatisfaction
S	high knowledge outflow (marketing and sales)	subsidiary transfers much knowledge concerning customers and market developments	same as as-is role	transfers knowledge in a form that does not match headquarters' expectations → output conflict	prevented: headquarters being up to date regarding customers and market developments	responsible sales manager leaves the company; dissatisfaction

Table 13: Perceptions of the Chinese Subsidiary's Role and their Implications

5.2.7 USA

5.2.7.1 Perceptions of the Role Dimensions

The US-American subsidiary of Construc was acquired in 1994.[150] As for all subsidiaries of Construc, a large extent of autonomy and independence are expected from the subsidiary by headquarters. The subsidiary carries out the full range of value chain activities. The results of the questionnaire comparing headquarters and subsidiary respondents' assessments of the four subsidiary role dimensions are presented in Figure 37.

---

[150] It should be noted that now the focus is on Construc, which is a division of Company B, while so far, the subsidiaries of Autocomp were described that belong to Company A.

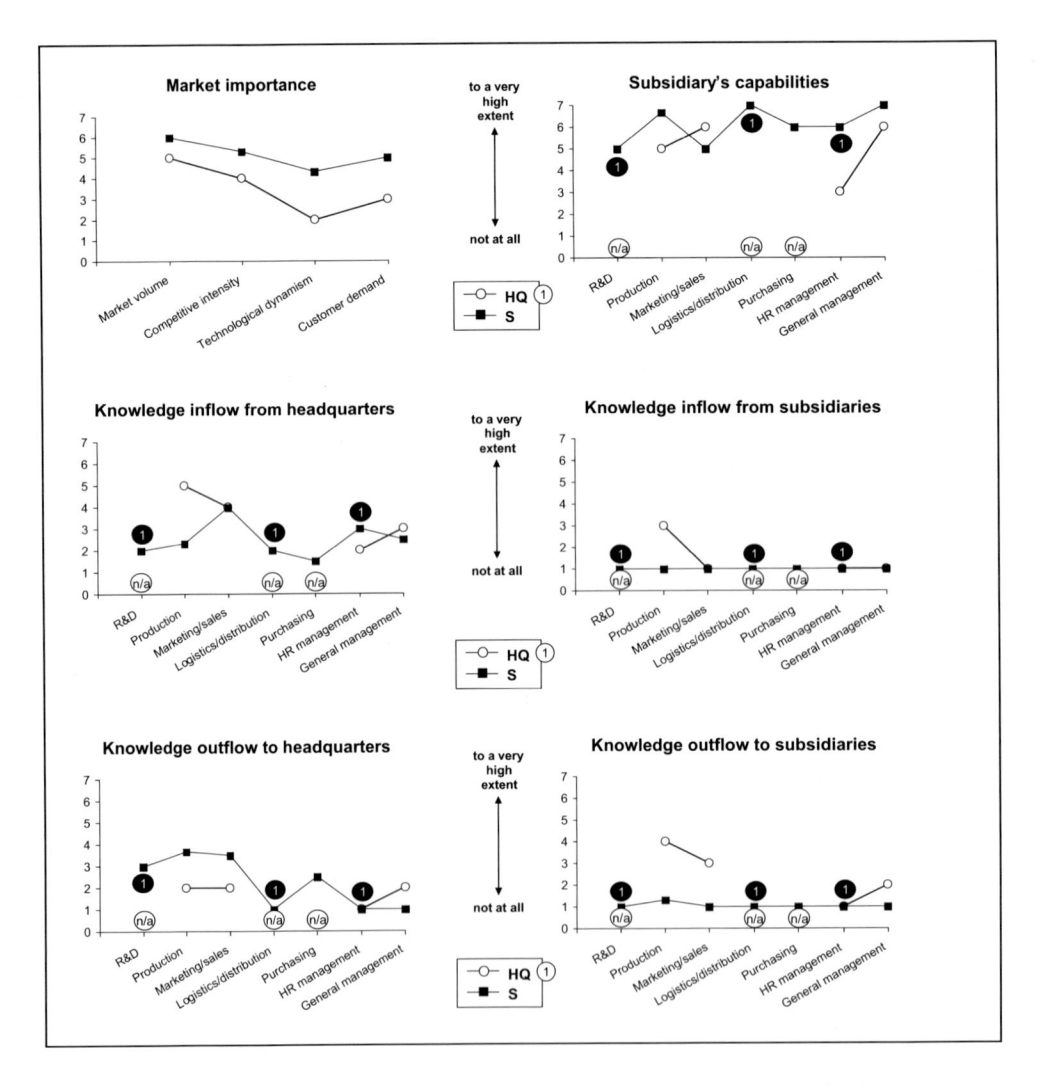

Figure 37: Questionnaire Results for the Role of Construc's US-American Subsidiary

Market importance. Subsidiary respondents consistently rate all aspects associated with market importance higher than headquarters does. From headquarters' perspective, the subsidiary's ratings are too high, particularly the assessment of technological dynamism (B2). Compared to other subsidiaries' markets, the market of the US-American subsidiary is known for traditional rather than innovative techniques (B2). In the interview, the subsidiary management confirms that the market does not require the subsidiary to apply a great variety of techniques (B3), so that no perception gap is identified.

Subsidiary's capabilities. (1) A perception gap concerning the subsidiary's production capabilities appears in the questionnaire results. Headquarters management rates the subsidiary's production capabilities lower than the subsidiary respondents. In the interviews, it is confirmed that from headquarters' perspective, there is a definite possibility to improve the subsidiary's production capabilities (B2).[151] In contrast, the subsidiary management emphasizes the subsidiary's extensive experience and perceives its production capabilities as very high (B3). Consequently, a perception gap is identified between headquarters and the US-American subsidiary concerning production capabilities. (2) Headquarters' side rates the subsidiary's HR management capabilities considerably lower than the subsidiary respondents do. The reason for headquarters' low rating is the fact that headquarters management considers it necessary to decrease the turnover rate of the subsidiary's commercial staff (B2). The high turnover rate is partly attributed to cultural reasons and the generally higher job mobility of US-Americans (B2). To some extent, however, it is seen as caused by the way human resources are managed at the subsidiary (B2). The subsidiary management is aware of headquarters management's expectations concerning a decrease in the staff turnover rate (B3). In contrast to headquarters management, however, the subsidiary management does not attribute the high turnover rate to the subsidiary's low HR management capabilities. Rather, it is entirely attributed to cultural factors that cannot be influenced by the subsidiary (B3). Therefore, a perception gap is identified regarding the subsidiary's HR management capabilities.

Knowledge inflow from headquarters. Headquarters rates the inflow of production knowledge from headquarters to the subsidiary higher than the subsidiary does. The headquarters management confirms the high rating in the interview and relates it to the perceived need to improve the subsidiary's production capabilities (B2). The subsidiary's rating is interpreted as signifying the opinion that knowledge transfer from headquarters concerning production is not needed (B2). So far, the subsidiary has not actively inquired about production knowledge at headquarters; rather the transferred knowledge was "imposed upon" the subsidiary (B2). From the subsidiary's side, it is stated that headquarters provides a large amount of knowledge in an electronic database that, however, has been accessible to the subsidiary only for a short time (B3). At the same time, the knowledge that is transferred to the subsidiary in case the subsidiary needs support can help the subsidiary only in a few instances (B3). Overall, the subsidiary management perceives considerably less

---

[151] At the same time, headquarters management emphasizes that the subsidiary's performance is satisfying. Nevertheless, headquarters management is convinced that productivity could still be higher (B2).

knowledge inflow than is indicated by headquarters (B3).[152] Consequently, a perception gap is identified concerning the inflow of production knowledge from headquarters to the subsidiary.

Knowledge inflow from subsidiaries. Headquarters' questionnaire rating of knowledge inflow to the US-American subsidiary from other subsidiaries is higher than the subsidiary's rating. In the interview, the subsidiary management confirms the low rating (B3), while the headquarters management also admits that the rating could be lower (B2). Until one year before, the US-American subsidiary had been the only unit representing Construc on the American continent. Now, two further subsidiaries were established, and it is expected that they will build a network and exchange knowledge in the near future (B2). No perception gap exists between headquarters and the subsidiary regarding the knowledge inflow from other subsidiaries to the US-American subsidiary.

Knowledge outflow to headquarters. The subsidiary rates its knowledge outflow to headquarters higher than headquarters does in the areas of production and marketing and sales. From headquarters' perspective, the subsidiary's ratings are too high (B2). The subsidiary generally does not transfer much knowledge to headquarters; whenever knowledge is transferred, the outflow is enhanced and mediated by headquarters (B2). This perspective is indirectly confirmed by the subsidiary's side, as the subsidiary management concedes that their knowledge is available to those who actively retrieve it from the subsidiary (B3). Therefore, no perception gap exists concerning knowledge outflow to headquarters.

Knowledge outflow to subsidiaries. Regarding knowledge outflow to other subsidiaries, headquarters rates the subsidiary's contribution concerning production and marketing and sales higher than the subsidiary does. In the interview, however, the headquarters management concedes that a lower rating is justified for direct transfer since here as well the knowledge transfer is generally mediated by headquarters (B2). The subsidiary management confirms the low rating, so that no perception gap concerning knowledge outflow to other subsidiaries is identified (B3).

---

[152] This may partly be related to the fact that the subsidiary representatives would prefer direct personal communication of knowledge (B3).

5.2.7.2 Implications for the Headquarters-Subsidiary Relationship

Subsidiary's capabilities. (1) The subsidiary management judges the subsidiary's production capabilities higher than headquarters' side does. Its lower estimation of the subsidiary's production capabilities prompted headquarters to put energy in the development of these capabilities (B2). Although some progress has been made, it turned out difficult for headquarters to initiate improvements in the subsidiary's production process (B2). As the responsible people at the subsidiary are convinced of their high capabilities and their extensive experience, they initially showed reactance and resisted many of headquarters' attempts to transfer knowledge (B2, B3). They also refused to use new machinery that was developed by Company B (B2). Headquarters reacted to that situation by installing an expatriate manager as vice president of the subsidiary who is now responsible for increasing productivity (B2). (2) Since headquarters management judges the subsidiary's HR management capabilities lower than the subsidiary representatives, headquarters managers perceive a need to improve the subsidiary's capabilities in this area (B2). Many discussions have taken place between headquarters and subsidiary representatives concerning this issue (B2, B3). As the situation at the subsidiary did not improve in the way headquarters management expected, headquarters initiated a change in leadership of the HR management function in the commercial area at the US-American subsidiary (B2). Although the subsidiary's HR department now puts considerable effort in the decrease of the staff turnover rate, the effect of these efforts cannot be judged yet (B2, B3).

Knowledge inflow from headquarters. Headquarters respondents' higher perception of knowledge inflow to the subsidiary compared to subsidiary managers is reflected by the fact that the knowledge that is transferred by headquarters is not necessarily applied by the subsidiary (B2). According to the subsidiary's point of view, those knowledge transfers from headquarters that are beneficial for the subsidiary are applied. From headquarters' perspective, however, processes at the subsidiary are not adjusted to headquarters management's expectations.

5.2.7.3 Interpretation According to the Conceptual Framework

Subsidiary's capabilities. Capabilities can be associated with Katz and Kahn's role definition as the subsidiary's ability to show certain behavioural patterns. In the present case, from headquarters management's perspective, the subsidiary does not possess the necessary capabilities and therefore does not show the behaviour patterns that are expected by headquarters management. In their opinion, the low capabilities surface in the subsidiary's missing ability to carry out production and HR management activities as expected. Consequently, headquarters attempts to initiate improvements at the subsidiary in order to reach a higher capability level. Headquarters management expects the subsidiary to appreciate this support and follow headquarters' recommendations. The subsidiary managers, however, perceive the subsidiary's capabilities to be higher and see no need to improve the subsidiary's processes. The fact that the subsidiary resists headquarters' improvement efforts and does not show the will to advance the organization in these respects is experienced as conflict from headquarters' perspective. The subsidiary's resistance prevents the processes from being improved quickly.

Knowledge inflow from headquarters. As in the case involving Autocomp's Chinese subsidiary, the inflow of production knowledge from headquarters to the US-American subsidiary is intended to change the processes at the subsidiary. However, the subsidiary representatives do not perceive the same amount of knowledge inflow from headquarters and the subsidiary does not apply the transferred knowledge. The subsidiary's refusal or failure to apply the transferred knowledge is perceived as conflict from headquarters' point of view.[153]

The implications of the perception gaps between headquarters and the US-American subsidiary are presented in Table 14.

---

[153] Both the case involving Autocomp's Chinese subsidiary and the case involving Construc's US-American subsidiary reveal a perception gap regarding knowledge inflow from headquarters. Headquarters managers' intentions with this knowledge transfer are similar in both cases as are the subsidiaries' failures to apply the knowledge. However, the reasons for the emergence of the perception gaps appear to differ. While the Chinese subsidiary does not perceive the transferred knowledge because it is not delivered in the necessary form, the US-American subsidiary seems to neglect or disregard the knowledge transfer because it is not considered necessary.

Capabilities						
Unit	Perception		Role expectation	Implications		
	Dimension	Role behaviour		Conflictful behaviour	Outcome	Further implications
HQ	low capabilities (production, HR management)	production and HR management processes at the subsidiary are less than ideal	subsidiary carries out high quality production and HR management processes	-	-	expatriate manager with responsibility to increase productivity is placed at the subsidiary; manager responsible for HR management of commercial staff is replaced
S	high capabilities (production, HR management)	subsidiary carries out high quality production and HR management processes	same as as-is role	resists improvements in production and HR management processes → throughput conflict	prevented: increase in productivity and decrease of staff turnover rate	-

Knowledge inflow						
Unit	Perception		Role expectation	Implications		
	Dimension	Role behaviour		Conflictful behaviour	Outcome	Further implications
HQ	high knowledge inflow (production)	subsidiary does not apply the knowledge that it receives from headquarters	subsidiary applies all knowledge that is transferred and improves its processes	-	-	expatriate manager with responsibility to increase productivity is placed at the subsidiary
S	low knowledge inflow (production)	subsidiary applies the knowledge that it receives from headquarters whenever necessary	same as as-is role	resists improvements in production processes → throughput conflict	prevented: increase in productivity	

Table 14: Perceptions of the US-American Subsidiary's Role and their Implications

5.3 Perception Gaps Concerning the Subsidiary's Role

5.3.1 Subsidiary Role Dimensions in the Present Study

5.3.1.1 Overview

So far, the cases analyzed for the present study have been described separately. In the following, cross-sections of these cases will be examined along the different subsidiary role dimensions. A priori, the four dimensions of market importance, subsidiary's capabilities, knowledge inflow and knowledge outflow were selected in order to describe the subsidiary's role within the MNC. These dimensions are frequently considered in the IB literature. In the empirical study, the dimensions of product scope, autonomy and involvement in value chain activities emerged as relevant for the examined cases, and they were considered as well. In the conceptual part of this study, it was outlined that in the present context, subsidiary roles are understood as patterns of behaviours that are related to a specific position within the MNC according to Katz and Kahn (Kahn & Quinn 1970, p. 52; Katz & Kahn 1978, p. 188). It is apparent that not all role dimensions taken into account in the present study immediately match this definition (3.2.2). Consequently, in the following, the relation between each of the seven role dimensions and the definition of roles as patterns of behaviour will be discussed in the light of the empirical findings (5.3.1.2). Since the analysis focused on perception gaps between the subsidiary and headquarters, the review will as well emphasize those instances. Starting with the definition of the respective dimension, it will be determined to what extent the dimension corresponds to the understanding of roles as patterns of behaviour. Role dimensions that match the proposed role concept can be assumed to entail behavioural expectations with which the subsidiary is confronted. Dimensions that do not correspond to this concept are not necessarily associated with behavioural expectations, but may as well be indirectly related to such expectations. The behavioural expectations related to each role dimension will be determined and their appearance in the analyzed cases will be examined. Finally, the question will be addressed of whether the role concept proposed in the present study is appropriate for analyzing the roles of subsidiaries in MNCs (5.3.1.3).

5.3.1.2 Conceptual and Empirical Review of the Individual Dimensions

Market importance. According to Bartlett and Ghoshal, an important market is defined as possessing the four characteristics of high market volume, competitive intensity, customer demand and technological dynamism (Bartlett & Ghoshal 1986, p. 90). Obviously, these four features describe the environment in which the subsidiary is active rather than the subsidiary itself. Since they are not directly associated with the subsidiary's behaviour, a specific degree of any of the four characteristics does not automatically refer to a particular pattern of behaviour. Consequently, the dimension market importance does not correspond to the role concept according to Katz and Kahn. Nevertheless, it was argued above that the importance of a subsidiary's market might influence the behavioural expectations directed at the subsidiary in various ways, since headquarters may expect the subsidiary to reach specific goals in that market (3.3.3.2). However, the association of these expectations with the dimension is not straightforward, but also depends on other factors, such as the overall subsidiary strategy. In the present study, perception gaps regarding the importance of the subsidiary's market are identified in the cases involving the Hungarian and the Turkish subsidiaries. In the case involving the Hungarian subsidiary, neither headquarters nor the subsidiary respondents describe specific expectations concerning the subsidiary's behaviour that are based on the importance of the subsidiary's market. In the case involving the Turkish subsidiary, behavioural expectations are described in relation to the perception of market importance: The Turkish subsidiary rates market importance higher than headquarters and at the same time, considers a high level of activity and fast reactions in the market more essential than headquarters does. However, it is not entirely clear whether these expectations can be distinctly attributed to the perception of market importance. Consequently, it seems difficult to consider the dimension market importance as a role characteristic in Katz and Kahn's terms. This is due to the lack of conceptual fit and the unclear behavioural expectations that are related to the dimension.

Subsidiary's capabilities. Since Bartlett and Ghoshal do not provide a clear definition for their dimension subsidiary capabilities, the definition provided by Day is referred to which describes capabilities as "complex bundles of skills and accumulated knowledge, exercised through organizational processes that enable firms to coordinate activities and make use of their assets" (Day 1994, p. 38). Although capabilities – as complex bundles of skills and knowledge – do not directly represent behaviour, they function as prerequisites that permit the subsidiary to show certain behaviour patterns. High capabilities may be associated with high expectations concerning the quality of the activities carried out, while low capabilities can be expected to result in low quality. The case involving Construc's US-American subsidiary is the only case in which a perception gap concerning the subsidiary's capabilities emerges. In this case, headquarters associates the relatively low quality of the subsidiary's production and HR management activities with relatively low capabilities in these areas. The subsidiary management judges the subsidiary's capabilities in both areas high and, accordingly, it assumes that the quality of its activities and processes in HR management and production is high as well. The perception of the subsidiary's capabilities is therefore closely connected to behavioural expectations concerning the subsidiary's activities. Despite the fact that capabilities are related to the quality of the subsidiary's behaviour rather than the behaviour as such, they have a clear connection with the behaviour pattern shown by the subsidiary.

Knowledge inflow. Gupta and Govindarajan define knowledge inflow as "transfer of either expertise (e.g., skills and capabilities) or external market data of strategic value" (Gupta & Govindarajan 1991, p. 773) from headquarters or other organizational units to the focal subsidiary. Rather than the subsidiary's behaviour, the dimension knowledge inflow describes the behaviour that is shown by other units as they transfer knowledge to the focal subsidiary. Consequently, the dimension does not correspond to the proposed role concept. Nevertheless, an indirect relation to the subsidiary's behaviour pattern can be constructed when the goals of knowledge transfers to a unit are taken into account: The expectations with which the receiving subsidiary is confronted can be assumed to concern the application of the transferred knowledge in the subsidiary's activities and processes (cp. 3.2.2). A perception gap regarding the role dimension knowledge inflow is identified in three of the analyzed cases and in two of them, the outlined relationship is observed. No behavioural expectations are mentioned in relation to the knowledge transfer from headquarters to Autocomp's Turkish subsidiary. In the cases involving Autocomp's Chinese subsidiary and Construc's US-American subsidiary, knowledge is transferred from headquarters to the subsidiary with the intention to improve the processes at the subsidiary or to adjust them to headquarters representatives' expectations. Rather than defining it as part of the subsidiary's role, knowledge transfer to a subsidiary may be seen as a means to bring the subsidiary closer to the role that is envisioned for it. In the relationship between Construc's headquarters and the US-American subsidiary, the knowledge transfer aims at improving the subsidiary's capabilities and thereby enabling it to play the role that it is intended to play. In the case involving Autocomp's Chinese subsidiary, the knowledge transfer is supposed to adjust the subsidiary's processes and the activities that are carried out by the subsidiary to headquarters management's conception of these activities and processes. Consequently, an indirect connection between knowledge inflow and expectations regarding the subsidiary's behaviour can be logically established and is observed in the analyzed cases. Nevertheless, knowledge inflow does not appear to be an appropriate characteristic that describes the subsidiary's role when the proposed role concept is adhered to.

Knowledge outflow. Representing the reverse process compared to knowledge inflow, knowledge outflow is defined as transfer of knowledge from the focal subsidiary to other organizational units. Knowledge outflow is the first of the portrayed dimensions that directly corresponds to the role concept by Katz and Kahn, as it describes the subsidiary's behaviour in terms of the provision of knowledge to other units. When the subsidiary's role implies a high degree of knowledge transfer to other units, the behavioural expectations that the subsidiary encounters directly concern this knowledge transfer. Perception gaps regarding knowledge outflow are identified in three of the presented cases. In the cases involving Autocomp's Polish and Turkish subsidiaries, headquarters management does not perceive much knowledge outflow. At the same time, however, headquarters representatives do not consider knowledge outflow in the respective areas as part of the subsidiaries' roles and, accordingly, do not expect more knowledge outflow than is perceived. In the relationship between Autocomp's headquarters and the Chinese subsidiary, the situation is different: Headquarters management does not perceive much knowledge outflow either, but considers it part of the subsidiary's role to provide a considerable amount of knowledge to headquarters. Consequently, headquarters managers' expectations regarding the knowledge outflow from the Chinese subsidiary and thereby the fulfilment of its role are disappointed. The dimension knowledge outflow corresponds to the role concept based on Katz and Kahn and can be easily associated with behavioural expectations with which members of the subsidiary's role set confront the subsidiary.[154]

Product scope. The dimension product scope is defined as the range of products that are manufactured at the subsidiary (cp. White & Poynter 1984, p. 59). As it describes the subsidiary's behaviour in terms of production, this dimension corresponds to the proposed role concept. The relationship of the dimension with behavioural expectations is obvious: The subsidiary is expected to produce the range of products that belong to its product scope. All subsidiaries analyzed in the present study fulfil headquarters representatives' behavioural expectations in this respect. This finding is not surprising since in both firms, the production of each product requires specific machinery at the subsidiary's site and thereby an investment that has to be approved by headquarters at least. Consequently, the subsidiaries' current role in terms of product scope can be controlled by headquarters and is obvious to both sides so that a perception gap is rather unlikely.[155]

---

[154] In none of the cases, the knowledge inflow from, or outflow to, other subsidiaries seems to be relevant, although such knowledge flows do exist in certain areas and between several subsidiaries. For instance, there are perception gaps concerning the knowledge outflow from the subsidiary to other subsidiaries in the cases of the Turkish and the Polish subsidiary. However, in neither of the cases does the perception gap show any implications. The reason for this finding may be that the headquarters-subsidiary relationship rather than the subsidiary-subsidiary relationship was in the focus of the present study. Although a study that considers perception gaps between sister subsidiaries is also conceivable, this is not the focus of the present study. Another general issue regarding headquarters' ratings of knowledge exchange between subsidiaries is the fact that headquarters respondents may not be aware of the communication that takes place between the subsidiaries (A1, A3, A4, A6).

[155] There are, however, disagreements concerning the subsidiary's should-be product scope in the cases involving the Hungarian and the Turkish subsidiaries.

Involvement in value chain activities. The subsidiary's involvement in value chain activities is defined as referring to the range of value chain activities in which the subsidiary is involved and the extent to which it is involved. This definition describes the subsidiary's activities in relation to different functions and thereby is directly related to the subsidiary's behaviour. If the subsidiary's role includes a certain degree of involvement in a specific value chain function, headquarters representatives will expect the subsidiary to show activities in that field that match a particular pattern. Consequently, the dimension corresponds to the role concept by Katz and Kahn. In one of the analyzed cases, headquarters and subsidiary managers perceive the subsidiary's involvement in value chain activities differently.[156] The management of the Hungarian subsidiary perceives a higher degree of involvement in some value chain activities than headquarters management does. Both headquarters and the subsidiary act according to their managers' role perception: The Hungarian subsidiary attempts to initiate changes in the finance function and demands the acknowledgement of its involvement in marketing and sales activities by headquarters. Headquarters managers, perceiving no involvement of the subsidiary in the two functions, do not expect the subsidiary to show activities in these areas and do not pay attention to the activities that are carried out by the subsidiary. The dimension involvement in value chain activities can be interpreted as a characteristic of the subsidiary's role according to Katz and Kahn.

Autonomy. As introduced in 5.1.2, the present study understands autonomy as "the constrained freedom or independence available to or acquired by a subsidiary, which enables it to take certain decisions on its own behalf" (Young & Tavares 2004, p. 228). As such, it refers to the subsidiary's behaviour in terms of decision making. This reference to the subsidiary's behaviour is in line with the proposed role concept. A certain idea concerning the subsidiary's decision making behaviour is directly associated with behavioural expectations in this respect. The dimension autonomy plays a role in the case involving the Turkish subsidiary.[157] The subsidiary representatives perceive a higher degree of autonomy than headquarters representatives do and, consequently, assume a higher degree of freedom to take certain decisions independently. Headquarters managers, on the other hand, do not expect the subsidiary to engage in independent decision making behaviour. The dimension autonomy as characteristic of the subsidiary's role corresponds to the proposed role concept,

---

[156] Additionally, both in the case involving the Hungarian subsidiary and the case involving the Turkish subsidiary, a perception gap is identified regarding the subsidiary's should-be involvement in value chain activities.

[157] In the case involving the Mexican subsidiary, a perception gap is identified concerning the subsidiary's should-be autonomy.

since it is directly associated with the subsidiary's behaviour pattern and with behavioural expectations with which the subsidiary is confronted.

An overview of the described dimensions is provided in Table 15. For each dimension, the review, first, includes the definition. Second, it states to what extent the dimension corresponds to the theoretically determined role concept. (Does it describe the subsidiary's behaviour or something else? If it does not fully correspond to the role definition, is it at least associated with the subsidiary's behaviour or not?) Third, it indicates in what way the dimension is related to behavioural expectations. Finally, the expectations that are actually observed in the analyzed cases are described.

Dimension	Definition	Correspondence to the role concept (behaviour pattern)	Direct/indirect relation to behavioural expectations	Expectations observed in the present cases (in relation to perception gaps)
Market importance	"A large market is obviously important, and so is a competitor's home market or a market that is particularly sophisticated or technologically advanced" (Bartlett & Ghoshal 1986, p. 90)	• Describes characteristics of the market • No association with the subsidiary's behaviour pattern	May influence the goals that a subsidiary should fulfil and thereby determine the behavioural expectations with which a subsidiary is confronted	• Hungary: no behavioural expectations explicated • Turkey: subsidiary management considers much activity and high level effort necessary
Subsidiary's capabilities	"Complex bundles of skills and accumulated knowledge, exercised through organizational processes that enable firms to coordinate activities and make use of their assets" (Day 1994, p. 38)	• Provide the prerequisite for the subsidiary to show certain behaviour patterns • Association with the subsidiary's behaviour pattern	High/low capabilities are associated with high/low expectations concerning the quality of activities and processes	• USA: (relatively) low quality processes are associated with (relatively) low capabilities
Knowledge inflow	"Transfer of either expertise (e.g., skills and capabilities) or external market data of strategic value" (Gupta & Govindarajan 1991, p. 773) from other organizational units to the focal subsidiary	• Describes the behaviour pattern of other units • No association with the subsidiary's behaviour pattern	The subsidiary may be expected to apply the transferred knowledge in order to improve or adapt its activities and processes	• Turkey: no behavioural expectations explicated • China: subsidiary is expected to improve and adapt processes • USA: subsidiary is expected to improve and adapt processes
Knowledge outflow	"Transfer of either expertise (e.g., skills and capabilities) or external market data of strategic value" (Gupta & Govindarajan 1991, p. 773) from the focal subsidiary to other organizational units	• Describes the subsidiary's behaviour in terms of its knowledge transfer to other units • Corresponds to the role concept	Behavioural expectations directly concern the knowledge outflow from the subsidiary	• Poland: no behavioural expectations explicated • Turkey: no behavioural expectations explicated • China: high knowledge outflow expected
Product scope	"Latitude exercised by a subsidiary's business with regard to product line extensions and new product areas" (White & Poynter 1984, p. 59)	• Describes the subsidiary's behaviour in terms of production • Corresponds to the role concept	Behavioural expectations directly concern the subsidiary's production activities	• Hungary: subsidiary is expected to produce a narrow product range • Turkey: subsidiary is expected to produce a narrow product range

Involvement in value chain activities	Range of value chain activities in which the subsidiary is involved and the extent to which it is involved (includes, e.g., the incorporation of feedback from the subsidiary into a function)	• Describes the subsidiary's behaviour in terms of its activities in various functions • Corresponds to the role concept	Behavioural expectations directly concern the subsidiary's activities in the respective functions	• Hungary: subsidiary management expects acknowledgement of its activities in marketing and sales and finance • Hungary: subsidiary is not expected to be involved in purchasing • Turkey: subsidiary is not expected to be involved in all sales negotiations
Autonomy	"The constrained freedom or independence available to or acquired by a subsidiary, which enables it to take certain decisions on its own behalf" (Young & Tavares 2004, p. 228)	• Describes the subsidiary's behaviour in terms of decision making • Association with the subsidiary's behaviour pattern	High/low autonomy is associated with independent/dependent decision making behaviour	• Turkey: subsidiary is not expected to make decisions independently • Mexico: subsidiary not expected to make decisions independently

Table 15: Subsidiary Role Dimensions in the Present Study

5.3.1.3 Critical Reflection on the Proposed Subsidiary Role Concept

It was outlined above to what extent and how it is possible to associate the analyzed subsidiary role dimensions with Katz and Kahn's definition of roles. The analysis confirms that there are considerable differences between the subsidiary role dimensions taken into account in the IB literature and Katz and Kahn's role concept. In the IB literature, any characteristic that may vary between different subsidiaries seems to be considered a potential "subsidiary role dimension". In the present study, for instance, the dimension market importance that describes the environment in which the subsidiary is active and the dimension knowledge inflow that describes the behaviour of other units interacting with the subsidiary are included. The role theoretical concept proposed in the present study, in contrast, defines roles relatively narrowly as patterns of behaviour.

The analysis presented above addresses the relationship between the proposed role concept and the roles that subsidiaries play in MNCs against the background of the empirical findings of the present study. In general, it seems possible to define the relationship between headquarters and the subsidiary as a role relationship. Figure 38 (this figure was introduced in 3.1.3.2 and was developed further here) displays the different elements of a role relationship in the context of a role episode from a role theoretical perspective. In the following, it will be outlined whether these elements of a role relationship can be found in the headquarters-subsidiary relationships described in the empirical findings: The two main actors in the role episode are the role senders and the focal person. In the present study, headquarters is defined as a member of the role set and the chief role sender, while the focal subsidiary represents the focal person.

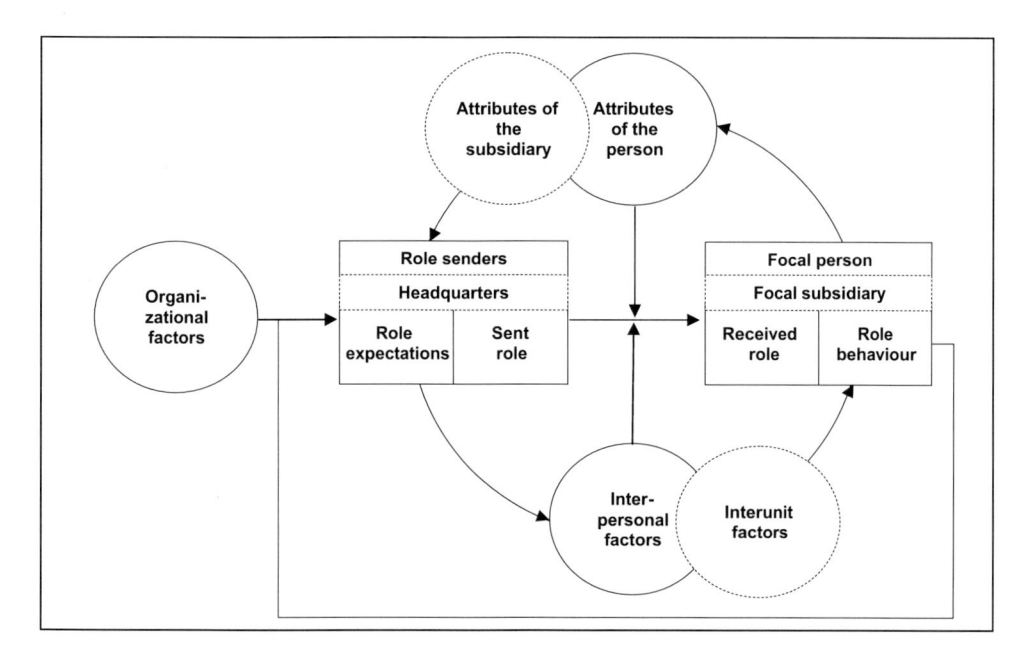

Figure 38: Factors Involved in a Role Episode between Headquarters and Subsidiary
Source: Adapted from Katz & Kahn 1978, p. 196.

Headquarters' side will be taken into account first. (1) Headquarters management holds certain expectations concerning the subsidiary's role behaviour. In the empirical findings of the present study, these expectations concern, for example, a certain amount of knowledge being sent by the subsidiary, the subsidiary not making decisions independently or the production of a specific range of products by the subsidiary. (2) These behavioural expectations are – or can be – sent to the subsidiary. For instance, the expectations referring to the production of a certain product scope are clearly determined and communicated to the subsidiaries in all of the presented cases. However, the expectations concerning the transfer of knowledge from the subsidiary to headquarters do not seem to be as unmistakable. In the case involving the Chinese subsidiary, one respondent states that the expectations in this respect were never clarified, although this would be necessary to create common understanding. Finally, headquarters representatives' expectations concerning the Turkish subsidiary's autonomy following the acquisition were not determined unambiguously. Following several conflictful episodes, the expectations were clarified one more time.

(3) Now, the subsidiary as role bearer will be considered. Although the question of how the subsidiary's role perception emerges is not in the study's focus, communication of a certain role by headquarters surfaces as an important factor. Two examples illustrate this assumption: In the case involving the Polish subsidiary, headquarters and the subsidiary managers' perceptions of the subsidiary's role are the most similar in any headquarters-subsidiary relationship analyzed. At the same time, respondents on both sides emphasize that this can be attributed to the good and frequent communication between headquarters and the subsidiary, which leaves hardly any room for misunderstandings of the subsidiary's role. In the cases involving the Hungarian and the Turkish subsidiary, headquarters representatives' role perception in terms of the subsidiary's product scope is implicitly communicated. By rejecting the subsidiaries' proposals for extensions of their product portfolios, headquarters reinforces that the subsidiaries' roles are seen as producing narrow product ranges. (4) The analysis presented above shows that the subsidiary acts according to its managers' role perception. For instance, the representatives of the Hungarian subsidiary perceive the subsidiary as being involved in finance issues and consequently present suggestions for improvement in that field to headquarters. Managers at the US-American subsidiary perceive the subsidiary as being very capable in production issues and consequently design processes and carry out activities as they are used to without considering suggestions for improvement provided by headquarters.

To summarize, the empirical findings concerning the headquarters-subsidiary relationships examined in the present study correspond to the theoretical elements of a role relationship. This finding confirms that the proposed role concept based on Katz and Kahn can be applied to the roles of subsidiaries in MNCs. In the following, a definition of subsidiary roles in line with Katz and Kahn's model is assumed and perception gaps concerning the seven dimensions will be examined based on this prerequisite.

5.3.2 Perception Gaps in the Present Study

5.3.2.1 Overview

In the following, the perception gaps identified in the present study will be reviewed. A common conceptual structure will be presented which allows comparing the different occurrences of perception gaps with each other. On the one hand, perception gaps regarding the subsidiary's current role (as-is role) can be differentiated from perception gaps concerning the subsidiary's should-be role. On the other hand, expectations concerning the subsidiary's role behaviour can be used to further specify perception gaps regarding the subsidiary's current role. Finally, the usage of the concept perception gap in the present study will be critically reviewed.

5.3.2.2 Conceptual Structure of the Identified Perception Gaps

A subsidiary's role can be viewed from different perspectives. In the present study, the focus is on headquarters' and the subsidiary's perspective on this role. First, headquarters and subsidiary managers perceive the subsidiary's current role behaviour (as-is role) in a certain way. Second, they have specific expectations concerning how the subsidiary should enact its role. This expected role behaviour is termed the subsidiary's should-be role. Headquarters and subsidiary managers' perceptions and expectations regarding the subsidiary's role behaviour may be contrasted in a two-by-two matrix as displayed in Figure 39. In the present study, perception gaps are defined as differing perceptions on headquarters' and the subsidiary's side concerning the role which the subsidiary currently plays (as-is role; 2.3.3). In Figure 39, a perception gap according to this definition is reflected by a difference between the top and the bottom row in the left column of the matrix. In contrast, a gap in the right column of the matrix can be interpreted as a gap regarding the subsidiary's should-be role. Although such a gap is also conceivable, it is not the primary interest of the present study.

	Perceived role behaviour	Expected role behaviour	① If headquarters and subsidiary managers perceive the role behaviour shown by the subsidiary differently, a perception gap concerning the subsidiary's current role (as-is role) is observed. The study's focus is on this type of perception gap.	② If headquarters and subsidiary managers have different expectations regarding the role behaviour that the subsidiary should show, this may be interpreted as a gap concerning the subsidiary's should-be role. This type of gap is not the primary focus of the present study.
Head-quarters	↕ ①	↕ ②		
Sub-sidiary				

Figure 39: Perceived and Expected Role Behaviour[158]

---

[158] The labels "headquarters" and subsidiary" determine which perspective on the subsidiary's role behaviour is referred to in the respective row. The columns distinguish between the role behaviour that is actually perceived (as-is role) and the role behaviour that is expected (should-be role). It should be emphasized that the figure exclusively looks at the *subsidiary's* behaviour (4.1.3).

By definition, perception gaps are characterized by a gap between headquarters and subsidiary managers' perceptions of the role behaviour currently shown by the subsidiary. While the definition thereby determines a necessary precondition regarding headquarters and subsidiary managers' *perceptions* (left column in Figure 39), it does not refer to headquarters and subsidiary managers' *expectations* (right column in Figure 39). However, since the relationship between perceptions and expectations may play an important role for the implications of perception gaps, the expectations are also considered in the following. Although the gap concerning the perceived role behaviour is fixed, the expected role behaviour still allows for different constellations of the entire matrix. For instance, the role behaviour that is expected by either headquarters or subsidiary managers may correspond to the role behaviour which they perceive; or their expectations regarding the subsidiary's role behaviour may differ from their perceptions. Figure 40 displays a variety of the possible constellations. The role behaviour perceived by headquarters managers is represented by the letter X, while Q is used as a symbol for the role behaviour perceived by subsidiary managers. For the expected role behaviour, the letters X and Q signify expectations which correspond to the behaviour perceived by headquarters or subsidiary managers, while E stands for expectations that differ from the behaviour perceived by either headquarters or subsidiary managers.[159]

A	Perceived role behaviour	Expected role behaviour		B	Perceived role behaviour	Expected role behaviour		C	Perceived role behaviour	Expected role behaviour
Head-quarters	X	X		Head-quarters	X	Q		Head-quarters	X	Q
Sub-sidiary	Q	Q		Sub-sidiary	Q	X		Sub-sidiary	Q	Q

D	Perceived role behaviour	Expected role behaviour		E	Perceived role behaviour	Expected role behaviour		F	Perceived role behaviour	Expected role behaviour
Head-quarters	X	X		Head-quarters	X	X		Head-quarters	X	E
Sub-sidiary	Q	X		Sub-sidiary	Q	E		Sub-sidiary	Q	Q

Figure 40: Constellations of Perception Gaps

---

[159] The three letters are chosen because their differing shapes make it easy to distinguish them.

In the empirical study, perception gaps regarding the subsidiary's current role are identified in five of the six included cases. In the following, the different instances of perception gaps are associated with the constellations introduced in Figure 40.[160] (A) Situation A occurs in the case involving the Polish and the Turkish subsidiaries. Although a perception gap exists regarding the subsidiary's role behaviour, both sides perceive what they expect. (B) Situation B is not found in the presented cases. This constellation seems rather unlikely, since it assumes that both sides perceive the subsidiary's role behaviour in a certain way, and each side expects exactly what the other side perceives. (C) Next, a situation is described in which headquarters management expects the same role behaviour as the subsidiary management. While the subsidiary managers have the impression that the subsidiary's behaviour corresponds to this expectation, headquarters representatives perceive the subsidiary behave differently. This constellation appears in the cases involving the Chinese and the US-American subsidiaries. (D) Situation D represents the reverse of the previous situation: Both sides expect the same behaviour of the subsidiary. Headquarters managers perceive the subsidiary acting the expected way, but the subsidiary managers perceive a differing behaviour. This situation is not observed in the present study. (E) In the next constellation, headquarters management's perceptions and expectations match. The subsidiary managers, however, perceive the subsidiary's behaviour differently than headquarters managers and expect the subsidiary's role still to be different. The cases involving the Hungarian and the Turkish subsidiaries show this pattern. (F) Finally, the reverse situation is taken into account. Here, the subsidiary managers perceive the subsidiary's role behaviour in the same way as they expect it to be. Headquarters representatives, however, perceive the subsidiary's role behaviour in a different way and expect a third kind of role behaviour from the subsidiary. This constellation is found in the cases involving the Turkish and the US-American subsidiaries.[161]

So far, perception gaps regarding the subsidiary's current role have been described. In addition, two other types of gaps should be mentioned. (1) First, a perception gap exists concerning the examined role dimension without any behaviour or behavioural expectations being attached to the dimension in two cases. The respective dimensions are market importance and knowledge inflow. These dimensions were described above as not fitting the proposed subsidiary role concept. This explains the lack of behavioural implications. (2) Second, in a number of cases, gaps are identified that concern the subsidiary's should-be

---

[160] The analysis of whether there are differences in the implications of the perception gaps depending on which constellation is observed will be presented in 5.4.2.
[161] Each subsidiary can appear repeatedly since several perception gaps may exist in each case.

role. In these cases, headquarters and subsidiary managers perceive the subsidiary's role behaviour identically but expect different role behaviours. In the case involving the Mexican subsidiary, headquarters and subsidiary respondents agree that the subsidiary's role has to change – they do not agree, however, in terms of the role the subsidiary should play. In the cases involving the Hungarian and the Turkish subsidiaries, headquarters and subsidiary managers agree in their perception of the subsidiaries' current role regarding product scope. In both cases, headquarters managers' perceptions correspond to their expectations, while the subsidiary representatives envision a different role.[162]

After this conceptual classification of the perception gaps identified in the present study, the usage of the concept perception gap in the present study is critically reviewed.

5.3.2.3 Critical Review of Perception Gaps

Two aspects of the application of the perception gap concept in the present study will be critically reviewed.

(1) The first aspect concerns the scope of the perception gaps taken into account. Subsidiary roles were defined as patterns of behaviour that are expected in relation to a subsidiary's position in the MNC. When perception gaps, in the present study, are defined as differences in perception between headquarters and subsidiary managers concerning the role behaviour currently shown by the subsidiary, only part of the abovementioned definition of subsidiary roles is covered. To consider the subsidiary's role enactment as the role which the subsidiary currently plays may be reproached, since it disregards the anticipatory element in the proposed role definition. Instead of the *expected* behaviour pattern, the *shown* behaviour pattern is taken into account. As an alternative for the subsidiary's role enactment, the expectations regarding its role may be claimed to correspond better to the theoretical role concept. Nevertheless, the assignments of role enactment to the current role and role expectations to the should-be role are defended. While the role expectations are only able to reflect the subsidiary's current role when the subsidiary's role enactment matches them, the subsidiary's role enactment is related to the subsidiary's momentary role. Therefore, headquarters and subsidiary representatives' perceptions of the subsidiary's role behaviour are interpreted as their perceptions of the subsidiary's current role.

---

[162] Although situations A, B, E and F also exhibit differing role expectations on headquarters' and the subsidiary's side, these situations are not explicitly considered as gaps regarding the subsidiary's should-be role, but first as perception gaps concerning the subsidiary's current role.

(2) Second, the methodical determination of perception gaps may be challenged. In the present study, perception gaps are determined through a combination of questionnaire results and interviews. However, there is no clear indication as to when a perception gap exists. It is conceivable that the present study identifies a perception gap although headquarters and subsidiary respondents might find a common value in between the values they indicate in the questionnaire and in the interviews if they spoke to each other directly. However, most of the described perception gaps seem to be meaningful. This will become clear in the following, when the implications of the perception gaps for the headquarters-subsidiary relationship are outlined.

5.4 Implications of Perception Gaps for the Headquarters-Subsidiary Relationship

5.4.1 The Empirical Findings in the Context of the International Business Literature

5.4.1.1 Overview

In the following, the empirical findings regarding implications of perception gaps concerning the subsidiary's role will be considered in the context of the IB literature. In particular, it will be examined as to what extent an application of the proposed conceptual framework in the context of the IB literature leads to meaningful conclusions about the implications of perception gaps concerning the subsidiary's role for the headquarters-subsidiary relationship. In 3.3, potential implications of perception gaps were derived by combining the ideas of the proposed framework with empirical and conceptual contributions of the IB literature. The empirical findings of the present study will be related to the developed suggestions. Since they are closely connected in the empirical findings, the role dimensions of subsidiary autonomy and involvement in value chain activities will be considered together.

5.4.1.2 Importance of the Subsidiary's Market

The empirical findings reveal meaningful perception gaps concerning the market characteristic of competitive intensity in the cases involving the Hungarian subsidiary and the

Turkish subsidiary.[163] In terms of implications, the IB literature proposes a positive relationship between the strategic importance of a subsidiary's market and headquarters' investment in the respective subsidiary (Bartlett & Ghoshal 1991, pp. 105–111). This relationship is determined not only for financial investment, but also for other types of resources, such as intangible or human resources (Furu 2001, p. 138; Luo 2003, pp. 293–294). It is proposed that differing perceptions of the importance of the subsidiary's market may imply differing expectations concerning the distribution of resources to the subsidiary and that this may result in input conflict. This assumption is confirmed by the present cases: Both the Hungarian and the Turkish subsidiaries state that they have to put much effort into persuading headquarters that resources are needed, and neither of them received much investment in the preceding years (A1, A10, A13; examples include financial investments in new buildings or machines, but also investments of temporal resources). This observation supports the assumption that input conflict may follow when subsidiary managers perceive the importance of the subsidiary's market higher than headquarters managers do. None of the analyzed cases confirms the emergence of process conflict that is also derived.

5.4.1.3 Product Scope

Although headquarters and subsidiary representatives agree in their perceptions of the respective subsidiaries' product scope in all headquarters-subsidiary relationships, they have differing expectations concerning the subsidiaries' should-be product scopes in two cases. In the cases involving the Turkish and the Hungarian subsidiaries, subsidiary management considers an extension of the subsidiary's product portfolio necessary while headquarters representatives do not share this expectation. From headquarters' perspective, the subsidiaries' future product scopes are identical to their current product scopes. Due to their differing ideas regarding the subsidiary's should-be product scope, headquarters representatives prevent the subsidiary from playing the should-be role that its management envisions. However, since no perception gap regarding the subsidiary's current role is identified, no implications of such a perception gap can be observed.

---

[163] In the interviews, the higher perception of competitive intensity by subsidiary managers is generally being associated with the subsidiary's more immediate exposition to the competition in the market and the concurrent pressure exerted by headquarters (A3, A4, A9, A10). While this situation is similar for all subsidiaries, the Hungarian and the Turkish subsidiary may be particularly aware of it, since each of them lost an important customer in the previous year. Due to the dominance of few large customers in Autocomp's business, this implies considerable difficulties for the subsidiaries to fill their capacities.

5.4.1.4 Subsidiary's Capabilities

The relationship between Construc's headquarters and its US-American subsidiary is the only case in which perception gaps concerning the subsidiary's capabilities are detected. The subsidiary management perceives higher capabilities in the areas of production and HR management than headquarters management. The IB literature relates a subsidiary's capabilities to the unit's processes as well as its results and the amount of resources it receives – i.e., to its throughput, output and input. Higher capabilities are associated with a higher quality of processes (Tasoluk, Yaprak & Calantone 2007, p. 337), higher performance (Delios & Beamish 2001, p. 1029; Luo 2002, p. 194) and higher input of resources (Bartlett & Ghoshal 1991, pp. 105–111; Furu 2001, p. 143; Lusk 1972, p. 567). In combination with the conceptual framework, the IB literature provides argumentation for the emergence of conflict regarding throughput, output and input in the case of a perception gap concerning a subsidiary's capabilities. In the present case, the subsidiary's processes are in the focus. When headquarters managers perceive a subsidiary as less capable than the subsidiary managers do, the IB literature (in combination with the proposed role theoretical framework) suggests that headquarters managers may attempt to change the way processes are carried out at the subsidiary. This is observed in the case involving the US-American subsidiary: Headquarters managers perceive a need to improve production as well as HR processes at the subsidiary. The subsidiary managers, however, judge the subsidiary's capabilities as high and consequently resist headquarters' efforts.[164] No confirmation is found for the emergence of input conflict and output conflict for which argumentation was presented as well.

5.4.1.5 Knowledge Inflow to the Subsidiary

Perception gaps concerning the dimension inflow of knowledge to the subsidiary are identified in the cases involving the Turkish, the Chinese and the US-American subsidiaries. In all three cases, headquarters managers perceive more knowledge inflow to the subsidiary than subsidiary managers do. The case involving the Turkish subsidiary differs from the two other cases, because the transfer is not associated with an intention to change the processes at the Turkish subsidiary. Since no specific expectations are connected with the knowledge

---

[164] This behaviour is also in line with the IB literature, which suggests that higher capabilities are frequently associated with a higher degree of autonomy (Young & Tavares 2004, p. 217).

flow, the difference in perception does not show any particular implications for the headquarters-subsidiary relationship. In contrast, the knowledge transfers to the Chinese subsidiary and the US-American subsidiary are associated with explicit expectations that headquarters managers have concerning the effect of the knowledge transfer. In both cases, the knowledge is intended to change and improve the processes at the subsidiary.

From the IB literature's perspective, knowledge inflow to the subsidiary can be associated with the categories input, throughput and output in the following way. First, knowledge inflow can be directly classified as distribution of resources to a subsidiary (input) (Luo & Zhao 2004, p. 98). When process improvements are aimed at, the knowledge inflow is obviously related to expectations concerning the subsidiary's processes (throughput) (Harzing & Noorderhaven 2006b, p. 200; Kostova 1999, p. 308; Taggart 1997a, p. 52); and finally, it may be related to the subsidiary's goals (output) in the sense that it should allow the subsidiary to achieve a higher performance (Luo 2003, p. 294; Monteiro, Arvidsson & Birkinshaw 2004, p. B6). When headquarters managers perceive more knowledge inflow to the subsidiary than subsidiary managers do, reasoning was provided for the emergence of conflict regarding input, throughput as well as output. In the present context, changes in the subsidiary are aimed at in both cases. The subsidiaries' failure to apply the transferred knowledge is perceived as conflictful by headquarters managers as it prevents improvements in the subsidiary's processes. Consequently, the proposition that throughput conflict may arise is confirmed, whereas conflict concerning input or output is not relevant.

5.4.1.6 Knowledge Outflow from the Subsidiary

Knowledge outflow refers to knowledge that is generated by the subsidiary and transferred to other units. Perception gaps regarding this dimension are identified in the cases involving Autocomp's Polish subsidiary, the Turkish subsidiary and the Chinese subsidiary. In all three cases, the subsidiary managers perceive higher knowledge outflow than headquarters managers do. In terms of implications of this perception gap, the IB literature proposes that input conflict, throughput conflict and goal conflict may arise when the knowledge outflow is judged higher on the subsidiary's side than on headquarters' side. The argumentations may be summarized as follows: First, headquarters is assumed to provide a subsidiary that generates a large amount of knowledge for the entire SBU with more resources (input) (Bartlett & Ghoshal 1991, p. 109). Second, higher outflow of knowledge can also be associated with a higher degree of autonomy of the subsidiary (throughput) (Gupta &

Govindarajan 1991, pp. 783–785). Finally, knowledge outflow from the subsidiary may be seen as contribution to the fulfilment of the subsidiary's goals (output).

In the cases involving the Polish and the Turkish subsidiaries, the perception gaps do not show any concrete implications. In both cases, the lack of implications seems to be related to the fact that headquarters' as well as the subsidiary's side perceive exactly the behaviour that they expect.[165] In the case involving the Chinese subsidiary, headquarters managers perceive less outflow of knowledge from the subsidiary to headquarters than is expected. The emerging conflict concerns the subsidiary's processes, since it is inferred by headquarters representatives that the activities at the subsidiary do not correspond to headquarters management's expectations. The assumption that less knowledge outflow is associated with headquarters' attempt to control processes at the subsidiary closely is confirmed by the case involving the Chinese subsidiary (Gupta & Govindarajan 1991, pp. 783–785). Headquarters tries to prescribe processes and activities that are to be carried out by the subsidiary in detail as the subsidiary is not trusted to act independently (A8). No indication is found for input or output conflict.

5.4.1.7 Subsidiary's Autonomy and Involvement in Value Chain Activities

The case involving Autocomp's Turkish subsidiary is the only case in the present study in which a perception gap appears concerning the subsidiary's autonomy. After the subsidiary's acquisition, the subsidiary's management perceived the subsidiary's autonomy to be higher than headquarters managers did.[166] The dimension involvement in value chain activities was considered in addition to autonomy, since even a subsidiary that is not autonomous may be involved in certain value chain activities to varying degrees.[167] A perception gap concerning involvement in value chain activities is identified in the case involving Autocomp's Hungarian subsidiary.[168] The subsidiary managers perceive a higher degree of involvement than headquarters managers do. As both autonomy and involvement in value chain activities are

---

[165] This relationship will be outlined in more detail in 5.4.2.2.
[166] In general, it is found in the IB literature that subsidiaries that were established through acquisition possess a higher degree of autonomy than other subsidiaries do (Garnier 1982, p. 900; Young & Tavares 2004, p. 217).
[167] The dimension involvement in value chain activities was defined based on the empirical findings of the present study. In the analyzed cases, the overall responsibility for the functions for which involvement in value chain activities is an issue is held by headquarters, which is accepted by all sides. The discussions here revolve around the exact design of the relationship between headquarters and subsidiary in the context of the respective functions.
[168] The Turkish subsidiary disagrees with headquarters regarding its should-be involvement.

related to the subsidiary's processes, implications of perception gaps are expected to involve throughput conflict (Young & Tavares 2004, p. 229). This corresponds to the findings of the present study: In the case involving the Turkish subsidiary, conflict emerges as the subsidiary makes decisions in certain functions independently instead of referring to headquarters. In the case involving the Hungarian subsidiary, conflict arises as the subsidiary managers have the impression that their contribution to several value chain activities is not taken seriously.

5.4.1.8 Conclusion

In the previous paragraphs, it was examined as to what extent combining the proposed conceptual framework with contributions from the IB literature leads to meaningful conclusions about the implications of perception gaps concerning the subsidiary's role for the headquarters-subsidiary relationship. Although the analyzed cases do not cover the full range of proposed relationships, the empirical findings correspond to the ideas formulated beforehand. This confirms the assumption that the developed approach is applicable in the context of the IB literature. The particularity of the present study's approach is the fact that it offers explanations that consider the individual level. While the IB literature generally refers to relationships between headquarters and subsidiary on a rather abstract level, the framework presented here lifts the surface and brings the perceptions and expectations of the individual managers into effect. The empirical findings of the present study show that despite this focus on the individual manager, conclusions can be drawn that concern the level of organizational units, in particular, the headquarters-subsidiary relationship. In the following, the appearance of the conceptual framework in the context of the examined headquarters-subsidiary relationships will be analyzed in depth. A fine-grained investigation of the conceptual framework's assertions will be conducted.

5.4.2 Fit of the Conceptual Framework in the Light of the Empirical Findings

5.4.2.1 Overview

The conceptual framework proposed in the present study suggests that a perception gap between the role occupant and a member of the role set concerning the occupant's role will lead to conflict between the role occupant and the respective member of the role set. This relationship crystallizes almost automatically from the definitions of roles, perception gaps and conflict that are combined in the conceptual framework (3.3.3.1). Although this proposition seems very clear from a theoretical perspective, it has to be empirically tested in the present study for two reasons: First, Katz and Kahn merely provide the definitions of role and conflict, but do not explicate the abovementioned relationship. Second, the present study is the first attempt to apply Katz and Kahn's theoretical approach to the study of subsidiary roles. Below, the main research question will be addressed and the implications of perception gaps will be analyzed. The following questions will be taken into account: Do perception gaps always lead to conflict? Of what nature is the resulting conflict? Do perception gaps only lead to conflict or are there other implications as well?

5.4.2.2 Conflict as Implication of Perception Gaps

Since the conceptual framework highlights conflict as consequence of perception gaps between headquarters and subsidiary, it will be examined as to whether conflict always follows in a case where a perception gap exists. The conceptual model assumes that the subsidiary as role bearer and headquarters as member of the role set show behaviour that matches their respective role perception and the related expectations (Figure 41). In a case where headquarters and subsidiary managers perceive the subsidiary's role differently, the behaviour of one side will probably not match the other side's expectations. By definition, this situation represents an instance of conflict, when A considers the fact that B acts according to A's role expectations as an outcome that is to be attained, while B behaves differently and thereby prevents the outcome desired by A. This theoretical expectation is confirmed by the empirical findings of the present study. Perception gaps concerning the subsidiary's current role always lead to headquarters-subsidiary conflict, with one exception: The situation labelled constellation (A) above does not result in conflict despite the existence of a perception gap (Figure 40; 5.3.2.2). Although headquarters and subsidiary managers perceive the subsidiary's role behaviour differently, representatives of both sides perceive exactly what they expect, so that no cause for conflict exists.[169]

---

[169] For instance, the relationship between German headquarters and the Polish subsidiary of Autocomp represents such a case. Subsidiary managers consider it part of the subsidiary's role to provide knowledge regarding HR management to headquarters. They not only expect, but also perceive such knowledge transfer. In contrast, headquarters managers neither expect nor perceive the transfer of HR management knowledge from the subsidiary to headquarters.

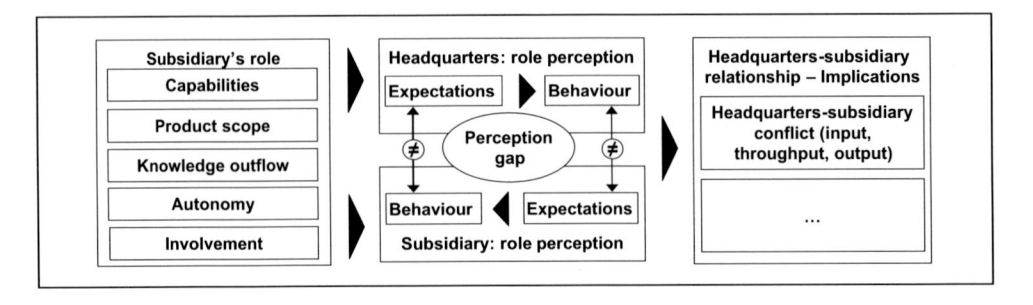

Figure 41: Proposed Conceptual Framework

The situation differs for the two other types of gaps that are determined. (1) First, there are several cases in which perception gaps concern dimensions that do not represent characteristics of the subsidiary's role as defined in the present study. It has to be distinguished whether the perception of these dimensions is still associated with expectations regarding the subsidiary's behaviour or not. There are two instances of gaps in which headquarters and subsidiary representatives perceive a dimension differently but where their perception is not associated with behavioural expectations for the subsidiary (Hungary subsidiary: market importance; Turkish subsidiary: knowledge inflow). Since no behaviour is shown and no behaviour is expected, in these instances, there is no reason for conflict to emerge. However, there are three instances in which the perceptions of market importance and knowledge inflow are indirectly associated with behavioural expectations (Turkish subsidiary: market importance; Chinese and US-American subsidiaries: knowledge inflow). In these cases, conflict emerges. (2) Second, the instances of differing ideas regarding the subsidiary's should-be role are considered. Here, the gap does not refer to the perception of the subsidiary's role behaviour, but concerns a situation in the future. In all analyzed cases in which headquarters and subsidiary representatives do not agree in their conception of the subsidiary's should-be role, conflict arises (Hungarian and Turkish subsidiaries: product scope and involvement in value chain activities; Mexican subsidiary: autonomy).

Overall, the analyzed cases support the theoretical assumption proposing conflict as an implication of perception gaps. Differentiating the three types of gaps mentioned above, the following conclusions can be drawn.

Consequently, both sides perceive what they expect and neither party considers its expectations disappointed.

(1) Perception gaps regarding subsidiary role dimensions corresponding to the role concept proposed in the present study result in headquarters-subsidiary conflict. However, conflict follows only when at least one of the involved parties expects role behaviour that differs from the role behaviour that is perceived.

(2) Perception gaps regarding dimensions that do not correspond to the role concept proposed in the present study also lead to conflict when behavioural expectations are associated with the dimensions.

(3) Differing ideas concerning the subsidiary's should-be role also lead to conflict.

5.4.2.3 Role Related Conflict and Further Implications

Now, a closer look will be taken at the specific types of conflict that emerge from perception gaps. Particular attention will be paid to the question whether the subsequent conflict is exclusively related to issues of role enactment or extends to other issues as well. For this purpose, the implications observed in the analyzed cases are summarized in Table 16, Table 17 and Table 18. The three tables represent a structured summary of the implications reported in the tables concluding each case description in 5.2. The different "categories" of gaps will be taken into account separately.

Dimensions corresponding to the role definition. First, perception gaps will be considered that concern the behaviour of the subsidiary in relation to its role for those dimensions that correspond to the role concept in the present study. The overview in Table 16 shows that the implications that are immediately associated with the perception gaps in all cases constitute conflict regarding role behaviour. Either headquarters or the subsidiary acts in a way that does not correspond to the other side's role expectations. In some instances, the subsidiary does not behave according to headquarters representatives' role perception and from their perspective, consequently, does not fulfil the function that it should fulfil. In some other instances, the subsidiary's side perceives headquarters as acting in a way that prevents the subsidiary from playing its role properly. While these implications are very close to the issue of role perception, each perception gap has further implications. Four types of further implications are found in the present study. The first type is identified in two instances in which headquarters management's expectations concerning the subsidiary's role enactment are disappointed. In both instances, headquarters takes measures in order to compel the subsidiary to enact its role as envisioned by headquarters.

In the case involving the US-American subsidiary, these measures consist of changes in management positions. In the case involving the Chinese subsidiary, headquarters on the one hand, exerts pressure on the subsidiary and on the other hand, strengthens the concerned function at the subsidiary by additional personnel resources. Despite these changes, the responsible sales manager in China left the company during the present study. Instead of an implication of the perception gap, his departure seems to be a consequence of headquarters' measures to change the subsidiary's role enactment. The second type of implication is also related to headquarters' dissatisfaction with the subsidiary's role behaviour. This type is found in relation to the Turkish subsidiary and a perception gap that existed in the past. In this case, the conflict was resolved through the accommodation of both sides' perceptions and the definition of a common solution. A further type of implication is observed in the cases involving the Hungarian and the Chinese subsidiaries. In both cases, dissatisfaction arises among the involved parties. Representatives of the Hungarian subsidiary perceive headquarters' behaviour as inhibiting the subsidiary in its proper role enactment. Since headquarters is in the more powerful position and the subsidiary cannot enforce its expectations, the consequences are frustration and dissatisfaction among the subsidiary managers. In the case involving the Chinese subsidiary, both headquarters' and the subsidiary's side experience dissatisfaction as neither side appears to be able to communicate its expectations to the other party. Finally, the Turkish subsidiary representatives' acceptance of headquarters' responsibility for customers belonging to a global key account represents a cognitive implication following the role related conflict.

Dimensions not corresponding to the role concept. Although the dimensions market importance and knowledge inflow are not directly associated with behavioural implications for the subsidiary, they may be indirectly related to the subsidiary's behaviour (Table 17). In the present study, there are two instances of perception gaps where these dimensions are not associated with behavioural implications, while they are related to behavioural expectations in three instances. As for the dimensions corresponding to the conceptual framework, the resulting conflict is related to the fact that one side's expectations concerning the other side's behaviour are not fulfilled. Further implications are observed as well: In the case involving the US-American subsidiary, the changes in management positions are considered to prompt the subsidiary to play its role as expected by headquarters. This implication falls into the first category identified above. In the case involving the Chinese subsidiary, a new pattern is observed: Instead of bringing the subsidiary closer to its envisioned role, headquarters seems to redefine the subsidiary's role according to the behaviour that is shown by the subsidiary by decreasing the subsidiary's responsibilities. In addition, cognitive implications are observed in this case that fall into the fourth category identified above: Headquarters representatives perceive the Chinese subsidiary as unwilling or incapable.

Subsidiary's should-be role. In all cases in which headquarters and subsidiary managers perceive the subsidiary's should-be role differently, conflict arises concerning the realization of the should-be role according to the subsidiary management's expectations (Table 18). Four of the six instances of differing ideas regarding the subsidiary's future role concern functions that are organizationally centralized at headquarters. All four instances are related to the fact that the subsidiaries would like to play a more significant role in these functions. The perception gaps concerning the subsidiary's should-be product scope in the cases involving the Hungarian and the Turkish subsidiaries do not show any further implications. In all other instances, further implications are observed. In the case involving the Hungarian subsidiary, dissatisfaction among subsidiary managers is identified as further implication. The Turkish subsidiary's loss of a long-time customer was mentioned in relation to the perception gap regarding the subsidiary's should-be role, but the causality cannot be clearly determined. While a decision was made to increase the number of people working for the Mexican subsidiary's sales office, it is unclear whether this measure supports headquarters management's or the subsidiary management's idea of the subsidiary's autonomy.

In the conceptual part of the present study, a classification of conflict types in input, throughput and output conflict is suggested. It is possible to classify the observed instances of headquarters-subsidiary conflict into one of these categories. However, the differentiation of conflict on this basis does not seem helpful for the further analysis. Consequently, the implications of perception gaps are merely differentiated in "directly related to role behaviour" and "further implications".

The main conclusions regarding the empirically observed implications of perception gaps concerning the subsidiary's role can be summarized as follows.[170]

(1) Conflict is confirmed as the main implication of perception gaps. Conflict is observed as implication of (A) perception gaps concerning role dimensions which correspond to the role concept, (B) perception gaps regarding dimensions which do not correspond to the

---

[170] It should be noted that the summary presented here is exclusively based on the empirical findings of the present study. The structure that is introduced will be used in 5.4.2.5 in order to abstract from the cases and to extend the conceptual framework presented in 3.3.3.1.

role concept as well as (C) gaps regarding the subsidiary's should-be role. There are, however, some differences between these three types of gaps.

(A) Conflict that results from perception gaps concerning role dimensions which correspond to the role concept primarily concerns the role enactment. In all analyzed cases, there are further implications that follow the role related conflict.

(B) Conflict as well results from perception gaps concerning role dimensions that do not correspond to the role concept when behavioural expectations are related to the perception of the dimension. In two of the three cases, further implications following the conflict regarding the role enactment are observed.

(C) Conflict that arises due to differing ideas regarding the subsidiary's should-be role concerns the subsidiary's transition from the present role to a different role in the future. Further implications follow the conflict in four of the six instances.

(2) As outlined above, in many cases, conflict is not the final point, but further implications following the conflictful behaviour can be observed. These further implications can be structured into behavioural, cognitive and affective implications.

(A) Behavioural implications

- Headquarters takes measures to bring the subsidiary closer to the role envisioned by headquarters.
- The conflict is resolved and a solution is found that accommodates both sides' role perceptions.
- Headquarters redefines the subsidiary's role according to the subsidiary's role behaviour.

(B) Cognitive implications

- Headquarters and subsidiary managers accept a common solution.
- Headquarters and subsidiary managers develop a certain opinion regarding the other party.

(C) Affective implications

- Frustration and dissatisfaction are observed when the options to alter the subsidiary's role in a specific direction are unclear.

Dimension (Case)	Conflicttful behaviour	Prevented outcome	Further implications	Conflict type
Capabilities (USA)	Subsidiary resists improvements in production and HR management processes	Increase of productivity and decrease of staff turnover rate → **role enactment according to headquarters management's expectations**	• Expatriate manager with responsibility to increase productivity is located at the subsidiary • Manager responsible for HR management of commercial staff is replaced	Through-put
Knowledge outflow (CHI)	Subsidiary transfers knowledge in a form that does not match headquarters management's expectations	Transfer of the expected data on customers and market developments from the subsidiary to headquarters → **role enactment according to headquarters management's expectations**	• Headquarters exerts a lot of pressure on the subsidiary • Headquarters strengthens the sales function through a new general manager and support staff • Responsible sales manager leaves the subsidiary • Dissatisfaction	Output
Knowledge outflow (POL/TUR)	(behaviour corresponds to expectations)	-	-	-
Involvement in value chain activities (HUN)	Headquarters does not provide subsidiary with current information (e.g., sales)	Subsidiary's chance to enter meetings with customers possessing current information on the customer relationship → **role enactment according to subsidiary management's expectations**	• Subsidiary managers are dissatisfied as they do not feel taken seriously	Input
Involvement in value chain activities (HUN)	Headquarters does not take subsidiary's suggestions to save costs or to improve financial returns into account	Implementation of subsidiary's suggestions → **role enactment according to subsidiary management's expectations**	• Subsidiary managers are dissatisfied as they do not feel taken seriously	Output
Autonomy (TUR)	Subsidiary sustains direct relationships with customers	Subsidiary's integration in the centralized marketing and sales key account organization → **role enactment according to headquarters management's expectations**	• Headquarters' responsibility for global key account customers is accepted • Subsidiary receives regional sales responsibility	Through-put
Autonomy (TUR)	Subsidiary purchases raw material without central sales' knowledge	Subsidiary's integration in the centralized purchasing organization and abidance by transactions requiring consent → **role enactment according to headquarters management's expectations**	• Subsidiary receives responsibility for purchasing part of its raw material	Through-put

Table 16: Implications of Perception Gaps – Dimensions Corresponding to the Role Definition

Dimension (Case)	Conflictful behaviour	Prevented outcome	Further implications	Conflict type
Market importance (TUR)	Headquarters reacts slowly to subsidiary's requests concerning feasibility and certification	Subsidiary's fast reaction to potential customers' requests **(gap does not directly concern behaviour pattern)**	-	Input
Knowledge inflow (CHI)	Subsidiary does not apply the transferred knowledge	Realization of activities and processes as expected **(gap does not directly concern behaviour pattern)**	• Headquarters takes responsibilities back from subsidiary • Subsidiary is perceived as unwilling or incapable • Dissatisfaction	Through-put
Knowledge inflow (USA)	Subsidiary resists improvements in production processes	Increase in productivity **(gap does not directly concern behaviour pattern)**	• Expatriate manager with responsibility to increase productivity is located at the subsidiary	Through-put

Table 17: Implications of Perception Gaps – Dimensions not Corresponding to the Role Definition

Dimension (Case)	Conflictful behaviour	Prevented outcome	Further implications	Conflict type
Product scope (HUN)	Headquarters rejects the subsidiary's investment proposals	Extension of product portfolio → **realization of should-be role according to the subsidiary management's expectations**	-	Input
Product scope (TUR)	Headquarters rejects the subsidiary's investment proposals	Extension of product portfolio → **realization of should-be role according to the subsidiary management's expectations**	-	Input
Involvement in value chain activities (HUN)	Headquarters does not consult the subsidiary when entering agreements with customers or suppliers	Consideration of the subsidiary's needs in contracts with suppliers → **realization of should-be role according to the subsidiary management's expectations**	Subsidiary managers are dissatisfied as they do not feel taken seriously	Through-put
Involvement in value chain activities (TUR)	Headquarters does not involve the subsidiary in sales negotiations	Subsidiary's managing director cannot contribute to the process → **realization of should-be role according to the subsidiary management's expectations**	Loss of a long-time customer of the subsidiary (causality unclear)	Through-put
Autonomy (MEX)	Headquarters is too involved in local decisions ("micro-management")	Subsidiary managers' independent decision making and contribution through own ideas → **realization of should-be role according to the subsidiary management's expectations**	Decision to increase number of people in the sales office	Through-put
Autonomy (MEX)	Subsidiary does not comply with headquarters' instructions	Realization of measures intended by headquarters → **realization of should-be role according to headquarters management's expectations**	Decision to increase number of people in the sales office	Through-put

Table 18: Implications of Perception Gaps – Subsidiary's Should-be Role

5.4.2.4 Critical Review of the Conceptual Framework

In the following, the fit of the conceptual framework that was developed based on Katz and Kahn's open system approach will be reviewed in the light of the empirical findings of the present study. The framework defines subsidiary roles as well as headquarters-subsidiary conflict in behavioural terms and proposes that perception gaps regarding the subsidiary's role lead to headquarters-subsidiary conflict. The empirical findings of the present study support this proposition if the definitions determined in the framework are accepted. The acceptance of these definitions, however, is not self-evident: First, many dimensions that represent characteristics of the subsidiary's role according to the IB literature do not match the role concept because they are not limited to behaviour patterns shown by the subsidiary. Second, the conflict definition is also incompatible with some approaches to conflict in the literature (2.4.1). In the light of the general conflict literature, Katz and Kahn's definition of conflict as observable behaviour is rather narrow. In particular, the conflict literature presents a cognitive and an affective dimension in addition to the behavioural dimension considered by Katz and Kahn.[171]

When subsidiary roles are defined as behaviour patterns, the immediate consequences of perception gaps represent conflictful behaviour as assumed by the conceptual framework. However, in addition to conflict as immediate consequence, further implications are identified that follow the role related conflict and that cannot be restricted to the behavioural level. Although the majority of further implications can be classified as behavioural, there are also some instances of affective and cognitive implications.[172] In its present form, the conceptual framework ends with conflict as an immediate consequence of perception gaps and does not explain any further implications independent of their level. Therefore, the proposed framework is extended below in order to include further implications following the role related conflict.

---

[171] The present study agrees with Katz and Kahn's assumption that cognitive and affective aspects may be helpful to understand the conflict but seem inappropriate to define it (Katz & Kahn 1978, p. 613).

[172] Some further comments concerning the cognitive level are offered, since it plays a role in the empirical findings of the present study in several forms. First, the perceptions of the subsidiary's role as well as the related expectations concerning role behaviour represent cognitive concepts. Perception gaps are entirely cognitive. In addition, the data collection via questionnaire and interviews leads to a focus on the respondents' conscious thoughts. Respondents can only report what they are aware of, so that the identified implications of perception gaps can be related to a cognitive level as well. While many contributions in the literature define conflict in terms of disagreement (2.4.1), in the present study, disagreement (in the form of a perception gap) is merely the basis on which "actual" conflict, i.e., observable conflictful behaviour, develops.

5.4.2.5 Extension of the Conceptual Framework

Overall, the proposed conceptual framework fits the empirical findings. As was outlined above, the role concept can be applied to subsidiary roles; for those role dimensions that correspond to the role concept, the identified perception gaps result in headquarters-subsidiary conflict, when at least one side's expectations regarding the subsidiary's role enactment are disappointed. The emerging conflict is role related, so that its nature is determined by the behavioural expectations associated with the role. In addition, however, the empirical findings of the present study indicate various types of further implications. These further implications can mainly be classified as behavioural, but they also include instances of cognitive and affective implications (5.4.2.3). It will be attempted to extend the conceptual framework in order to incorporate further implications that follow the role related conflict. Since very few instances of cognitive and behavioural implications were reported, these levels cannot be examined in detail. The focus of the following extension will therefore be on the behavioural level.

The behavioural reactions following the role related headquarters-subsidiary conflict seem to be directed at this conflict with the intention to alter the situation. Therefore, they are interpreted as conflict management measures and literature on conflict management is taken into account in the search for a structure of the observed implications.[173] The frequently applied taxonomy of conflict handling intentions by Thomas will be considered (Thomas 1992a, p. 266). In the following, it will be analyzed whether this taxonomy can be associated with the observed behavioural reactions following the role related conflict and whether the interpretation of these reactions as conflict management measures is justified. The taxonomy is presented in Figure 42.

---

[173] Katz and Kahn as well address the issue of conflict management. However, instead of classifying the involved parties' behaviour, they consider the potential targets at which the behaviour may be directed (Katz & Kahn 1978, pp. 641–649).

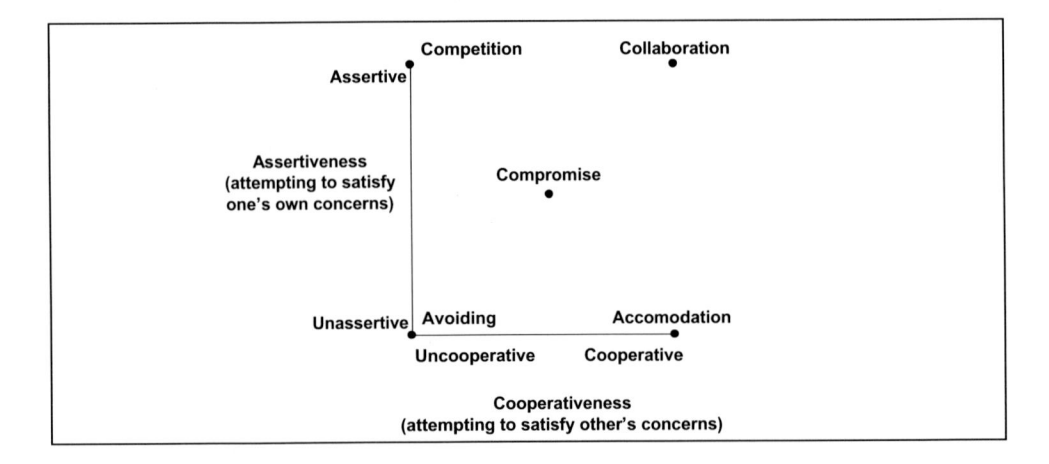

```
                    Competition         Collaboration
           Assertive •                      •

    Assertiveness
    (attempting to satisfy      Compromise
    one's own concerns)             •


           Unassertive  Avoiding        Accomodation
                    •                      •
                    Uncooperative    Cooperative

                        Cooperativeness
               (attempting to satisfy other's concerns)
```

Figure 42: Two-dimensional Taxonomy of Conflict Handling Intentions
Source: Thomas 1992a, p. 266.

While Thomas first refers to "conflict handling modes", he later emphasizes that the five terms of avoiding, accommodation, competition, collaboration and compromise represent intentions that do not automatically imply a causal relation to the mode by which the conflict is finally handled (Thomas 1992a, p. 269). They, however, do motivate the behaviour that is shown by the respective parties in terms of conflict management. In the present study, mainly measures taken by headquarters to manage the role related conflict are observed as further implications of perception gaps. This may be due to the fact that headquarters has more power than the subsidiary to act as intended (cp. 5.4.2.3).

In the following, it will be examined whether the behaviours shown by headquarters following the role related conflict can be traced back to the five conflict handling intentions proposed by Thomas. (1) The first type of behavioural implications consists of headquarters taking measures to bring the subsidiary closer to the role envisioned by headquarters management. In the cases examined for the present study, this includes changes in management positions and the increase of personnel resources for certain functions. In this situation, headquarters intends to satisfy its own concerns and seems to consider the subsidiary's concerns only to a limited extent. In other words, from headquarters' perspective, the behaviour is assertive and mainly uncooperative, leading to the intention termed "competition" in the taxonomy. Although this name does not fully fit the actions taken by headquarters, the intention may be interpreted as going in that direction. (2) Second, headquarters is found to redefine the subsidiary's role according to the subsidiary's behaviour. In the present study, responsibilities are taken back from the subsidiary to headquarters. This behaviour can be described as "accommodation". The subsidiary's concerns are taken into account but not headquarters' own concerns.[174] (3) Third, there are instances where headquarters and the subsidiary resolve the conflict by determining a solution that lies in between both sides' role perception. This behaviour can be defined as "compromise", since it reflects the concerns of both headquarters and the subsidiary to some extent, but not to the full extent.[175]

While the term competition does not fully fit headquarters' behaviours, the terms accommodation and compromise describe the observed behaviours well. Competition appears to be more appropriate for a relationship between equal partners that are not hierarchically related. In the case of a headquarters-subsidiary relationship, headquarters may be assumed to possess more power than the subsidiary to realize its intentions and if necessary enforce them.[176] Overall, it is concluded that it is possible to interpret the observed behavioural reactions to the role related headquarters-subsidiary conflict as conflict management measures that are motivated by one of the five conflict handling intentions presented by Thomas (Thomas 1992a).

Although it can be imagined that cognitive as well as affective issues also play a role in the context of conflict management, these levels remain vague. Cognitive processes, for example, appear in the form of the conflict management intentions that motivate the conflict management behaviour of the involved parties. Emotional reactions, such as frustration and dissatisfaction, arise, for instance, when no possibility exists to take such measures. However, it cannot be assumed that all possible implications on these levels can be explained in that way. The small number of instances that appear in the present study do not allow a more detailed analysis. The extended framework is summarized in Figure 43.[177] Although it cannot be claimed that the extended framework is complete in the sense that it describes all possible implications of perception gaps, it accommodates the empirical findings

---

[174] Katz and Kahn note that a change in the involved parties' role expectations is likely if the costs of conflict are high, and the parties doubt their ability to resolve their differences otherwise (Katz & Kahn 1978, p. 645). In such a situation, organizational pressures to avoid open conflict are assumed strong.
[175] It was argued above that the leaving of the responsible sales manager from the Chinese subsidiary constitutes a consequence of the pressure exerted by headquarters following the role related conflict rather than a direct implication of the conflict. Nevertheless, the sales manager's behaviour could be interpreted as an instance of avoiding behaviour according to the taxonomy.
[176] For instance, it can hardly be imagined that the subsidiary decides that a change of management at headquarters is necessary.
[177] For examples of the three dimensions of further implications, see 5.4.2.3.

of the present study and leaves room for further conflict management modes that were not observed in the analyzed cases.

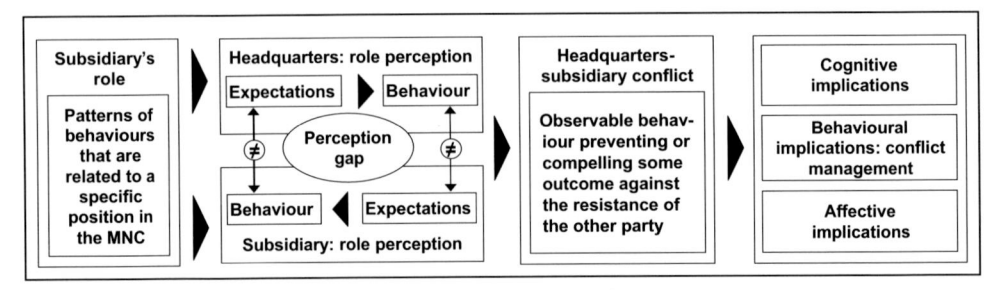

Figure 43: Extended Conceptual Framework
Source: Kahn & Quinn 1970, p. 52; Katz & Kahn 1978, p. 613.

5.4.2.6 Conclusion

The preceding paragraphs examined to what extent the proposed mechanisms linking role perceptions, expectations and behaviour are valid for subsidiary roles. Overall, the conceptual framework developed in the present study seems applicable to subsidiaries as role bearers. Corresponding to the conceptual framework, the empirical findings show that headquarters-subsidiary conflict always follows when a perception gap regarding the subsidiary's role exists between headquarters and subsidiary representatives and when at least one of the involved parties expects role behaviour that differs from the role behaviour that is perceived. This relationship applies for dimensions that correspond to the proposed role definition as well as for dimensions that do not correspond to this definition as long as behavioural expectations are associated with the respective dimension. Headquarters-subsidiary conflict that results from perception gaps regarding the subsidiary's role is generally role related, i.e., it concerns the subsidiary's role enactment or headquarters' behaviour as interrelated partner. Further implications appear to follow the role related conflict in most cases; behavioural consequences constitute the majority of identified further implications. All behavioural consequences reported in the present study can be interpreted as conflict management measures addressing the headquarters-subsidiary conflict. In few cases, respondents referred to further implications on an affective and a cognitive level as well. In contrast to the behavioural implications, no specific interpretation can be provided for the affective and cognitive implications due to their small number. The conceptual framework relating perception gaps regarding the subsidiary's role to headquarters-subsidiary conflict is extended in order to include the role related conflict's further implications.[178] The further implications of the role related conflict on a behavioural level can be interpreted as conflict management measures. These behavioural implications may be accompanied by cognitive and affective consequences.

---

[178] Differing ideas concerning the subsidiary's should-be role also lead to conflict. In these cases, the emerging conflict concerns the subsidiary's prohibited transition from the present role to a different role in the future.

6. Discussion

6.1 Limitations of the Present Study

6.1.1 Scope of the Study

The scope of each study is necessarily limited. Three limitations of the present study will be addressed in the following: the focus of the research question, the subsidiary role characteristics that were considered and the implications of perception gaps that were identified.

(1) First, the scope of the study is limited due to the research question's focus on implications of perception gaps. In comparison with the overview of the research field surrounding perception gaps regarding the subsidiary's role (Figure 6), the present study does not include an analysis of the factors influencing perception gaps. Although the question why perception gaps emerge is briefly reflected from a theoretical perspective (3.3.2), conditions that increase the likelihood of perception gaps are not empirically studied. However, it is necessary to know the factors influencing perception gaps in order to be able to control their emergence in headquarters-subsidiary relationships and to prevent potentially negative implications. Nevertheless, due to the extensiveness of the research field, a decision had to be made to focus on one section. The consequences were taken into account because they constitute the practical relevance of the study of perception gaps.

(2) The second limitation concerns the characteristics of the subsidiary's role that were considered. For the present study, a priori, four dimensions of subsidiary roles that are frequently used in the IB literature were selected. In the course of the interviews, three additional dimensions turned out to be relevant and were consequently included in the analysis. On the one side, the consideration of seven dimensions provides a more detailed picture of the subsidiary's role than the reference to only one typology and its two or three dimensions that is commonly found in the IB literature. On the other side, however, even seven dimensions are not capable of describing the subsidiary's role comprehensively. Although the three additional dimensions can be assumed to represent aspects that appeared particularly relevant in the analyzed cases, it is possible that other issues were not taken into account. However, since the subsidiary role concept is quite abstract, the consideration of distinct dimensions appears as a viable way for the empirical study of subsidiary roles.

(3) Third, the implications of perception gaps are considered. Although it was one of the present study's main goals to determine the implications of perception gaps, it seems unlikely that the analyzed cases reflect the full range of potential consequences. While the present study focused on a relatively small number of cases, a larger scale study might have revealed a broader scope of implications. Nevertheless, the present study represents a first step towards more extensive knowledge of the potential implications of perception gaps.

6.1.2 Conceptual Issues

Three issues that limit the study on a conceptual level will be discussed: the need to reconcile the individual and the organizational levels of analysis, the role concept and the failure to explain cognitive and affective implications of the role related headquarters-subsidiary conflict.

(1) The dichotomy between individual members of an organization and organizational units that they are part of was discussed in 3.2.1.3. Two issues were addressed: first, the question of whether the role concept can be meaningfully applied to subsidiaries, and second, how conclusions can be drawn from data collected from individuals to the organizational unit. While the first question seems to be confirmed by the results of the present study, the second issue remains. In the following, it will be discussed to what extent it limits the present study. It is common practice in the IB literature to survey or to interview one top manager of, for instance, a subsidiary and to interpret the findings as the subsidiary's perception or the subsidiary's behaviour (e.g., Birkinshaw & Morrison 1995; Ghoshal & Nohria 1989; Taggart 1997b). The present study tried to address this issue by involving multiple respondents of each organizational unit in the questionnaire and the interview part of the study. Although this approach had the advantage of reflecting the unit's perspective by more than one opinion, it did not overcome the general problem. Instead of inferring from one individual to the entire unit, the standpoint of a group of individuals was generalized and attributed to the respective unit; the generalization was only built on a broader basis.[179] Furthermore, an additional problem arose that is evaded by the single respondent method: In several instances, the respondents of the same unit did not share the

---

[179] One aspect that supports the use of generalizations is the fact that respondents of one unit also frequently referred to the other unit rather generally and – with few exceptions – did not consider individual differences between members of the other unit.

same opinion but had different opinions.[180] In the present study, this difficulty could be solved, since it was possible to associate the different opinions with different functional areas; the perception of each group was taken into account separately. To summarize, the problem associated with the need to generalize from individuals and attribute their opinion to organizational units could not be solved in the present study, but was moderated by the consideration of a larger group of respondents in each unit.

(2) A second conceptual issue concerns the role concept. The socially constructed nature of roles makes them hard to grasp and almost impossible to determine. In the present study, roles were defined according to Katz and Kahn as patterns of behaviours that are associated with a social position (Kahn & Quinn 1970, p. 52; Katz & Kahn 1978, p. 188). Although this definition seems rather straightforward, difficulties arose when the respondents' role perceptions were to be assessed. In particular, the differentiation of role behaviour and role expectation entailed some ambiguity. Katz and Kahn do not elaborate on the situation in which the behaviour pattern that is expected in relation to a certain position, i.e., the role, does not correspond to the behaviour actually shown. It is unclear as to how such a situation should be interpreted – is the *expected* behaviour pattern still the role? Or is it the behaviour pattern that is actually *shown* and *perceived* by the involved parties?[181] The present study decided to consider the perceived role behaviour as the role that the subsidiary currently plays. In case the expected behaviour differs from the perceived behaviour, the expected behaviour is defined as the subsidiary's should-be role. Although this solution may not resolve the issue completely, it provided a practicable way to approach the research question posed.

(3) The present study aimed at providing a structure for the implications of perception gaps between headquarters and subsidiary representatives. The framework developed based on Katz and Kahn's open system approach seems to accomplish this goal to a considerable extent (5.4.2). The initially developed framework determined conflict as the main implication of perception gaps regarding the subsidiary's role, which was confirmed by the empirical findings. However, the findings showed that further implications might follow the headquarters-subsidiary conflict that partly pertain to a behavioural level, but also include

---

[180] Nevertheless, this finding supports the criticism that cautions against the generalization of individual opinions.
[181] The difficulty encountered here is to some extent rooted in the research topic of the present study. The role concept is the central concept of the present study. At the same time, this concept is questioned by the main research question, since it implies that "the role" does not exist, but rather it is a socially constructed variable that depends on subjective perception.

cognitive and affective aspects. The initial framework was consequently extended in order to include these further implications. However, since the extended framework was developed ex post from the empirical findings, it still requires empirical testing.

6.1.3 Methodological Issues

Several methodological limitations of the present study will be discussed: the difficulties to generalize from case studies, the applied methods, the study's focus on MNCs headquartered in Germany and the heterogeneity of the analyzed cases.

(1) Although it was argued that a qualitative multiple case study design was most suitable for addressing the goals of the present study (4.1.1), research designs based on case studies generally involve certain limitations. The most obvious issue is the generalization of the empirical findings (4.4.4). Case study designs typically include a relatively small number of cases that are selected for specific reasons such as their typicality, their accessibility or because they are unique (Merkens 2004, p. 166; Yin 2003, pp. 40–42). However, the small sample size and non-random choice of cases and subjects involve problems for the generalization of the findings of case study research (see, for instance, the contributions in Gomm, Hammersley & Foster 2000b). It is obvious that these conditions do not allow for statistical generalization based on error probabilities. Although it was argued in 4.4.4 that case studies may permit "analytic generalization" instead (Yin 2003, p. 10), the possibilities to generalize the results of the present study are limited.

(2) Further issues concern the methods that were applied in the empirical study. First, the questionnaire is considered that was used to assess headquarters and subsidiary respondents' evaluation of the subsidiary's role. It may be considered problematic to apply a standardized questionnaire for both companies and for all subsidiaries. Since the companies differed in terms of industry and the subsidiaries were not identical regarding their involvement in value chain activities, it may be argued that the questionnaire should have emphasized different types of capabilities or knowledge flows in each case. Furthermore, the posed questions allowed some degree of interpretation: It turned out that respondents sometimes had different ideas concerning issues, such as the scope of the question and certain expressions.[182] Overall, however, the questionnaire fulfilled its goal as a means to

---

[182] For instance, a group of headquarters representatives of Autocomp misinterpreted the term "interference". Apparently, one respondent had already answered the questionnaire and wanted

identify perception gaps in the examined cases. The additional interviews with representatives of each unit shed light on respondents' (mis)understandings of the questionnaire and allowed clarification of the respondents' opinions. Nevertheless, the findings of the interviews are not free from doubt. Although it was argued that semi-structured interviews were the means of choice to determine implications of perception gaps (4.2.2), interviews may generally be criticized for subjectivity in terms of data collection as well as data analysis (on biases in research interviews, see, e.g., Boyd Jr. & Westfall 1970; Hildum & Brown 1956).

(3) The empirical study focused on MNCs headquartered in Germany – mainly due to pragmatic reasons: German MNCs were most easily accessible for the present study. While the developed conceptual framework is not country-specific, the focus on German MNCs as well as the selection of subsidiaries from a relatively small number of countries may have resulted in certain particularities in the empirical findings.[183] The IB literature provides a large number of studies that hypothesize and confirm differences in many organizational and managerial issues depending on where an MNC is based (e.g., Chung, Gibbons & Schoch 1999; Ouchi 1981), where a subsidiary is located (e.g., Welge 1981a) and the constellation of headquarters-subsidiary location (e.g., Herbert 1999). Culturally based differences range from issues pertaining to knowledge transfer (e.g., Javidan et al. 2005) and the development of trust (e.g., Doney, Cannon & Mullen 1998) to staffing practices (e.g., Harzing 2001b). Consequently, it seems likely that the perceptions of role behaviour and behavioural expectations are influenced by culture as well. Although the importance of cultural factors is acknowledged, the present study is not able to determine the role that culture played in this context.

(4) While the argumentation outlined above criticizes mainly the focus on MNCs from one particular country and the concurrent neglect of potential variation, the sample of subsidiaries may also be criticized for too much variation. In addition to their location in different countries and cultures, the subsidiaries differed in terms of other characteristics, such as mode of establishment, local vs. expatriate management and size; furthermore, the subsidiaries belonged to two different companies. On the one side, this dissimilarity may

---

to confirm his understanding of the term with some other respondents. While discussing, the group determined to understand interference as "interaction", which was not the originally intended meaning.

[183] Although the number of subsidiaries restricted the number of included countries to six, the dispersion of these subsidiaries is quite broad. The six subsidiaries cover four of the eight cultural zones proposed by Ronen and Shenkar (Ronen & Shenkar 1985, p. 449).

have resulted in variance in the empirical findings and potentially masked results that would have surfaced in a more homogeneous sample. On the other side, the individual subgroups are too small to allow interpreting differences between them.

6.2 Implications for the International Business Literature

6.2.1 Knowledge about Subsidiary Roles

The present study contributes to the IB literature's knowledge about the perception of subsidiary roles. While the IB literature frequently refers to "the subsidiary's role", the empirical findings of the present study reinforce the supposition that a subsidiary cannot be associated with one specific role. Several earlier contributions in the IB literature hinted at this condition. For instance, it was found that elements of different roles can coexist in a subsidiary at the same time (Pearce & Tavares 2002, p. 84; Tavares & Young 2006, p. 596). In the present study, such coexistence was observed in different functional areas of a subsidiary: While a subsidiary, for example, may be highly capable in production, its marketing and sales capabilities may be low. This provides argumentation for the internal differentiation of subsidiary roles. At the same time, reasoning can be presented which nourishes the presumption that the subsidiary's role may differ depending on the environment in which the subsidiary acts. While a subsidiary is confronted with one set of role expectations within the network MNC, it may be faced with a completely different set of expectations in the context of its local business network (Johanson, Pahlberg & Thilenius 1996, p. 253; Miles & Perreault Jr. 1980, p. 138).

Neither the former perspective that highlights the concurrent coexistence of elements of different roles in a subsidiary nor the latter notion of different subsidiary roles in different contexts was in the focus of the present study. Instead, the present study illustrated a third perspective: It emphasized the perception of headquarters representatives on the one side and subsidiary representatives on the other side regarding rather narrow elements of the subsidiary's role. The empirical findings show that even when a specific role dimension in a particular functional area is concerned, headquarters and subsidiary representatives' perceptions of this dimension may differ. Furthermore, the empirical findings point at an even higher degree of complexity: In several instances, the role behaviour that is perceived by headquarters or subsidiary representatives does not match the expectations prevailing in the respective unit. This hints at a need to differentiate between the role that is currently enacted by a subsidiary and the role that is expected or envisioned for the future. The situation is complicated further by the differing degrees of awareness that one unit's members may have of the perceptions and ideas held by the members of the other unit.

In summary, this review highlights the difficulties that are associated with the subsidiary role concept. While the concept is frequently used in a broad and superficial way, it seems to be crucial to take a much more differentiated approach. Subsidiary roles should be specified in terms of issues, such as the functional area which they relate to, the context for which they are relevant, the question of whether the subsidiary's current or its should-be role is concerned and the question of which perspective is taken.

6.2.2 Conceptual Contribution

The present study contributes to the IB literature in several ways on a conceptual level. The following aspects will be discussed below: the transfer of Katz and Kahn's open system approach to network MNCs, the application of the role theoretical framework to subsidiary roles, the use of the conflict model for headquarters-subsidiary conflict and the integration of these different elements in a consistent framework.

(1) The first conceptual contribution of the present study can be seen in establishing the transferability of Katz and Kahn's social psychological open system approach to network MNCs (3.2). While the present study used only a small part of the entire approach, the theoretical model is much broader and offers a variety of possibilities; for instance, it may be applied in order to analyze an organization's relationships with its environment, power and authority in an organization, motivation or organizational change (Katz & Kahn 1978). The present study can be considered exemplary in the sense that it showed the usefulness of two components of Katz and Kahn's approach: the role theoretical framework that was applied to subsidiary roles and the conflict model that was used to consider headquarters-subsidiary conflict. These applications will be described in more detail below.

(2) As mentioned above, Katz and Kahn's open system approach provides a theoretical basis for the study of subsidiary roles. So far, research on subsidiary roles had only been theoretically grounded to a limited extent. The present study empirically tested and confirmed the applicability of the role theoretical model to subsidiary roles. However, one issue has to be kept in mind: When the role theoretical model based on Katz and Kahn is to

be applied to subsidiaries in network MNCs, then the considered characteristics of subsidiary roles have to correspond to Katz and Kahn's role definition. This definition describes roles as patterns of behaviour that are expected in relation to a certain position in a social system (Kahn & Quinn 1970, p. 52; Katz & Kahn 1978, p. 188). Many subsidiary role dimensions referred to in the IB literature do not match this definition, and the role theoretical framework does therefore not cover them. It can be concluded that, in general, a consistent definition of subsidiary roles is necessary in order to grasp the concept theoretically. Defining subsidiary roles according to Katz and Kahn, for instance, allows using the role theoretical framework in order to draw conclusions about subsidiary roles.

(3) In addition to the role theoretical framework, the present study transfers the conflict model presented by Katz and Kahn to headquarters-subsidiary conflict (3.2.3). Other contributions in the IB literature do not explicate their conceptual understanding of headquarters-subsidiary conflict. Implicitly, they define conflict as cognitive construct in terms of disagreement concerning goals and priorities, processes and conditions of the headquarters-subsidiary relationship (Pahl & Roth 1993, p. 150; Roth & Nigh 1992, p. 285) or as differing interests (Johanson, Pahlberg & Thilenius 1996, p. 259). Consequently, the present study differs from these contributions in two ways. First, it clarifies the conceptual understanding of conflict. This makes the approach taken towards headquarters-subsidiary conflict transparent and comprehensible. Thereby it presents a model of headquarters-subsidiary conflict that can be consistently applied. Second, defining headquarters-subsidiary conflict in terms of interfering behaviour is judged appropriate. Following Katz and Kahn's argumentation, the present study assumes that cognitive and affective aspects can help to understand the conflict but that they seem unfit to define conflict between organizational units (Katz & Kahn 1978, p. 613). Future IB research may consider this reasoning.[184]

(4) Finally, the present study integrated the role theoretical framework and the conflict model into a new framework that can be used to explain the implications of perception gaps regarding the subsidiary's role. As prescribed by Katz and Kahn's approach, this framework describes subsidiary roles as behaviour patterns and defines headquarters-subsidiary conflict

---

[184] If conflict was defined as disagreement, every perception gap would already represent an instance of conflict. However, the empirical findings showed that the involved parties are not even aware of some perception gaps and that these perception gaps are not experienced as conflict. Defining conflict as disagreement would include instances of conflict that would not intuitively be classified as conflict. Such a situation can be found, for example, in the cases involving the Turkish and the Polish subsidiaries: The subsidiary's behaviour is perceived differently, but the perceptions correspond to the respective expectations, and no further implications follow.

in terms of observable behaviour. In the light of the empirical findings, the framework was developed further in order to include implications for the headquarters-subsidiary relationship that follow the headquarters-subsidiary conflict. This framework can be used in the IB literature in order to study perceptions of subsidiary roles and the implications of perception gaps.

6.2.3 Methodological Implications

Several methodological issues associated with the assessment of subsidiary roles in the IB literature are highlighted.

(1) It is common practice in IB research that studies of subsidiary roles either focus on headquarters' perspective or on the subsidiary's perspective (e.g., Birkinshaw & Morrison 1995, p. 740; Taggart 1997a, p. 59). While this practice was criticized before (footnote 89; Schmid 2004, p. 248), and empirical studies confirm the existence of perceptual differences between headquarters and subsidiary representatives, the empirical findings of the present study provide further indication for associated problems: Assuming that the opinion collected from one side also represents the other side's point of view may result in a distorted picture of the actual subsidiary roles. Every headquarters-subsidiary relationship analyzed in the present study shows perception gaps concerning at least one subsidiary role attribute. This finding once more highlights the need for a more comprehensive approach to studying subsidiary roles. It seems necessary that both headquarters' and the subsidiary's side are included in the empirical procedure.

(2) Previous studies of subsidiary roles presume that each subsidiary plays one role that can be detected across the functional areas of the subsidiary. Gupta and Govindarajan explicitly include a broad range of value chain activities in the assessment of their role dimensions: In order to determine the knowledge inflow to a subsidiary and the knowledge outflow from a subsidiary, knowledge flows in nine (and later in seven) different functional areas are evaluated and their average is considered the subsidiary's position on the respective dimension (Gupta & Govindarajan 1994, p. 450). Although not as explicitly as Gupta and Govindarajan, Bartlett and Ghoshal also include a mixture of functional areas in the dimension subsidiary capabilities. They assume that capabilities can manifest themselves in any functional area of the subsidiary (Bartlett & Ghoshal 1986, p. 90). Ghoshal assesses the dimension by asking respondents to indicate the overall level of "technological and

managerial capabilities" at the respective subsidiary (Ghoshal 1986, p. 538). Consequently, both these typologies as well as empirical studies based on them assume that the subsidiary's overall location on a certain dimension can be determined (e.g., Harzing & Noorderhaven 2006b, p. 203). In contrast to this assumption, the empirical findings of the present study corroborate the suspicion that subsidiaries do not "play the same role" in every function, but that these roles may be very different. It is concluded that future studies should take a more differentiated approach to subsidiary roles.

(3) It can be frequently observed in IB research that the opinion or perception of one top manager is assessed and interpreted as representing the entire unit. The findings of the present study suggest that this may be problematic. Although overall, the responses obtained from members of the same unit were rather similar, in some instances, different representatives replied differently. Since variation between the individual respondents may have significant implications for the meaning of the obtained data, it is recommended that studies that refer to perceptual data consider more than one opinion. As was discussed above, this approach does not eliminate the issue of inferring to the entire unit, but it moderates the problem (6.1.3).

(4) Most contributions focusing on subsidiary roles are based on quantitative survey data. In the present study, the questionnaire was very helpful as a first indication of perception gaps. Furthermore, the results served as a basis for discussion in the interviews. While the questionnaire results were beneficial in this respect, it would have been problematic to consider them in isolation. Especially the lack of control over respondents' understanding of the posed questions became noticeable: The interviews revealed that respondents relatively often interpreted questions in different ways in terms of scope or meaning (6.1.3). This led to the fact that the questionnaire results showed some large differences between headquarters and subsidiary that were exposed as artefacts in the interviews; at the same time, other, not very sizable, differences seemed to be much more relevant from the respondents' point of view. It has to be emphasized that the present study did not operationalize the four role dimensions any differently than is commonly the case in studies in IB research, so that this issue can be inferred to many contributions in the field. It is concluded that questionnaires should be employed more carefully when studying subsidiary roles, and interviews should be used in order to confirm or complement survey data.

6.3 Avenues for Future Research

6.3.1 Research on Perception Gaps Concerning the Subsidiary's Role

In 2.3.2.3, a framework was presented that structures the research field surrounding the issue of perception gaps regarding the subsidiary's role. In comparison with this framework, the present study only covers a small section and thereby leaves room for future studies. The focus of the present study could be extended in several ways:

(1) The concept "subsidiary role" unites a large number of diverse aspects that are relevant for the headquarters-subsidiary relationship. The dimensions of the subsidiary role typologies presented above (2.2.2) provide a tentative summary of the variety of issues that may be considered part of a subsidiary's role. Although the typologies cannot be integrated into one comprehensive framework of subsidiary roles (Schmid, Bäurle & Kutschker 1998, p. 89), they can serve as a starting point for studies taking into account different dimensions of subsidiary roles. Since the individual dimensions refer to a variety of aspects, it could be expected that they differ in the probability with which perception gaps between headquarters and subsidiary exist. The present study did not include enough cases to allow the analysis of likelihoods for the different dimensions. Nevertheless, the findings indicate that some characteristics of the subsidiary's current role, such as decision making autonomy, knowledge outflow and capabilities seem to be particularly prone to perception gaps due to their subjective nature (Denrell, Arvidsson & Zander 2004, p. 1493). In contrast, the subsidiary's current product scope is perceived identically in all cases.[185]

(2) Perception gaps may have various causes. Particularly, the study by Denrell et al. hints at a relatively broad range of influencing factors (Denrell, Arvidsson & Zander 2004). However, additional factors could be imagined complementing those mentioned so far in the subsidiary role research stream. In Figure 6, the proposed influencing factors are grouped into several categories. Each category opens up a new area of potential influencing factors. First, influencing factors at the level of the perceiving individuals should be considered: Perception gaps may not only be influenced by information, knowledge and experience, but also, for instance, by motivation, goals or personal relationships (Birkinshaw et al. 2000, pp. 322, 327). Next, characteristics of the perceived issue can be considered. When taking "subsidiary capabilities" as an example, the clarity with which a capability can be defined, the ease with

---

[185] However, differing ideas are identified concerning the should-be development of this dimension in the future.

which it can be evaluated as well as the ease with which it can be articulated may influence the consensus between headquarters and subsidiary managers. In addition, questions as to whether the capability is regularly used and whether it has been acquired by the subsidiary or transferred by headquarters could be relevant. The range of subsidiary characteristics studied so far includes subsidiary age, market importance and perceived profitability. This spectrum could be broadened by other factors such as size, autonomy or number of expatriates. At the level of the headquarters-subsidiary relationship, communication frequency and cultural distance were examined. Here, for instance, the overall number of subsidiaries, the mode of headquarters' control of the subsidiary or the question of how communication takes place could be considered (Rodrigues 1995). Finally, characteristics of the MNC headquarters might be relevant. In this category, the general MNC strategy is considered. Further potential factors include the country in which headquarters are located, the mindset of headquarters managers and the general internationalization philosophy (Perlmutter 1969). These ideas still do not amount to a complete list of influencing factors that might have an effect on perception gaps. However, the identified categories of influencing factors refer to further possible variables and make it clear that the present study and previous research can be extended and complemented.[186]

(3) The present study's focus was on the implications of perception gaps. Nevertheless, also this area could be extended. The developed framework could serve as a basis for a more systematic approach to identify implications of perception gaps. While the present study highlighted role related headquarters-subsidiary conflict as an immediate consequence of perception gaps regarding the subsidiary's role, the further implications following this conflict might be elaborated. When it is assumed that the further implications can be interpreted as measures to manage the role related conflict, the question may be addressed as to which conflict management strategy is most functional for the headquarters-subsidiary relationship under which circumstances. In addition to the behavioural consequences, the cognitive and the affective levels should be taken into account in more detail.[187]

---

[186] Although influencing factors were not included in the scope of the present study, the empirical findings hint at various influencing factors that may have had an influence on the existence of perception gaps. These factors included cultural differences, geographic distance, characteristics of the involved persons, the quality of the personal relationships between headquarters and subsidiary managers, as well as communication, personal visits and the subsidiary's mode of establishment.

[187] Two previously conducted studies by Birkinshaw et al. and Chini et al. empirically examine consequences of perception gaps as well (Birkinshaw et al. 2000; Chini, Ambos & Wehle 2005). Birkinshaw et al. identified the degree of headquarters' control over the subsidiary and

6.3.2 Theoretical Consolidation

Previous research on perception gaps concerning subsidiary roles had only been theoretically grounded to a limited extent (Schmid 2004, p. 247). The present study encountered this lack of theoretical foundation in the subsidiary role literature by drawing on the social psychological open system approach presented by Katz and Kahn (Katz & Kahn 1978). The applicability of the approach for network MNCs in general and subsidiary roles in particular was conceptually established and empirically tested. Although the developed conceptual framework is supported by the empirical findings of the present study, further developments are necessary. First, several issues included in the conceptual framework should be specified. This concerns, for instance, an unambiguous definition of the concepts defined as the subsidiary's current role and its relationship with the subsidiary's perceived behaviour as well as expectations regarding this behaviour. In this context, the concepts as-is role and should-be role should be consolidated. Furthermore, the applicability of the conceptual framework to the roles of subsidiaries in network MNCs should be replicated by other studies. The conditions and circumstances under which the framework is applicable have to be spelled out. Finally, the conceptual framework's usefulness for addressing various questions has to be clarified.

6.3.3 Methodological Approaches

The research designs applied in previous studies of perception gaps were mostly quantitative. The main results were attained by questionnaires that were mailed to the participants. As an exception, Birkinshaw et al. administer the questionnaires in person, which gives them more control over who actually answers the questions and, at the same time, validates the answers (Birkinshaw et al. 2000, pp. 333–334). The studies by Arvidsson and Asakawa additionally conduct interviews with some of the questionnaire respondents. Arvidsson aims at confirming the questionnaire results and their interpretation as well as receiving a better idea of the appearance of the concepts in reality (Arvidsson 1999, p. 130).

---

headquarters-subsidiary cooperation as behavioural implications of the perception gap (Birkinshaw et al. 2000). While decreased cooperation was found to be a consequence of increased control, headquarters' increased control may be interpreted as a conflict management measure by headquarters according to the present study's framework. Chini et al. detected dissatisfaction as implication of perception gaps, which was also found in the present study (Chini, Ambos & Wehle 2005).

Asakawa also intends to confirm the questionnaire results and at the same time tries to address the dynamic nature of the analyzed phenomena (Asakawa 2001, p. 740).

The present study also combined a questionnaire with interviews but differs from the previous studies by more strongly emphasizing the contribution of the interviews. Although this in-depth approach provided more detailed insight in the ideas which headquarters and subsidiary representatives associate with a subsidiary's role as well as the mechanisms by which perception gaps result in conflict and further implications, additional qualitative research could still extend this knowledge base (Morgan & Smircich 1980, pp. 497–499). As was mentioned above, for instance, the role concept that is part of the conceptual framework needs further clarification, which can probably only be reached by detailed analysis of the interrelations in specific cases. In addition to the specification of conceptual issues via qualitative approaches, empirical tests of the proposed conceptual framework in a large-scale quantitative study are suggested. Such a test can help to determine the opportunities and limitations of the conceptual framework developed in the present study.

The present study considered not only headquarters' and the subsidiary's perspective, but also referred to several respondents in each unit. It was acknowledged in 6.1.2 that this approach does not finally solve the dichotomy between individual responses and the inference to the entire unit. Nevertheless, it allowed valuable insights in the diversity of opinions that may exist within one unit. Consequently, it is strongly recommended to future studies that want to highlight cognitive concepts on the level of the organizational unit to assess more than one opinion in the unit.

6.4 Managerial Implications

As Starbuck and Mezias contend, "researchers and managers live in different worlds" (Starbuck & Mezias 1996, p. 104). Nevertheless, it will be attempted to identify several issues of the present study that may be relevant for managers in MNCs.

So far, no definite judgement was offered concerning the valuation of perception gaps and their implications from the MNC's perspective. Differing perceptions of the subsidiary's role as such cannot be considered positive or negative; rather, their consequences are decisive.[188] The present study showed that perception gaps generally lead to role related conflict between headquarters and the subsidiary. The general conflict literature asserts that functional as well as dysfunctional implications of conflict are conceivable (Jehn & Mannix 2001; Litterer 1966, pp. 179–180; Rahim 2002, p. 211). This is expected to be true for headquarters-subsidiary conflict as well, although some authors claim that the negative rather than the positive implications of conflict usually prevail (Johanson, Pahlberg & Thilenius 1996, p. 254; Roth & Nigh 1992, p. 286).

In general, managers seem to have two options of how to handle perception gaps. (1) The first option is to try to avoid them. Although the present study did not explicitly focus on the conditions surrounding the emergence of perception gaps, several ideas can be developed that may be helpful for reducing perception gaps. For that purpose, the empirical findings of the present study are combined with recommendations found in the literature: While some factors that seem to affect perception gaps, such as cultural differences, geographical distance and characteristics of the involved persons, cannot be intentionally influenced, other influencing factors are in the managers' grip. A clear role definition that unambiguously determines rights and responsibilities may contribute to the prevention of perception gaps (Hulbert, Brandt & Richers 1980, p. 13). However, it seems advisable that such a definition is not dictated by headquarters, but that it is attempted to develop consent that is acceptable for both sides. Communication appears to be a central means in order to avoid perception gaps between headquarters and subsidiary managers. Frequent and open exchange as well as the discussion of the ideas and perspectives emerging on each side may establish a common understanding of the subsidiary's role. Even if gaps appear, they can be bridged through frank interaction. While regular and open communication may positively influence the quality of a headquarters-subsidiary relationship, personal contact in the form of visits to each others' location could even enhance this effect. Particular attention regarding the perceptions of subsidiary roles may be necessary for headquarters-subsidiary relationships which involve acquired subsidiaries that had already developed a certain structure and "identity". While some acquisitions require a high degree of adjustment on the side of the newly acquired unit (Haspeslagh & Jemison 1991, pp. 145–166), the subsidiary managers may possess a predetermined idea of the subsidiary's role which may not be easily altered

---

[188] While most authors focus on the negative consequences of perception gaps, Birkinshaw et al. note the possibility that under certain conditions, perception gaps might also provide momentum for MNC development (Birkinshaw et al. 2000, p. 340).

(Garnier 1982, p. 900).[189] Furthermore, perception gaps especially emerge in functions for which headquarters and the subsidiary share responsibility. Although it may be difficult to define unambiguously the degree to which the subsidiary is involved in the respective function, it seems to be worthwhile to put effort into a clear determination of duties and responsibilities.

(2) The second option that managers have in dealing with perception gaps is to try to manage the resulting role related conflict in a constructive way. It is generally assumed that the question of whether the functional or dysfunctional implications of conflict prevail mainly depends on the way in which conflict is managed (Alper, Tjosvold & Law 2000, p. 625; Hignite, Margavio & Chin 2002, p. 316; Kelly 2006, p. 27; Thomas 1976, pp. 891–892). Thomas assumes that the functionality of a certain conflict handling mode depends on the two dimensions "choice of beneficiary" and "time frame" (Thomas 1992a, p. 270). With regard to the first dimension, one can try to optimize the welfare of one of the involved parties, both parties or a larger system of which the parties are members. In the case of headquarters-subsidiary conflict, probably the welfare of the larger system, i.e., the MNC should be aimed at. When time as the second dimension is considered, Thomas differentiates short-term and long-term goals. Although he acknowledges, that certain conditions may necessitate pragmatic answers which allow coping with the current conditions, he advocates collaboration in the long-term (Thomas 1992a, p. 271). Collaboration as the most beneficial conflict management strategy is promoted by a considerable number of researchers (e.g., Blake & Mouton 1964; Brown 1983; Eiseman 1978; Fisher, Ury & Patton 1991; Likert & Likert 1976; Rubin, Pruitt & Kim 1994). Not only theoretical contributions, but also empirical findings support this assumption. The results indicate that collaboration can lead to superior outcomes for the involved individuals (e.g., satisfaction and self-esteem), for their relationship (e.g., trust and respect) and for the entire organization (e.g., more open exchange of information and more integrative decisions; Thomas 1992a, p. 271, 1992b, pp. 682–690). However, although collaboration or cooperation may be the most functional solution for the entire system in the long term, the individual actors may find other modes, such as competition, more attractive in the short term. It is therefore crucial to organize structural variables of the headquarters-subsidiary

---

[189] The IB literature confirms a positive relationship between subsidiaries that were established through acquisition (versus greenfield establishments) and the subsidiary's autonomy (Young & Tavares 2004, p. 217). However, it should be kept in mind that there are various alternatives for integrating acquired subsidiaries which imply differing requirements for the adjustment of the subsidiary's role (see, for instance, Haspeslagh & Jemison 1991, pp. 145–166).

relationship in a way that provides incentives for collaboration (Katz & Kahn 1978, p. 644; Thomas 1992a, p. 271).

6.5 Summary

Two goals were formulated at the outset of the present study. (1) First, the study intended to identify implications of perception gaps between headquarters and subsidiary managers concerning the subsidiary's role within the MNC for the headquarters-subsidiary relationship. In the empirical study, headquarters-subsidiary conflict was distinguished as the immediate consequence of perception gaps concerning role dimensions that correspond to the role definition determined in the conceptual framework. This role related conflict was found to have further implications for the headquarters-subsidiary relationship – not only at a behavioural level, but also at an affective level and a cognitive level. Overall, the empirical findings allowed more insight into the behavioural level than into the affective and cognitive levels. The behavioural implications following the role related conflict could be interpreted as conflict management measures directed at the role related conflict. Although it cannot be claimed that the present study uncovered all possible implications of perception gaps, it is supposed to constitute a first step in that direction. However, particularly the affective and cognitive levels of implications following the role related conflict require more attention.

(2) The second goal was of a conceptual nature. Since the theoretical foundation of the literature on subsidiary roles is generally limited, the study aimed at developing a conceptual framework that can be applied in order to analyze headquarters-subsidiary relationships and, in particular, the subsidiary role concept. The applicability of the proposed framework was theoretically established and empirically tested. Nevertheless, the present study must be understood as merely a first initiative towards a theoretical foundation for research on the roles of subsidiaries in network MNCs. The developed framework has to be further tested and extended.

To summarize, the present study contributes to the literature on subsidiary roles in two ways: First, it provides novel insights regarding the perceptions of subsidiary roles in network MNCs and the implication of perception gaps between headquarters and subsidiary managers. Second, it proposes a conceptual framework that can be used to analyze subsidiary roles from a theoretical perspective.

Appendix

Appendix A Questionnaire Results on Disagreement and Interference

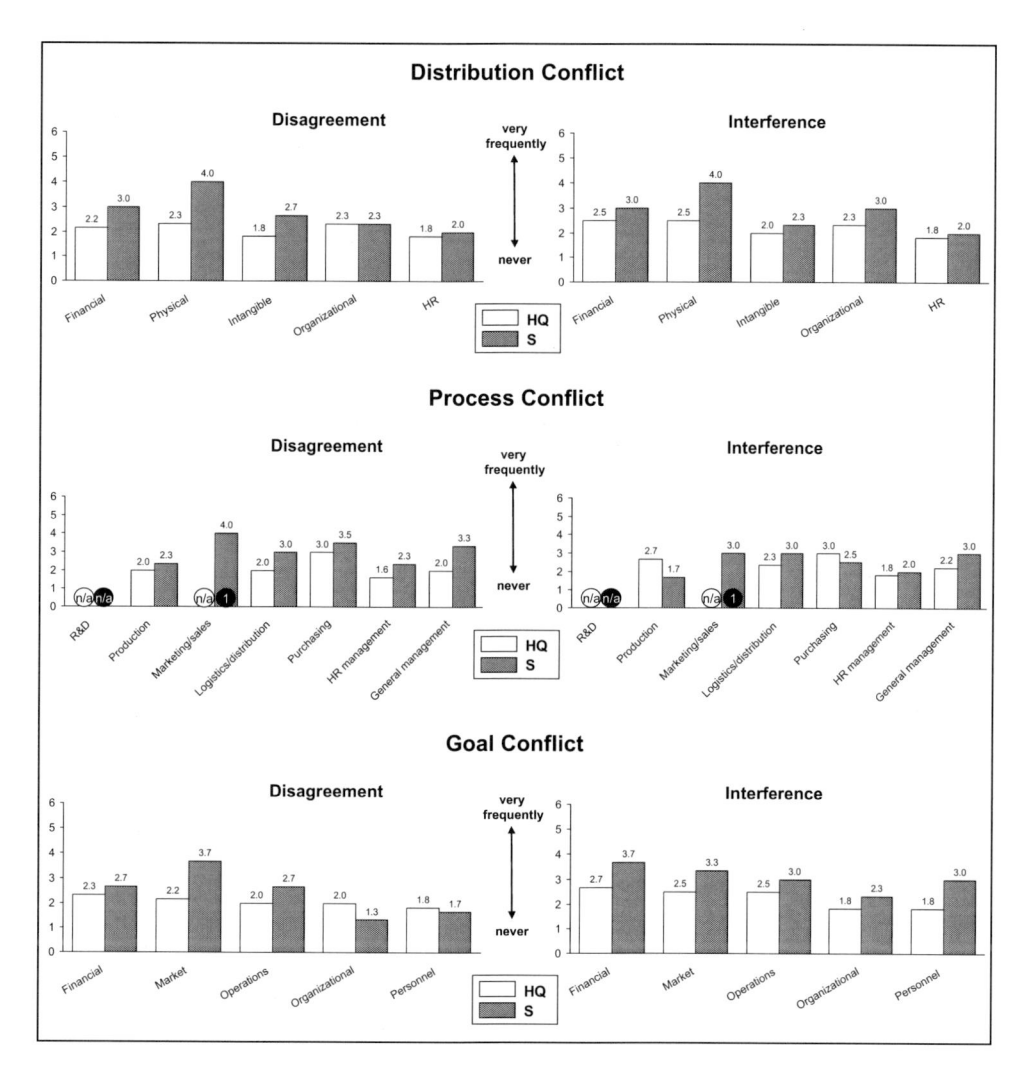

Distribution Conflict

Disagreement (very frequently ↕ never):
- Financial: HQ 2.2, S 3.0
- Physical: HQ 2.3, S 4.0
- Intangible: HQ 1.8, S 2.7
- Organizational: HQ 2.3, S 2.3
- HR: HQ 1.8, S 2.0

Interference:
- Financial: HQ 2.5, S 3.0
- Physical: HQ 2.5, S 4.0
- Intangible: HQ 2.0, S 2.3
- Organizational: HQ 2.3, S 3.0
- HR: HQ 1.8, S 2.0

Process Conflict

Disagreement:
- R&D: n/a, n/a
- Production: HQ 2.0, S 2.3
- Marketing/sales: n/a, 4.0
- Logistics/distribution: HQ 2.0, S 3.0
- Purchasing: HQ 3.0, S 3.5
- HR management: HQ 1.6, S 2.3
- General management: HQ 2.0, S 3.3

Interference:
- R&D: n/a, n/a
- Production: HQ 2.7, S 1.7
- Marketing/sales: n/a, 3.0
- Logistics/distribution: HQ 2.3, S 3.0
- Purchasing: HQ 3.0, S 2.5
- HR management: HQ 1.8, S 2.0
- General management: HQ 2.2, S 3.0

Goal Conflict

Disagreement:
- Financial: HQ 2.3, S 2.7
- Market: HQ 2.2, S 3.7
- Operations: HQ 2.0, S 2.7
- Organizational: HQ 2.0, S 1.3
- Personnel: HQ 1.8, S 1.7

Interference:
- Financial: HQ 2.7, S 3.7
- Market: HQ 2.5, S 3.3
- Operations: HQ 2.5, S 3.0
- Organizational: HQ 1.8, S 2.3
- Personnel: HQ 1.8, S 3.0

Appendix A - 1: Questionnaire Results Concerning Conflict between Autocomp's Headquarters and the Hungarian Subsidiary

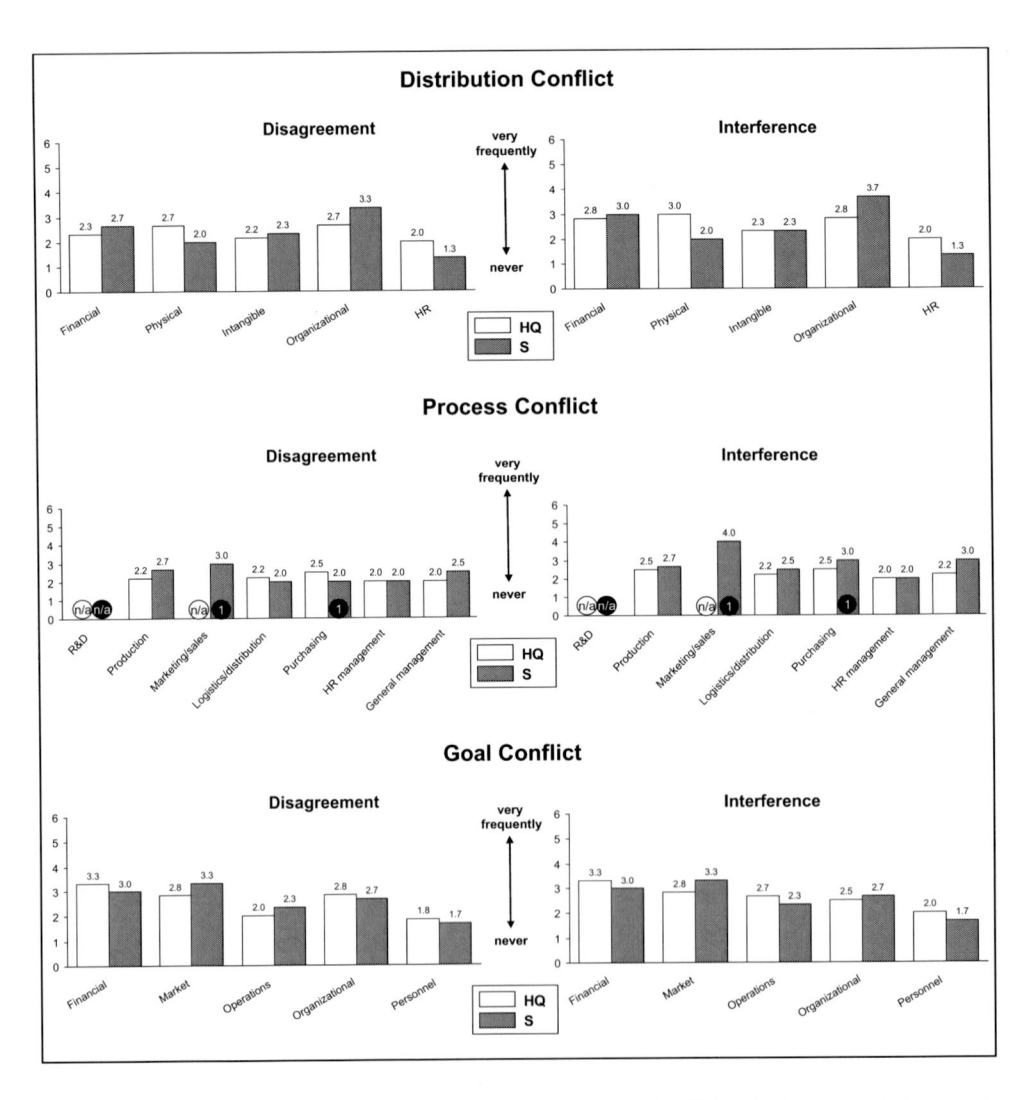

Distribution Conflict

Disagreement

Category	HQ	S
Financial	2.3	2.7
Physical	2.7	2.0
Intangible	2.2	2.3
Organizational	2.7	3.3
HR	2.0	1.3

Interference

Category	HQ	S
Financial	2.8	3.0
Physical	3.0	2.0
Intangible	2.3	2.3
Organizational	2.8	3.7
HR	2.0	1.3

Process Conflict

Disagreement

Category	HQ	S
R&D	n/a	n/a
Production	2.2	2.7
Marketing/sales	n/a	3.0
Logistics/distribution	2.2	2.0
Purchasing	2.5	2.0
HR management	2.0	2.0
General management	2.0	2.5

Interference

Category	HQ	S
R&D	n/a	n/a
Production	2.5	2.7
Marketing/sales	n/a	4.0
Logistics/distribution	2.2	2.5
Purchasing	2.5	3.0
HR management	2.0	2.0
General management	2.2	3.0

Goal Conflict

Disagreement

Category	HQ	S
Financial	3.3	3.0
Market	2.8	3.3
Operations	2.0	2.3
Organizational	2.8	2.7
Personnel	1.8	1.7

Interference

Category	HQ	S
Financial	3.3	3.0
Market	2.8	3.3
Operations	2.7	2.3
Organizational	2.5	2.7
Personnel	2.0	1.7

Appendix A - 2: Questionnaire Results Concerning Conflict between Autocomp's Headquarters and the Polish Subsidiary

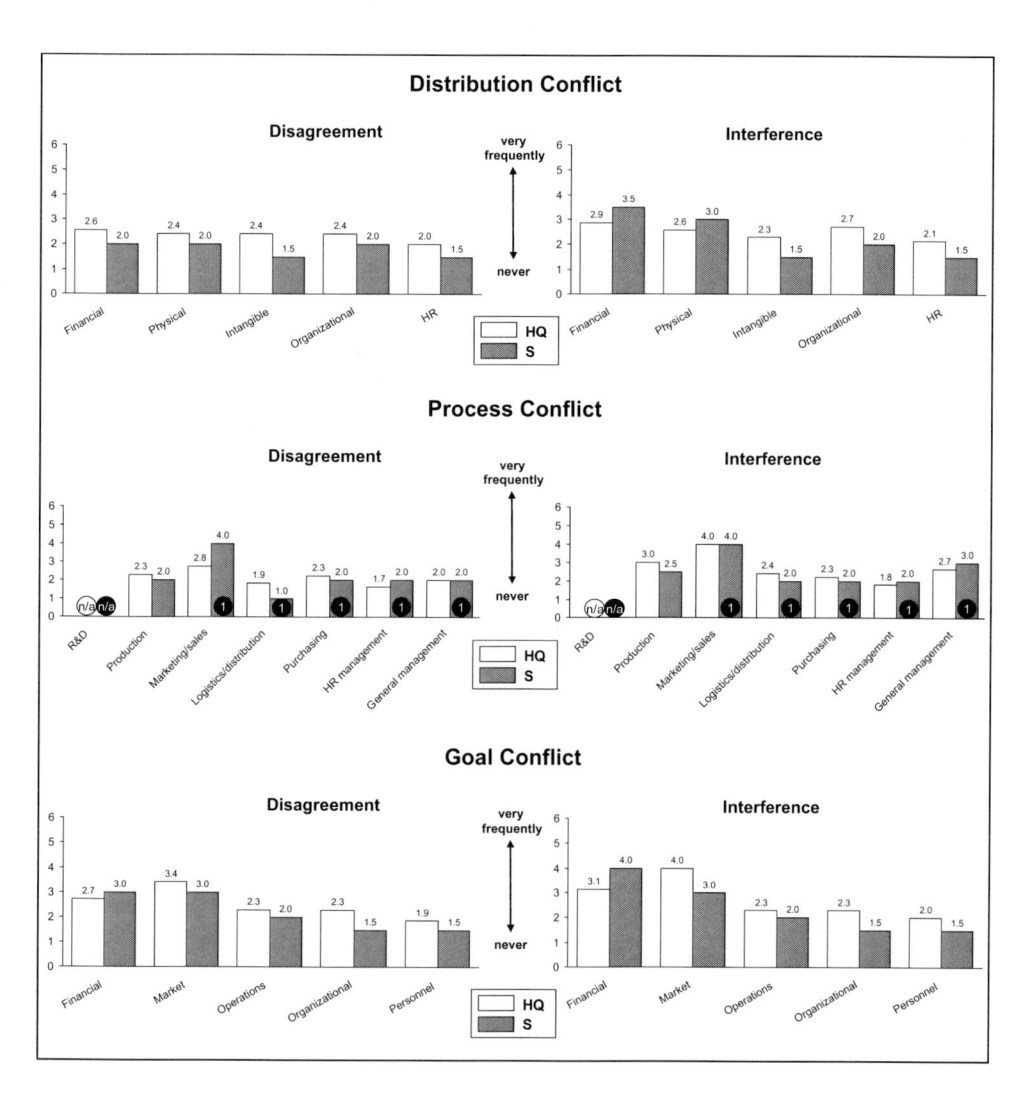

Distribution Conflict

Disagreement

Category	HQ	S
Financial	2.6	2.0
Physical	2.4	2.0
Intangible	2.4	1.5
Organizational	2.4	2.0
HR	2.0	1.5

Interference

Category	HQ	S
Financial	2.9	3.5
Physical	2.6	3.0
Intangible	2.3	1.5
Organizational	2.7	2.0
HR	2.1	1.5

Process Conflict

Disagreement

Category	HQ	S
R&D	n/a	n/a
Production	2.3	2.0
Marketing/sales	2.8	4.0
Logistics/distribution	1.9	1.0
Purchasing	2.3	2.0
HR management	1.7	2.0
General management	2.0	2.0

Interference

Category	HQ	S
R&D	n/a	n/a
Production	3.0	2.5
Marketing/sales	4.0	4.0
Logistics/distribution	2.4	2.0
Purchasing	2.3	2.0
HR management	1.8	2.0
General management	2.7	3.0

Goal Conflict

Disagreement

Category	HQ	S
Financial	2.7	3.0
Market	3.4	3.0
Operations	2.3	2.0
Organizational	2.3	1.5
Personnel	1.9	1.5

Interference

Category	HQ	S
Financial	3.1	4.0
Market	4.0	3.0
Operations	2.3	2.0
Organizational	2.3	1.5
Personnel	2.0	1.5

Appendix A - 3: Questionnaire Results Concerning Conflict between Autocomp's Headquarters and the Turkish Subsidiary

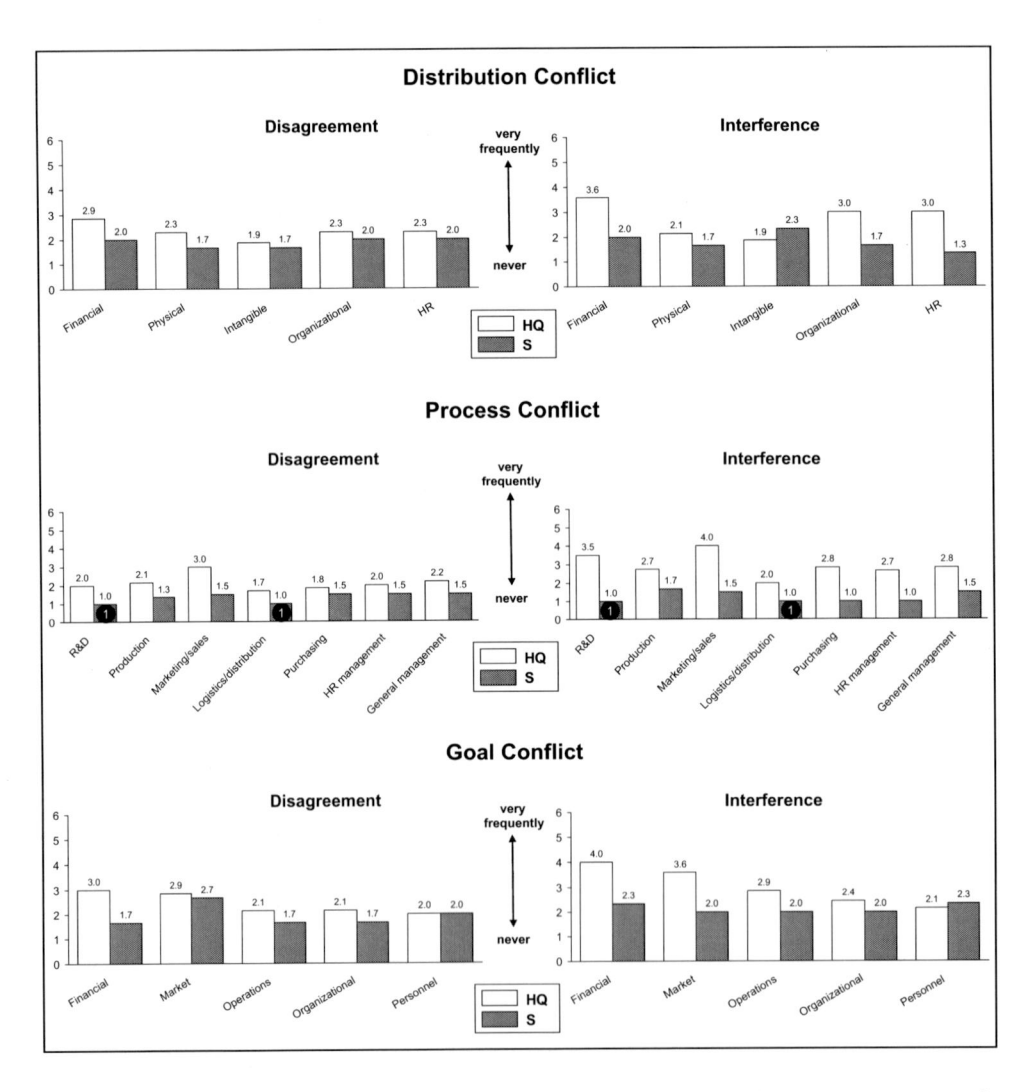

Distribution Conflict

Disagreement

Category	HQ	S
Financial	2.9	2.0
Physical	2.3	1.7
Intangible	1.9	1.7
Organizational	2.3	2.0
HR	2.3	2.0

Interference

Category	HQ	S
Financial	3.6	2.0
Physical	2.1	1.7
Intangible	1.9	2.3
Organizational	3.0	1.7
HR	3.0	1.3

Process Conflict

Disagreement

Category	HQ	S
R&D	2.0	1.0
Production	2.1	1.3
Marketing/sales	3.0	1.5
Logistics/distribution	1.7	1.0
Purchasing	1.8	1.5
HR management	2.0	1.5
General management	2.2	1.5

Interference

Category	HQ	S
R&D	3.5	1.0
Production	2.7	1.7
Marketing/sales	4.0	1.5
Logistics/distribution	2.0	1.0
Purchasing	2.8	1.0
HR management	2.7	1.0
General management	2.8	1.5

Goal Conflict

Disagreement

Category	HQ	S
Financial	3.0	1.7
Market	2.9	2.7
Operations	2.1	1.7
Organizational	2.1	1.7
Personnel	2.0	2.0

Interference

Category	HQ	S
Financial	4.0	2.3
Market	3.6	2.0
Operations	2.9	2.0
Organizational	2.4	2.0
Personnel	2.1	2.3

Scale: very frequently ↔ never

Appendix A - 4: Questionnaire Results Concerning Conflict between Autocomp's Headquarters and the Mexican Subsidiary

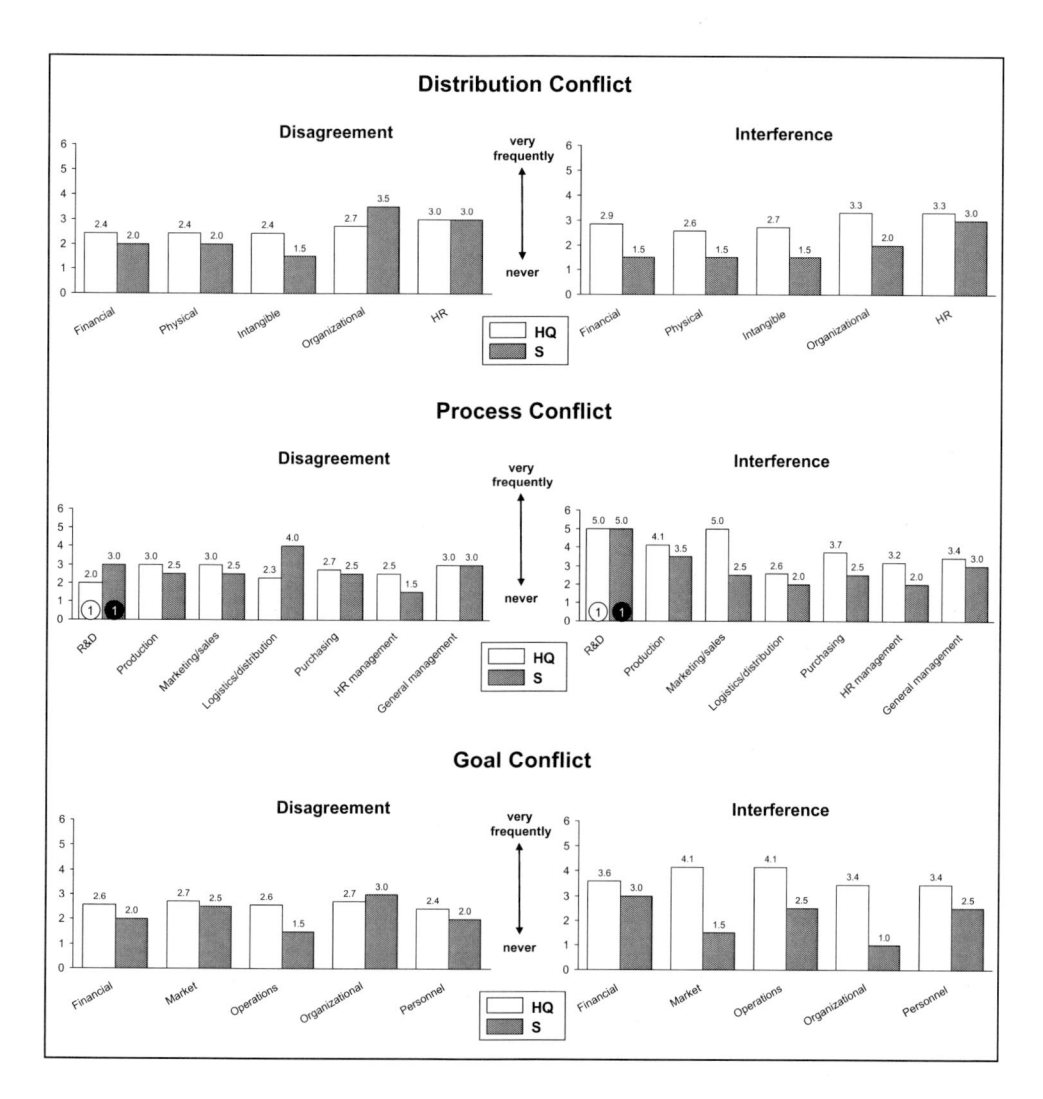

Appendix A - 5: Questionnaire Results Concerning Conflict between Autocomp's Headquarters and the Chinese Subsidiary

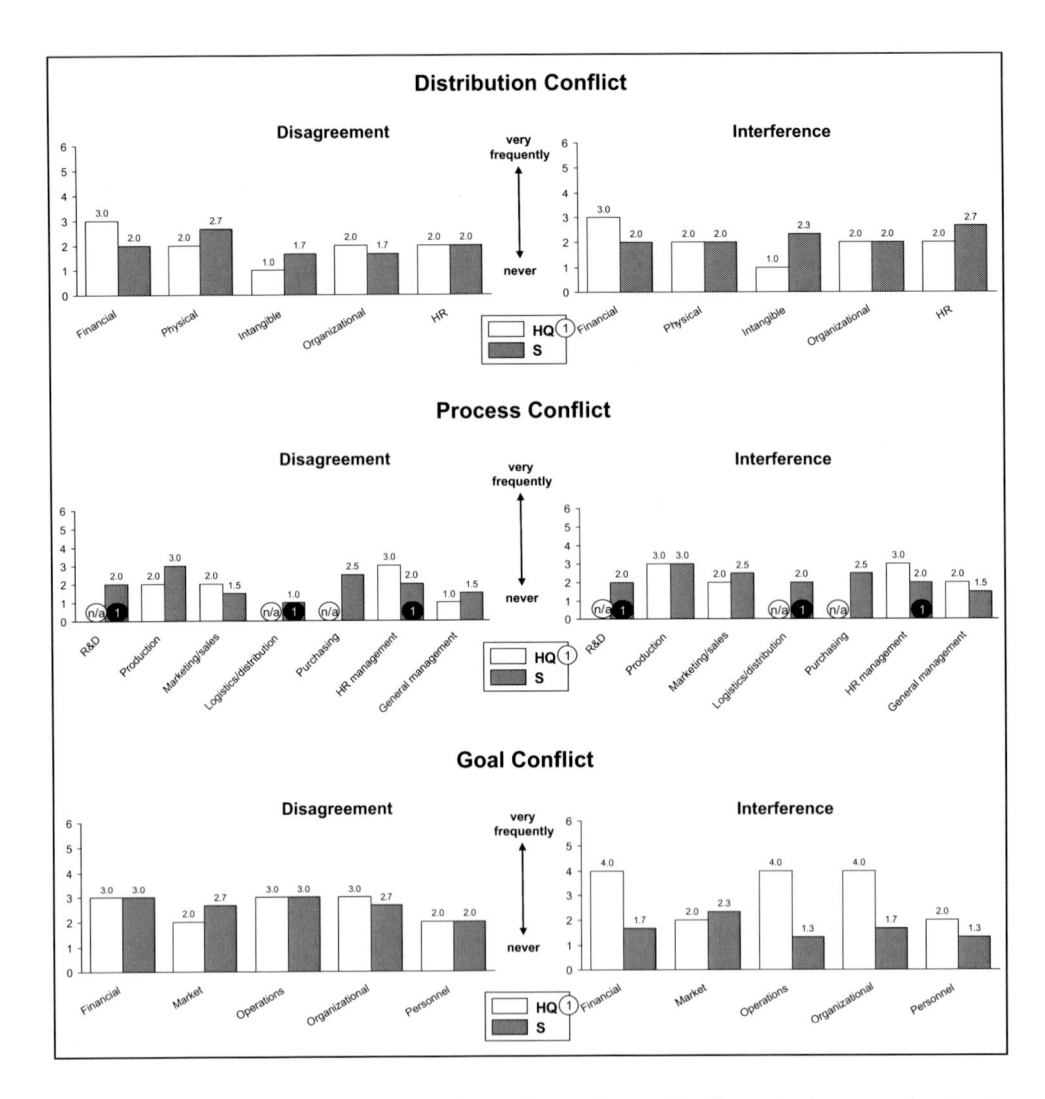

Distribution Conflict

Disagreement

Category	HQ	S
Financial	3.0	2.0
Physical	2.0	2.7
Intangible	1.0	1.7
Organizational	2.0	1.7
HR	2.0	2.0

Interference

Category	HQ	S
Financial	3.0	2.0
Physical	2.0	2.0
Intangible	1.0	2.3
Organizational	2.0	2.0
HR	2.0	2.7

Process Conflict

Disagreement

Category	HQ	S
R&D	n/a	2.0
Production	2.0	3.0
Marketing/sales	2.0	1.5
Logistics/distribution	n/a	1.0
Purchasing	n/a	2.5
HR management	3.0	2.0
General management	1.0	1.5

Interference

Category	HQ	S
R&D	n/a	2.0
Production	3.0	3.0
Marketing/sales	2.0	2.5
Logistics/distribution	n/a	2.0
Purchasing	n/a	2.5
HR management	3.0	2.0
General management	2.0	1.5

Goal Conflict

Disagreement

Category	HQ	S
Financial	3.0	3.0
Market	2.0	2.7
Operations	3.0	3.0
Organizational	3.0	2.7
Personnel	2.0	2.0

Interference

Category	HQ	S
Financial	4.0	1.7
Market	2.0	2.3
Operations	4.0	1.3
Organizational	4.0	1.7
Personnel	2.0	1.3

Appendix A - 6: Questionnaire Results Concerning Conflict between Construc's Headquarters and the US-American Subsidiary

Appendix B   Final Code List

Categories	Codes	Definition
Subsidiary country (COU)		
China	CHI	Subsidiary is located in China.
Hungary	HUN	Subsidiary is located in Hungary.
Mexico	MEX	Subsidiary is located in Mexico.
Poland	POL	Subsidiary is located in Poland.
Romania	ROM	Subsidiary is located in Romania.
Turkey	TUR	Subsidiary is located in Turkey.
UAE	UAE	Subsidiary is located in UAE.
USA	USA	Subsidiary is located in USA.
Perception gaps (PG)		
HQ>S	HQ>S	Headquarters managers rate the respective characteristic higher than subsidiary managers do.
S>S	S>HQ	Subsidiary managers rate the respective characteristic higher than headquarters managers do.
Subsidiary's market (SM)		
Market volume	SM Vol.	Respondent talks about the volume of the subsidiary's market.
Competitive intensity	SM Comp.Int.	Respondent talks about the competitive intensity of the subsidiary's market.
Technological dynamism	SM Tech.Dyn.	Respondent talks about the technological dynamism of the subsidiary's market.
Customer demand	SM Cust.Dem.	Respondent talks about the customer demand in the subsidiary's market.
Subsidiary's functions (SF)		
R&D	R&D	Respondent talks about the subsidiary's/headquarters' R&D activities.
Production	Prod.	Respondent talks about the subsidiary's/headquarters' production activities.
Marketing/sales	Mark./Sal.	Respondent talks about the subsidiary's/headquarters' marketing/sales activities.
Logistics/distribution	Log./Dist.	Respondent talks about the subsidiary's/headquarters' logistics/distribution activities.
Purchasing	Purch.	Respondent talks about the subsidiary's/headquarters' purchasing activities.
HR management	HR Mgmt.	Respondent talks about the subsidiary's/headquarters' HR management activities.
General management	Gen.Mgmt.	Respondent talks about the subsidiary's/headquarters' general management activities.
IT	IT	Respondent talks about the subsidiary's/headquarters' IT activities.
Product management	Prod.Mgmt.	Respondent talks about the subsidiary's/headquarters' product management activities.
Subsidiary's capabilities (SC)		
Subsidiary's capabilities	SC (& SF-code)	Respondent talks about the subsidiary's capabilities. The subsidiary's capabilities will generally be considered in relation to activities in a specific function.
Knowledge inflow HQ → S (KI-HQ-S)		

Knowledge inflow from HQ to the focal subsidiary	KI-HQ-S (& SF-code)	Respondent talks about knowledge inflow from HQ to the focal subsidiary. Knowledge inflow from HQ to the focal subsidiary will generally be considered in relation to activities in a specific function.
Knowledge inflow S → S (KI-S-S)		
Knowledge inflow from other subsidiaries to the focal subsidiary	KI-S-S (& SF-code)	Respondent talks about knowledge inflow from other subsidiaries to the focal subsidiary. Knowledge inflow from other subsidiaries to the focal subsidiary will generally be considered in relation to activities in a specific function.
Knowledge outflow S → HQ (KO-S-HQ)		
Knowledge outflow from the focal subsidiary to headquarters	KO-S-HQ (& SF-code)	Respondent talks about knowledge outflow from the focal subsidiary to headquarters. Knowledge outflow from the focal subsidiary to headquarters will generally be considered in relation to activities in a specific function.
Knowledge outflow S → S (KO-S-S)		
Knowledge outflow from the focal subsidiary to other subsidiaries	KO-S-S (& SF-code)	Respondent talks about knowledge outflow from the focal subsidiary to other subsidiaries. Knowledge outflow from the focal subsidiary to other subsidiaries will generally be considered in relation to activities in a specific function.
"New" role dimensions		
(Decision making) autonomy	Auton.	Respondent talks about the subsidiary's autonomy.
Involvement in value chain activities	Involv.Val.Ch.Act.	Respondent talks about the subsidiary's involvement in specific value chain activities.
Products scope	Prod. scope	Respondent talks about the subsidiary's product scope.
Conflict		
Disagreement	Disagr.	Respondent talks about disagreement between headquarters and the subsidiary. → The disagreement is open. That means that the involved parties are aware of the differing opinion. Disagreement will be considered in relation to specific conflict areas.
Emotional Conflict	Emot.Con.	Respondent talks about emotional conflict between headquarters and the subsidiary. → Emotional conflict is understood as tension, anger, dissatisfaction of one of the involved parties. Emotional conflict will be considered in relation to specific conflict areas.
Interference	Interf.	Respondent talks about interference between headquarters and the subsidiary. → Interference means that one of the involved parties interferes with the goals of the other party or blocks the other party. Interference will be considered in relation to specific conflict areas.
Headquarters conflict	HQ-Conf.	Respondent talks about conflict that is experienced by headquarters representatives. → Headquarters conflict is always identified with specific other categories: disagreement/interference, conflict issues.
Subsidiary conflict	S-Conf.	Respondent talks about conflict that is experienced by subsidiary representatives. → Subsidiary conflict is always identified with specific other

			categories: disagreement/interference, conflict issues.
Distribution conflict (DC)			
	Financial resources	DC Fin.R.	Respondent talks about headquarters-subsidiary conflict concerning financial resources.
	Physical resources	DC Phys.R.	Respondent talks about headquarters-subsidiary conflict concerning physical resources.
	Intangible resources	DC Intan.Rs.	Respondent talks about headquarters-subsidiary conflict concerning intangible resources.
	Organizational resources	DC Org.R.	Respondent talks about headquarters-subsidiary conflict concerning organizational resources.
	HR resources	DC Hum.R.	Respondent talks about headquarters-subsidiary conflict concerning HR resources.
Process conflict (PC)			
	Process conflict	PC (& SF-code)	Respondent talks about process conflict. Process conflict will generally be considered in relation to activities in a specific function.
Goal conflict (GC)			
	Financial goals	GC Fin.G.	Respondent talks about headquarters-subsidiary conflict concerning the subsidiary's financial goals.
	Market related goals	GC Mark.G.	Respondent talks about headquarters-subsidiary conflict concerning the subsidiary's market related goals.
	Operations related goals	GC Ops.G.	Respondent talks about headquarters-subsidiary conflict concerning the subsidiary's operations related goals.
	Organizational develop. goals	GC Org.G.	Respondent talks about headquarters-subsidiary conflict concerning the subsidiary's organizational development goals.
	Personnel development goals	GC Pers.G.	Respondent talks about headquarters-subsidiary conflict concerning the subsidiary's personnel development goals.
Other			
	Results of the questionnaire: Subjectivity/perspective	Subj./Persp.	Respondent explains the results showing in the questionnaire by the specific perspective of the respondents (HQ vs. S; personal; temporal…).
	"Reality": Persons	Person	Respondent explains certain situations or occurrences with the personality of the involved persons.
	Method: Questionnaire	Quest.	Respondent comments on the questionnaire – ambiguity of the questions….
Influencing factors/explanations			
	Distance	Dist.	Respondent refers to the distance between HQ and S – geographically and figuratively.
	Visits	Visits	Respondent talks about visits by HQ representatives at S locations
	Communication	Commu.	Respondent talks about the communication between HQ and S managers (frequency, quality…).
	Culture	Cult.	Respondent talks about cultural differences, specifics of home and host country.
	Centralization	Centr.	Respondent talks about centralization of value chain activities.
	Information flow	Inf.Fl.	Respondent talks about the flow of information between organizational units.
	Overall role of subsidiary	Overall role	Respondent talks about the subsidiary's overall role.

References

Abdel-Halim, Ahmed A. (1981): Effects of Role Stress-Job Design-Technology Interaction on Employee Work Satisfaction. In: Academy of Management Journal. Vol. 24, No. 2, pp. 260–273.

Abernethy, Margaret A., Wai Fong, Chua, Luckett, Peter F. & Selto, Frank H. (1999): Research in Managerial Accounting: Learning from Others' Experiences. In: Accounting & Finance. Vol. 39, No. 1, pp. 1–27.

Adenfelt, Maria & Lagerström, Katarina (2006): Knowledge Development and Sharing in Multinational Corporations: The Case of a Centre of Excellence and a Transnational Team. In: International Business Review. Vol. 15, No. 4, pp. 381–400.

Aiken, Michael & Hage, Jerald (1968): Organizational Interdependence and Intra-Organizational Structure. In: American Sociological Review. Vol. 33, No. 6, pp. 912–930.

Allen, Vernon L. & Van de Vliert, Evert (1984): A Role Theoretical Perspective on Transition Processes. In: Allen, Vernon L. & Van de Vliert, Evert (eds.): Role Transitions. Plenum, New York, London, pp. 3–18.

Alper, Steve, Tjosvold, Dean & Law, Kenneth S. (2000): Conflict Management, Efficacy, and Performance in Organizational Teams. In: Personnel Psychology. Vol. 53, No. 3, pp. 625–642.

Alter, Catherine (1990): An Exploratory Study of Conflicts and Coordination in Interorganizational Service Delivery System. In: Academy of Management Journal. Vol. 33, No. 3, pp. 478–502.

Amason, Allen C. & Sapienza, Harry J. (1997): The Effects of Top Management Team Size and Interaction Norms on Cognitive and Affective Conflict. In: Journal of Management. Vol. 23, No. 4, pp. 495–516.

Amason, Allen C. & Schweiger, David (1997): The Effect of Conflict on Strategic Decision Making Effectiveness and Organizational Performance. In: De Dreu, Carsten K. W. & Van de Vliert, Evert (eds.): Using Conflict in Organizations. Sage, London, pp. 101–115.

Ambos, Björn & Reitsperger, Wolf (2004): Offshore Centers of Excellence: Social Control and Success. In: Management International Review. Vol. 44, No. 2, pp. 51–65.

Amit, Raphael & Schoemaker, Paul J. H. (1993): Strategic Assets and Organizational Rent. In: Strategic Management Journal. Vol. 14, No. 1, pp. 33–46.

Ammeter, Anthony P., Douglas, Ceasar, Ferris, Gerald R. & Goka, Heather (2004): A Social Relationship Conceptualization of Trust and Accountability in Organizations. In: Human Resource Management Review. Vol. 14, No. 1, pp. 47–65.

Andersen, Poul Houman & Skaates, Maria Anne (2004): Ensuring Validity in Qualitative International Business Research. In: Marschan-Piekkari, Rebecca & Welch, Catherine (eds.): Handbook of Qualitative Research Methods for International Business. Edward Elgar, Cheltenham, Northampton, pp. 464–485.

Anderson, Helen, Havila, Virpi, Andersen, Poul & Halinen, Aino (1998): Position and Role-Conceptualizing Dynamics in Business Networks. In: Scandinavian Journal of Management. Vol. 14, No. 3, pp. 167–186.

Anderson, James C. & Narus, James A. (1990): A Model of Distributor Firm and Manufacturer Firm Working Partnerships. In: Journal of Marketing. Vol. 54, No. 1, pp. 42–58.

Andersson, Ulf, Björkman, Ingmar & Forsgren, Mats (2005): Managing Subsidiary Knowledge Creation: The Effect of Control Mechanisms on Subsidiary Local Embeddedness. In: International Business Review. Vol. 14, No. 5, pp. 521–538.

Andersson, Ulf & Forsgren, Mats (2000): In Search of Centre of Excellence: Network Embeddedness and Subsidiary Roles in Multinational Corporations. In: Management International Review. Vol. 40, No. 4, pp. 329–350.

Andersson, Ulf & Forsgren, Mats (2002): Integration in the Multinational Corporation: The Problem of Subsidiary Embeddedness. In: McNaughton, Rob B. & Green, Milford B. (eds.): Global Competition and Global Networks. Ashgate, Aldershot, pp. 343–365.

Andersson, Ulf, Forsgren, Mats & Holm, Ulf (2002): The Strategic Impact of External Networks: Subsidiary Performance and Competence Development in the Multinational Corporation. In: Strategic Management Journal. Vol. 23, No. 11, pp. 979–996.

Arvidsson, Niklas (1999): The Ignorant MNE. The Role of Perception Gaps in Knowledge Management. Stockholm School of Economics, Stockholm.

Asakawa, Kazuhiro (2001): Organizational Tension in International R&D Management: The Case of Japanese Firms. In: Research Policy. Vol. 30, No. 5, pp. 735–757.

Ashmos, Donde P. & Huber, George P. (1987): The Systems Paradigm in Organization Theory: Correcting the Record and Suggesting the Future. In: Academy of Management Review. Vol. 12, No. 4, pp. 607–621.

Astley, W. Graham & Van de Ven, Andrew H. (1983): Central Perspectives and Debates in Organization Theory. In: Administrative Science Quarterly. Vol. 28, No. 2, pp. 245–273.

Au, Kevin Y. & Fukuda, John (2002): Boundary Spanning Behaviors of Expatriates. In: Journal of World Business. Vol. 37, No. 4, pp. 285–296.

Audi, Robert (ed. 2001): The Cambridge Dictionary of Philosophy. Cambridge University Press, Cambridge.

Bamberger, Ingolf & Wrona, Thomas (1996): Der Ressourcenansatz und seine Bedeutung für die strategische Unternehmensführung. In: Zfbf: Schmalenbachs Zeitschrift für betriebswirtschaftliche Forschung. Vol. 48, No. 2, pp. 130–153.

Bamberger, Ingolf & Wrona, Thomas (2004): Strategische Unternehmensführung. Vahlen, Munich.

Barclay, Donald W. (1991): Interdepartmental Conflict in Organizational Buying: The Impact of the Organizational Context. In: Journal of Marketing Research. Vol. 28, No. 2, pp. 145–159.

Barki, Henri & Hartwick, Jon (2001): Interpersonal Conflict and its Management in Information System Development. In: MIS Quarterly. Vol. 25, No. 2, pp. 195–228.

Barki, Henri & Hartwick, Jon (2004): Conceptualizing the Construct of Interpersonal Conflict. In: International Journal of Conflict Management. Vol. 15, No. 3, pp. 216–244.

Bartlett, Christopher A. (1984): Organization and Control of Global Enterprises: Influences, Characteristics and Guidelines. Harvard Business School, Boston.

Bartlett, Christopher A. & Ghoshal, Sumantra (1986): Tap Your Subsidiaries for Global Reach. In: Harvard Business Review. Vol. 64, No. 6, pp. 87–94.

Bartlett, Christopher A. & Ghoshal, Sumantra (1990): Managing Innovations in the Transnational Corporation. In: Bartlett, Christopher A., Doz, Yves L. & Hedlund, Gunnar (eds.): Managing the Global Firm. Routledge, London, pp. 215–255.

Bartlett, Christopher A. & Ghoshal, Sumantra (1991): Managing across Borders: The Transnational Solution. Harvard Business School Press, Boston.

Bateman, Thomas S., O'Neill, Hugh & Kenworthy-U'Ren, Amy (2002): A Hierarchical Taxonomy of Top Managers' Goals. In: Journal of Applied Psychology. Vol. 87, No. 6, pp. 1134–1148.

Belbin, R. Meredith (1981): Management Teams: Why They Succeed or Fail. Heinemann, London (reprinted by Butterworth Heinemann, Oxford).

Belbin, R. Meredith (1993): Team Roles at Work: A Strategy for Human Resource Management. Butterworth Heinemann, Oxford.

Benito, Gabriel R. G., Grøgaard, Brigitte & Narula, Rajneesh (2003): Environmental Influences on MNE Subsidiary Roles: Economic Integration and the Nordic Countries. In: Journal of International Business Studies. Vol. 34, No. 5, pp. 443–456.

Berger, Peter & Luckmann, Thomas (1966): The Social Construction of Reality: A Treatise on the Sociology of Knowledge. Penguin Books, London.

Berkel, Karl (1984): Konfliktforschung und Konfliktbewältigung. Ein organisationspsychologischer Ansatz. Duncker & Humblot, Berlin.

Berkel, Karl (1992): Interpersonelle Konflikte. In: Gaugler, Eduard (ed.): Handwörterbuch des Personalwesens. 2nd edition. Schäffer-Poeschel, Stuttgart, pp. 1085–1094.

Berkel, Karl (2003): Konflikte in und zwischen Gruppen. In: von Rosenstiel, Lutz, Regnet, Erika & Domsch, Michael E. (eds.): Führung von Mitarbeitern. 5th edition. Schäffer-Poeschel, Stuttgart, pp. 397–414.

Bible, Bond L. & McComas, James D. (1963): Role Consensus and Teacher Effectiveness. In: Social Forces. Vol. 42, No. 2, pp. 225–233.

Bick, Markus (2004): Knowledge Management Support System – Nachhaltige Einführung organisationsspezifischen Wissensmanagements. Universität Duisburg-Essen, Essen.

Biddle, Bruce J. (1986): Recent Developments in Role Theory. In: Annual Review of Sociology. Vol. 12, pp. 67–92.

Birkinshaw, Julian (1996): How Multinational Subsidiary Mandates Are Gained and Lost. In: Journal of International Business Studies. Vol. 27, No. 3, pp. 467–495.

Birkinshaw, Julian (1997): Entrepreneurship in Multinational Corporations: The Characteristics of Subsidiary Initiative. In: Strategic Management Journal. Vol. 18, No. 3, pp. 207–229.

Birkinshaw, Julian (2000): Entrepreneurship in the Global Firm. Sage, London et al.

Birkinshaw, Julian (2001): Strategy and Management in MNE Subsidiaries. In: Rugman, Alan M. & Brewer, Thomas L. (eds.): Oxford Handbook of International Business. Oxford University Press, Oxford, pp. 380–401.

Birkinshaw, Julian, Bouquet, Cyril & Ambos, Tina (2006): Attention HQ. In: Business Strategy Review. Vol. 17, No. 3, pp. 4–9.

Birkinshaw, Julian, Bouquet, Cyril & Ambos, Tina C. (2007): Managing Executive Attention in the Global Company. In: Sloan Management Review. Vol. 48, No. 4, pp. 39–45.

Birkinshaw, Julian, Holm, Ulf, Thilenius, Peter & Arvidsson, Niklas (2000): Consequences of Perception Gaps in the Headquarters-Subsidiary Relationship. In: International Business Review. Vol. 9, No. 3, pp. 321–344.

Birkinshaw, Julian & Hood, Neil (1998a): Introduction and Overview. In: Birkinshaw, Julian & Hood, Neil (eds.): Multinational Corporate Evolution and Subsidiary Development. Macmillan, Houndsmill et al., pp. 1–19.

Birkinshaw, Julian & Hood, Neil (eds., 1998b): Multinational Corporate Evolution and Subsidiary Development. Macmillan, Houndsmill et al.

Birkinshaw, Julian & Hood, Neil (1998c): Multinational Subsidiary Evolution: Capability and Charter Change in Foreign-Owned Subsidiary Companies. In: Academy of Management Review. Vol. 23, No. 4, pp. 773–795.

Birkinshaw, Julian & Hood, Neil (2000): Characteristics of Foreign Subsidiaries in Industry Clusters. In: Journal of International Business Studies. Vol. 31, No. 1, pp. 141–154.

Birkinshaw, Julian, Hood, Neil & Young, Stephen (2005): Subsidiary Entrepreneurship, Internal and External Competitive Forces, and Subsidiary Performance. In: International Business Review. Vol. 14, No. 2, pp. 227–248.

Birkinshaw, Julian M. & Morrison, Allen J. (1995): Configurations of Strategy and Structure in Subsidiaries of Multinational Subsidiaries. In: Journal of International Business Studies. Vol. 26, No. 4, pp. 729–753.

Björkman, Ingmar, Barner-Rasmussen, Wilhelm & Li, Li (2004): Managing Knowledge Transfer in MNCs: The Impact of Headquarters Control Mechanisms. In: Journal of International Business Studies. Vol. 35, No. 5, pp. 443–455.

Blake, Robert R. & Mouton, Jane S. (1964): The Managerial Grid. Gulf, Houston.

Blazejewski, Susanne (2006): Transferring Value-Infused Organizational Practices in Multinational Companies: A Conflict Perspective. In: Geppert, Mike & Mayer, Michael (eds.): Global, National and Local Practices in Multinational Companies. Palgrave Macmillan, Houndsmill & New York, pp. 63–104.

Bogdan, Robert C. & Biklen, Sari Knopp (1992): Qualitative Research for Education: An Introduction to Theory and Methods. 2nd edition. Allyn and Bacon, Boston et al.

Bonoma, Thomas V. (1985): Case Research in Marketing: Opportunities, Problems, and a Process. In: Journal of Marketing Research. Vol. 22, No. 2, pp. 199–208.

Borgatti, Stephen P. & Foster, Pacey C. (2003): The Network Paradigm in Organizational Research: A Review and Typology. In: Journal of Management. Vol. 29, No. 6, pp. 991–1013.

Bortz, Jürgen & Döring, Nicola (2002): Forschungsmethoden und Evaluation für Human- und Sozialwissenschaftler. Springer, Berlin.

Böttcher, Roland (1996): Global Network Management. Gabler, Wiesbaden.

Boyd Jr., Harper W. & Westfall, Ralph (1970): Interviewer Bias Once More Revisited. In: Journal of Marketing Research. Vol. 7, No. 2, pp. 249–253.

Brandt, William K. & Hulbert, James M. (1976): Patterns of Communications in the Multinational Corporation: An Empirical Study. In: Journal of International Business Studies. Vol. 7, No. 1, pp. 57–64.

Brass, Daniel J., Galaskiewicz, Joseph, Greve, Henrich R. & Wenpin, Tsai (2004): Taking Stock of Networks and Organizations: A Multilevel Perspective. In: Academy of Management Journal. Vol. 47, No. 6, pp. 795–817.

Breiger, Ronald L. (1974): The Duality of Persons and Groups. In: Social Forces. Vol. 53, No. 2, pp. 181–190.

Brock, David M. & Barry, David (2003): What if Planning Were Really Strategic? Exploring the Strategy-Planning Relationship in Multinationals. In: International Business Review. Vol. 12, No. 5, pp. 543–561.

Brooking, Annie (1999): Corporate Memory: Strategies for Knowledge Management. International Thomson Business Press, London.

Brown, L. David (1983): Managing Conflict at Organizational Interfaces. Addison-Wesley, Reading.

Brühl, Rolf & Buch, Sabrina (2006): Einheitliche Gütekriterien in der empirischen Forschung? – Objektivität, Reliabilität und Validität in der Diskussion. Working Paper, No. 20, ESCP-EAP European School of Management Berlin.

Bryman, Alan (1992): Quantitative and Qualitative Research: Further Reflections on Their Integration. In: Brannen, Julia (ed.): Mixing Methods: Qualitative and Quantitative Research. Avebury, Aldershot et al., pp. 57–78.

Bryman, Alan (2004): Social Research Methods. Oxford University Press, Oxford et al.

Burrell, Gibson & Morgan, Gareth (1979): Sociological Paradigms and Organisational Analysis: Elements of the Sociology of Corporate Life. Heinemann, London.

Butler, Richard (1995): Time in Organizations: Its Experience, Explanations and Effects. In: Organization Studies. Vol. 16, No. 6, pp. 925–950.

Carr, Adrian, Durant, Rita & Downs, Alexis (2004): Emergent Strategy Development, Abduction, and Pragmatism: New Lessons for Corporations. In: Human Systems Management. Vol. 23, No. 2, pp. 79–91.

Chakravarthy, Balaji S. (1982): Adaptation: A Promising Metaphor for Strategic Management. In: Academy of Management Review. Vol. 7, No. 1, pp. 35–44.

Chan, Chi-fai & Holbert, Neil Bruce (2001): Marketing Home and Away: Perceptions of Managers in Headquarters and Subsidiaries. In: Journal of World Business. Vol. 36, No. 2, pp. 205–221.

Chang, Sea-Jin & Rosenzweig, Philip M. (1998): Functional and Line of Business Evolution Processes in MNC Subsidiaries: Sony in the USA, 1972-1995. In: Birkinshaw, Julian & Hood, Neil (eds.): Multinational Corporate Evolution and Subsidiary Development. Macmillan, Houndsmill et al., pp. 299–332.

Chatterjee, Savan & Wernerfelt, Birger (1991): The Link between Resources and Type of Diversification: Theory and Evidence. In: Strategic Management Journal. Vol. 12, No. 1, pp. 33–48.

Chenet, Pierre, Tynan, Caroline & Money, Arthur (1999): Service Performance Gap: Re-Evaluation and Redevelopment. In: Journal of Business Research. Vol. 46, No. 2, pp. 133–147.

Chi Cui, Charles, Ball, Derrick F. & Coyne, John (2002): Working Effectively in Strategic Alliances through Managerial Fit between Partners: Some Evidence from Sino-British Joint Ventures and the Implications for R&D Professionals. In: R&D Management. Vol. 32, No. 4, pp. 343–357.

Child, John (1987): Information Technology, Organization, and the Response to Strategic Challenges. In: California Management Review. Vol. 30, No. 1, pp. 33–50.

Chini, Tina, Ambos, Björn & Wehle, Katrin (2005): The Headquarters-Subsidiaries Trench: Tracing Perception Gaps within the Multinational Corporation. In: European Management Journal. Vol. 23, No. 2, pp. 145–153.

Chung, Hong Lai, Gibbons, Patrick T. & Schoch, Herbert P. (2006): The Management of Information and Managers in Subsidiaries of Multinational Corporations. In: British Journal of Management. Vol. 17, No. 2, pp. 153–165.

Chung, Lai Hong, Gibbons, Patrick T. & Schoch, Herbert P. (1999): The Influence of Subsidiary Context and Head Office Strategic Management Style on Control of MNCs: The Experience in Australia. In: Accounting Auditing & Accountability Journal. Vol. 13, No. 5, pp. 647–666.

Cohen, Wesley M. & Levinthal, Daniel A. (1990): Absorptive Capacity: A New Perspective on Learning and Innovation. In: Administrative Science Quarterly. Vol. 35, No. 1, pp. 128–152.

Collins, Frank (1982): Managerial Accounting Systems and Organizational Control: A Role Perspective. In: Accounting, Organizations and Society. Vol. 7, No. 2, pp. 107–122.

Connor, Patrick E. & Bloomfield, Stefan D. (1975): Organizational Design: A Goal Approach. In: Academy of Management Proceedings. Academy of Management, pp. 122–124.

Cook, Thomas D. & Campbell, Donald T. (1979): Quasi-Experimentation: Design and Analysis Issues for Field Settings. Houghton Mifflin, Boston et al.

Cox, Julie Wolfram & Hassard, John (2005): Triangulation in Organizational Research: A Re-Presentation. In: Organization. Vol. 12, No. 1, pp. 109–133.

Cox, Kathleen B. (2003): The Effects of Intrapersonal, Intragroup, and Intergroup Conflict on Team Performance Effectiveness and Work Satisfaction. In: Nursing Administration Quarterly. Vol. 27, No. 2, pp. 153–163.

Creswell, John W. (2003): Research Design: Qualitative, Quantitative, and Mixed Methods Approaches. 2nd edition. Sage, Thousand Oaks.

Cronin, Matthew A. & Weingart, Laurie R. (2007): Representational Gaps, Information Processing, and Conflict in Functionally Diverse Teams. In: Academy of Management Review. Vol. 32, No. 3, pp. 761–773.

Crookell, Harold (1987): Managing Canadian Subsidiaries in a Free Trade Environment. In: Sloan Management Review. Vol. 29, No. 1, pp. 71–76.

Currie, Graeme & Procter, Stephen J. (2005): The Antecedents of Middle Managers' Strategic Contribution: The Case of a Professional Bureaucracy. In: Journal of Management Studies. Vol. 42, No. 7, pp. 1325–1356.

Cyert, Richard M. & March, James G. (1963): A Behavioral Theory of the Firm. Prentice-Hall, Englewood Cliffs.

D'Cruz, Joseph (1986): Strategic Management of Subsidiaries. In: Etemad, Hamid G. & Séguin, Dulude (eds.): Managing the Multinational Subsidiary: Response to Environmental Changes and to Host Nation R&D Policies. Croom Helm, London, pp. 75–89.

Daniels, John D. & Cannice, Mark V. (2004): Interview Studies in International Business Research. In: Marschan-Piekkari, Rebecca & Welch, Catherine (eds.): Handbook of Qualitative Research Methods for International Business. Edward Elgar, Cheltenham, Northampton, pp. 185–206.

Daniels, John D., Pitts, Robert A. & Tretter, Marietta J. (1984): Strategy and Structure of U.S. Multinationals: An Exploratory Study. In: Academy of Management Journal. Vol. 27, No. 2, pp. 292–307.

Daub, Matthias (2009): Coordination of Service Offshoring Subsidiaries in Multinational Corporations. Gabler, Wiesbaden.

Davenport, Thomas H., De Long, David W. & Beers, Michael C. (1998): Successful Knowledge Management Projects. In: Sloan Management Review. Vol. 39, No. 2, pp. 43–57.

Day, George S. (1994): The Capabilities of Market-Driven Organizations. In: Journal of Marketing. Vol. 58, No. 4, pp. 37–52.

De Dreu, Carsten K. W. & Van Vianen, Annelies E. M. (2001): Managing Relationship Conflict and the Effectiveness of Organizational Teams. In: Journal of Organizational Behavior. Vol. 22, No. 3, pp. 309–328.

De Dreu, Carsten K. W. & Weingart, Laurie R. (2003): Task versus Relationship Conflict, Team Performance, and Team Member Satisfaction: A Meta-Analysis. In: Journal of Applied Psychology. Vol. 88, No. 4, pp. 741–749.

De Meyer, Arnoud (1993): Management of an International Network of Industrial R&D Laboratories. In: R&D Management. Vol. 23, No. 2, pp. 109–120.

Delany, Ed (1998): Strategic Development of Multinational Subsidiaries in Ireland. In: Birkinshaw, Julian & Hood, Neil (eds.): Multinational Corporate Evolution and Subsidiary Development. Macmillan, Houndsmill et al., pp. 239–267.

Delios, Andrew & Beamish, Paul W. (2001): Survival and Profitability: The Roles of Experience and Intangible Assets in Foreign Subsidiary Performance. In: Academy of Management Journal. Vol. 44, No. 5, pp. 1028–1038.

Denrell, Jerker, Arvidsson, Niklas & Zander, Udo (2004): Managing Knowledge in the Dark: An Empirical Study of the Reliability of Capability Evaluations. In: Management Science. Vol. 50, No. 11, pp. 1491–1503.

Denzin, Norman & Lincoln, Yvonna S. (2000): The Discipline and Practice of Qualitative Research. In: Denzin, Norman & Lincoln, Yvonna S. (eds.): Handbook of Qualitative Research. 2nd edition. Sage, Thousand Oaks et al., pp. 1–29.

Desmidt, Sebastian & Heene, Aimé (2007): Mission Statement Perception: Are We All on the Same Wavelength? A Case Study in a Flemish Hospital. In: Health Care Management Review. Vol. 32, No. 1, pp. 77–87.

Deutsch, Morton (1969): Conflicts: Productive and Destructive. In: Journal of Social Issues. Vol. 25, No. 1, pp. 7–41.

Deutsch, Morton (1980): Fifty Years of Conflict. In: Festinger, Leon (ed.): Four Decades of Social Psychology. Oxford University Press, New York, pp. 46–77.

Deutsch, Morton (1990): Sixty Years of Conflict. In: The International Journal of Conflict Management. Vol. 1, No. 3, pp. 237–263.

Dev, Chekitan S. & Olsen, Michael D. (1989): Applying Role Theory in Developing a Framework for the Management of Customer Interactions in Hospitality Businesses. In: International Journal of Hospitality Management. Vol. 8, No. 1, pp. 19–33.

Dillman, Don A. (2007): Mail and Internet Surveys: The Tailored Design Method. 2nd edition. Wiley, New York.

Doney, Patricia M., Cannon, Joseph P. & Mullen, Michael R. (1998): Understanding the Influence of National Culture on the Development of Trust. In: Academy of Management Review. Vol. 23, No. 3, pp. 601–620.

Donohue, William A. & Kolt, Robert (1992): Managing Interpersonal Conflict. Sage, Newbury Park.

Dorow, Wolfgang (1978): Unternehmungskonflikte als Gegenstand unternehmungspolitischer Forschung. Duncker & Humblot, Berlin.

Dorow, Wolfgang (1981): Values and Conflict Behavior. An Exploration of Conceptual Relationships. In: Dlugos, Günter, Weiermeier, Klaus & Dorow, Wolfgang (eds.):

Management under Differing Value Systems. De Gruyter, Berlin & New York, pp. 677–702.

Dorow, Wolfgang & Grunwald, Wolfgang (1980): Konflikte in Organisationen. In: Neubauer, Rainer & Von Rosenstiel, Lutz (eds.): Handbuch der Angewandten Psychologie. Verlag Moderne Industrie, Munich, pp. 509–530.

Dörrenbächer, Christoph & Geppert, Mike (2006): Micro-Politics and Conflicts in Multinational Corporations: Current Debates, Re-Framing, and Contributions of This Special Issue. In: Journal of International Management. Vol. 12, No. 3, pp. 251–265.

Doty, D. Harold, Bhattacharya, Mousumi, Wheatley, Kathleen K. & Sutcliffe, Kathleen M. (2006): Divergence between Informant and Archival Measures of the Environment: Real Differences, Artifact, or Perceptual Error? In: Journal of Business Research. Vol. 59, No. 2, pp. 268–277.

Doz, Yves L. & Prahalad, Coimbatore K. (1981): Headquarters Influence and Strategic Control in MNCs. In: Sloan Management Review. Vol. 23, No. 1, pp. 15–29.

Doz, Yves L. & Prahalad, Coimbatore K. (1984): Patterns of Strategic Control within Multinational Corporations. In: Journal of International Business Studies. Vol. 15, No. 2, pp. 55–72.

Doz, Yves L., Santos, José & Williamson, Peter (2001): From Global to Metanational. Harvard Business School Publishing, Boston.

Doz, Yves. L. & Prahalad, Coimbatore K. (1991): Managing DMNCs: A Search for a New Paradigm. In: Strategic Management Journal. Vol. 12, No. 4, pp. 145–164.

Easterbrook, Steve M., Beck, Eevi E., Goodlet, James S, Plowman, Lydia, Sharples, Mike & Wood, Charles C. (1993): A Survey of Empirical Studies of Conflict. In: Easterbrook, Steve M. (ed.): Cooperation or Conflict? Springer, London, pp. 1–68.

Eckert, Stefan & Rossmeissl, Frank (2007): Local Heroes, Regional Champions or Global Mandates? Empirical Evidence on the Dynamics of German MNC Subsidiary Roles in Central Europe. In: Journal of East-West Business. Vol. 13, No. 2/3, pp. 191–218.

Egelhoff, William G. (1982): Strategy and Structure in Multinational Corporations: An Information-Processing Approach. In: Administrative Science Quarterly. Vol. 27, No. 3, pp. 435–458.

Eiseman, Jeffrey W. (1978): Reconciling "Incompatible" Positions. In: Journal of Applied Behavioural Science. Vol. 14, No. 2, pp. 133–150.

Eisenhardt, Kathleen M. (1989): Building Theories from Case Study Research. In: Academy of Management Review. Vol. 14, No. 4, pp. 532–550.

Eisenhardt, Kathleen M. & Graebner, Melissa (2007): Theory Building from Cases. Opportunities and Challenges. In: Academy of Management Journal. Vol. 50, No. 1, pp. 25–32.

England, George W. & Lee, Raymond (1971): Organizational Goals and Expected Behavior among American, Japanese and Korean Managers – A Comparative Study. In: Academy of Management Journal. Vol. 14, No. 4, pp. 425–438.

England, Geroge W. (1967): Organizational Goals and Expected Behavior of American Managers. In: Academy of Management Journal. Vol. 10, No. 2, pp. 107–117.

Ensign, Prescott C. (1999): The Multinational Corporation as a Coordinated Network: Organizing and Managing Differently. In: Thunderbird International Business Review. Vol. 41, No. 3, pp. 291–322.

Etzioni, Amitai (1960): Two Approaches to Organizational Analysis: A Critique and a Suggestion. In: Administrative Science Quarterly. Vol. 5, No. 2, pp. 257–278.

Feinberg, Susan E. (2000): Do World Product Mandates Really Matter? In: Journal of International Business Studies. Vol. 31, No. 1, pp. 155–167.

Ferdows, Kasra (1989): Mapping International Factory Networks. In: Ferdows, Kasra (ed.): Managing International Manufacturing. North-Holland/Elsevier, Amsterdam, pp. 3–21.

Ferdows, Kasra (1997): Making the Most of Foreign Factories. In: Harvard Business Review. Vol. 75, No. 2, pp. 73–86.

Ferguson, Charles K. & Kelley, Harold H. (1964): Significant Factors in Overevaluations of Own-Group Product. In: Journal of Abnormal and Social Psychology. Vol. 69, No. 2, pp. 223–228.

Fey, Carl F. & Beamish, Paul W. (2000): Joint Venture Conflict: The Case of Russian International Joint Ventures. In: International Business Review. Vol. 9, No. 2, pp. 139–162.

Fink, Clinton F. (1968): Some Conceptual Difficulties in the Theory of Social Conflict. In: Journal of Conflict Resolution. Vol. 12, No. 4, pp. 412–460.

Fisher, Roger, Ury, William & Patton, Bruce (1991): Getting to YES: Negotiating Agreement without Giving in. 2nd edition. Houghton Mifflin, Boston.

Fisher, Ronald J. (1990): The Social Psychology of Intergroup and International Conflict Resolution. Springer, New York et al.

Flick, Uwe (2003): Konstruktivismus. In: Flick, Uwe, von Kardorff, Ernst & Steinke, Ines (eds.): Qualitative Forschung. Rowolt, Reinbek, pp. 150–164.

Flick, Uwe (2004): Design and Process in Qualitative Research. In: Flick, Uwe, von Kardorff, Ernst & Steinke, Ines (eds.): A Companion to Qualitative Research. Sage, London et al., pp. 146–152.

Floyd, Steven W. & Lane, Peter J. (2000): Strategizing throughout the Organization: Managing Role Conflict in Strategic Renewal. In: Academy of Management Review. Vol. 25, No. 1, pp. 154–177.

Ford, Dianne P. & Chan, Yolande E. (2003): Knowledge Sharing in a Multi-Cultural Setting: A Case Study. In: Knowledge Management Research & Practice. Vol. 1, No. 1, pp. 11–27.

Forsgren, Mats (1989): Managing the Internationalization Process. The Swedish Case. Routledge, London.

Forsgren, Mats, Holm, Ulf & Johanson, Jan (1995): Division Headquarters Go Abroad – A Step in the Internationalization of the Multinational Corporation. In: Journal of Management Studies. Vol. 32, No. 4, pp. 475–491.

Forsgren, Mats & Pedersen, Torben (1996): Are there any Centres of Excellence among Foreign-Owned Firms in Denmark? 22nd Annual Conference of the European International Business Academy (EIBA), Stockholm.

Forsgren, Mats & Pedersen, Torben (1997): Centres of Excellence in Multinational Companies: The Case of Denmark. Working Paper, No. 2, Institute of International Economics and Management, Copenhagen Business School.

Franko, Lawrence G. (1974): The Move toward A Multidivisional Structure in European Organizations. In: Administrative Science Quarterly. Vol. 19, No. 4, pp. 493–506.

French, Wendell & Henning, Dale (1966): The Authority-Influence Role of the Functional Specialist in Management. In: Academy of Management Journal. Vol. 9, No. 3, pp. 187–203.

Friedman, Raymond A. & Podolny, Joel (1992): Differentiation of Boundary Spanning Roles: Labor Negotiations and Implications for Role Conflict. In: Administrative Science Quarterly. Vol. 37, No. 1, pp. 28–47.

Frost, Dean E. (1983): Role Perceptions and Behavior of the Immediate Superior: Moderating Effects on the Prediction of Leadership Effectiveness. In: Organizational Behavior and Human Performance. Vol. 31, No. 1, pp. 123–142.

Frost, Tony S., Birkinshaw, Julian M. & Ensign, Prescott C. (2002): Centers of Excellence in Multinational Corporations. In: Strategic Management Journal. Vol. 23, No. 11, pp. 997–1018.

Furu, Patrick (2001): Drivers of Competence Development in Different Types of Multinational R&D Subsidiaries. In: Scandinavian Journal of Management. Vol. 17, No. 1, pp. 133–149.

Gabris, Gerald T. & Mitchell, Kenneth (1991): The Everyday Organization: A Diagnostic Model for Assessing Adaptation Cycles. In: Public Administration Quarterly. Vol. 14, No. 4, pp. 498–518.

Galunic, D. Charles & Eisenhardt, Kathleen M. (1996): The Evolution of Intracorporate Domains: Divisional Charter Losses in High-Technology, Multidivisional Corporations. In: Organization Science. Vol. 7, No. 3, pp. 255–282.

Garnier, Gérard H. (1982): Context and Decision Making Autonomy in the Foreign Affiliates of U.S. Multinational Corporations. In: Academy of Management Journal. Vol. 25, No. 4, pp. 893–908.

Garnier, Gérard H. (1984): The Autonomy of Foreign Subsidiaries: Environmental and National Influences. In: Journal of General Management. Vol. 10, No. 1, pp. 57–82.

Gates, Stephen R. & Egelhoff, William G. (1986): Centralization in Headquarters-Subsidiary Relationships. In: Journal of International Business Studies. Vol. 17, No. 2, pp. 71–92.

Geertz, Clifford A. (1973): The Interpretation of Cultures. Basic Books, New York.

Geringer, J. Michael & Herbert, Louis (1991): Measuring Performance of International Joint Ventures. In: Journal of International Business Studies. Vol. 22, No. 2, pp. 249–264.

Ghauri, Pervez & Grønhaug, Kjell (2005): Research Methods in Business Studies. 3rd edition. Prentice Hall, London.

Ghoshal, Sumantra (1986): The Innovative Multinational: A Differentiated Network of Organizational Roles and Management Roles. Graduate School of Business Administration. Harvard University, Cambridge.

Ghoshal, Sumantra & Bartlett, Christopher A. (1990): The Multinational Corporation as an Interorganizational Network. In: Academy of Management Review. Vol. 15, No. 4, pp. 603–625.

Ghoshal, Sumantra & Nohria, Nitin (1987): Multinational Corporations as Differentiated Networks. Working Paper, No. 87/13, INSEAD.

Ghoshal, Sumantra & Nohria, Nitin (1989): Internal Differentiation within Multinational Corporations. In: Strategic Management Journal. Vol. 10, No. 4, pp. 323–337.

Ghoshal, Sumantra & Nohria, Nitin (1993): Horses for Courses: Organizational Forms for Multinational Corporations. In: Sloan Management Review. Vol. 34, No. 2, pp. 23–35.

Gilbert, Dirk Ulrich (1998): Konfliktmanagement in international tätigen Unternehmen. Ein diskurs-ethischer Ansatz zur Regelung von Konflikten im interkulturellen Management. Verlag Wissenschaft und Praxis, Sternenfels, Berlin.

Gläser, Jochen & Laudel, Grit (1999): Theoriegeleitete Textanalyse? Das Potential einer variablenorientierten qualitativen Inhaltsanalyse. Wissenschaftszentrum Berlin für Sozialforschung, Berlin.

Glaum, Martin (1996): Internationalisierung und Unternehmenserfolg. Gabler, Wiesbaden.

Gomm, Roger, Hammersley, Martyn & Foster, Peter (2000a): Case Study and Generalization. In: Gomm, Roger, Hammersley, Martyn & Foster, Peter (eds.): Case Study Method. Sage, London et al., pp. 98–115.

Gomm, Roger, Hammersley, Martyn & Foster, Peter (eds., 2000b): Case Study Method. Sage, London et al.

Gong, Yaping, Shenkar, Oded, Luo, Yadong & Nyaw, Mee-Kau (2001): Role Conflict and Ambiguity of CEOs in International Joint Ventures: A Transaction Cost Perspective. In: Journal of Applied Psychology. Vol. 86, No. 4, pp. 764–773.

Gouthier, Matthias & Schmid, Stefan (2003): Customers and Customer Relationships in Service Firms: The Perspective of the Resource-Based View. In: Marketing Theory. Vol. 3, No. 1, pp. 119–143.

Granovetter, Mark S. (1985): Economic Action and Social Structure: The Problem of Embeddedness. In: American Journal of Sociology. Vol. 91, No. 3, pp. 481–510.

Grant, Robert M. (1991): The Resource-Based Theory of Competitive Advantage: Implications for Strategy Formulation. In: California Management Review. Vol. 33, No. 3, pp. 114–135.

Greenberg, Jerald & Baron, Robert A. (1997): Behavior in Organizations. 6th edition. Prentice-Hall, Englewood Cliffs.

Grinyer, Peter H. & Spender, J. C. (1979): Recipes, Crises, and Adaptation in Mature Business. In: International Studies of Management & Organization. Vol. 9, No. 3, pp. 113–133.

Gross, Edward (1969): The Definition of Organizational Goals. In: British Journal of Sociology. Vol. 20, No. 3, pp. 277–294.

Gross, N., Mason, W.S. & McEachern, A.W. (eds., 1958): Explorations in Role Analysis – Studies in the School Superintendency Role. Wiley, New York.

Grover, Steven L. (1993): Why Professionals Lie: The Impact of Professional Role Conflict on Reporting Accuracy. In: Organizational Behavior and Human Decision Processes. Vol. 55, No. 2, pp. 251–272.

Grunwald, Wolfgang & Redel, Wolfgang (1989): Soziale Konflikte. In: Roth, Erwin (ed.): Organisationspsychologie (Enzyklopädie der Psychologie, D, III, 3). Hogrefe, Göttingen, pp. 529–551.

Gupta, Anil K. & Govindarajan, Vijay (1991): Knowledge Flows and the Structure of Control within Multinational Corporations. In: Academy of Management Review. Vol. 16, No. 4, pp. 768–792.

Gupta, Anil K. & Govindarajan, Vijay (1994): Organizing for Knowledge Flows within MNCs. In: International Business Review. Vol. 3, No. 4, pp. 443–457.

Gupta, Anil K. & Govindarajan, Vijay (2000): Knowledge Flows within Multinational Corporations. In: Strategic Management Journal. Vol. 21, No. 4, pp. 473–496.

Gupta, Anil K., Govindarajan, Vijay & Malhotra, Ayesha (1996): Feedback-Seeking Behavior of Subsidiary Presidents in Multinational Corporations. Academy of Management Proceedings, Cincinnati, Academy of Management.

Gurteen, David (1998): Knowledge, Creativity and Innovation. In: Journal of Knowledge Management. Vol. 2, No. 1, pp. 5–13.

Hacking, Ian (1999): The Social Construction of What? Harvard University Press, Cambridge.

Håkansson, Håkan & Snehota, Ivan (1995): Developing Relationships in Business Networks. Routledge, London.

Hall, Richard (1993): A Framework Linking Intangible Resources and Capabilities to Sustainable Competitive Advantage. In: Strategic Management Journal. Vol. 14, No. 8, pp. 607–618.

Hammersley, Martyn (1992): Deconstructing the Qualitative-Quantitative Divide. In: Brannen, Julia (ed.): Mixing Methods: Qualitative and Quantitative Research. Avebury, Aldershot et al., pp. 39–55.

Hansen, Morten T., Mors, Marie Louise & Løvås, Bjørn (2005): Knowledge Sharing in Organizations: Multiple Networks, Multiple Phases. In: Academy of Management Journal. Vol. 48, No. 5, pp. 776–793.

Hartley, Jean (2004): Case Study Research. In: Cassell, Catherine & Symon, Gillian (eds.): Essential Guide to Qualitative Methods in Organizational Research. Sage, London et al., pp. 323–333.

Hartman, Sandra J., White, Michael C. & Crino, Michael D. (1986): Environmental Volatility, System Adaptation, Planning Requirements, and Information-Processing Strategies: An Integrative Model. In: Decision Sciences. Vol. 17, No. 4, pp. 454–474.

Harvard Business School (1977): Yoshida Kogyo K. K. HBS Case Services.

Harvey, Michael & Novicevic, Milorad M. (2001): The Impact of Hypercompetitive "Timescapes" on the Development of a Global Mindset. In: Management Decision. Vol. 39, No. 6, pp. 448–460.

Harzing, Anne-Wil (1999): Managing the Multinationals: An International Study of Control Mechanisms. Elgar, Cheltenham.

Harzing, Anne-Wil (2000): An Empirical Analysis and Extension of the Bartlett and Ghoshal Typology of Multinational Companies. In: Journal of International Business Studies. Vol. 31, No. 1, pp. 101–119.

Harzing, Anne-Wil (2001a): Of Bears, Bumble-Bees, and Spiders: The Role of Expatriates in Controlling Foreign Subsidiaries. In: Journal of World Business. Vol. 36, No. 4, pp. 366–379.

Harzing, Anne-Wil (2001b): Who's in Charge? An Empirical Study of Executive Staffing Practices in Foreign Subsidiaries. In: Human Resource Management. Vol. 40, No. 2, pp. 139–158.

Harzing, Anne-Wil & Noorderhaven, Niels (2006a): Geographical Distance and the Role and Management of Subsidiaries: The Case of Subsidiaries Down-Under. In: Asia Pacific Journal of Management. Vol. 23, No. 2, pp. 167–185.

Harzing, Anne-Wil & Noorderhaven, Niels (2006b): Knowledge Flows in MNCs: An Empirical Test and Extension of Gupta and Govindarajan's Typology of Subsidiary Roles. In: International Business Review. Vol. 15, No. 3, pp. 195–214.

Haspeslagh, Philippe C. & Jemison, David B. (1991): Managing Acquisitions. The Free Press, New York.

Hedlund, Gunnar (1986): The Hypermodern MNC – A Heterarchy? In: Human Resource Management. Vol. 25, No. 1, pp. 9–35.

Heider, Fritz (1958): The Psychology of Interpersonal Relations. Wiley, New York.

Heiss, Jerold (1981): Social Roles. In: Rosenberg, Morris & Turner, Ralph H. (eds.): Social Psychology. Social Perspectives. Basic Books, New York, pp. 94–129.

Henning, Dale A. & Moseley, Roger L. (1970): Authority Role of a Functional Manager: The Controller. In: Administrative Science Quarterly. Vol. 15, No. 4, pp. 482–489.

Herbert, Theodore T. (1999): Multinational Strategic Planning: Matching Central Expectations to Local Realities. In: Long Range Planning. Vol. 32, No. 1, pp. 81–87.

Higgins, F. Tory & Bargh, John A. (1987): Social Cognition and Social Perception. In: Annual Review of Psychology. Vol. 38, p. 369.

Hignite, Michael A., Margavio, Thomas M. & Chin, Jerry M. (2002): Assessing the Conflict Resolution Profiles of Emerging Information Systems Professionals. In: Journal of Information Systems Education. Vol. 13, No. 4, pp. 315–324.

Hildum, Donald C. & Brown, Roger W. (1956): Verbal Reinforcement and Interviewer Bias. In: Journal of Abnormal and Social Psychology. Vol. 53, No. 1, pp. 108–111.

Hoffman, Richard C. (1994): Generic Strategies for Subsidiaries of Multinational Corporations. In: Journal of Managerial Issues. Vol. 6, No. 1, pp. 69–87.

Holm, Ulf, Johanson, Jan & Thilenius, Peter (1995): Headquarters' Knowledge of Subsidiary Network Contexts in the Multinational Corporation. In: International Studies of Management & Organization. Vol. 25, No. 1/2, pp. 97–119.

Holm, Ulf & Pedersen, Torben (2000a): The Centres of Excellence Project – Methods and Some Empirical Findings. In: Holm, Ulf & Pedersen, Torben (eds.): The Emergence and Impact of MNC Centres of Excellence: A Subsidiary Perspective. Macmillan, Basingstoke, pp. 23–41.

Holm, Ulf & Pedersen, Torben (2000b): The Emergence and Impact of MNC Centres of Excellence: A Subsidiary Perspective. Macmillan, Basingstoke.

Holmlund, Maria & Strandvik, Tore (1999): Perception Configurations in Business Relationships. In: Management Decision. Vol. 37, No. 9/10, pp. 686–696.

Holtbrügge, Dirk (2005): Configuration and Co-ordination of Value Activities in German Multinational Corporations. In: European Management Journal. Vol. 23, No. 5, pp. 564–575.

Hood, Neil & Taggart, James H. (1999): Subsidiary Development in German and Japanese Manufacturing Subsidiaries in the British Isles. In: Regional Studies. Vol. 33, No. 6, pp. 513–528.

House, Robert J. (1970): Role Conflict and Multiple Authority in Complex Organizations. In: California Management Review. Vol. 12, No. 4, pp. 53–60.

Hulbert, James M., Brandt, William K. & Richers, Raimar (1980): Marketing Planning in the Multinational Subsidiary: Practices and Problems. In: Journal of Marketing. Vol. 44, No. 3, pp. 7–15.

Inderst, Roman, Muller, Holger M. & Warneryd, Karl (2005): Influence Costs and Hierarchy. In: Economics of Governance. Vol. 6, No. 2, pp. 177–197.

Jacobson, Eugene, Charters, W. W. & Lieberman, Seymour (1951): The Use of the Role Concept in the Study of Complex Organizations. In: Journal of Social Issues. Vol. 7, pp. 18–27.

Jameson, Jessica Katz (1999): toward a Comprehensive Model for the Assessment and Management of Intraorganizational Conflict: Developing the Framework. In: International Journal of Conflict Management. Vol. 10, No. 3, pp. 268–294.

Jarillo, J. Carlos & Martinez, Jon I. (1990): Different Roles for Subsidiaries: The Case of Multinational Corporations in Spain. In: Strategic Management Journal. Vol. 11, No. 7, pp. 501–512.

Javidan, Mansour, Stahl, Günter K., Brodbeck, Felix & Wilderom, Celeste P. M. (2005): Cross-Border Transfer of Knowledge: Cultural Lessons from Project GLOBE. In: Academy of Management Executive. Vol. 19, No. 2, pp. 59–76.

Jehn, Karen A. (1995): A Multimethod Examination of the Benefits and Detriments of Intragroup Conflict. In: Administrative Science Quarterly. Vol. 40, No. 2, pp. 256–282.

Jehn, Karen A. (1997): A Qualitative Analysis of Conflict Types and Dimensions in Organizational Groups. In: Administrative Science Quarterly. Vol. 42, No. 3, pp. 530–557.

Jehn, Karen A. & Mannix, Elizabeth A. (2001): The Dynamic Nature of Conflict: A Longitudinal Study of Intragroup Conflict and Group Performance. In: Academy of Management Journal. Vol. 44, No. 2, pp. 238–251.

Johanson, Jan, Pahlberg, Cecilia & Thilenius, Peter (1996): Conflict and Control in MNC New Product Introduction. In: Journal of Market Focused Management. Vol. 1, No. 3, pp. 249–265.

Johnston, Stewart (2005): Headquarters and Subsidiaries in Multinational Corporations. Palgrave Macmillan, Houndsmill et al.

Jones, Robert E. & Deckro, Richard F. (1993): The Social Psychology of Project Management Conflict. In: European Journal of Operational Research. Vol. 64, No. 2, pp. 216–228.

Kabanoff, Boris (1985): Potential Influence Structures as Sources of Interpersonal Conflict in Groups and Organizations. In: Organizational Behavior and Human Decision Processes. Vol. 36, No. 1, pp. 113–141.

Kahn, Robert L. & Quinn, Robert P. (1970): Role Stress: A Framework for Analysis. In: McLean, Alan A. (ed.): Mental Health and Work Organizations. Rand McNally, Chicago, pp. 50–115.

Kahn, Robert L., Wolfe, Donald M., Quinn, Robert P., Snoek, J. Diedrick & Rosenthal, Robert A. (1964): Organizational Stress: Studies in Role Conflict and Ambiguity. Wiley, New York.

Kaplan, Robert S. & Norton, David P. (1992): The Balanced Scorecard – Measures That Drive Performance. In: Harvard Business Review. Vol. 70, No. 1, pp. 71–79.

Kaplan, Robert S. & Norton, David P. (1996): Linking the Balanced Scorecard to Strategy. In: California Management Review. Vol. 39, No. 1, pp. 53–79.

Kaplan, Robert S. & Norton, David P. (2007): Using the Balanced Scorecard as a Strategic Management System. In: Harvard Business Review. Vol. 85, No. 7/8, pp. 150–161.

Kast, Fremont E. & Rosenzweig, James E. (1967): System Concepts: Pervasiveness and Potential. In: Management International Review. Vol. 7, No. 4/5, pp. 87–110.

Kast, Fremont E. & Rosenzweig, James E. (1972): General System Theory: Applications for Organization and Management. In: Academy of Management Journal. Vol. 15, No. 4, pp. 447–465.

Katz, Daniel & Kahn, Robert L. (1978): The Social Psychology of Organizations. 2nd edition. Wiley, New York.

Kaufman, Allen, Wood, Craig H. & Theyel, Gregory (2000): Collaboration and Technology Linkages: A Strategic Supplier Typology. In: Strategic Management Journal. Vol. 21, No. 6, pp. 649–663.

Kaufmann, Lutz & Roessing, Soenke (2005): Managing Conflict of Interests between Headquarters and Their Subsidiaries Regarding Technology Transfer to Emerging Markets – A Framework. In: Journal of World Business. Vol. 40, No. 3, pp. 235–253.

Keating, Patrick J. (1995): A Framework for Classifying and Evaluating the Theoretical Contributions of Case Research in Management Accounting. In: Journal of Management Accounting Research. Vol. 7, No. 3, pp. 66–86.

Kelley, Harold H. (1967): Attribution Theory in Social Psychology. In: Levine, Daniel S. (ed.): Nebraska Symposium on Motivation. Vol. 15. University of Nebraska Press, Lincoln, pp. 191–238.

Kelly, Jacinta (2006): An Overview of Conflict. In: Dimensions of Critical Care Nursing. Vol. 25, No. 1, pp. 22–28.

Kiel, Geoffrey C., Hendry, Kevin & Nicholson, Gavin J. (2006): Corporate Governance Options for the Local Subsidiaries of Multinational Enterprises. In: Corporate Governance: An International Review. Vol. 14, No. 6, pp. 568–576.

Kim, Bongjin, Prescott, John E. & Kim, Sung Min (2005): Differentiated Governance of Foreign Subsidiaries in Transnational Corporations: An Agency Theory Perspective. In: Journal of International Management. Vol. 11, No. 1, pp. 43–66.

Kim, W. Chan & Mauborgne, Renee A. (1993): Procedural Justice, Attitudes, and Subsidiary Top Management Compliance with Multinationals' Corporate Strategic Decisions. In: Academy of Management Journal. Vol. 36, No. 3, pp. 502–526.

King, Nigel (1994): The Qualitative Research Interview. In: Cassell, Catherine & Symon, Gillian (eds.): Qualitative Methods in Organizational Research: A Practical Guide. Sage London et al., pp. 14–36.

Kirk, Jerome & Miller, Marc L. (1986): Reliability and Validity in Qualitative Research. Sage, Beverly Hills.

Knight, Louise & Harland, Christine (2005): Managing Supply Networks: Organizational Roles in Network Management. In: European Management Journal. Vol. 23, No. 3, pp. 281–292.

Knoblauch, Hubert (2004): The Future Prospects of Qualitative Research. In: Flick, Uwe, von Kardorff, Ernst & Steinke, Ines (eds.): A Companion to Qualitative Research. Sage, London et al., pp. 354–358.

Kobrin, Stephen J. (1991): An Empirical Analysis of the Determinants of Global Integration. In: Strategic Management Journal. Vol. 12, No. 4, pp. 17–31.

Kogut, Bruce (1989): A Note on Global Strategies. In: Strategic Management Journal. Vol. 10, No. 4, pp. 383–389.

Kogut, Bruce & Singh, Harbir (1988): The Effect of National Culture on the Choice of Entry Mode. In: Journal of International Business Studies. Vol. 19, No. 3, pp. 411–432.

Kogut, Bruce & Zander, Udo (1993): Knowledge of the Firm and the Evolutionary Theory of the Multinational Corporation. In: Journal of International Business Studies. Vol. 24, No. 4, pp. 625–645.

Kogut, Bruce & Zander, Udo (2003): Knowledge of the Firm and the Evolutionary Theory of the Multinational Corporation. In: Journal of International Business Studies. Vol. 34, No. 6, pp. 516–529.

Korhonen, Antti (2001): Strategic Financial Management in a Multinational Financial Conglomerate: A Multiple Goal Stochastic Programming Approach. In: European Journal of Operational Research. Vol. 128, No. 2, pp. 418–434.

Kostova, Tatiana (1998): The Quality of Inter-Unit Relationships in MNEs as a Source of Competitive Advantage. In: Hitt, Michael A., Ricart i Costa, Joan E. & Nixon, Robert D. (eds.): New Managerial Mindsets: Organizational Transformation and Strategy Implementation. Wiley, Chichester et al., pp. 299–324.

Kostova, Tatiana (1999): Transnational Transfer of Strategic Organizational Practices: A Contextual Perspective. In: Academy of Management Review. Vol. 24, No. 2, pp. 308–324.

Kowal, Sabine & O'Connell, Daniel C. (2004): The Transcription of Conversations. In: Flick, Uwe, von Kardoff, Ernst & Steinke, Ines (eds.): A Companion to Qualitative Research. Sage, London et al., pp. 248–252.

Kuester, Sabine, Homburg, Christian & Robertson, Thomas S. (1999): Retaliatory Behavior to New Product Entry. In: Journal of Marketing. Vol. 63, No. 4, pp. 90–106.

Kutschker, Michael & Schmid, Stefan (2008): Internationales Management. 6th edition. Oldenbourg, Munich & Wien.

Kutschker, Michael, Schurig, Andreas & Schmid, Stefan (2001): The Existence of Centers of Excellence in Multinational Corporations: Results from an International Research Project. Diskussionsbeitrag, No. 154, Wirtschaftswissenschaftliche Fakultät Ingolstadt.

Kutschker, Michael, Schurig, Andreas & Schmid, Stefan (2002): Centres of Excellence in MNCs – An Empirical Analysis from Seven European Countries. In: Larimo, Jorma (ed.): Current European Research in International Business. Vol. 86. Vaasan Yliopiston Julkaisuja, Vaasa, pp. 224–245.

Kvale, Steinar (1988): The 1000-Page Question. In: Phenomenology & Pedagogy. Vol. 6, No. 2, pp. 90–106.

Kvale, Steinar (1996): Interviews: An Introduction to Qualitative Research Interviewing. Sage, Thousand Oaks et al.

Kwak, Nojin & Radler, Barry (2002): A Comparison between Mail and Web Surveys: Response Pattern, Respondent Profile, and Data Quality. In: Journal of Official Statistics. Vol. 18, No. 2, pp. 257–274.

Lado, Augustine A., Boyd, Nancy G. & Wright, Peter (1992): A Competency-Based Model of Sustainable Competitive Advantage: toward a Conceptual Integration. In: Journal of Management. Vol. 18, No. 1, pp. 77–91.

Lamnek, Siegfried (2005): Qualitative Sozialforschung. 4th edition. Beltz, Weinheim, Basel.

Lane, Peter J., Koka, Balaji R. & Pathak, Seemantini (2006): The Reification of Absorptive Capacity: A Critical Review and Rejuvenation of the Construct. In: Academy of Management Review. Vol. 31, No. 4, pp. 833–863.

Lane, Peter J. & Lubatkin, Michael (1998): Relative Absorptive Capacity and Interorganizational Learning. In: Strategic Management Journal. Vol. 19, No. 5, pp. 461–477.

Lawrence, Paul R. & Lorsch, Jay W. (1967): Organization and Environment. Harvard University Press, Cambridge.

Lee, Thomas W. (1999): Using Qualitative Methods in Organizational Research. Sage, London et al.

Leksell, Laurent & Lindgren, Ulf (1982): The Board of Directors in Foreign Subsidiaries. In: Journal of International Business Studies. Vol. 13, No. 1, pp. 27–38.

Levinson, Daniel J. (1959): Role, Personality, and Social Structure in the Organizational Setting. In: Journal of Abnormal and Social Psychology. Vol. 58, pp. 170–180.

Lewicki, Roy J., Weiss, Stephen E. & Lewin, David (1992): Models of Conflict, Negotiation and Third Party Intervention: A Review and Synthesis. In: Journal of Organizational Behavior. Vol. 13, No. 3, pp. 209–252.

Lewin, Kurt (1935): A Dynamic Theory of Personality. McGraw-Hill, New York.

Lewin, Kurt (1951): Field Theory in Social Science. Harper & Brothers, New York.

Likert, Rensis & Likert, Jane G. (1976): New Ways of Managing Conflict. McGraw-Hill, New York.

Lilienthal, David (1960): The Multinational Corporation. In: Anshen, Melvin & Bach, George Leland (eds.): Management and Corporations 1985. A Symposium Held on the Occasion of the 10th Anniversary of the Graduate School of Industrial Administration, Carnegie Institute of Technology. Greenwood Press, Westport, pp. 119–158.

Lin, Lihui, Geng, Xianjun & Whinston, Andrew B. (2005): A Sender-Receiver Framework for Knowledge Transfer. In: MIS Quarterly. Vol. 29, No. 2, pp. 197–219.

Lincoln, Yvonna S. & Guba, Egon G. (1985): Naturalistic Inquiry. Sage, London.

Lipparini, Andrea & Fratocchi, Luciano (1999): The Capabilities of the Transnational Firm: Accessing Knowledge and Leveraging Inter-firm. In: European Management Journal. Vol. 17, No. 6, pp. 655–667.

Litterer, Joseph A. (1966): Conflict in Organization: A Re-Examination. In: Academy of Management Journal. Vol. 9, No. 3, pp. 178–186.

Luhmann, Niklas (1995): Social Systems. Stanford University Press, Stanford.

Lumsden, Joanna & Morgan, Wendy (2005): Online-Questionnaire Design: Establishing Guidelines and Evaluating Existing Support. 16th Annual Conference of the Information Resources Management Association. National Research Council of Canada, San Diego.

Luo, Xueming, Slotegraaf, Rebecca J. & Pan, Xing (2006): Cross-Functional "Coopetition": The Simultaneous Role of Cooperation and Competition within Firms. In: Journal of Marketing. Vol. 70, No. 2, pp. 67–80.

Luo, Yadong (2002): Organizational Dynamics and Global Integration: A Perspective from Subsidiary Managers. In: Journal of International Management. Vol. 8, No. 2, pp. 189–215.

Luo, Yadong (2003): Market-Seeking MNEs in an Emerging Market: How Parent-Subsidiary Links Shape Overseas Success. In: Journal of International Business Studies. Vol. 34, No. 3, pp. 290–309.

Luo, Yadong & Zhao, Hongxin (2004): Corporate Link and Competitive Strategy in Multinational Enterprises: A Perspective from Subsidiaries Seeking Host Market Penetration. In: Journal of International Management. Vol. 10, No. 1, pp. 77–105.

Lusk, Edward J. (1972): Discriminant Analysis as Applied to the Resource Allocation Decision. In: Accounting Review. Vol. 47, No. 3, pp. 567–575.

Lysonski, Steven J. & Johnson, Eugene M. (1983): The Sales Manager as a Boundary Spanner: A Role Theory Analysis. In: Journal of Personal Selling & Sales Management. Vol. 3, No. 2, pp. 8–21.

Lytle, Richard S. & Timmerman, John E. (2006): Service Orientation and Performance: An Organizational Perspective. In: Journal of Services Marketing. Vol. 20, No. 2, pp. 136–147.

Macharzina, Klaus & Wolf, Joachim (2005): Unternehmensführung: Das internationale Managementwissen. 5th edition. Gabler, Wiesbaden.

Malim, Tony (1994): Cognitive Processes. Attention, Perception, Memory, Thinking and Language. Macmillan, Houndsmill & London.

Malnight, Thomas W. (1995): Globalization of an Ethnocentric Firm: An Evolutionary Perspective. In: Strategic Management Journal. Vol. 16, No. 2, pp. 119–141.

Malnight, Thomas W. (1996): The Transition from Decentralized to Network-Based MNC Structures: An Evolutionary Perspective. In: Journal of International Business Studies. Vol. 27, No. 1, pp. 43–65.

Manev, Ivan M. (2003): The Managerial Network in a Multinational Enterprise and the Resource Profiles of Subsidiaries. In: Journal of International Management. Vol. 9, No. 2, pp. 133–151.

Mantere, Saku (2008): Role Expectations and Middle Manager Strategic Agency. In: Journal of Management Studies. Vol. 45, No. 2, pp. 294–316.

Marcati, Alberto (1989): Configuration and Coordination – The Role of US Subsidiaries in the International Network of Italian Multinationals. In: Management International Review. Vol. 29, No. 3, pp. 35–50.

March, James G. & Simon, Herbert A. (1958): Organizations. Wiley, New York et al.

Marschan-Piekkari, Rebecca, Welch, Catherine, Penttinen, Heli & Tahvanainen, Marja (2004): Interviewing in the Multinational Corporation: Challenges of the Organisational Context. In: Marschan-Piekkari, Rebecca & Welch, Catherine (eds.): Handbook of Qualitative Research Methods for International Business. Edward Elgar, Cheltenham, Northampton, pp. 244–263.

Marshall, Catherine & Rossman, Gretchen B. (1989): Designing Qualitative Research. Sage, Newbury Park et al.

Martinez, Jon I. & Jarillo, J. Carlos (1991): Coordination Demands of International Strategies. In: Journal of International Business Studies. Vol. 22, No. 3, pp. 429–444.

Maxwell, Joseph A. (1996): Qualitative Research Design. Sage, Thousand Oaks.

Maynard-Moody, Steven & McClintock, Charles (1987): Weeding an Old Garden: toward a New Understanding of Organizational Goals. In: Administration & Society. Vol. 19, No. 1, pp. 125–142.

Mayring, Philipp (1997): Qualitative Inhaltsanalyse. 7th edition. Deutscher Studienverlag, Weinheim.

Mayring, Philipp (2002): Einführung in die qualitative Sozialforschung: Eine Anleitung zu qualitativem Denken. 5th edition. Beltz, Weinheim, Basel.

McCann, Joseph E. & Ferry, Diane L. (1979): An Approach for Assessing and Managing Inter-Unit Interdependence. In: Academy of Management Review. Vol. 4, No. 1, pp. 113–119.

McClelland, Kent (2004): The Collective Control of Perceptions: Constructing Order from Conflict. In: International Journal of Human-Computer Studies. Vol. 60, No. 1, pp. 65–99.

Melewar, T. C. & Saunders, John (1998): Global Corporate Visual Identity Systems. In: International Marketing Review. Vol. 15, No. 4, pp. 291–308.

Merkens, Hans (2004): Selection Procedures, Sampling, Case Construction. In: Flick, Uwe, von Kardorff, Ernst & Steinke, Ines (eds.): A Companion to Qualitative Research. Sage, London et al., pp. 165–171.

Merton, Robert K. (1957): The Role-Set: Problems in Sociological Theory. In: The British Journal of Sociology. Vol. 8, No. 2, pp. 106–120.

Messner, John I. & Sanvido, Victor E. (2001): An Information Model for Project Evaluation. In: Engineering Construction & Architectural Management. Vol. 8, No. 5/6, pp. 393–402.

Mezias, John M. (2002a): How to Identify Liabilities of Foreignness and Assess Their Effects on Multinational Corporations. In: Journal of International Management. Vol. 8, No. 3, pp. 265–282.

Mezias, John M. (2002b): Identifying Liabilities of Foreignness and Strategies to Minimize Their Effects: The Case of Labor Lawsuit Judgments in the United States. In: Strategic Management Journal. Vol. 23, No. 3, pp. 229–244.

Mezias, John M. & Starbuck, William H. (2003): Studying the Accuracy of Managers' Perceptions: A Research Odyssey. In: British Journal of Management. Vol. 14, No. 1, pp. 3–17.

Miles, Matthew B. & Huberman, A. Michael (1994): Qualitative Data Analysis: An Expanded Sourcebook. 2nd edition. Sage, Thousand Oaks.

Miles, Robert H. & Perreault Jr., William D. (1980): Organizational Role Conflict: Its Antecedents and Consequences. In: Katz, Daniel, Kahn, Robert L. & Adams, J. Stacy (eds.): The Study of Organizations. Jossey-Bass, San Francisco et al., pp. 136–156.

Miller, Danny & Friesen, Peter H. (1983): Organizations: A Quantum View. Prentice-Hall, Englewood Cliffs.

Miller, James G. (1978): Living Systems. McGraw-Hill, New York et al.

Minbaeva, Dana, Pedersen, Torben, Björkman, Ingmar, Fey, Carl F. & Park, Hyeon Jeong (2003): MNC Knowledge Transfer, Subsidiary Absorptive Capacity, and HRM. In: Journal of International Business Studies. Vol. 34, No. 6, pp. 586–599.

Miner, John B. (1984): The Validity and Usefulness of Theories in an Emerging Organizational Science. In: Academy of Management Review. Vol. 9, No. 2, pp. 296–306.

Monteiro, L. Felipe, Arvidsson, Niklas & Birkinshaw, Julian (2004): Knowledge Flows within Multinational Corporations: Why are Some Subsidiaries Isolated? Academy of Management Proceedings, Academy of Management.

Montgomery, James D. (1998): toward a Role-Theoretic Conception of Embeddedness. In: American Journal of Sociology. Vol. 104, No. 1, pp. 92–125.

Mooney, Ann C., Holahan, Patricia J. & Amason, Allen C. (2007): Don't Take It Personally: Exploring Cognitive Conflict as a Mediator of Affective Conflict. In: Journal of Management Studies. Vol. 44, No. 5, pp. 733–758.

Moore, Karl J. (2000): The Competence of Formally Appointed Centres of Excellence in the UK. In: Holm, Ulf & Pedersen, Torben (eds.): The Emergence and Impact of MNC Centres of Excellence: A Subsidiary Perspective. Macmillan, London, pp. 154–166.

Moore, Karl J. (2001): A Strategy for Subsidiaries: Centres of Excellences to Build Subsidiary Specific Advantages. In: Management International Review. Vol. 41, No. 3, pp. 275–290.

Moore, Karl J. & Heeler, Roger (1998): A Globalization Strategy for Subsidiaries – Subsidiary Specific Advantages. In: Journal of Transnational Management Development. Vol. 3, No. 2, pp. 1–14.

Morecroft, John D. W., Larsen, Erik R., Lomi, Alessandro & Ginsberg, Ari (1995): The Dynamics of Resource Sharing: A Metaphorical Model. In: System Dynamics Review. Vol. 11, No. 4, pp. 289–309.

Morgan, Gareth & Smircich, Linda (1980): The Case for Qualitative Research. In: Academy of Management Review. Vol. 5, No. 4, pp. 491–500.

Morin, Danielle (2001): Influence of Value for Money Audit on Public Administrations: Looking beyond Appearances. In: Financial Accountability & Management. Vol. 17, No. 2, pp. 99–117.

Mostyn, Barbara (1985): The Content Analysis of Qualitative Research Data: A Dynamic Approach. In: Brenner, Michael, Brown, Jennifer & Canter, David (eds.): The Research Interview. Academic Press, London et al., pp. 115–145.

Mucchielli, Jean-Louis (1998): Multinationales et Mondialisation. Inédit Economie, Editions du Seuil, Paris.

Mühlfeld, Claus & Reimann, Horst (1984): Soziale Rolle. In: Reimann, Horst, Giesen, Bernhard, Goetze, Dieter, Kiefer, Klaus, Meyer, Peter, Mühlfeld, Claus & Schmid, Michael (eds.): Basale Soziologie: Hauptprobleme. 3rd edition. Westdeutscher Verlag, Opladen, pp. 165–189.

Negandhi, Anant R. & Baliga, B. R. (1981): Internal Functioning of American, German and Japanese Multinational Corporations. In: Otterbeck, Lars (ed.): The Management of Headquarters-Subsidiary Relations in Multinational Corporations. Gower, Aldershot, pp. 107–120.

Nobel, Robert & Birkinshaw, Julian (1998): Innovation in Multinational Corporations: Control and Communication Patterns in International R&D. In: Strategic Management Journal. Vol. 19, No. 5, pp. 479–496.

Nonaka, Ikujiro (1994): A Dynamic Theory of Organizational Knowledge Creation. In: Organization Science. Vol. 5, No. 1, pp. 14–37.

O'Donnell, Sharon Watson (2000): Managing Foreign Subsidiaries: Agents of Headquarters, or an Interdependent Network? In: Strategic Management Journal. Vol. 21, No. 5, pp. 525–548.

O'Grady, Shawna & Lane, Henry W. (1996): The Psychic Distance Paradox. In: Journal of International Business Studies. Vol. 27, No. 2, pp. 309–333.

Otley, David T. & Berry, Anthony J. (1998): Case Study Research in Management Accounting and Control. In: Accounting Education. Vol. 7, pp. 105–127.

Otterbeck, Lars (1981): Concluding Remarks – And a Review of Subsidiary Autonomy. In: Otterbeck, Lars (ed.): The Management of Headquarters-Subsidiary Relations in Multinational Corporations. Gower, Aldershot, pp. 337–343.

Ouchi, William (1981): Comparing Japanese and American Companies. In: Theory Z. Addison-Wesley, Reading et al.

Pahl, Joy M. (1995): Power, Conflict, and Organizational Justice in the Multinational Corporation Headquarters-Subsidiary Relationship. College of Business Administration. University of South Carolina.

Pahl, Joy M. & Roth, Kendall (1993): Managing the Headquarters-Foreign Subsidiary Relationship: The Roles of Strategy, Conflict, and Integration. In: The International Journal of Conflict Management. Vol. 4, No. 2, pp. 139–165.

Pahlberg, Cecilia (1996a): Subsidiary-Headquarters Relationships in International Business Networks. Uppsala University, Uppsala.

Pahlberg, Cecilia (1996b): MNCs Differ – And so Do Subsidiaries. Department of Business Studies Uppsala University.

Papanastassiou, Marina & Pearce, Robert (1994): Determinants of the Market Strategies of US Companies. In: Journal of the Economics of Business. Vol. 1, No. 2, pp. 199–217.

Papanastassiou, Marina & Pearce, Robert (1997): Technology Sourcing and the Strategic Roles of Manufacturing Subsidiaries in the U.K.: Local Competences and Global Competitiveness. In: Management International Review. Vol. 37, No. 1, pp. 5–25.

Parker, Sharon K. (2000): From Passive to Proactive Motivation: The Importance of Flexible Role Orientations and Role Breadth Self-Efficacy. In: Applied Psychology: An International Review. Vol. 49, No. 3, pp. 447–469.

Parker, Sharon K. (2007): "That Is my Job": How Employees' Role Orientation Affects Their Job Performance. In: Human Relations. Vol. 60, No. 3, pp. 403–434.

Parsons, Talcott (1951): The Social System. Routledge, London.

Parsons, Talcott (1956a): Suggestions for a Sociological Approach to the Theory of Organizations – I. In: Administrative Science Quarterly. Vol. 1, No. 1, pp. 63–85.

Parsons, Talcott (1956b): Suggestions for a Sociological Approach to the Theory of Organizations – II. In: Administrative Science Quarterly. Vol. 1, No. 2, pp. 225–239.

Parsons, Talcott (1960): A Sociological Approach to the Theory of Formal Organizations. In: Parsons, Talcott (ed.): Structure and Process in Modern Societies. Free Press of Glencoe, New York, pp. 16–58.

Paterson, S. L. & Brock, David M. (2002): The Development of Subsidiary-Management Research: Review and Theoretical Analysis. In: International Business Review. Vol. 11, No. 2, pp. 139–163.

Patton, Michael Quinn (1990): Qualitative Evaluation and Research Methods. 2nd edition. Sage, Newbury Park.

Pearce, Robert & Tavares, Ana Teresa (2002): On the Dynamics and Coexistence of Multiple Subsidiary Roles: An Investigation of Multinational Operations in the UK. In: Lundan, Sarianna M. (ed.): Network Knowledge in International Business. Elgar, Cheltenham, pp. 73–90.

Peery Jr., Newman S. (1972): General Systems Theory: An Inquiry into Its Social Philosophy. In: Academy of Management Journal. Vol. 15, pp. 495–510.

Peiró, José M., Martínez-Tur, Vicente & Ramos, José (2005): Employees' Overestimation of Functional and Relational Service Quality: A Gap Analysis. In: Service Industries Journal. Vol. 25, No. 6, pp. 773–788.

Perez-Lopez, Mark S., Lewis, Robin J. & Cash, Thomas F. (2001): The Relationship of Antifat Attitudes to Other Prejudicial and Gender-Related Attitudes. In: Journal of Applied Social Psychology. Vol. 31, No. 4, pp. 683–697.

Perlmutter, Howard V. (1969): The Tortuous Evolution of the Multinational Corporation. In: Columbia Journal of World Business. Vol. 4, No. 1, pp. 9–18.

Perrow, Charles (1961): The Analysis of Goals in Complex Organizations. In: American Sociological Review. Vol. 26, No. 6, pp. 854–866.

Perrow, Charles (1967): A Framework for the Comparative Analysis of Organizations. In: American Sociological Review. Vol. 32, No. 2, pp. 194–208.

Perrow, Charles (1968): Organizational Goals. In: Sills, David L. (ed.): International Encyclopedia of the Social Sciences. Vol. 11. MacMillan/Free Press, New York, pp. 305–311.

Peterson, Randall S., Martorana, Paul V., Smith, D. Brent & Owens, Pamela D. (2003): The Impact of Chief Executive Officer Personality on Top Management Team Dynamics: One Mechanism by which Leadership Affects Organizational Performance. In: Journal of Applied Psychology. Vol. 88, No. 5, pp. 795–808.

Pettigrew, Andrew (1968): Inter-Group Conflict and Role Strain. In: Journal of Management Studies. Vol. 5, No. 2, pp. 205–218.

Pfeffer, Jeffrey (1981): Power in Organizations. Pitman, Boston.

Pfeffer, Jeffrey & Salancik, Gerald R. (1978): The External Control of Organizations: A Resource Dependency Perspective. Harper & Row, New York.

Picard, Jacques (1980): Organizational Structures and Integrative Devices in European Multinational Corporations. In: Columbia Journal of World Business. Vol. 15, No. 1, pp. 30–35.

Pierce, Bernard & O'Dea, Tony (2003): Management Accounting Information and the Needs of Managers: Perceptions of Managers and Accountants Compared. In: British Accounting Review. Vol. 35, No. 3, pp. 257–290.

Plakoyiannaki, Emmanuella & Saren, Michael (2006): Time and the Customer Relationship Management Process: Conceptual and Methodological Insights. In: Journal of Business & Industrial Marketing. Vol. 21, No. 4, pp. 218–230.

Pondy, Louis R. (1967): Organizational Conflict: Concepts and Models. In: Administrative Science Quarterly. Vol. 12, No. 2, pp. 296–320.

Pondy, Louis R. (1992): Reflections on Organizational Conflict. In: Journal of Organizational Behavior. Vol. 13, No. 3, pp. 257–261.

Porter Liebeskind, Julia, Lumerman Oliver, Amalya, Zucker, Lynne & Brewer, Marilynn (1996): Social Networks, Learning, and Flexibility: Sourcing Scientific Knowledge in New Biotechnology Firms. In: Organization Science. Vol. 7, No. 4, pp. 428–443.

Porter, Michael E. (1985): Competitive Advantage: Creating and Sustaining Superior Performance. Free Press, New York.

Porter, Michael E. (1986): Competition in Global Industries: A Conceptual Framework. In: Porter, Michael E. (ed.): Competition in Global Industries. Harvard Business School Press, Boston, pp. 15–60.

Pouliot, Vincent (2007): "Sobjectivism": Toward a Constructivist Methodology. In: International Studies Quarterly. Vol. 51, No. 2, pp. 359–384.

Prahalad, Coimbatore K. & Doz, Yves L. (1981): Strategic Control – The Dilemma in Headquarters-Subsidiary Relationship. In: Otterbeck, Lars (ed.): The Management of Headquarters-Subsidiary Relations in Multinational Corporations. Gower, Aldershot, pp. 187–204.

Prahalad, Coimbatore K. & Doz, Yves L. (1987): The Multinational Mission. Balancing Local Demands and Global Vision. Free Press, New York.

Prashantham, Shameen & McNaughton, Rod B. (2006): Facilitation of Links between Multinational Subsidiaries and SMEs: The Scottish Technology and Collaboration (STAC) Initiative. In: International Business Review. Vol. 15, No. 5, pp. 447–462.

Prichard, Jane S. & Stanton, Neville A. (1999): Testing Belbin's Team Role Theory of Effective Groups. In: Journal of Management Development. Vol. 18, No. 7/8, pp. 652–665.

Pruitt, Dean G. & Rubin, Jeffrey Z. (1986): Social Conflict: Escalation, Stalemate, and Settlement. Random House, New York.

Putnam, Linda L. & Poole, M. Scott (1987): Conflict and Negotiation. In: Jablin, Fredric M., Putnam, Linda L., Roberts, Karlene H. & Porter, Lyman W. (eds.): Handbook of Organizational Communication. Sage, Newbury Park, pp. 549–599.

Rahim, M. Afzalur (1983): Measurement of Organizational Conflict. In: Journal of General Psychology. Vol. 109, pp. 189–199.

Rahim, M. Afzalur (1992): Managing Conflict in Organizations. 3rd edition. Praeger, Westport.

Rahim, M. Afzalur (2002): toward a Theory of Managing Organizational Conflict. In: International Journal of Conflict Management. Vol. 13, No. 3, pp. 206–235.

Raider, Holly & Krackhardt, David J. (2002): Intraorganizational Networks. In: Blackwell Companion to Organizations. pp. 58–74.

Randøy, Trond & Li, Jiatao (1998): Global Resource Flow and MNE Netwok Integration. In: Birkinshaw, Julian & Hood, Neil (eds.): Multinational Corporate Evolution and Subsidiary Development. Macmillan, Houndsmill et al., pp. 76–101.

Reichers, Arnon E. (1986): Conflict and Organizational Commitments. In: Journal of Applied Psychology. Vol. 71, No. 3, pp. 508–514.

Rizzo, John R., House, Robert J. & Lirtzman, Sidney I. (1970): Role Conflict and Ambiguity in Complex Organizations. In: Administrative Science Quarterly. Vol. 15, No. 2, pp. 150–163.

Rodrigues, Carl A. (1995): Headquarters-Foreign Subsidiary Control Relationships: Three Conceptual Frameworks. In: Empowerment in Organizations. Vol. 3, No. 3, pp. 25–34.

Ronen, Simcha & Shenkar, Oded (1985): Clustering Countries on Attitudinal Dimensions: A Review and Synthesis. In: Academy of Management Review. Vol. 10, No. 3, pp. 435–454.

Root, Franklin R. (1998): Entry Strategies for International Markets. Revised and expanded edition. Lexington Books/Macmillan, New York et al.

Roth, Kendall & Morrison, Allen J. (1992): Implementing Global Strategy: Characteristics of Global Subsidiary Mandates. In: Journal of International Business Studies. Vol. 23, No. 4, pp. 715–735.

Roth, Kendall & Nigh, Douglas (1992): The Effectiveness of Headquarters-Subsidiary Relationships: The Role of Coordination, Control, and Conflict. In: Journal of Business Research. Vol. 25, No. 4, pp. 277–301.

Roth, Kendall & Schweiger, David M. (1991): Global Strategy Implementation at the Business Unit Level: Operational Capabilities and Administrative Mechanisms. In: Journal of International Business Studies. Vol. 22, No. 3, pp. 369–402.

Rubin, Jeffrey Z., Pruitt, Dean G. & Kim, Sung Hee (1994): Social Conflict: Escalation, Stalemate, and Settlement. 2nd edition. McGraw-Hill, New York.

Ruekert, Robert W. & Walker, Orville C. Jr. (1987): Interactions between Marketing and R&D Departments in Implementing Different Business Strategies. In: Strategic Management Journal. Vol. 8, No. 3, pp. 233–248.

Rugman, Alan M. (ed. 1983): Multinationals and Technology Transfer. Praeger, New York.

Rüttinger, Bruno (1977): Konflikt und Konfliktlösen. Wilhelm Goldmann, Munich.

Rüttinger, Bruno & Sauer, Jürgen (2000): Konflikt und Konfliktlösen: Kritische Situationen erkennen und bewältigen. 3rd edition. Rosenberger Fachverlag, Leonberg.

Sarbin, Theodore R. & Allen, Vernon L. (1968): Role Theory. In: Gardner, Lindzey & Aronson, Elliot (eds.): The Handbook of Social Psychology. 2nd edition. Vol. 1. Addison-Wesley, Reading, pp. 488–567.

Sashittal, Hemant C. & Jassawalla, Avan R. (1998): Why Managers Do What They Do. In: Management Decision. Vol. 36, No. 8, pp. 533–542.

Scharfstein, David S. & Stein, Jeremy C. (2000): The Dark Side of Internal Capital Markets: Divisional Rent-Seeking and Inefficient Investment. In: Journal of Finance. Vol. 55, No. 6, pp. 2537–2564.

Schilling, Jan (2006): On the Pragmatics of Qualitative Assessment. In: European Journal of Psychological Assessment. Vol. 22, No. 1, pp. 28–37.

Schmid, Stefan (2000): Foreign Subsidiaries as Centres of Competence – Empirical Evidence from Japanese Multinationals. In: Larimo, Jorma & Kock, Sören (eds.): Recent Studies in Interorganizational and International Business Research. Vol. 58. Vaasan Yliopiston Julkaisuja, Vaasa, pp. 182–204.

Schmid, Stefan (2003): How Multinational Corporations Can Upgrade Foreign Subsidiaries: A Case Study from Central and Eastern Europe. In: Stüting, Heinz-Jürgen, Dorow, Wolfgang, Claassen, Frank & Blazejewski, Susanne (eds.): Change Management in Transition Economies: Integrating Corporate Strategy, Structure and Culture. Palgrave/Macmillan, Houndmills et al., pp. 273–290.

Schmid, Stefan (2004): The Roles of Foreign Subsidiaries in Network MNCs – A Critical Review of the Literature and Some Directions for Future Research. In: Larimo, Jorma (ed.): European Research on Foreign Direct Investment and International Human Resource Management. Vaasan Yliopiston Julkaisuja, Vaasa, pp. 237–255.

Schmid, Stefan, Bäurle, Iris & Kutschker, Michael (1998): Tochtergesellschaften in international tätigen Unternehmungen – Ein "State-of-the-Art" unterschiedlicher Rollentypologien. Diskussionsbeitrag, No. 104, Wirtschaftswissenschaftliche Fakultät Ingolstadt.

Schmid, Stefan & Daniel, Andrea (2007): Are Subsidiary Roles a Matter of Perception? A Review of the Literature and Avenues for Future Research. Working Paper, No. 30, ESCP-EAP European School of Management Berlin.

Schmid, Stefan & Daub, Matthias (2005): Service Offshoring Subsidiaries – Towards a Typology. Working Paper, No. 12, ESCP-EAP European School of Management Berlin.

Schmid, Stefan & Kutschker, Michael (2003): Rollentypologien für ausländische Tochtergesellschaften in Multinationalen Unternehmungen. In: Holtbrügge, Dirk (ed.): Management Multinationaler Unternehmungen. Festschrift zum 60. Geburtstag von Martin K. Welge. Physika/Springer, Heidelberg, pp. 161–182.

Schmid, Stefan & Schurig, Andreas (2003): The Development of Critical Capabilities in Foreign Subsidiaries: Disentangling the Role of the Subsidiary's Business Network. In: International Business Review. Vol. 12, No. 6, pp. 755–782.

Schmid, Stefan, Schurig, Andreas & Kutschker, Michael (2002): The MNC as a Network: A Closer Look at Intra-organizational Flows. In: Lundan, Sarianna M. (ed.): Network Knowledge in International Business. Elgar, Cheltenham, Northampton, pp. 45–72.

Schmidt, Stuart M. & Kochan, Thomas A. (1972): Conflict: toward Conceptual Clarity. In: Administrative Science Quarterly. Vol. 17, No. 3, pp. 359–370.

Schneider, Susan C. & Angelmar, Reinhard (1993): Cognition in Organizational Analysis: Who's Minding the Store? In: Organization Studies. Vol. 14, No. 3, pp. 347–374.

Schnell, Rainer, Hill, Paul Bernhard & Esser, Elke (2005): Methoden der empirischen Sozialforschung. 7th edition. Oldenbourg, Munich, Wien.

Scholl, Wolfgang (2004): Grundkonzepte der Organisation. In: Schuler, Heinz (ed.): Organisationspsychologie. 3rd edition. Huber, Bern et al., pp. 515–556.

Schulz, Martin (2001): The Uncertain Relevance of Newness: Organizational Learning and Knowledge Flows. In: Academy of Management Journal. Vol. 44, No. 4, pp. 661–681.

Schulz, Martin (2003): Pathways of Relevance: Exploring Inflows of Knowledge into Subunits of Multinational Corporations. In: Organization Science. Vol. 14, No. 4, pp. 440–459.

Schwenk, Charles R. (1990): Conflict in Organizational Decision Making: An Exploratory Study of its Effects in For-Profit and Not-For-Profit Organizations. In: Management Science. Vol. 36, No. 4, pp. 436–448.

Seale, Clive (1999): The Quality of Qualitative Research. Sage, London.

Sell, Jane, Lovaglia, Michael J., Mannix, Elizabeth A., Samuelson, Charles D. & Wilson, Rick K. (2004): Investigating Conflict, Power, and Status within and among Groups. In: Small Group Research. Vol. 35, No. 1, pp. 44–72.

Shenkar, Oded & Zeira, Yoram (1987): Human Resources Management in International Joint Ventures: Directions for Research. In: Academy of Management Review. Vol. 12, No. 3, pp. 546–557.

Shenkar, Oded & Zeira, Yoram (1992): Role Conflict and Role Ambiguity of Chief Executive Officers in International Joint Ventures. In: Journal of International Business Studies. Vol. 23, No. 1, pp. 55–75.

Shibutani, Tamotsu (1968): A Cybernetic Approach to Motivation. In: Buckley, Walter (ed.): Modern Systems Research for the Behavioural Scientist. Aldine, Chicago, pp. 303–336.

Shuy, Roger W. (2001): In-Person versus Telephone Interviewing. In: Gubrium, Jaber F. & Holstein, James A. (eds.): Handbook of Interview Research. Sage, Thousand Oaks et al., pp. 537–555.

Silverman, David (2000): Doing Qualitative Research: A Practical Handbook. Sage, London.

Simon, Herbert A. (1964): On the Concept of Organizational Goal. In: Administrative Science Quarterly. Vol. 9, No. 1, pp. 1-22.

Simons, Tony L. & Peterson, Randall S. (2000): Task Conflict and Relationship Conflict in Top Management Teams: The Pivotal Role of Intragroup Trust. In: Journal of Applied Psychology. Vol. 85, No. 1, pp. 102–111.

Smith, Kenwyn K. (1989): The Movement of Conflict in Organizations: The Joint Dynamics of Splitting and Triangulation. In: Administrative Science Quarterly. Vol. 34, No. 1, pp. 1–20.

Smith, Stuart, Tranfield, David, Bessant, John, Levy, Paul & Ley, Clive (1992): Organization Design for the Factory of the Future. In: International Studies of Management & Organization. Vol. 22, No. 4, pp. 61–68.

Solomon, Michael R., Surprenant, Carol, Czepiel, John A. & Gutman, Evelyn G. (1985): A Role Theory Perspective on Dyadic Interactions: The Service Encounter. In: Journal of Marketing. Vol. 49, No. 1, pp. 99–111.

Stake, Robert E. (2000): Case Studies. In: Denzin, Norman & Lincoln, Yvonna S. (eds.): Handbook of Qualitative Research. 2nd edition., Thousand Oaks et al. pp. 435–454.

Starbuck, William H. & Mezias, John M. (1996): Opening Pandora's Box: Studying the Accuracy of Managers' Perceptions. In: Journal of Organizational Behavior. Vol. 17, No. 2, pp. 99–117.

Steensma, H. Kevin & Lyles, Marjorie A. (2000): Explaining IJV Survival in a Transitional Economy through Social Exchange and Knowledge-Based Perspectives. In: Strategic Management Journal. Vol. 21, No. 8, pp. 831–851.

Steinke, Ines (1999): Kriterien qualitativer Forschung – Ansätze zur Bewertung qualitativ-empirischer Sozialforschung. Juventa, Weinheim, Munich.

Steinke, Ines (2004): Quality Criteria in Qualitative Research. In: Flick, Uwe, von Kardorff, Ernst & Steinke, Ines (eds.): A Companion to Qualitative Research. Sage, London et al., pp. 184–190.

Sternberg, Robert J. (2006): Cognitive Psychology. 4th edition. Thomson, Belmont.

Stopford, John M. & Wells, Louis T. (1972): Managing the Multinational Enterprise: Organization of the Firm and Ownership of the Subsidiaries. Basic Books, New York.

Stöttinger, Barbara & Schlegelmilch, Bodo B. (1998): Explaining Export Development through Psychic Distance: Enlightening or Elusive? In: International Marketing Review. Vol. 15, No. 5, pp. 357–372.

Stöttinger, Barbara & Schlegelmilch, Bodo B. (2000): Psychic Distance: A Concept Past Its Due Date? In: International Marketing Review. Vol. 17, No. 2/3, pp. 169–173.

Surlemont, Bernard (1998): A Typology of Centres within Multinational Corporations: An Empirical Investigation. In: Birkinshaw, Julian & Hood, Neil (eds.): Multinational Corporate Evolution and Subsidiary Development. Macmillan, Houndsmill et al., pp. 162–188.

Sutcliffe, Kathleen M. (1994): What Executives Notice: Accurate Perceptions in Top Management Teams. In: Academy of Management Journal. Vol. 37, No. 5, pp. 1360–1378.

Sutcliffe, Kathleen M. & Huber, George P. (1998): Firm and Industry as Determinants of Executive Perceptions of the Environment. In: Strategic Management Journal. Vol. 19, No. 8, pp. 793–807.

Sydow, Joerg (1992): Strategische Netzwerke: Evolution und Organisation. Gabler, Wiesbaden.

Szulanski, Gabriel (1996): Exploring Internal Stickiness: Impediments to the Transfer of Best Practice within the Firm. In: Strategic Management Journal. Vol. 17, Special Issue, pp. 27–43.

Szulanski, Gabriel & Cappetta, Rossella (2003): Stickiness: Conceptualizing, Measuring, and Predicting Difficulties in the Transfer of Knowledge within Organizations. In: Easterby-Smith, Mark & Lyles, Marjorie A. (eds.): The Blackwell Handbook of Organizational Learning and Knowledge. Blackwell, Malden et al., pp. 513–534.

Taggart, James (1999): MNC Subsidiary Performance, Risk, and Corporate Expectations. In: International Business Review. Vol. 8, No. 2, pp. 233–255.

Taggart, James H. (1997a): Autonomy and Procedural Justice: A Framework for Evaluating Subsidiary Strategy. In: Journal of International Business Studies. Vol. 28, No. 1, pp. 51–76.

Taggart, James H. (1997b): An Evaluation of the Integration-Responsiveness Framework: MNC Manufacturing Subsidiaries in the UK. In: Management International Review. Vol. 37, No. 4, pp. 295–318.

Taggart, James H. (1998): Strategy Shifts in MNC Subsidiaries. In: Strategic Management Journal. Vol. 19, No. 7, pp. 663–681.

Taggart, James & Hood, Neil (1999): Determinants of Autonomy in Multinational Corporation Subsidiaries. In: European Management Journal. Vol. 17, No. 2, pp. 226–236.

Tasoluk, Burcu, Yaprak, Attila & Calantone, Roger J. (2007): Conflict and Collaboration in Headquarters-Subsidiary Relationships: An Agency Theory Perspective on Product Rollouts in an Emerging Market. In: International Journal of Conflict Management. Vol. 17, No. 4, pp. 332–351.

Tavares, Ana Teresa & Pearce, Robert (2002): Product Mandate Subsidiaries and High Value-Added Scope in MNEs' Operations in the UK: An EU-based Comparative Investigation. In: McDonald, Frank, Tüselmann, Heinz & Wheeler, Colin (eds.): International Business. Adjusting to New Challenges and Opportunities. Palgrave, Houndsmill, pp. 76–87.

Tavares, Ana Teresa & Young, Stephen (2006): Sourcing Patterns of Foreign-Owned Multinational Subsidiaries in Europe. In: Regional Studies. Vol. 40, No. 6, pp. 583–599.

Teece, David J. (1977): Technology Transfer by Multinational Firms: The Resource Cost of Transferring Technological Know-How. In: Economic Journal. Vol. 87, pp. 242–261.

Thomas, Alexander & Schenk, Eberhard (2001): Beruflich in China. Vandenhoeck & Ruprecht, Göttingen.

Thomas, Edwin J. & Biddle, Bruce J. (1966): Basic Concepts for Classifying the Phenomena of Role. In: Biddle, Bruce J. & Thomas, Edwin J. (eds.): Role Theory: Concepts and Research. Wiley, New York et al., pp. 23–45.

Thomas, Kenneth W. (1976): Conflict and Conflict Management. In: Dunnette, Marvin D. (ed.): Handbook of Industrial and Organizational Psychology. Rand McNally, Chicago, pp. 889–935.

Thomas, Kenneth W. (1992a): Conflict and Conflict Management: Reflections and Update. In: Journal of Organizational Behavior. Vol. 13, No. 3, pp. 265–274.

Thomas, Kenneth W. (1992b): Conflict and Negotiation Processes in Organizations. In: Dunnette, Marvin D. & Hough, Leaetta M. (eds.): Handbook of Industrial and Organizational Psychology. 3rd edition. Consulting Psychologists Press, Palo Alto, pp. 651–717.

Thompson, James D. (2004): Organizations in Action. Transaction, New Brunswick, London.

Thompson, James D. & McEwen, Willlam J. (1958): Organizational Goals and Environment: Goal-Setting as an Interaction Process. In: American Sociological Review. Vol. 23, No. 1, pp. 23–31.

Titscher, Stefan, Meyer, Michael, Wodak, Ruth & Vetter, Eva (2000): Methods of Text and Discourse Analysis. Sage, London et al.

Toffler, Barbara Ley (1981): Occupational Role Development: The Changing Determinants of Outcomes for the Individual. In: Administrative Science Quarterly. Vol. 26, No. 3, pp. 396–418.

Toyne, Brian (1978): Procurement-Related Perceptions of Corporate-Based and Foreign-Based Purchasing Managers. In: Journal of International Business Studies. Vol. 9, No. 3, pp. 39–54.

Tsai, Wenpin (2002): Social Structure of "Coopetition" within a Multiunit Organization: Coordination, Competition, and Intraorganizational Knowledge Sharing. In: Organization Science. Vol. 13, No. 2, pp. 179–190.

Tversky, Amos & Kahneman, Daniel (1982): Judgement under Uncertainty: Heuristics and Biases. In: Kahneman, Daniel, Slovic, Paul & Tversky, Amos (eds.): Judgement under Uncertainty. Cambridge University Press, Cambridge, pp. 3–20.

Vaaland, Terje I. & Håkansson, Håkan (2003): Exploring Interorganizational Conflict in Complex Projects. In: Industrial Marketing Management. Vol. 32, No. 2, pp. 127–138.

van de Ven, Andrew H. & Ferry, Diane L. (1980): Measuring and Assessing Organizations. Wiley, New York.

Venaik, Sunil, Midgley, David F. & Devinney, Timothy M. (2005): Dual Paths to Performance: The Impact of Global Pressures on MNC Subsidiary Conduct and Performance. In: Journal of International Business Studies. Vol. 36, No. 6, pp. 655–675.

Vereecke, Ann, Van Dierdonck, Roland & De Meyer, Arnoud (2006): A Typology of Plants in Global Manufacturing Networks. In: Management Science. Vol. 52, No. 11, pp. 1737–1750.

Vernon, Raymond, Wells, Louis T. & Rangan, Subramanian (1996): The Manager in the International Economy. 7th edition. Prentice Hall, London et al.

Victor, Bart & Blackburn, Richard S. (1987): Interdependence: An Alternative Conceptualization. In: Academy of Management Review. Vol. 12, No. 3, pp. 486–498.

Vollmer, Albert (2005): Konflikt: Eine Struktur- und Prozessqualität in der interorganisationalen Kooperation. Studentendruckerei, Zürich.

von Bertalanffy, Ludwig (1972): The History and Status of General Systems Theory. In: Academy of Management Journal. Vol. 15, No. 4, pp. 407–426.

von Glasersfeld, Ernst (1994): Einführung in den radikalen Konstruktivismus. In: Watzlawick, Paul (ed.): Die erfundene Wirklichkeit. Piper, Munich, Zürich, pp. 16–38.

Vora, Davina & Kostova, Tatiana (2007): A Model of Dual Organizational Identification in the Context of the Multinational Enterprise. In: Journal of Organizational Behavior. Vol. 28, No. 3, pp. 327–350.

Vora, Davina, Kostova, Tatiana & Roth, Kendall (2007): Roles of Subsidiary Managers in Multinational Corporations: The Effect of Dual Organizational Identification. In: Management International Review. Vol. 47, No. 4, pp. 595–620.

Wall Jr., James A. & Callister, Ronda Roberts (1995): Conflict and its Management. In: Journal of Management. Vol. 21, No. 3, pp. 515–558.

Waller, Mary J., Conte, Jeffrey M., Gibson, Cristina B. & Carpenter, Mason A. (2001): The Effect of Individual Perceptions of Deadlines on Team Performance. In: Academy of Management Review. Vol. 26, No. 4, pp. 586–600.

Waller, Mary J., Huber, George P. & Glick, William H. (1995): Functional Background as a Determinant of Executives' Selective Perception. In: Academy of Management Journal. Vol. 38, No. 4, pp. 943–974.

Walton, Richard E. & Dutton, John M. (1969): The Management of Interdepartmental Conflict: A Model and Review. In: Administrative Science Quarterly. Vol. 14, No. 1, pp. 73–84.

Walton, Richard E., Dutton, John M. & Cafferty, Thomas P. (1969): Organizational Context and Interdepartmental Conflict. In: Administrative Science Quarterly. Vol. 14, No. 4, pp. 522–542.

Weigand, Robert E. (1966): Identifying Industrial Buying Responsibility. In: Journal of Marketing Research. Vol. 3, No. 1, pp. 81–84.

Welge, Martin K. (1981a): A Comparison of Managerial Structures in German Subsidiaries in France, India, and the United States. In: Management International Review. Vol. 21, No. 2, pp. 5–21.

Welge, Martin K. (1981b): The Effective Design of Headquarters-Subsidiary Relationships in German MNCs. In: Otterbeck, Lars (ed.): The Management of Headquarters-Subsidiary Relations in Multinational Corporations. Gower, Aldershot, pp. 79–106.

Wernerfelt, Birger (1984): A Resource-Based View of the Firm. In: Strategic Management Journal. Vol. 5, No. 2, pp. 171–180.

White, Roderick E. & Poynter, Thomas A. (1984): Strategies for Foreign-Owned Subsidiaries in Canada. In: Business Quarterly. Vol. 49, No. 2, pp. 59–69.

White, Roderick E. & Poynter, Thomas A. (1989): Achieving Worldwide Advantage with the Horizontal Organization. In: Business Quarterly. Vol. 54, No. 2, pp. 55–60.

Wilkinson, Ian & Young, Louise (2004): Improvisation and Adaptation in International Business Research Interviews. In: Marschan-Piekkari, Rebecca & Welch, Catherine (eds.): Handbook of Qualitative Research Methods for International Business. Edward Elgar, Cheltenham, Northampton, pp. 207–223.

Witte, Erich H. (1994): Lehrbuch Sozialpsychologie. 2nd edition. Beltz, Psychologie-Verlags-Union, Weinheim.

Wolf, Joachim (1994): Internationales Personalmanagement: Kontext – Koordination – Erfolg. Gabler, Wiesbaden.

Wondolleck, Julia M. & Ryan, Clare M. (1999): What Hat Do I Wear Now? An Examination of Agency Roles in Collaborative Processes. In: Negotiation Journal. Vol. 15, No. 2, pp. 117–134.

Wright, Francis W., Madura, Jeff & Wiant, Kenneth J. (2002): The Differential Effects of Agency Costs on Multinational Corporations. In: Applied Financial Economics. Vol. 12, No. 5, pp. 347–359.

Wrona, Thomas (2006): Fortschritts- und Gütekriterien im Rahmen qualitativer Sozialforschung. In: Zelewski, Stephan & Akca, Naciye (eds.): Fortschritt in den Wirtschaftswissenschaften. Gabler, Wiesbaden, pp. 189–216.

Yeung, Henry Wai-chung (1995): Qualitative Personal Interviews in International Business Research: Some Lessons from a Study of Hong Kong Transnational Corporations. In: International Business Review. Vol. 4, No. 3, pp. 313–339.

Yin, Robert K. (1993): Applications of Case Study Research. Sage, Newbury Park.

Yin, Robert K. (2003): Case Study Research – Design and Methods. 3rd edition. Sage, Thousand Oaks et al.

Young, Angela M. & Hurlic, David (2007): Gender Enactment at Work: The Importance of Gender and Gender-Related Behavior to Person-Organizational Fit and Career Decisions. In: Journal of Managerial Psychology. Vol. 22, No. 2, pp. 168–187.

Young, Stephen & Hood, Neil (1994): Designing Developmental After-Care Programs for Inward Investors in the European Community. In: Transnational Corporations. Vol. 3, No. 2, pp. 45–72.

Young, Stephen, Hood, Neil & Dunlop, Stewart (1988): Global Strategies, Multinational Subsidiary Roles and Economic Impact in Scotland. In: Regional Studies. Vol. 22, No. 6, pp. 487–497.

Young, Stephen & Tavares, Ana Teresa (2004): Centralization and Autonomy: Back to the Future. In: International Business Review. Vol. 13, No. 2, pp. 215–237.

Yu, Chwo-Ming Joseph, Wong, Huang-Che & Chiao, Yu-Ching (2006): Local Linkages and Their Effects on Headquarters' Use of Process Controls. In: Journal of Business Research. Vol. 59, No. 12, pp. 1239–1247.

Zalan, Tatiana & Lewis, Geoffrey (2004): Writing about Methods in Qualitative Research: Towards a More Transparent Approach. In: Marschan-Piekkari, Rebecca & Welch, Catherine (eds.): Handbook of Qualitative Research Methods for International Business. Edward Elgar, Cheltenham, Northampton, pp. 507–528.

Zhao, Hongxin & Luo, Yadong (2005): Antecedents of Knowledge Sharing with Peer Subsidiaries in Other Countries: A Perspective from Subsidiary Managers in a Foreign Emerging Market. In: Management International Review. Vol. 45, No. 1, pp. 71–97.

Zimbardo, Philip G. (1995): Psychologie. 6th edition. Springer, Berlin et al.